AUTHENTIC TRANSCRIPTIONS WITH NOTES AND TABLATURE

Bob Seger & ... GREATEST HITS

Front cover photo by Caroline Greyshock

Back cover photo by Terrance Bert

Music transcriptions by Pete Billmann, Steve Gorenberg, Jeff Jacobson, Andrew Moore and David Stocker

ISBN 0-634-06885-7

7777 W. BLUEMOUND RD. P.O. BOX 13819 MILWAUKEE, WI 53213

Visit Hal Leonard Online at
www.halleonard.com

Understanding

Words and Music by Bob Seger

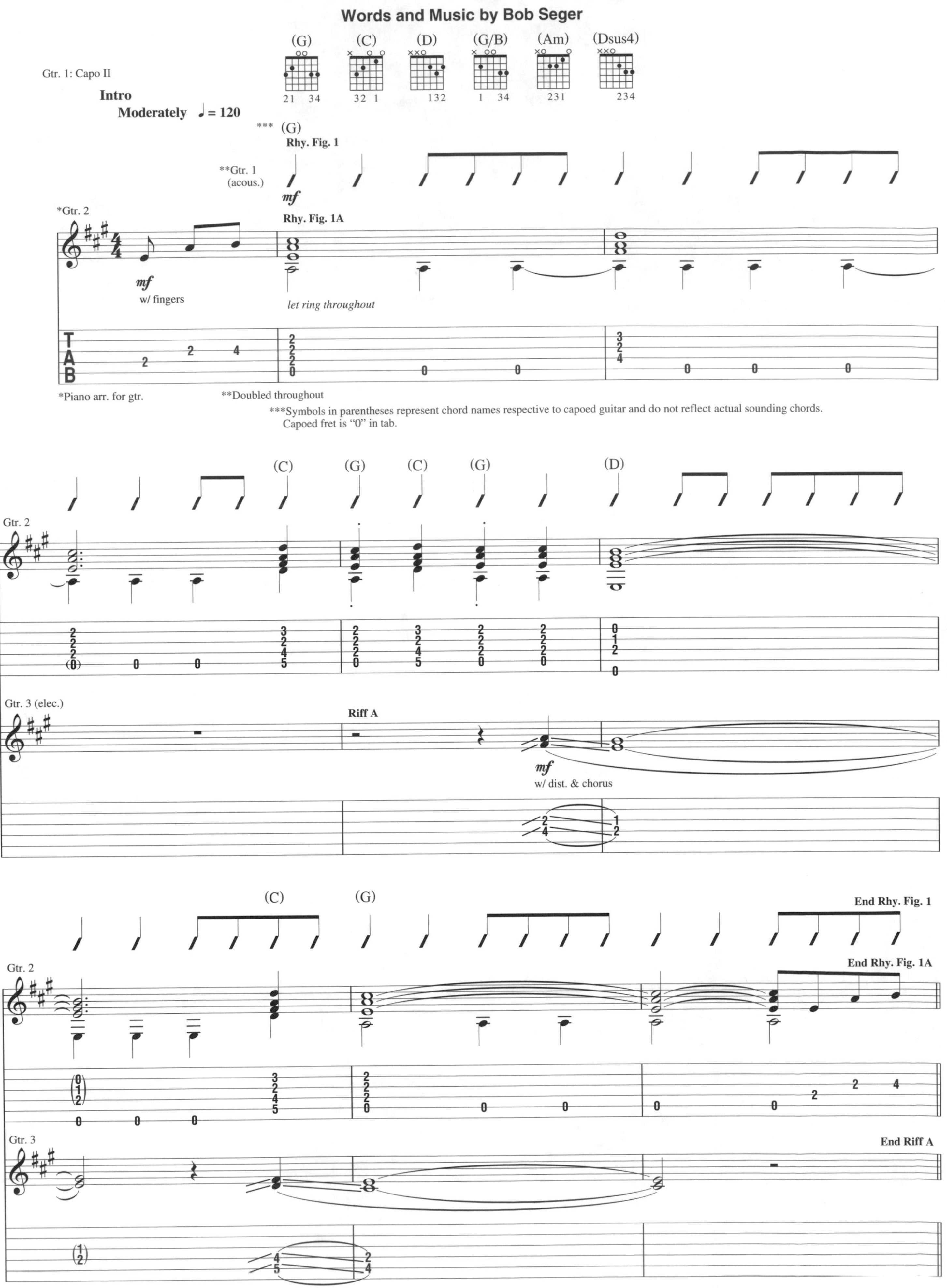

Verse
Gtr. 1: w/ Rhy. Fig. 1 (2 times)
Gtr. 2: w/ Rhy. Fig. 1A (1 7/8 times)
Gtr. 3 tacet
*A (G)
D/A (C/G)
A (G)
D (C)
1. It seems like on - ly yes - ter - day
I did - n't have a clue.
*Symbols in parentheses represent chord names respective to capoed guitar. Symbols above reflect actual sounding chords.
Chord symbols reflect overall harmony.
A (G) D (C) A (G)
E (D)
D (C)
I stood a - lone not know - in' where to turn.
A (G)
A (G)
D/A (C/G)
Now sud - den - ly I look a - round,
A (G)
D (C)
Gtr. 3: w/ Riff A
A (G) D (C) A (G)
E (D)
ev 'ry - thing looks new.
I don't know why but I
D (C)
A (G)
think I'm start - in' to learn,
mm.
Rhy. Fill 1
Gtr. 2
End Rhy. Fill 1
Chorus
C#m (Bm)
D (C)
A/E (G/D)
They call it un - der - stand - ing,
a will - ing - ness to grow.
Rhy. Fig. 2
Gtr. 1
Gtr. 2
**w/ echo set for dotted quarter-note regeneration w/ 1 repeat.

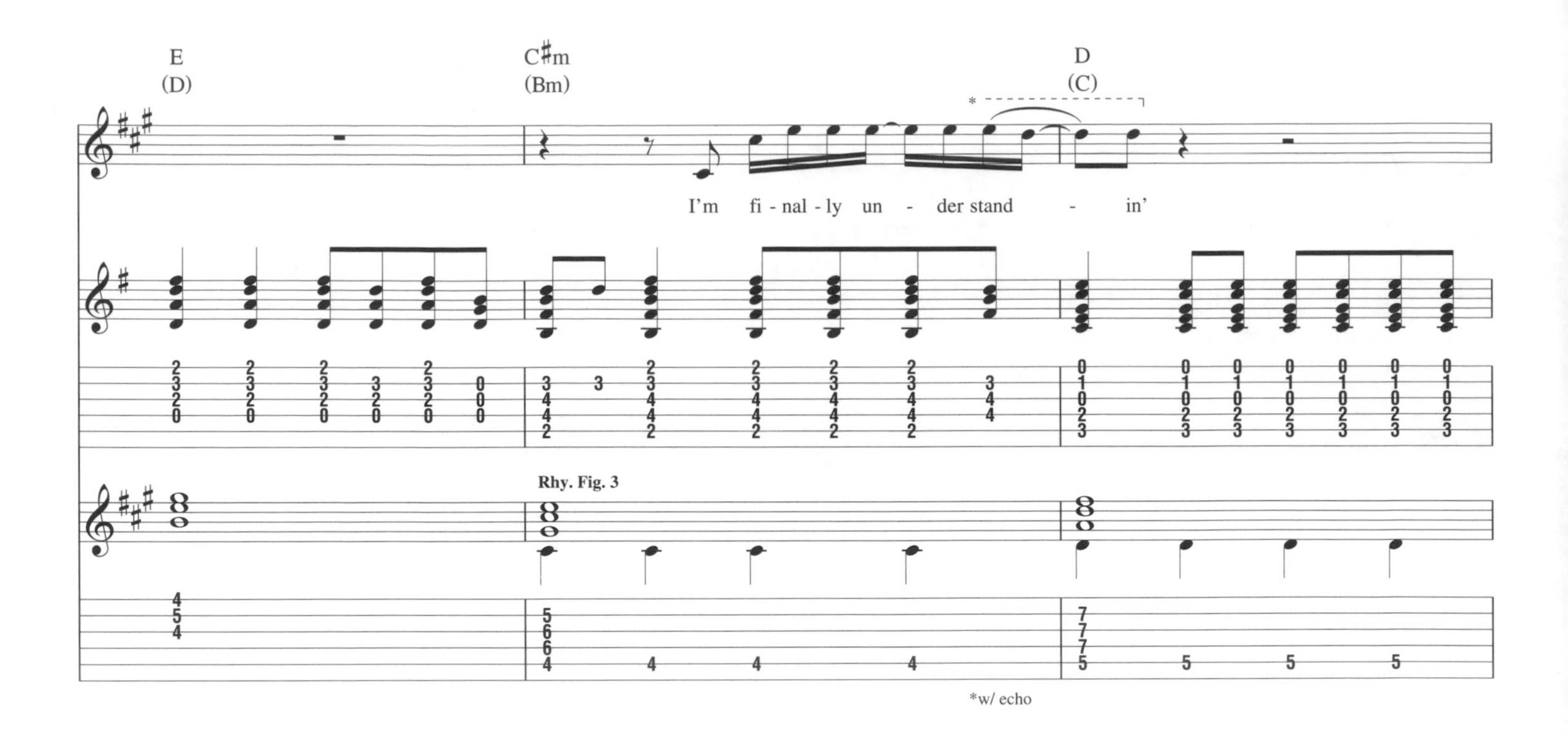
E
(D)
C♯m
(Bm)
D
(C)
I'm fi - nal - ly un - der stand - in'
Rhy. Fig. 3
*w/ echo

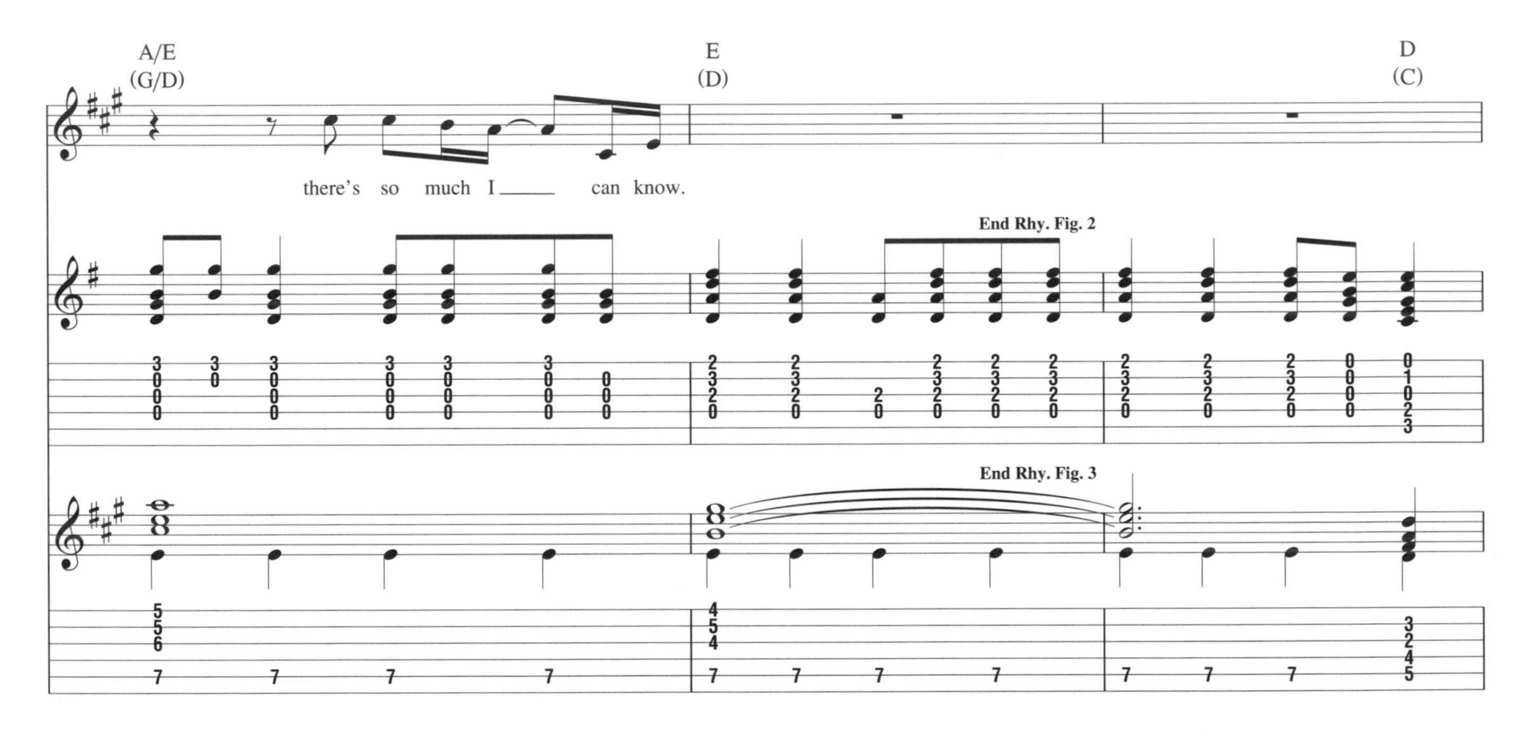
A/E
(G/D)
E
(D)
D
(C)
there's so much I can know.
End Rhy. Fig. 2
End Rhy. Fig. 3

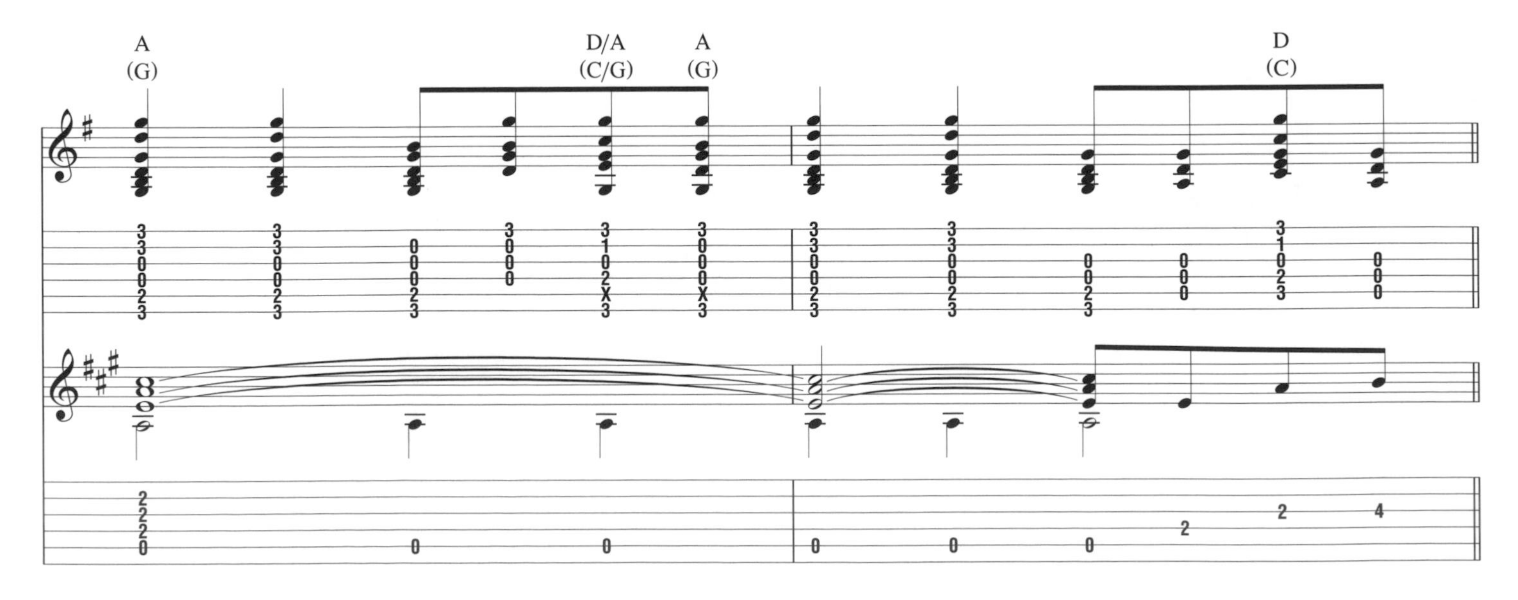
A
(G)
D/A
(C/G)
A
(G)
D
(C)

Verse
Gtr. 1: w/ Rhy. Fig. 1 (2 times)
Gtr. 2: w/ Rhy. Fig. 1A (1st 6 meas.)
A
(G)
D/A
(C/G)
A
(G)
D
(C)
2. Un - til the day you came a - long,
I used to just get lost.
Voc. Fig. 1
(Oo,
oo,
A
(G)
D
(C)
A
(G)
E
(D)
D
(C)
I on - ly heard the things I want - ed to hear.
End Voc. Fig. 1
Voc. Fig. 2
oo,
oo,
oo.
A
(G)
Bkgd. Voc.: w/ Voc. Fig. 1
Gtr. 2: w/ Rhy. Fig. 1A (1st 7 meas.)
A
(G)
D/A
(C/G)
It al - ways seemed like no one cared,
End Voc. Fig. 2
Gtr. 2
A
(G)
D
(C)
A
(G)
D
(C)
A
(G)
E
(D)
then you took the time.
And now I look and ev - 'ry -
Gtr. 3

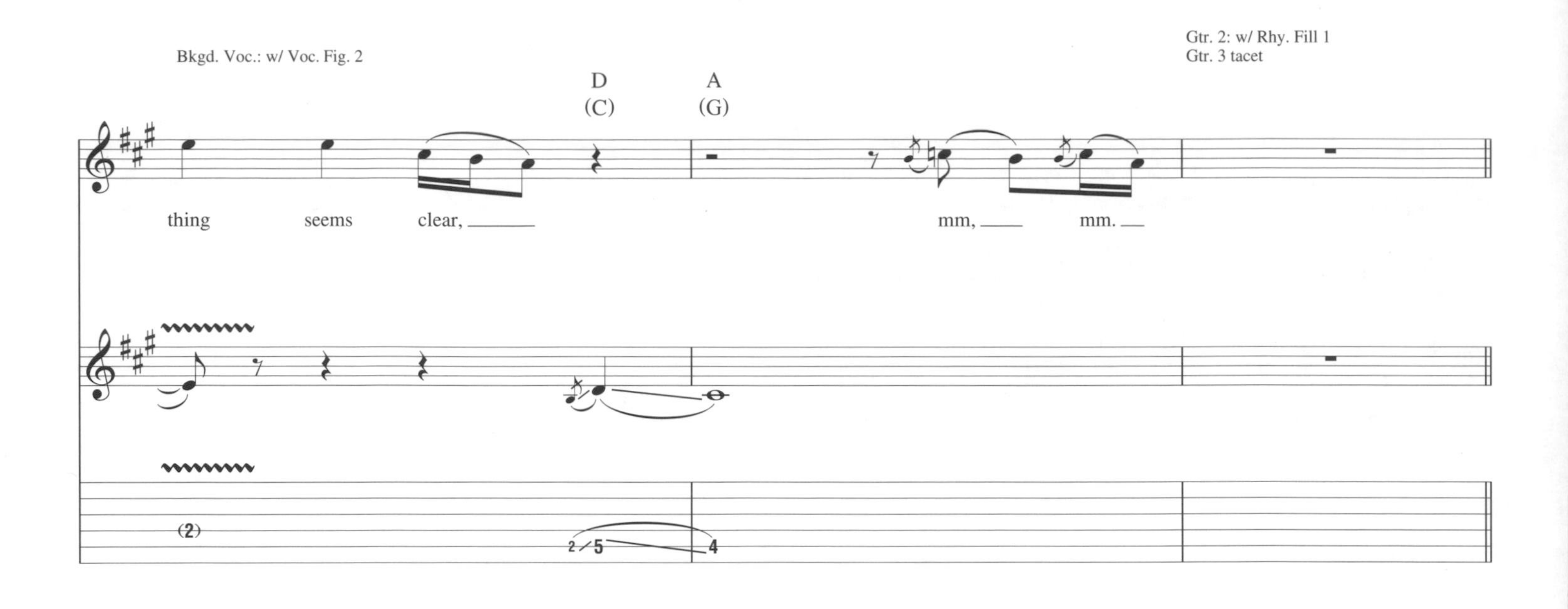
Bkgd. Voc.: w/ Voc. Fig. 2
Gtr. 2: w/ Rhy. Fill 1
Gtr. 3 tacet
D
(C)
A
(G)
thing seems clear,
mm, mm.
(2)
2 5
4

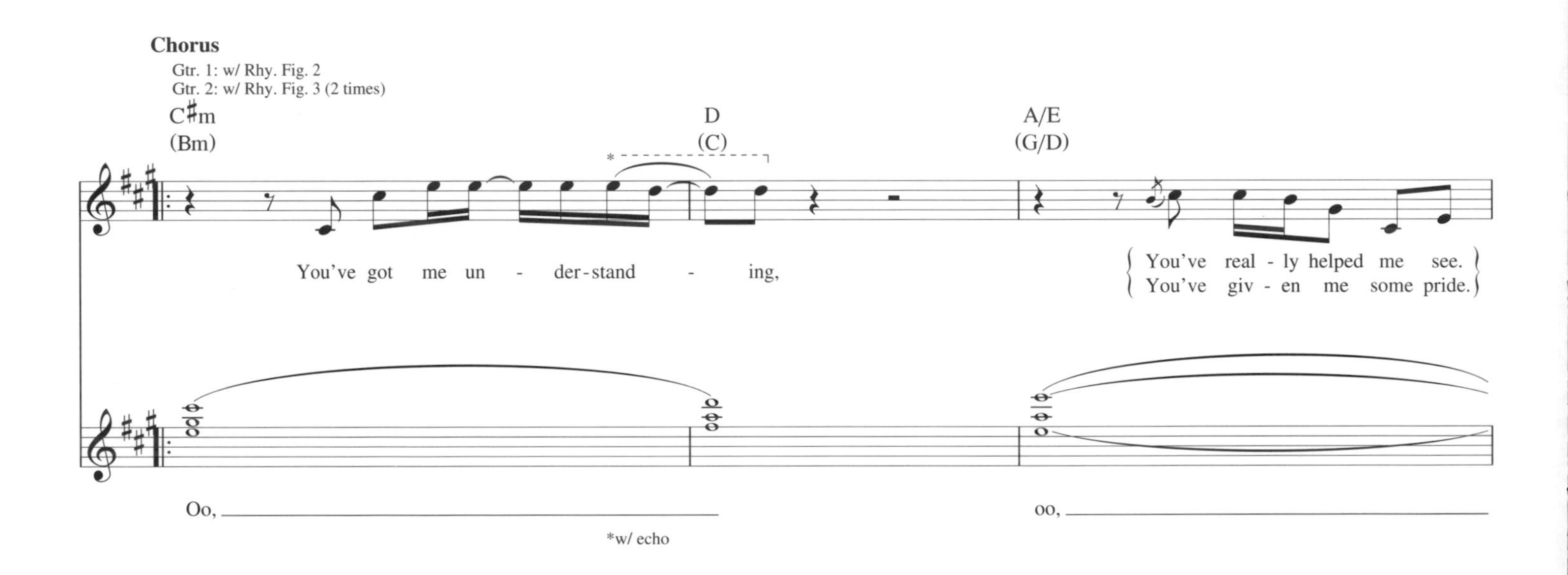
Chorus
Gtr. 1: w/ Rhy. Fig. 2
Gtr. 2: w/ Rhy. Fig. 3 (2 times)
C♯m
(Bm)
D
(C)
A/E
(G/D)
You've got me un - der-stand - ing,
You've real - ly helped me see.
You've giv - en me some pride.
Oo,
oo,
*w/ echo

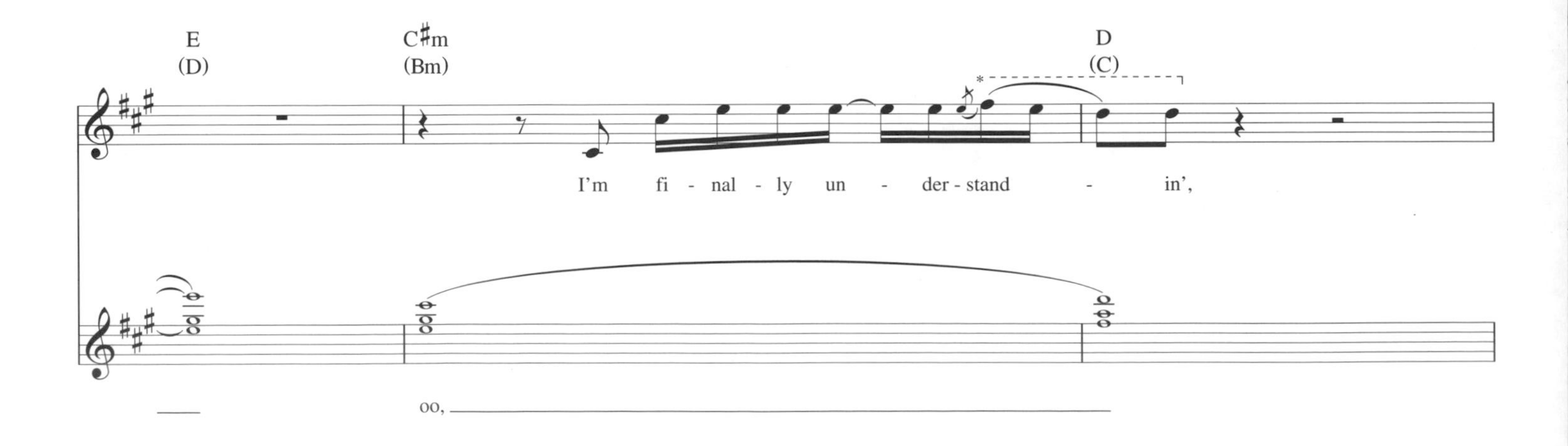
E
(D)
C♯m
(Bm)
D
(C)
I'm fi - nal - ly un - der-stand - in',
oo,

A/E
(G/D)
E
(D)
(D)
Gtr. 1
it's meant so much to me.
you're real - ly on my side,
real - ly on my
oo.
Gtr. 2
Interlude
D
(C)
A/C♯
(G/B)
side,
yeah,
yeah.
8va
loco
Bm
(Am)
Esus4
(Dsus4)
E
(D)
Oo.

Outro
Bkgd. Voc.: w/ Voc. Fig. 1
Gtr. 1: w/ Rhy. Fig. 1
2nd, 3rd & 4th times, Lead Voc., ad lib.
A
(G)
Got me un - der - stand - ing.
D/A
(C/G)
D
(C)
E
(D)
2nd, 3rd & 4th times, Gtr. 3: w/ Riff A
Un - der - stand - ing.
Play 4 times & fade
(You got me un - der - stand - in'.)
Mm, yeah.

The Fire Down Below

Words and Music by Bob Seger

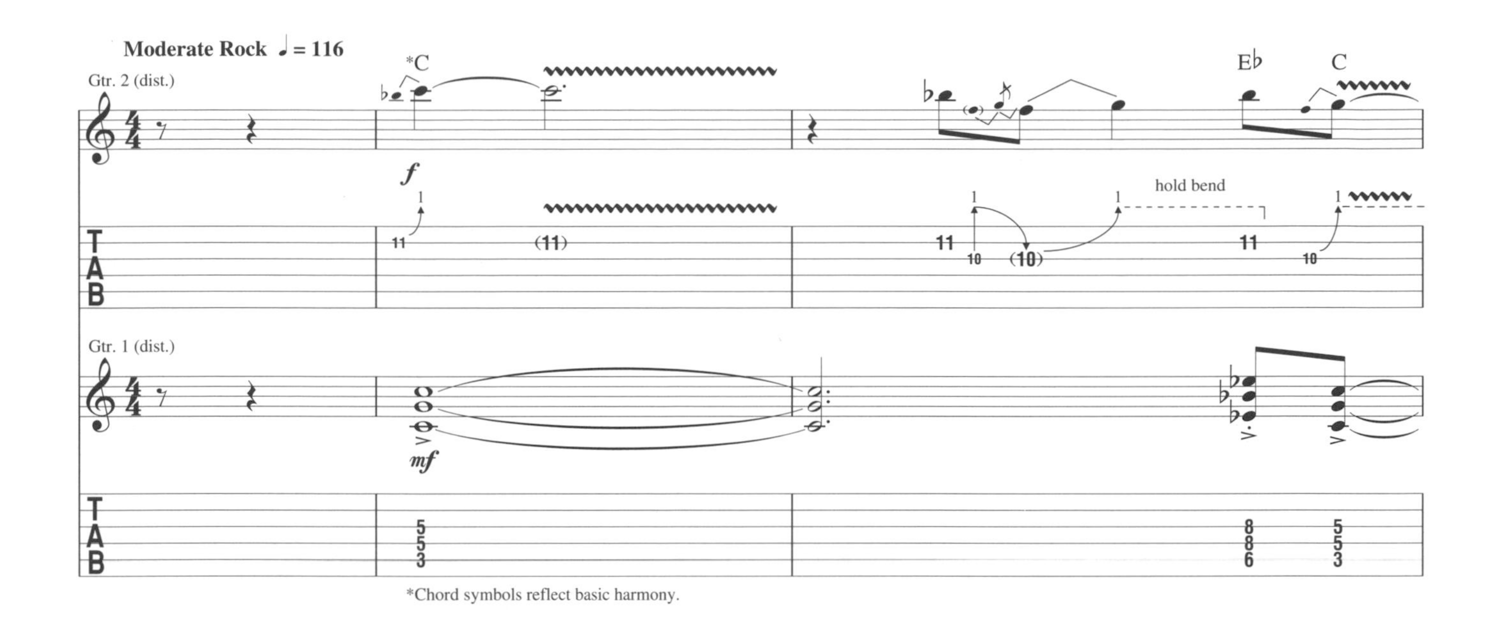

*Chord symbols reflect basic harmony.

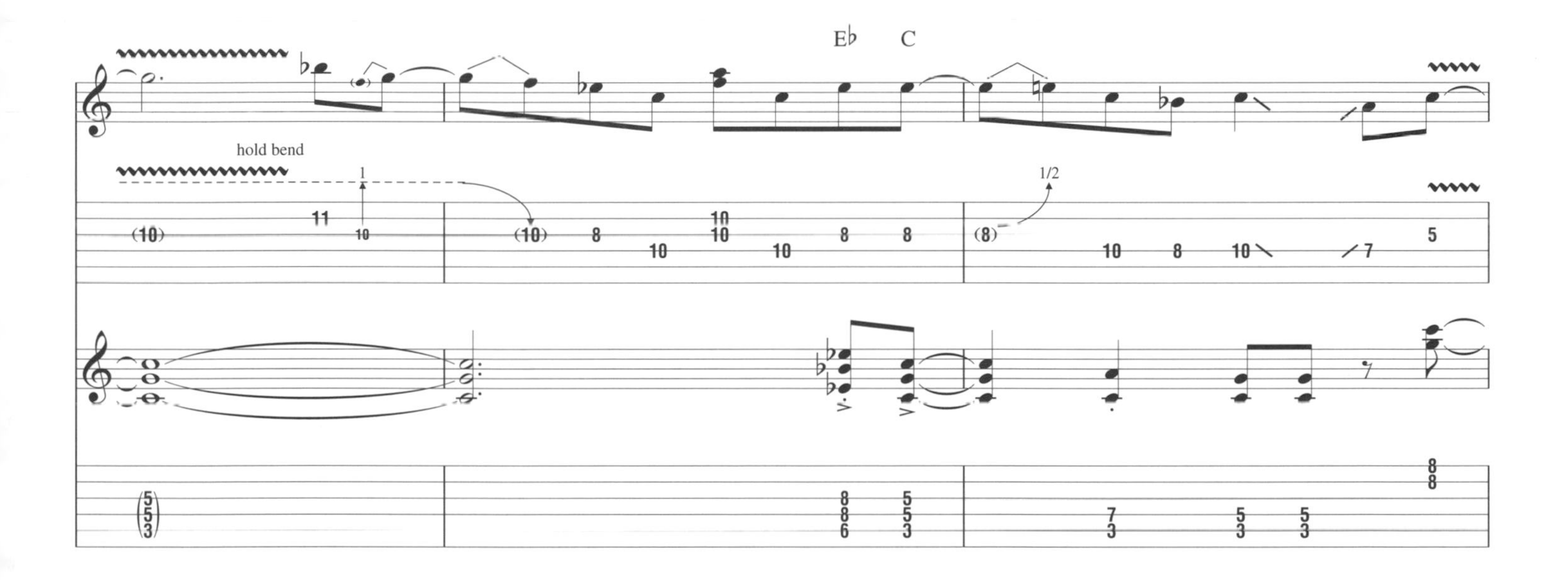

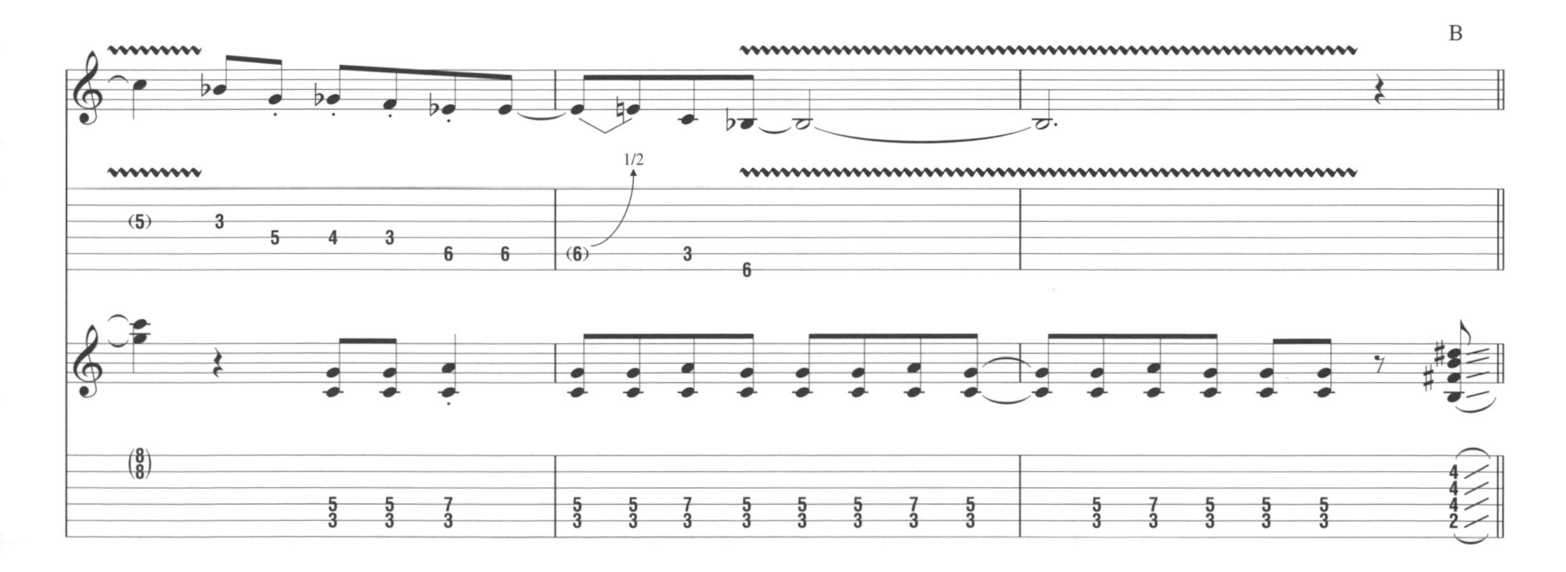

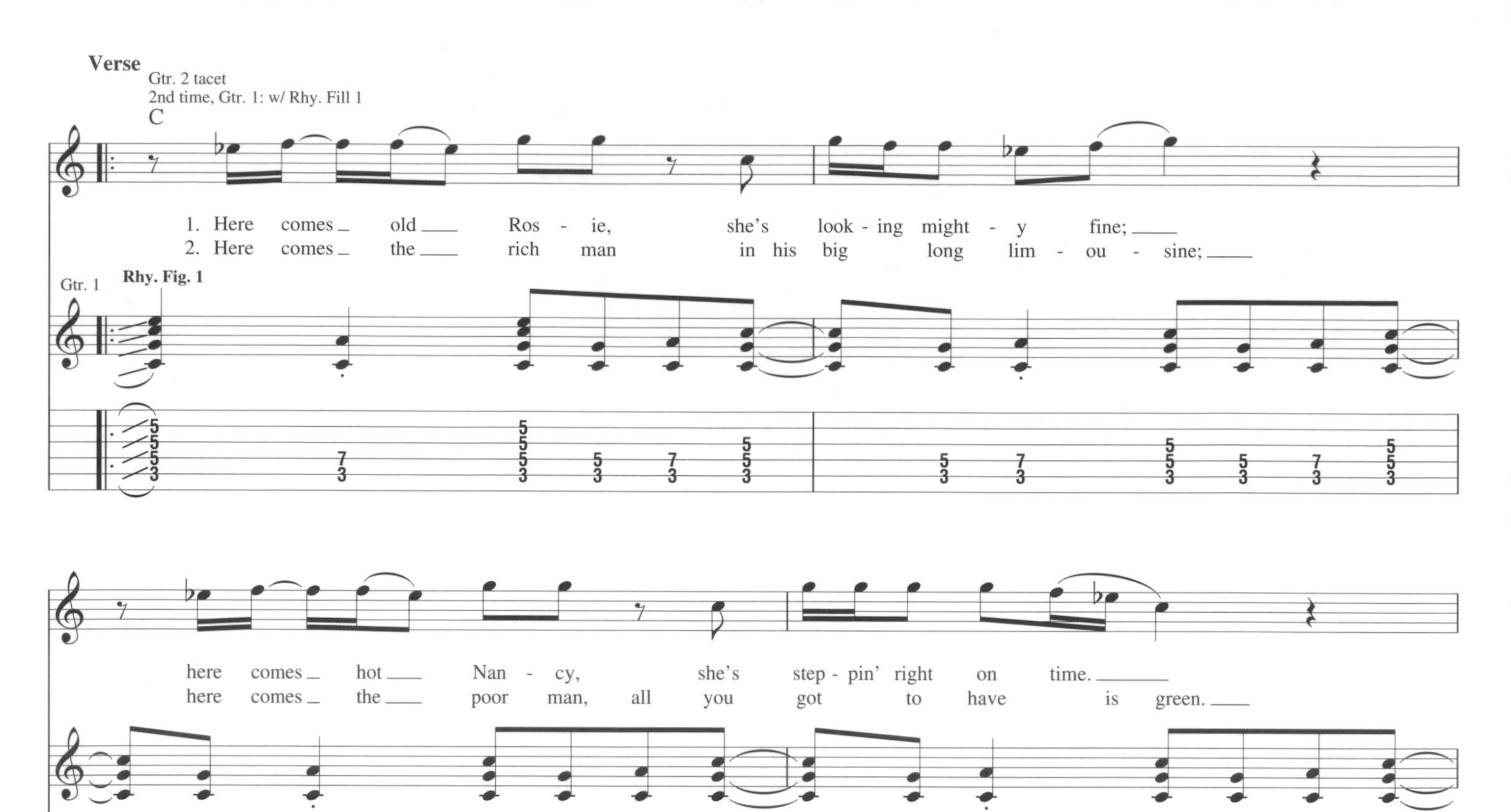
Verse
Gtr. 2 tacet
2nd time, Gtr. 1: w/ Rhy. Fill 1
C
1. Here comes old Ros - ie, she's look - ing might - y fine;
2. Here comes the rich man in his big long lim - ou - sine;
Gtr. 1
Rhy. Fig. 1
here comes hot Nan - cy, she's step - pin' right on time.
here comes the poor man, all you got to have is green.

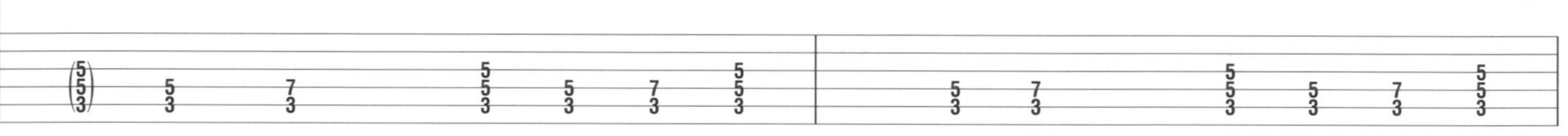

There go the street lights, bring - ing on the night;
Here comes the bank - er, and the law - yer and the cop;

here come the men, fac - es hid - den from the light.
one thing for cer - tain, it ain't nev - er gon - na stop.

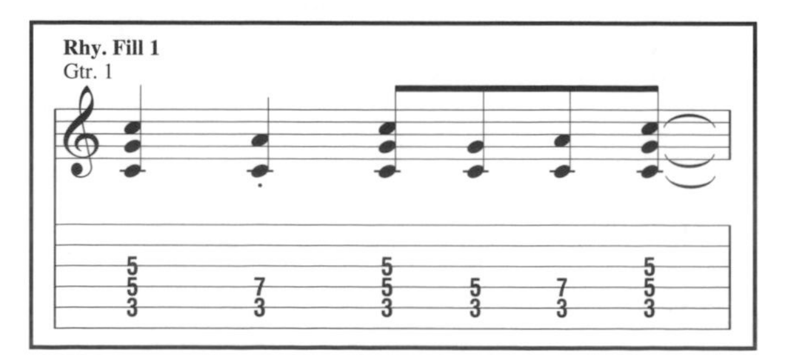
Rhy. Fill 1
Gtr. 1

F
Eb
All through the shad - ows,
oh, they come and they go,
When it all gets too heav - y,
that's when they come and they go,
C
they go,
with on - ly one
Gtr. 2
Gtr. 1
Gtr. 2 tacet
G
thing in com - mon,
F
they got the fi - re down be - low.
C
1.
Fill 1
End Fill 1
End Rhy. Fig. 1

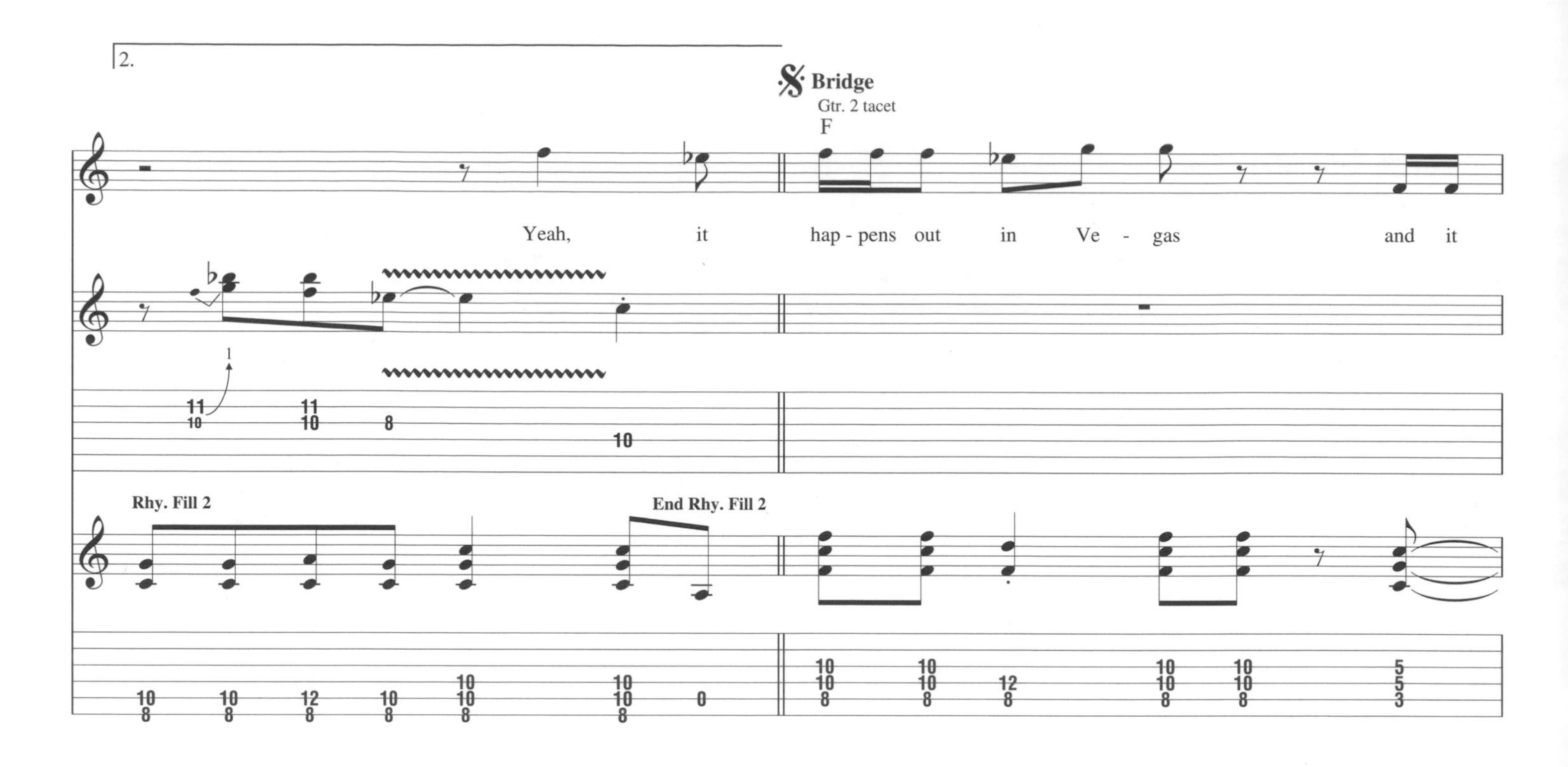

2.
Bridge
Gtr. 2 tacet
F
Yeah, it hap - pens out in Ve - gas and it
Rhy. Fill 2
End Rhy. Fill 2

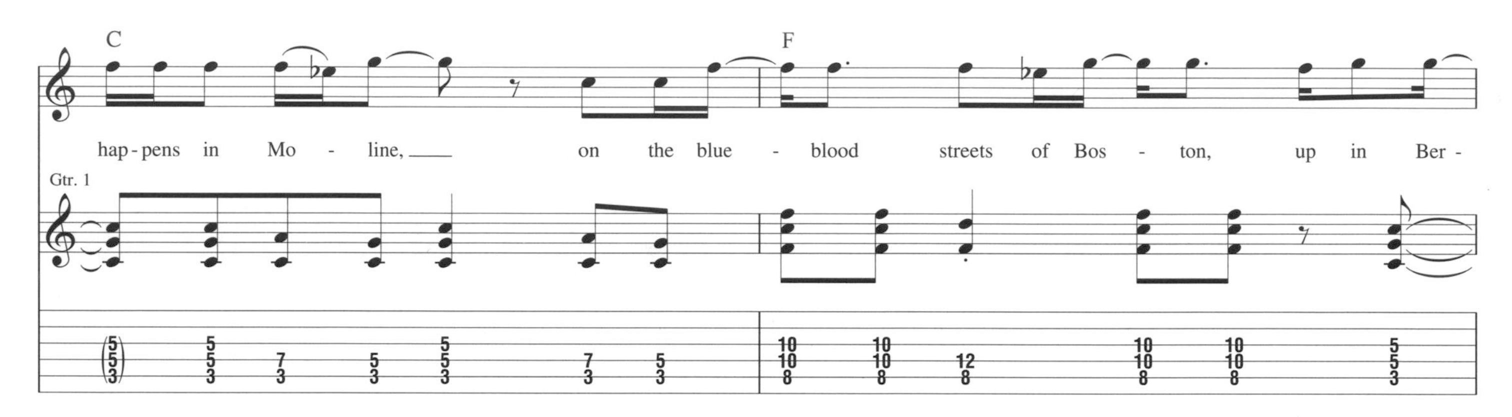

C
F
hap - pens in Mo - line, on the blue - blood streets of Bos - ton, up in Ber -
Gtr. 1

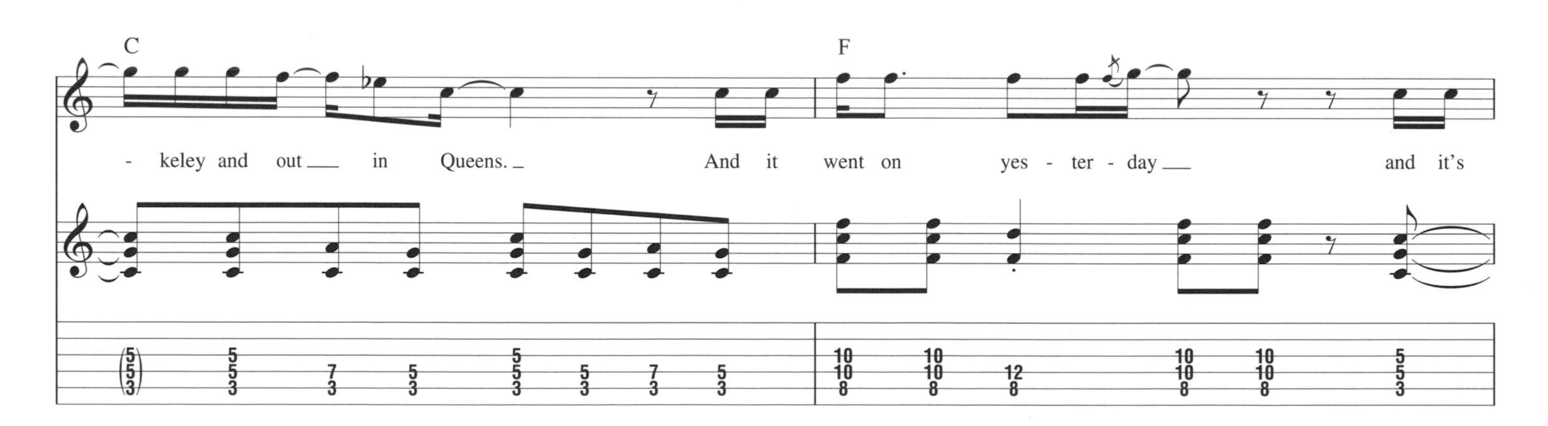

C
F
- keley and out in Queens. And it went on yes - ter - day and it's

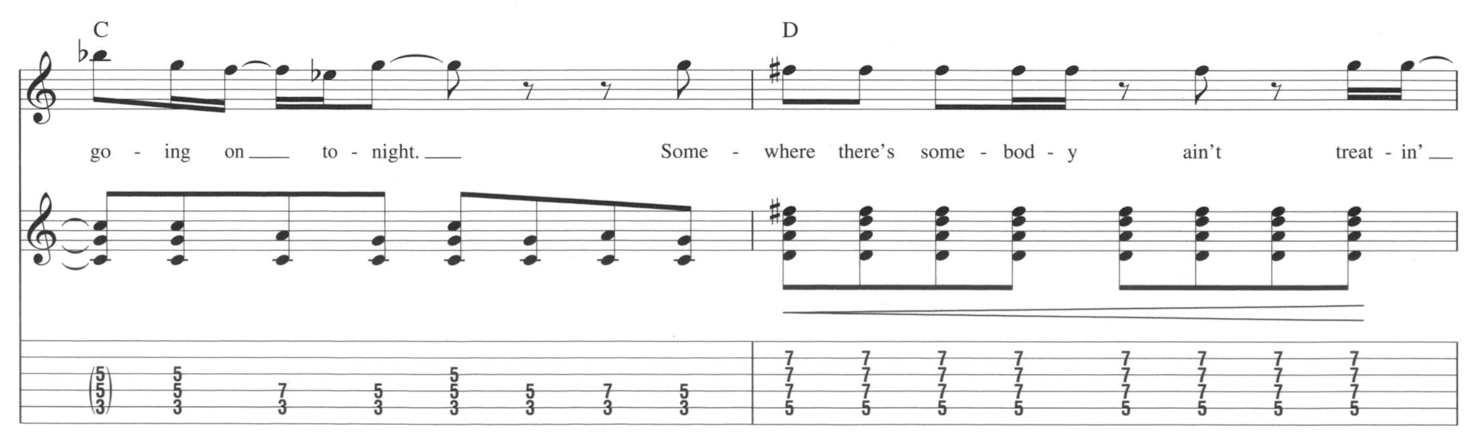

C
D
go - ing on to - night. Some - where there's some - bod - y ain't treat - in'

Verse

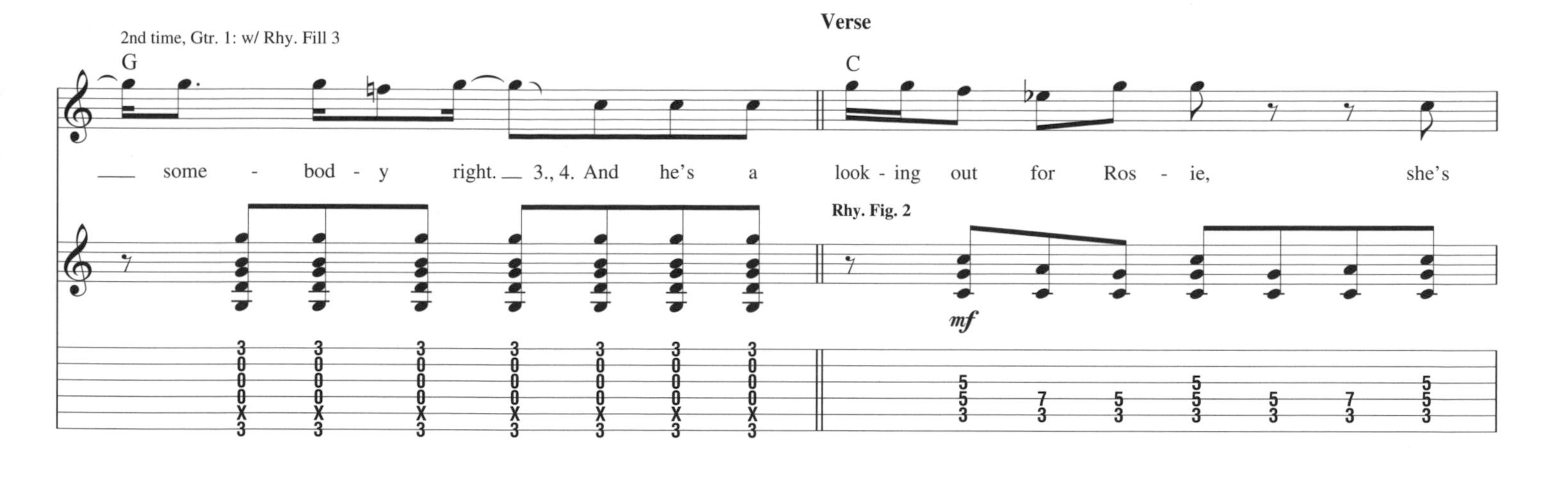
2nd time, Gtr. 1: w/ Rhy. Fill 3
G
C
some - bod - y right. 3., 4. And he's a look - ing out for Ros - ie, she's
Rhy. Fig. 2
mf

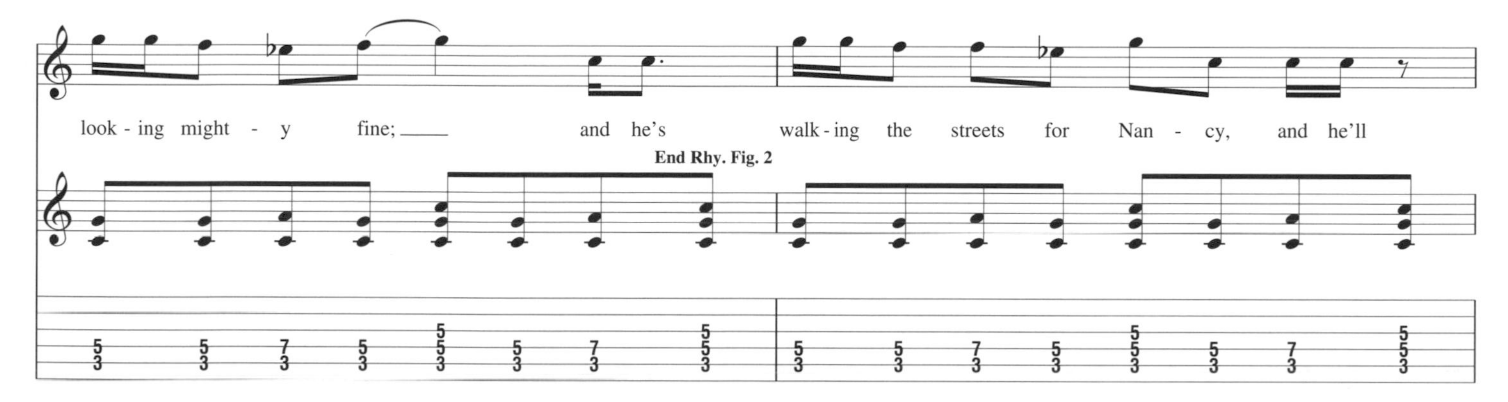
look - ing might - y fine; and he's walk - ing the streets for Nan - cy, and he'll
End Rhy. Fig. 2

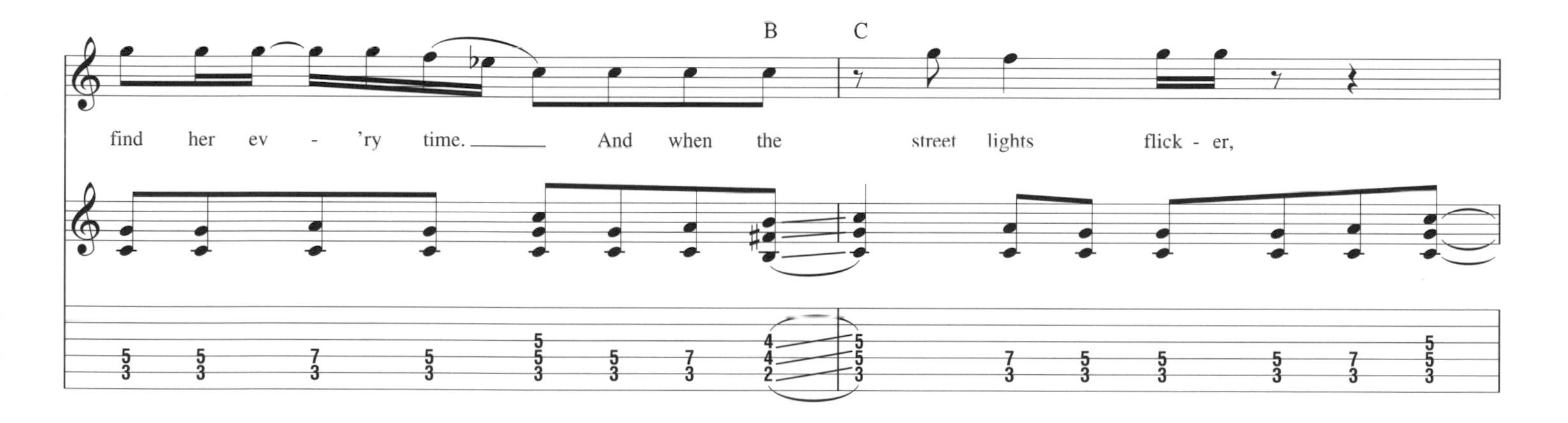
B
C
find her ev - 'ry time. And when the street lights flick - er,

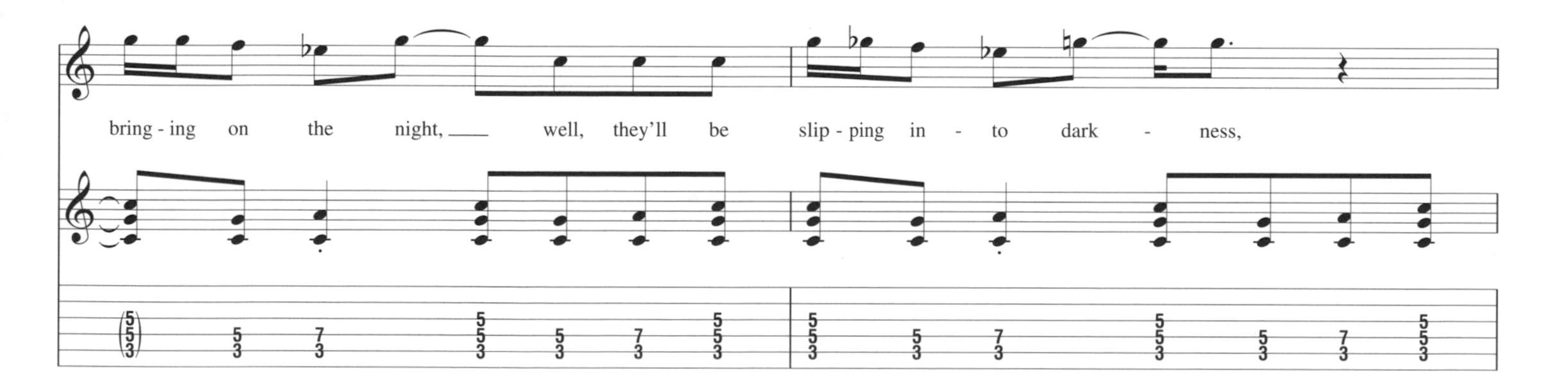
bring - ing on the night, well, they'll be slip - ping in - to dark - ness,

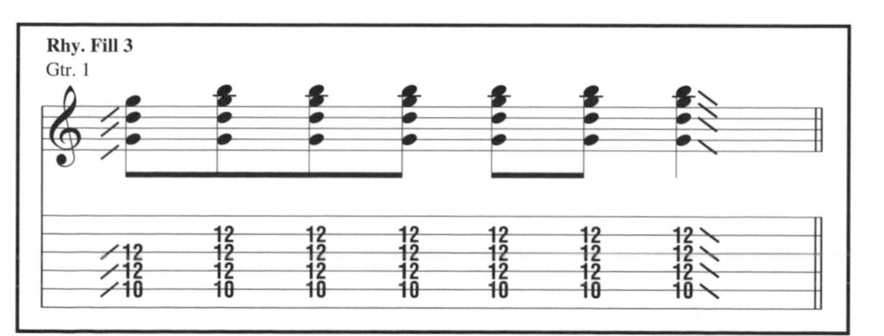
Rhy. Fill 3
Gtr. 1

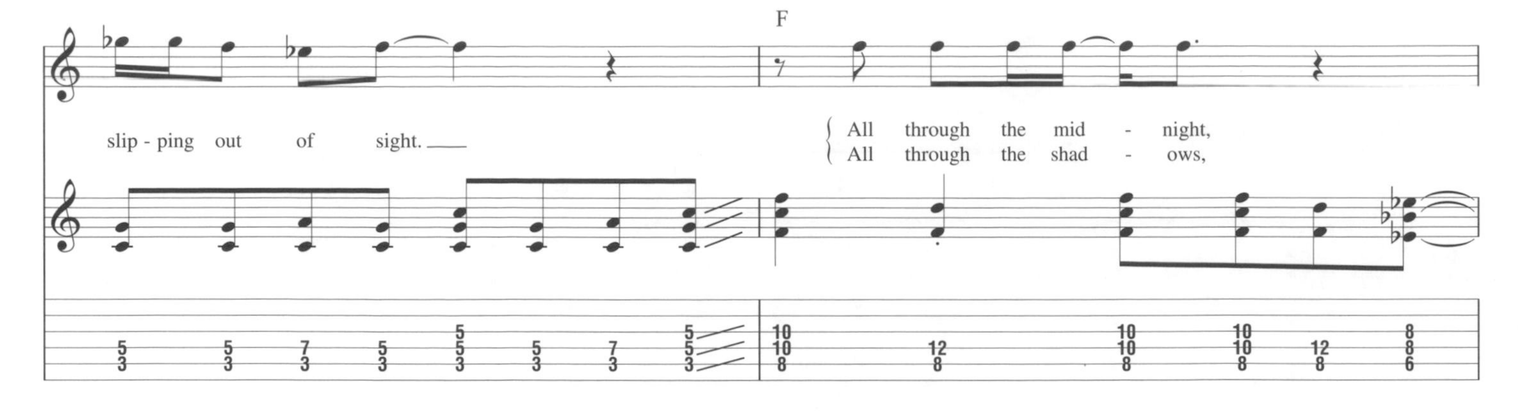
F
slip - ping out of sight.
All through the mid - night,
All through the shad - ows,

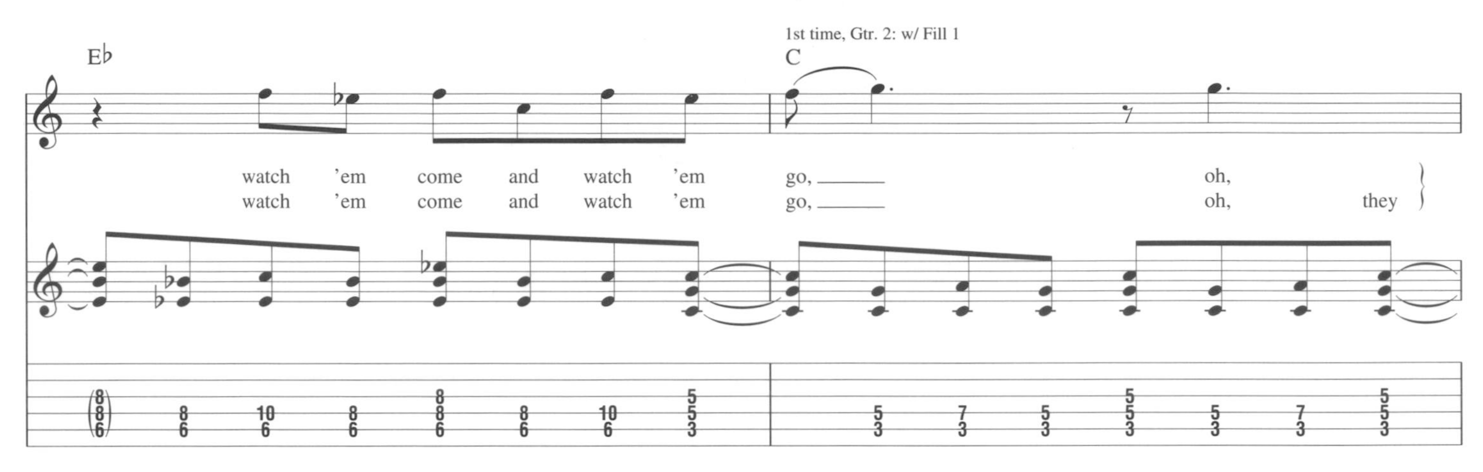
E♭
1st time, Gtr. 2: w/ Fill 1
C
watch 'em come and watch 'em go, oh,
watch 'em come and watch 'em go, oh, they

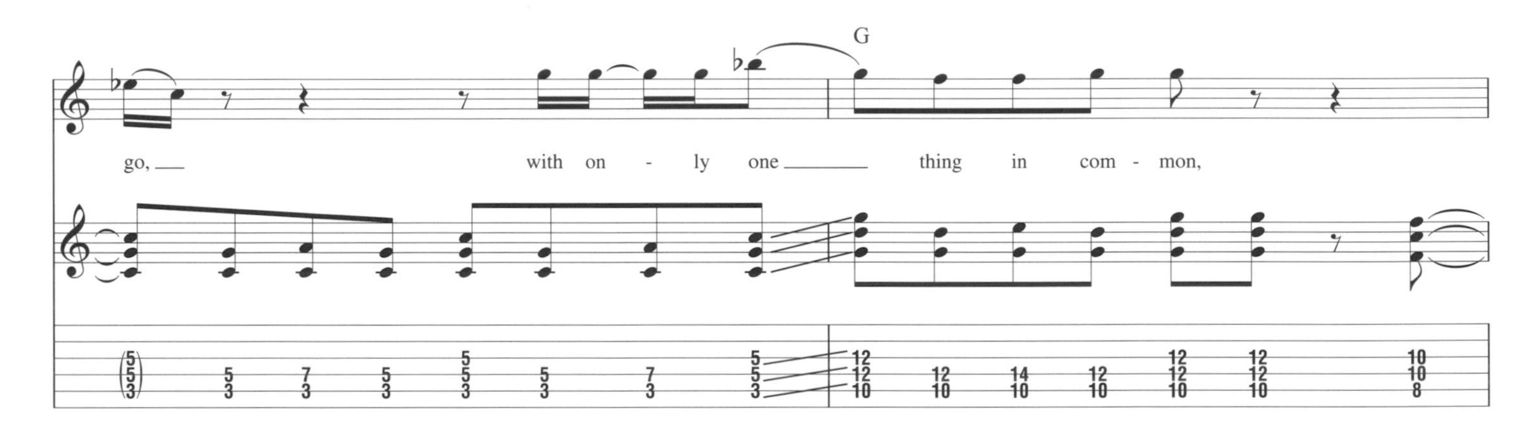
G
go, with on - ly one thing in com - mon,

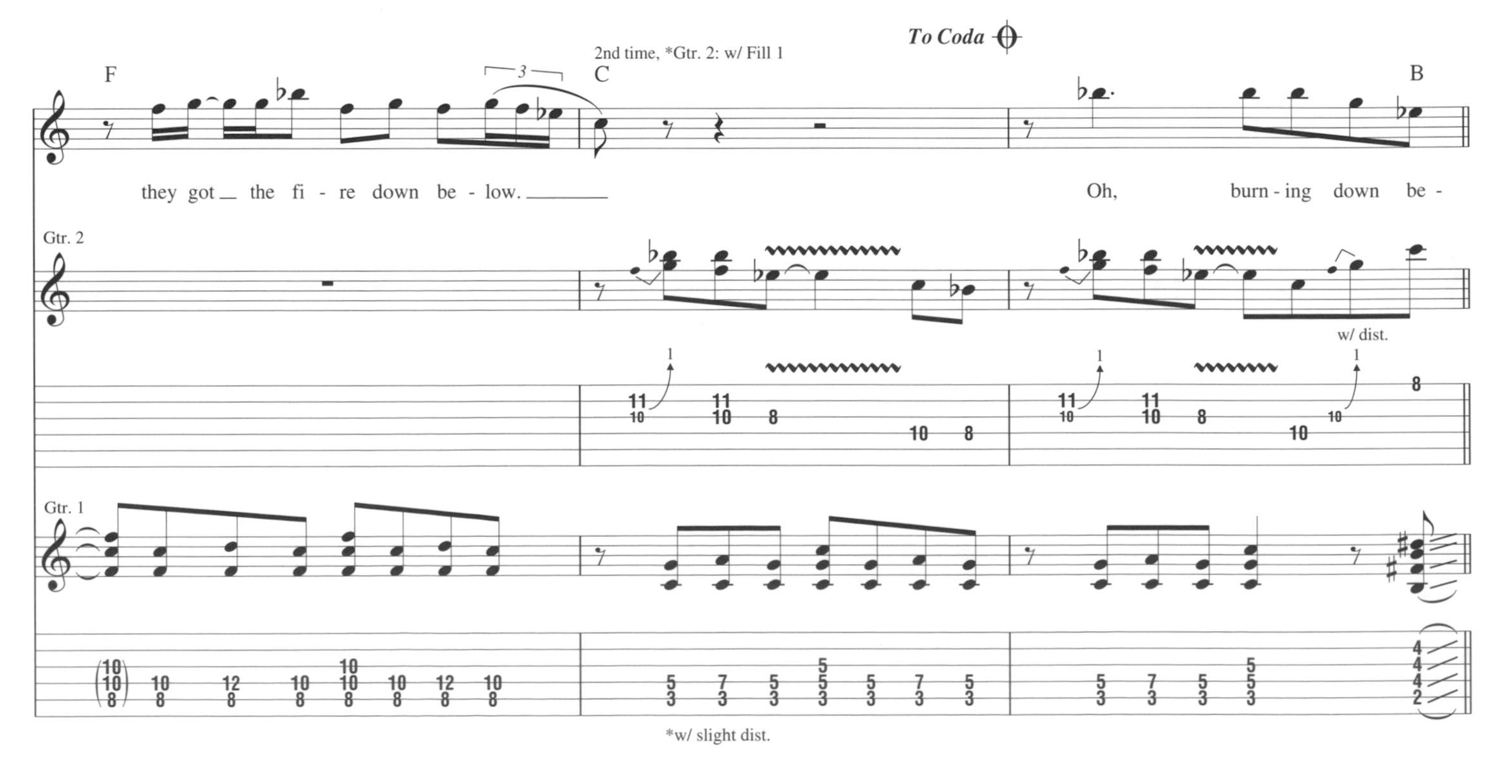
To Coda
2nd time, *Gtr. 2: w/ Fill 1
F
C
B
they got the fi - re down be - low.
Oh, burn - ing down be -
Gtr. 2
w/ dist.
Gtr. 1
*w/ slight dist.

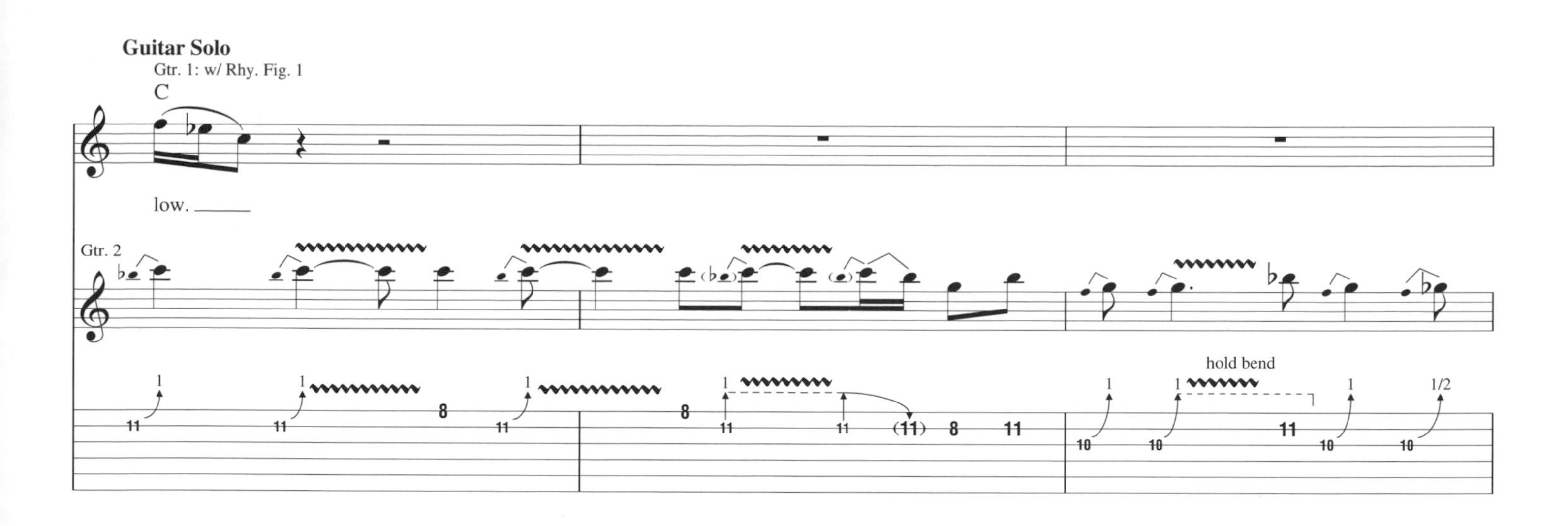
Guitar Solo
Gtr. 1: w/ Rhy. Fig. 1
C
low.
Gtr. 2
hold bend

let ring

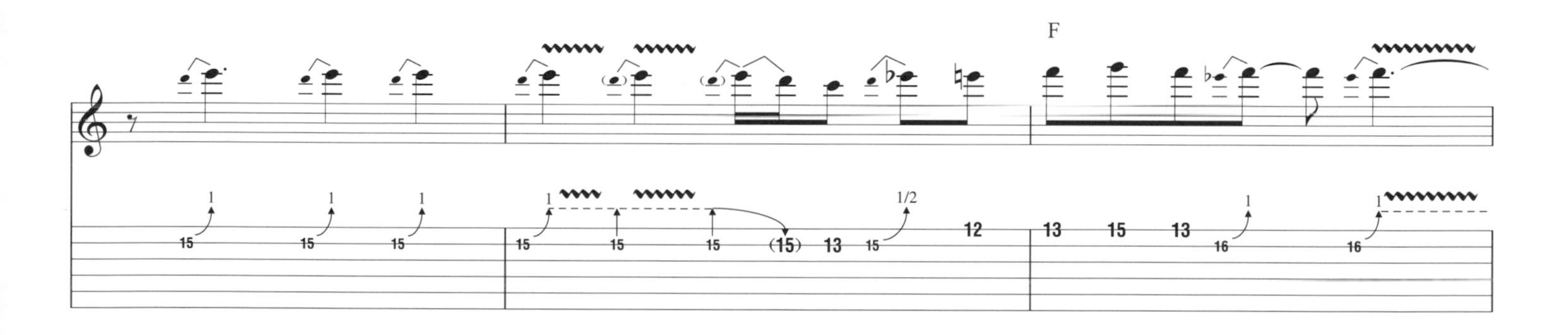
F

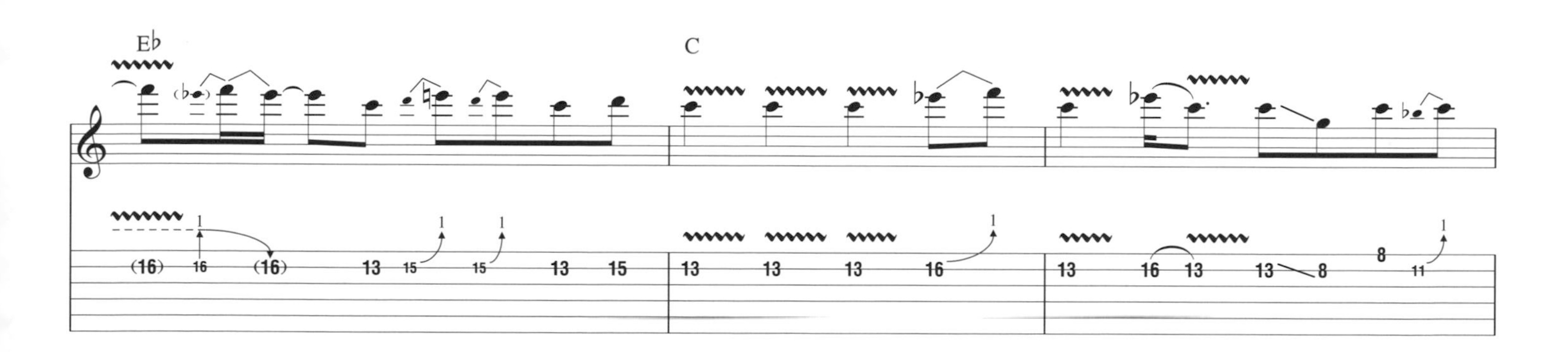
E♭
C

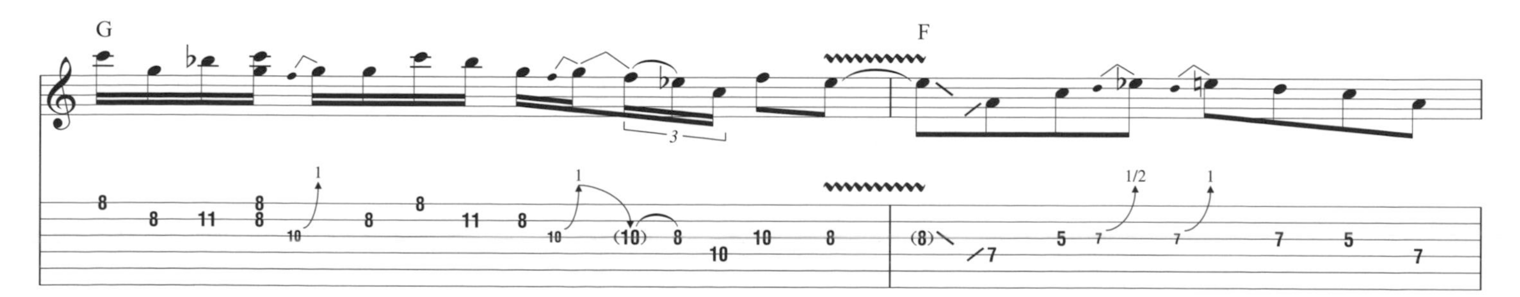
G
F

D.S. al Coda
C
Gtr. 1: w/ Rhy. Fill 2
Yeah, it

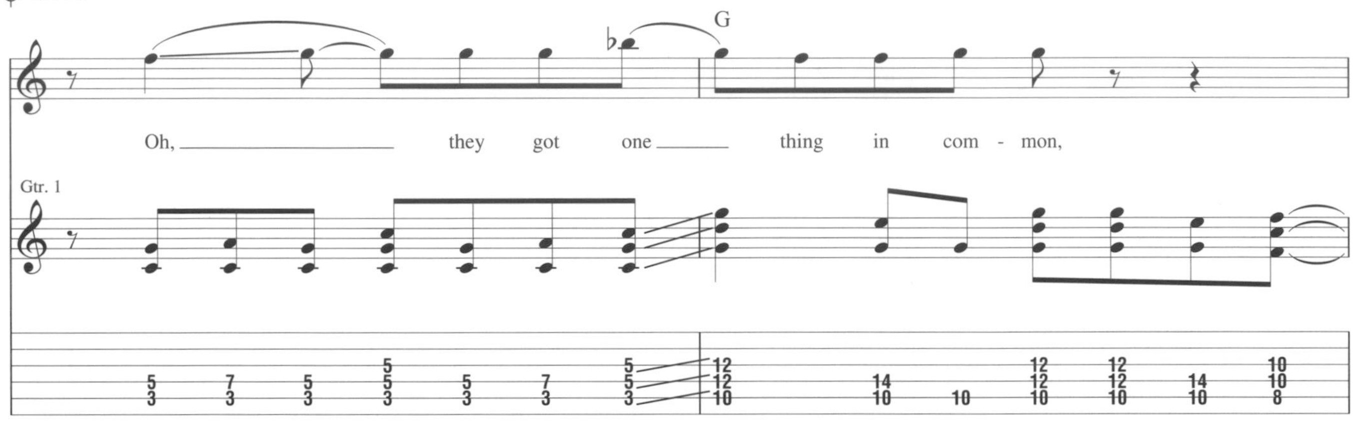
Coda
G
Oh, they got one thing in com - mon,
Gtr. 1

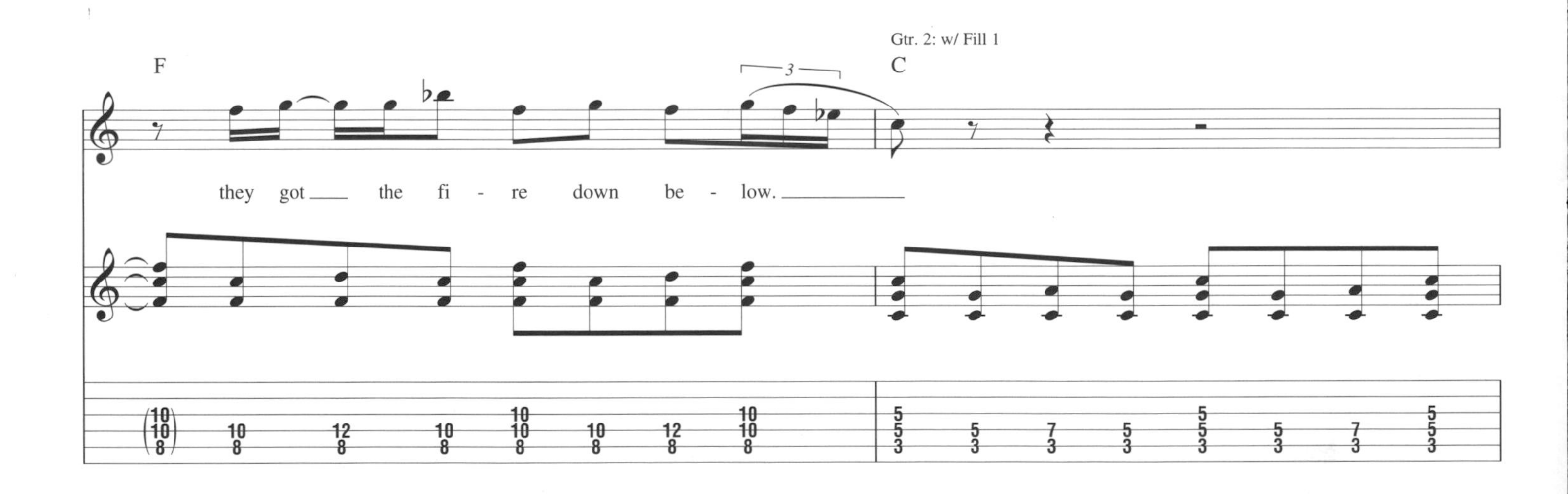
F
Gtr. 2: w/ Fill 1
C
they got the fi - re down be - low.

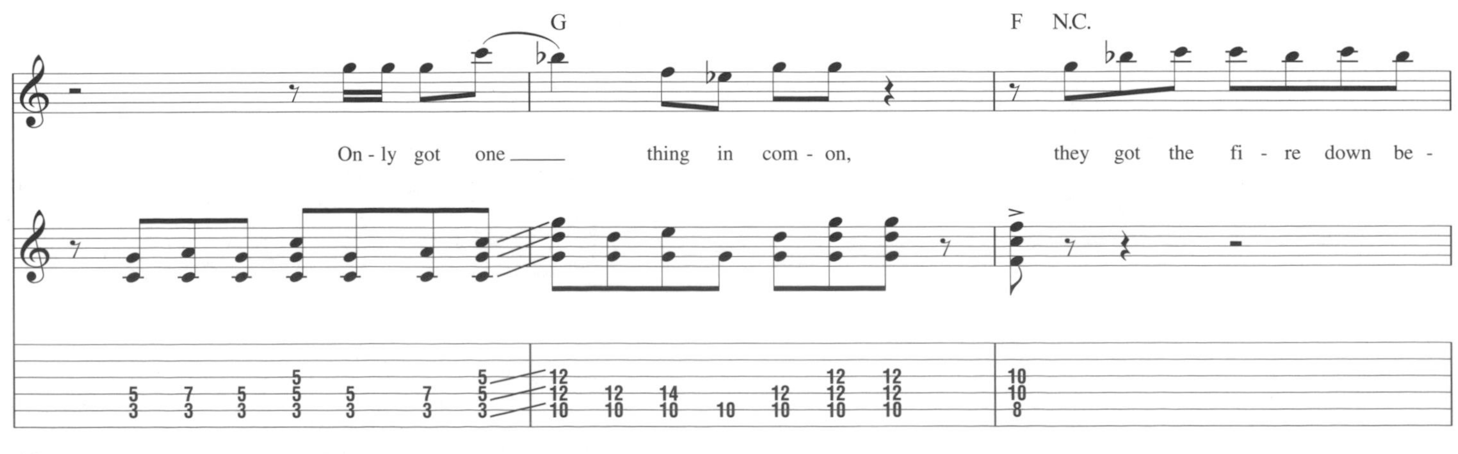
G
F N.C.
On - ly got one thing in com - on, they got the fi - re down be -

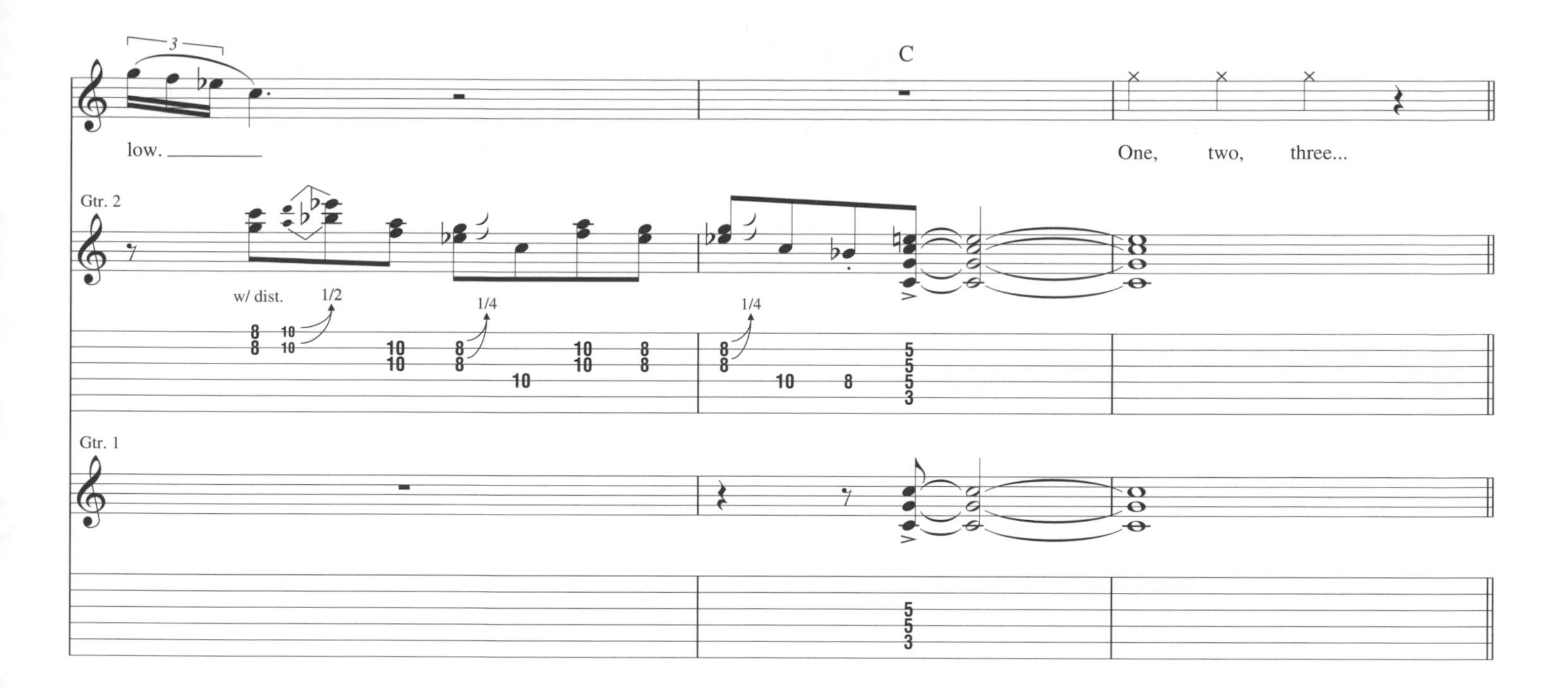
C
low.
One, two, three...
Gtr. 2
w/ dist.
1/2
1/4
1/4
Gtr. 1

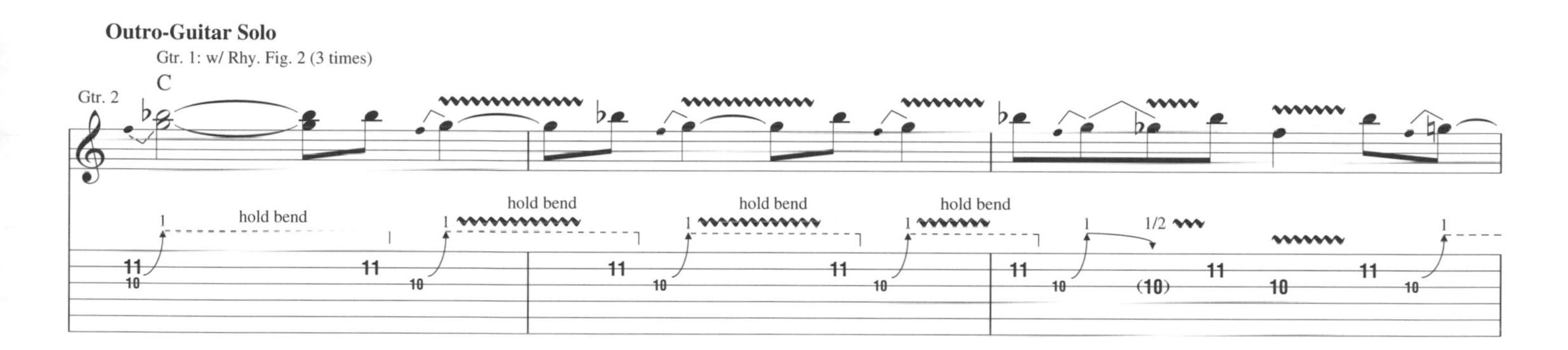
Outro-Guitar Solo
Gtr. 1: w/ Rhy. Fig. 2 (3 times)
C
Gtr. 2
hold bend
hold bend
hold bend
hold bend
1/2

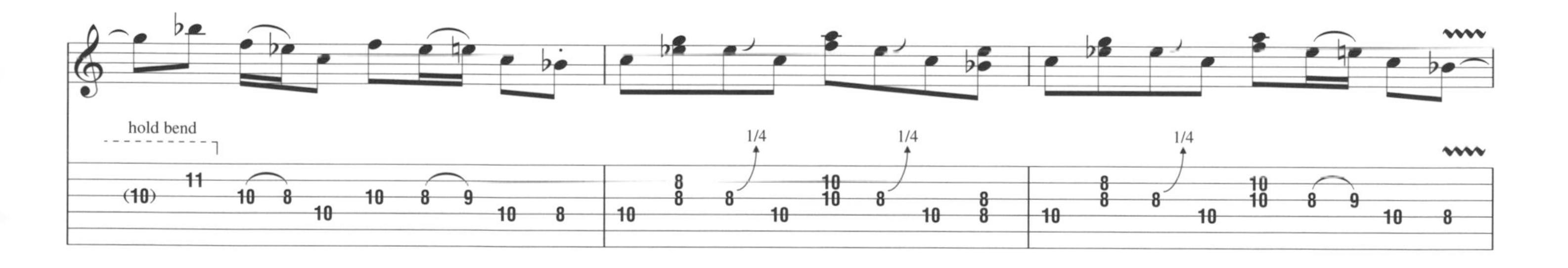
hold bend
1/4
1/4
1/4

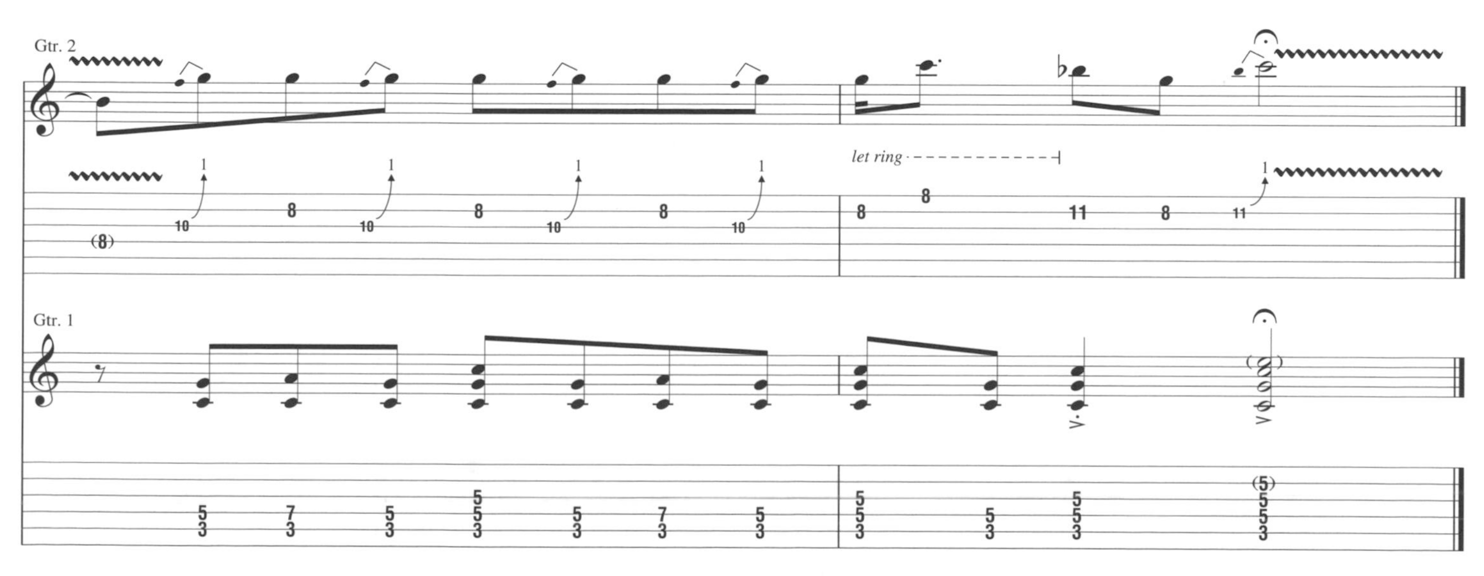
Gtr. 2
let ring
Gtr. 1

Her Strut

Words and Music by Bob Seger

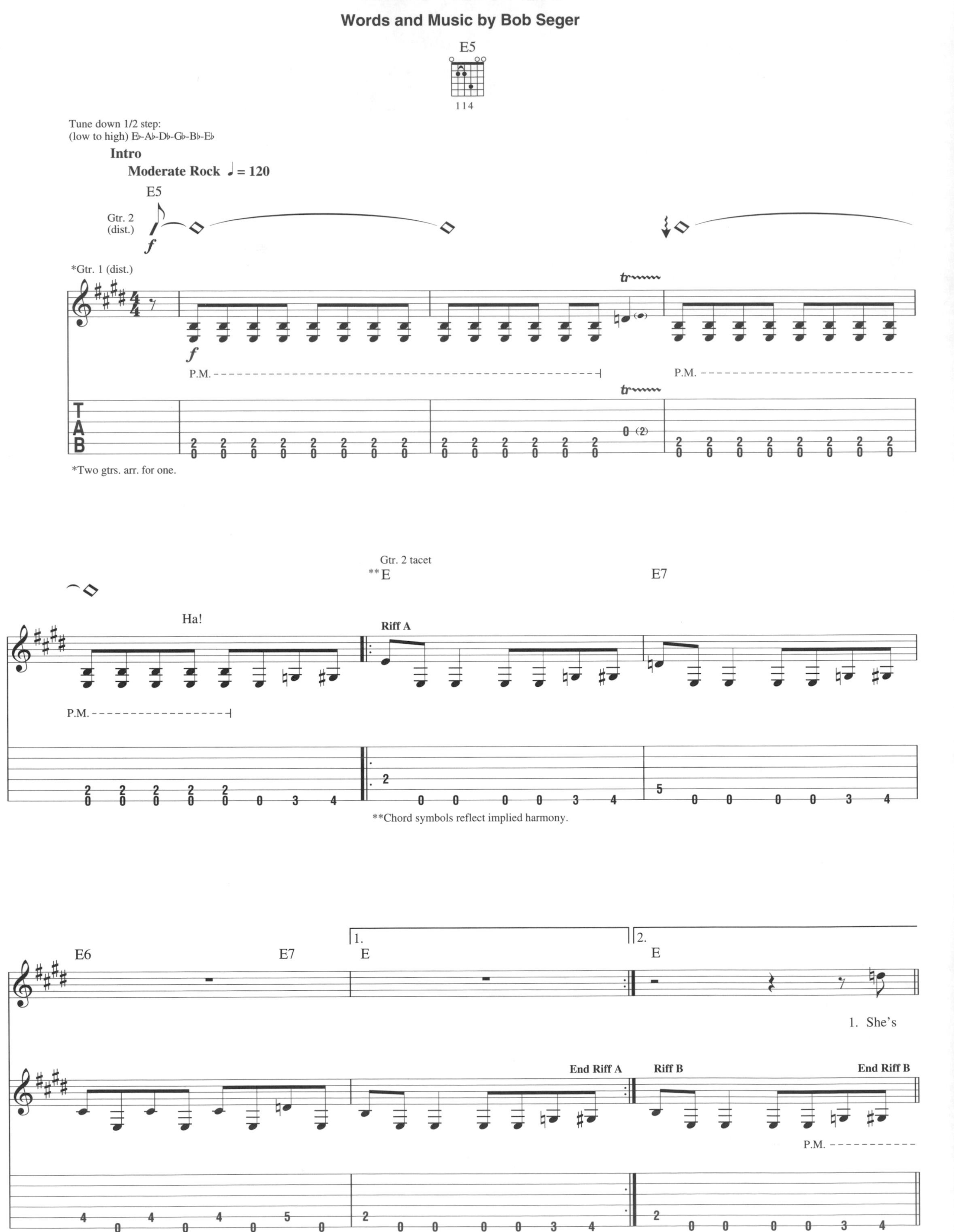

Verse
E
E7
to - tal - ly com - mit - ted to ma - jor in - de - pen - dence, but
times they'll want to leave her, just give up and leave her, but
Riff C
P.M.
E6
E7
E
she's a la - dy through and through. She
they would nev - er play that scene. In
gives them quite a bat tle, all that they can han - dle; she'll
spite of all her talk - ing, once she starts in walk - ing, the
bruise some, she'll hurt some, too. But,
la - dy will be all they ev - er dreamed.
End Riff C
1/4

Chorus

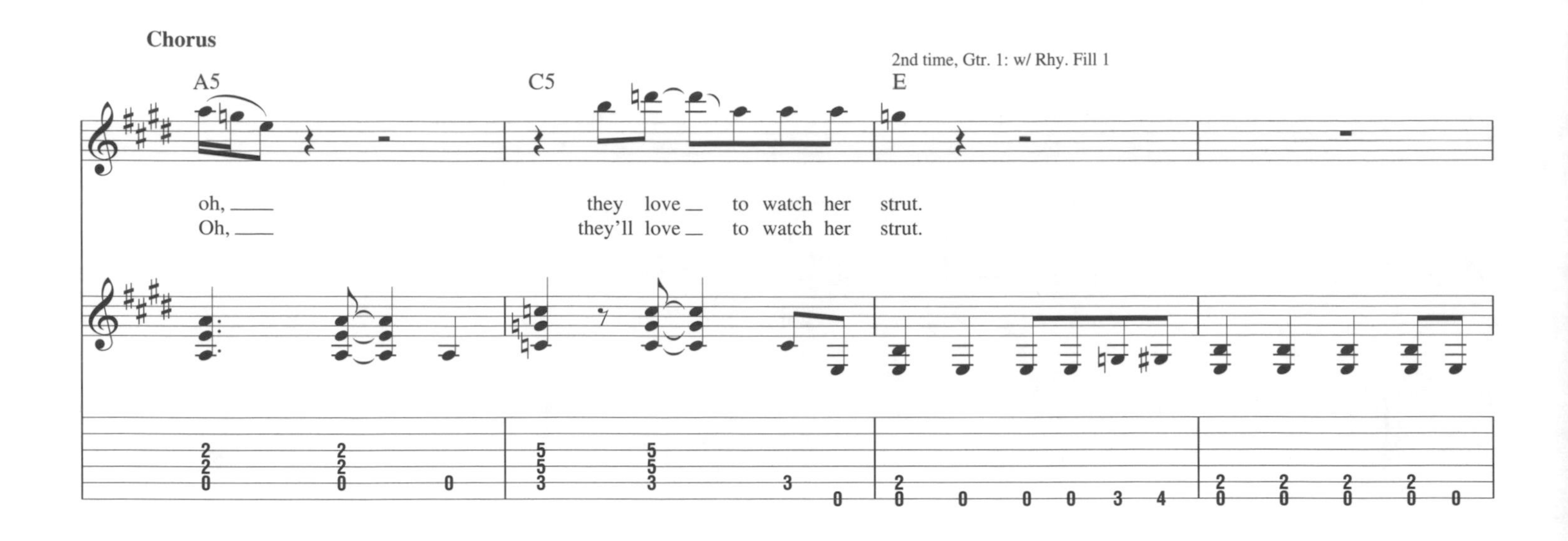

Interlude

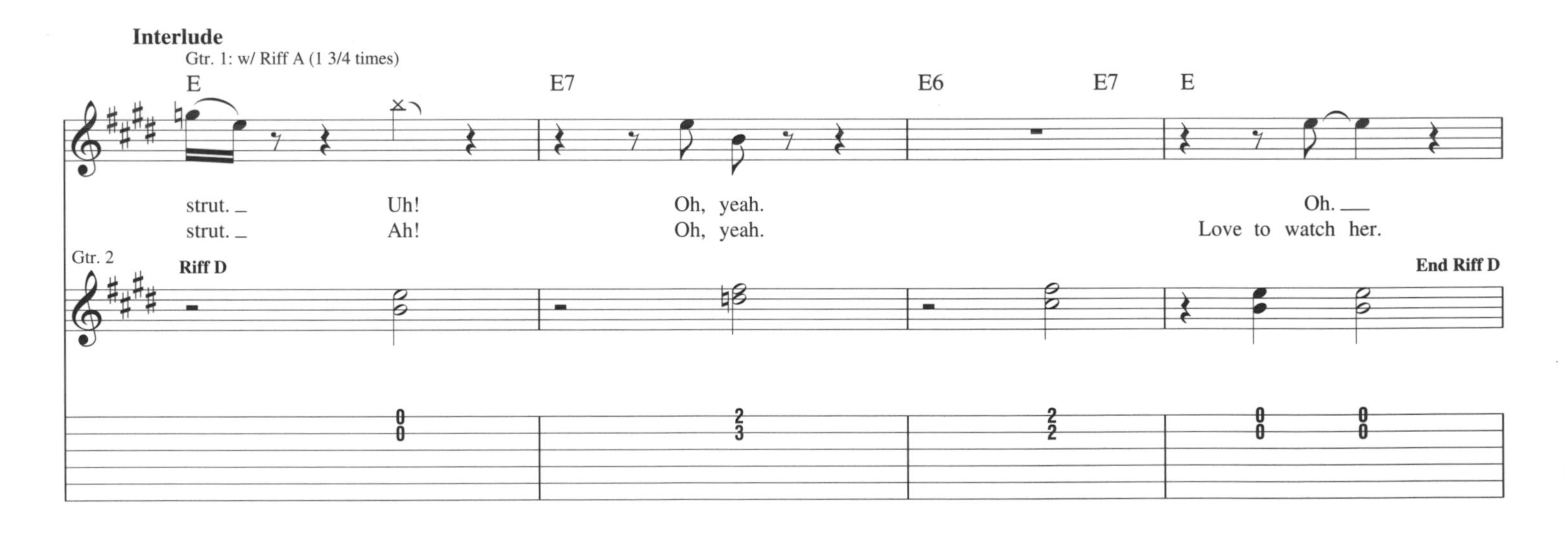

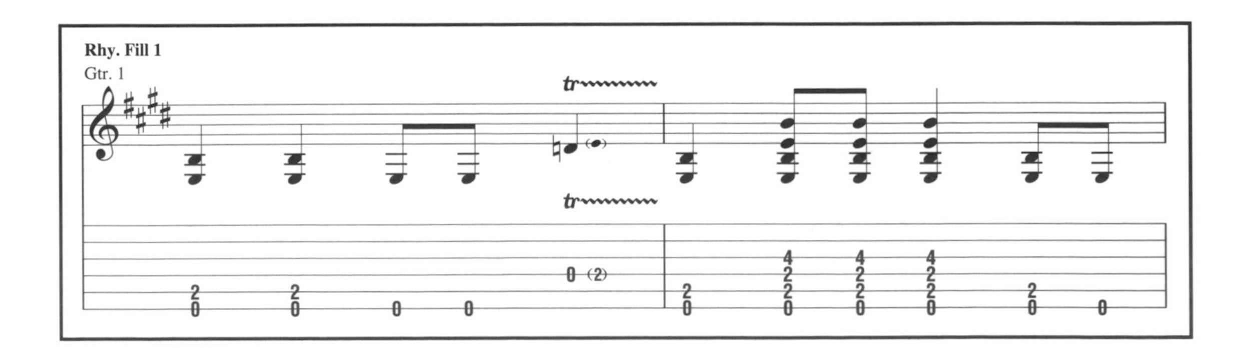

Gtr. 2: w/ Riff D
E7
E6
E7
1.
Gtr. 1: w/ Riff B
E
2. Some -
2.
Gtr. 1: w/ Riff B
E
Guitar Solo
Gtr. 1: w/ Riff C
E
E7
Watch her strut, now.
Gtr. 3 (dist.)
f
*w/ delay
delay off

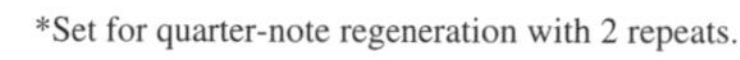
*Set for quarter-note regeneration with 2 repeats.

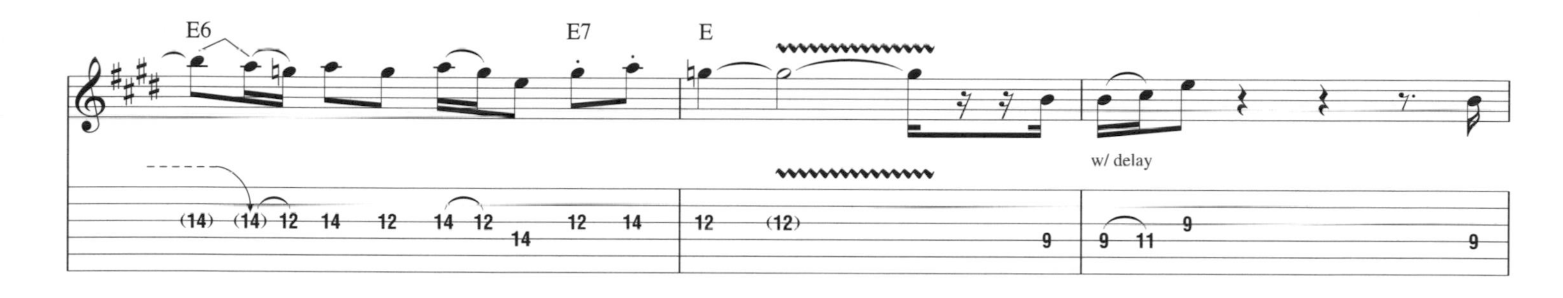
E6
E7
E
w/ delay

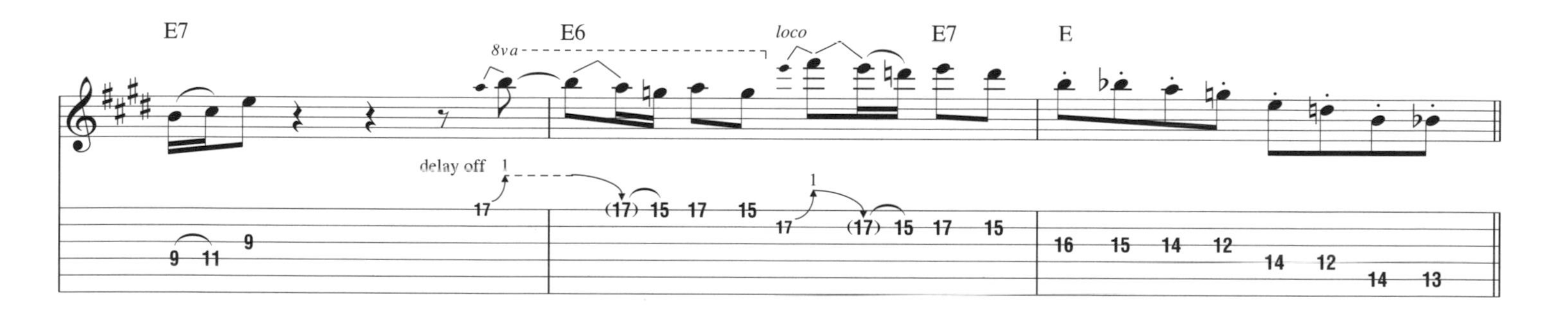
E7
8va
E6
loco
E7
E
delay off

Chorus
A5
Gtr. 3 tacet
C5
E5
Oh,
they love to watch her strut.
Gtr. 3
Gtr. 1

Gtr. 1: w/ Rhy. Fig. 1
G5 F#5 F5 E5 A5 C5 B5
Oh, they do re-spect her but
Gtr. 1
Interlude
Gtr. 1: w/ Riff A (2 times)
N.C. E E7 E6 E7 E
they love to watch her strut. Mm! Al-right. Ah.
Love her strut. Mm, hmm. Love to, love to love to watch her
Outro
Gtrs. 1 & *2: w/ Riffs A & D (till fade)
strut. Mm! Love to watch her
**Gtr. 4 (dist.)
Riff E
End Riff E
*Gtr. 2 played mp
**Doubled throughout
Gtr. 4: w/ Riff E (till fade)
strut! Al-right. They love her strut. Mm!
Love the la-dy's strut. Mm! They love to watch her
Begin fade
strut. Love to watch her strut. Uh.
Fade out
Oh, yeah. They love, they love to watch her strut.

Beautiful Loser
Words and Music by Bob Seger
B♭ C G Am D Em
Intro
Moderately ♩ = 115
Verse
*G
G Am
1. He wants to dream like a
Gtr. 1 (elec.)
Rhy. Fig. 1
mf
w/ clean tone
let ring throughout
Gtr. 2 (elec.)
Rhy. Fig. 1A
mp
w/ clean tone
let ring throughout
*Chord symbols reflect overall harmony.
C D G
young man with the wis - dom of an old man.

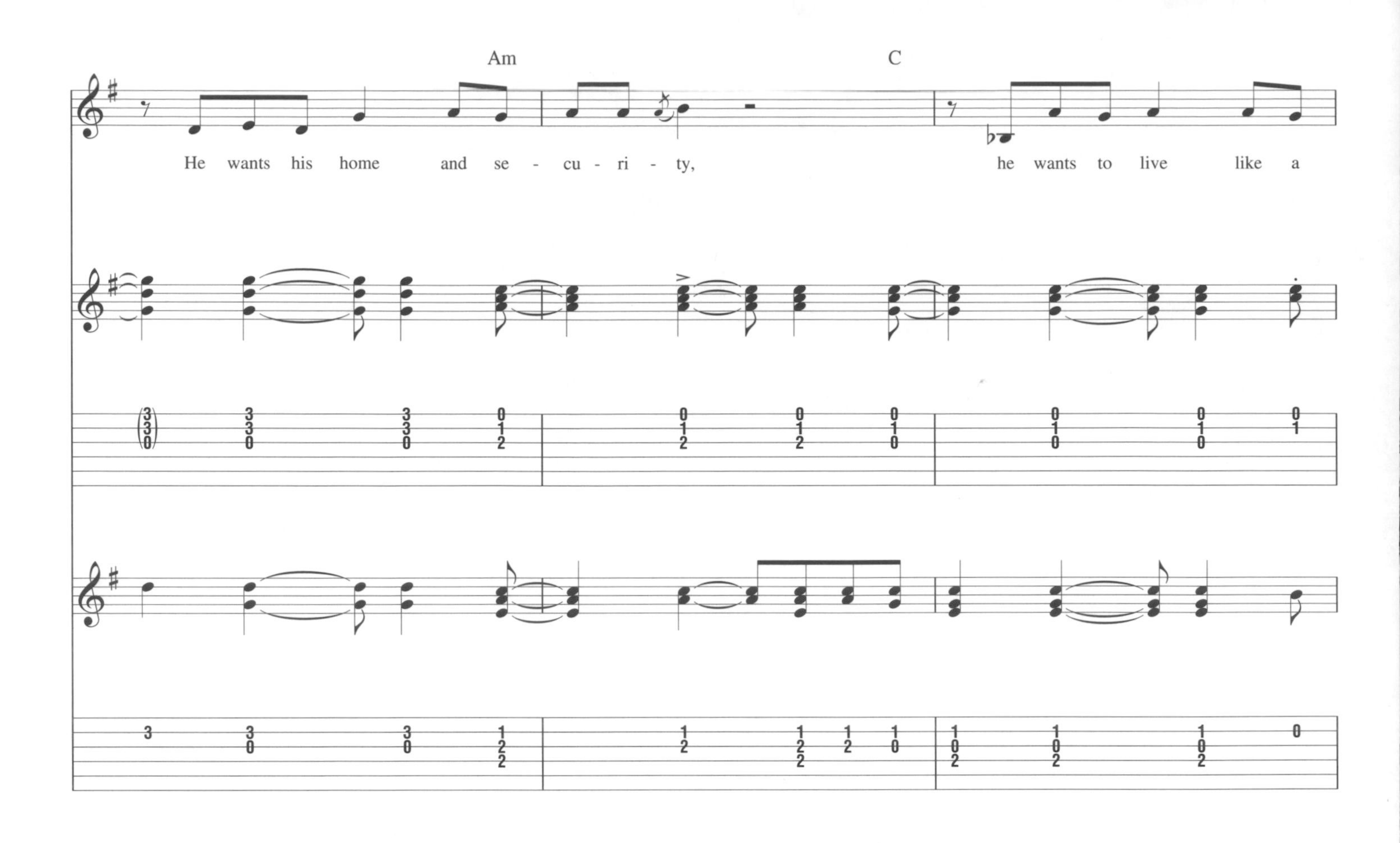

Am
C
He wants his home and se - cu - ri - ty,
he wants to live like a

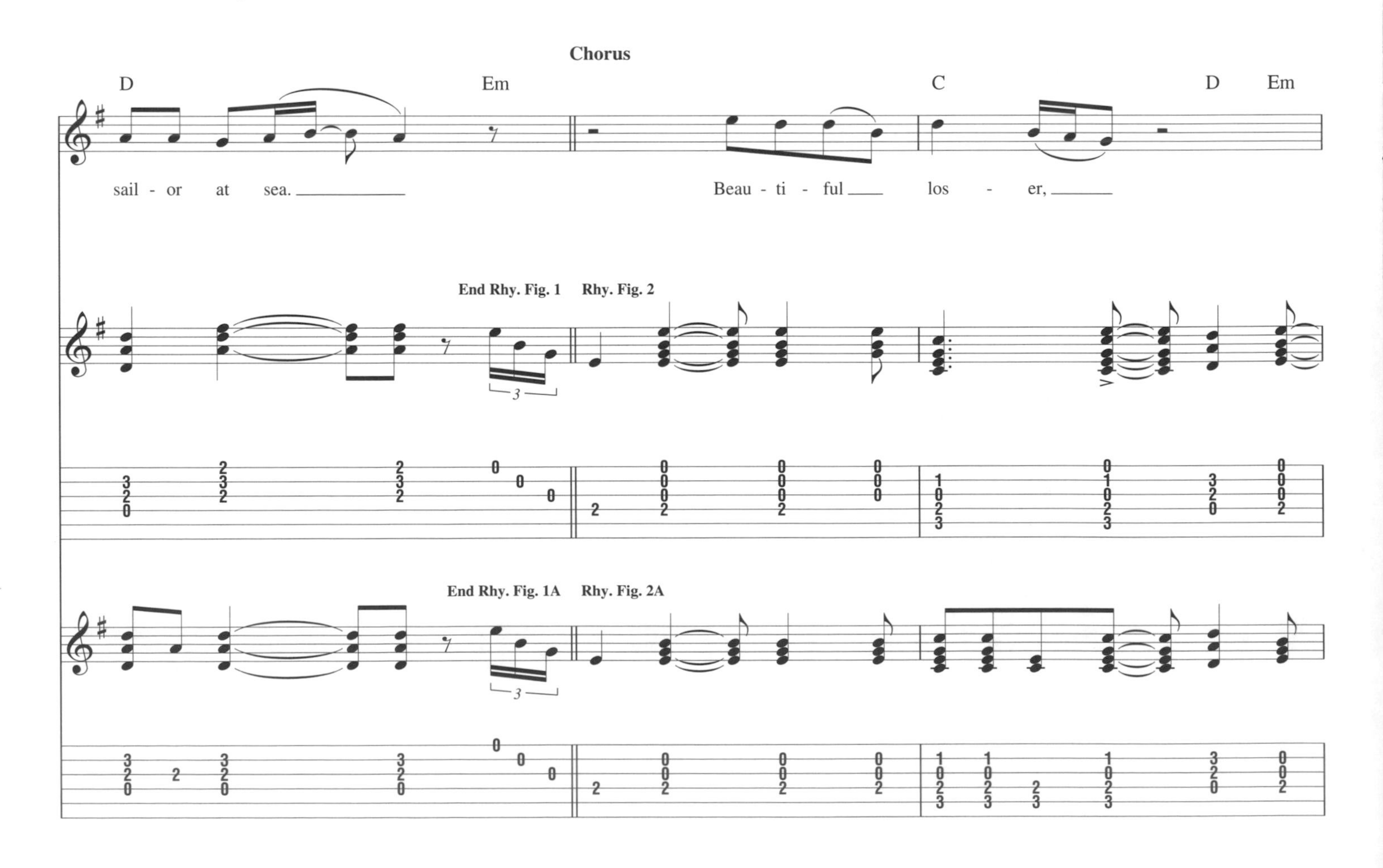

Chorus
D
Em
C
D
Em
sail - or at sea.
Beau - ti - ful
los - er,
End Rhy. Fig. 1
Rhy. Fig. 2
End Rhy. Fig. 1A
Rhy. Fig. 2A

A7
G
where you gon-na fall, when you re-al-ize you
1/2
1/2

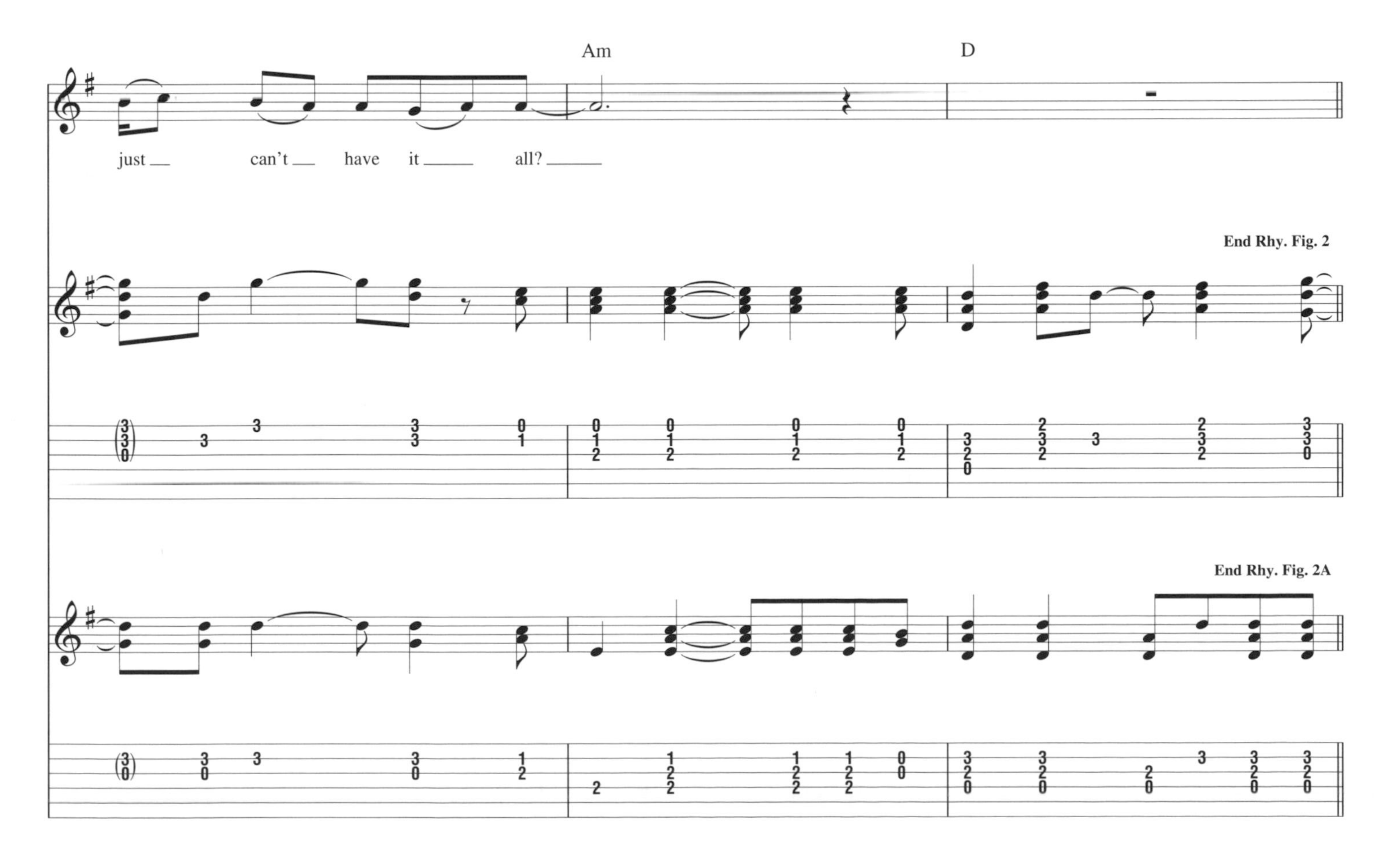
Am
D
just can't have it all?
End Rhy. Fig. 2
End Rhy. Fig. 2A

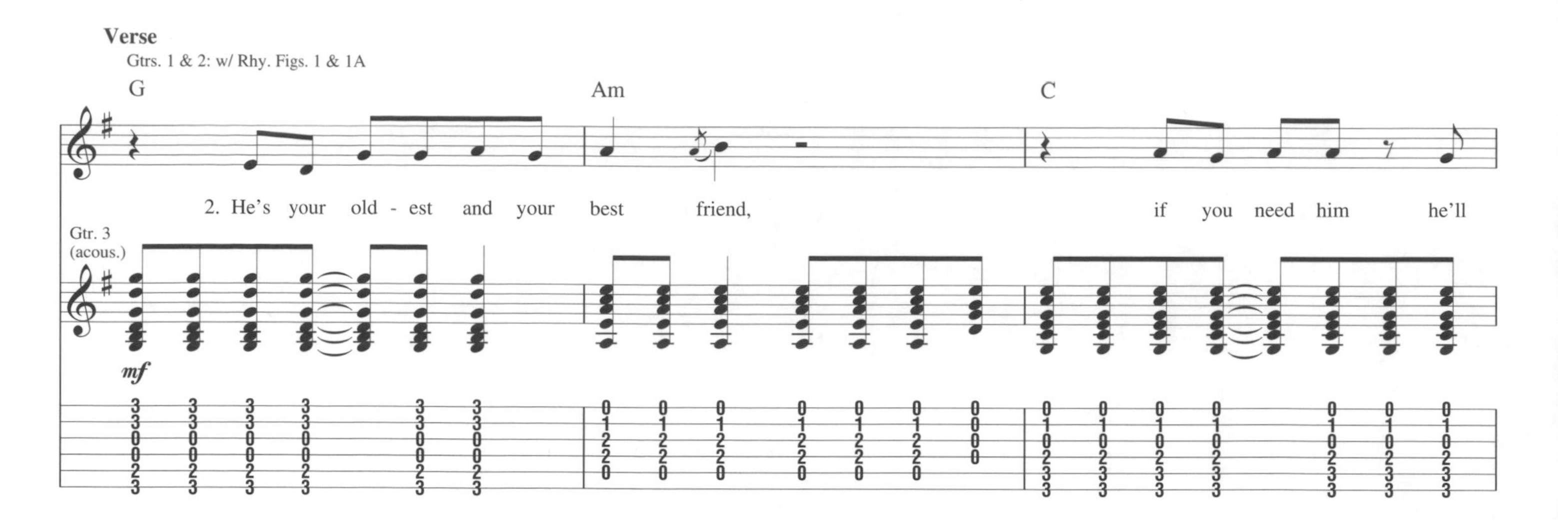
Verse
Gtrs. 1 & 2: w/ Rhy. Figs. 1 & 1A
G
Am
C
2. He's your old - est and your best friend, if you need him he'll
Gtr. 3 (acous.)
mf

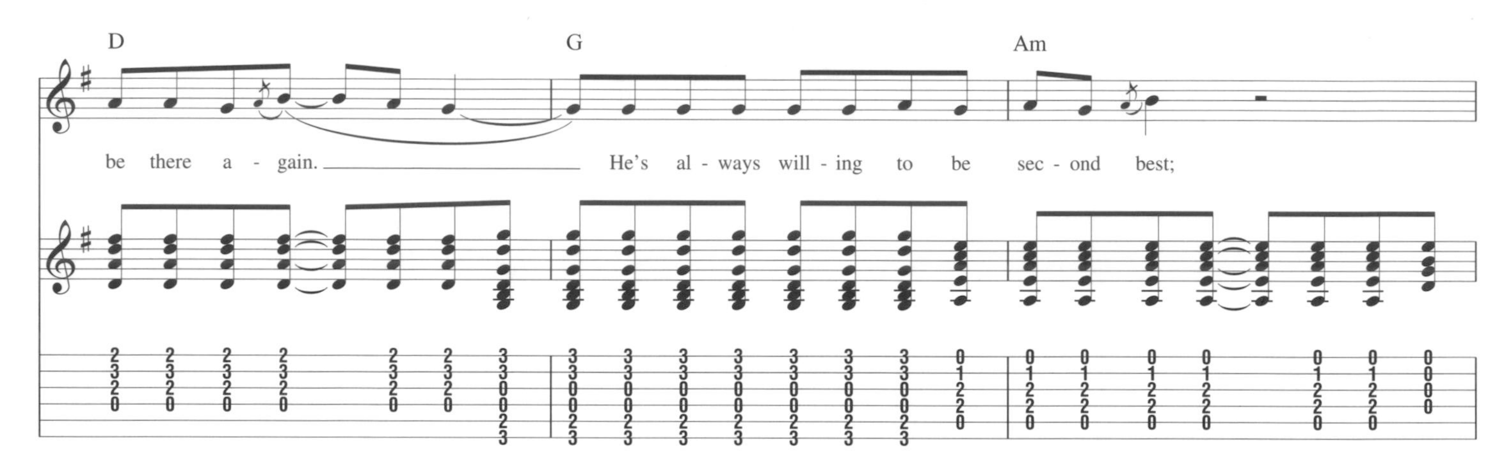
D
G
Am
be there a - gain. He's al - ways will - ing to be sec - ond best;

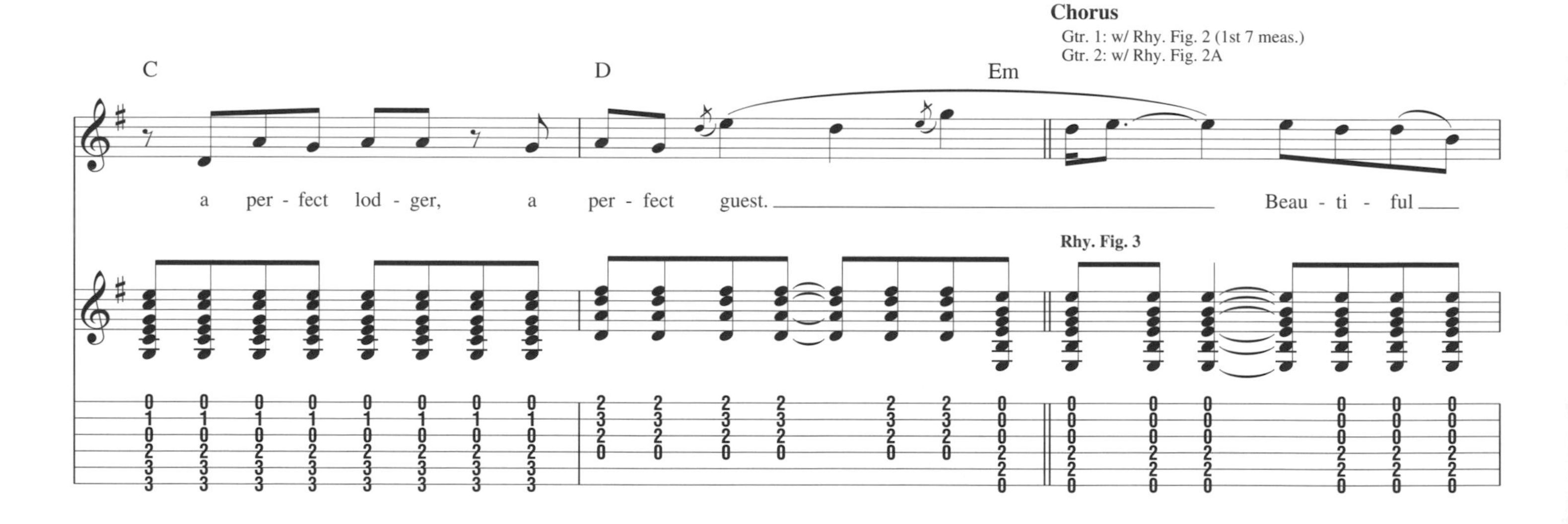
Chorus
Gtr. 1: w/ Rhy. Fig. 2 (1st 7 meas.)
Gtr. 2: w/ Rhy. Fig. 2A
C
D
Em
a per - fect lod - ger, a per - fect guest. Beau - ti - ful
Rhy. Fig. 3

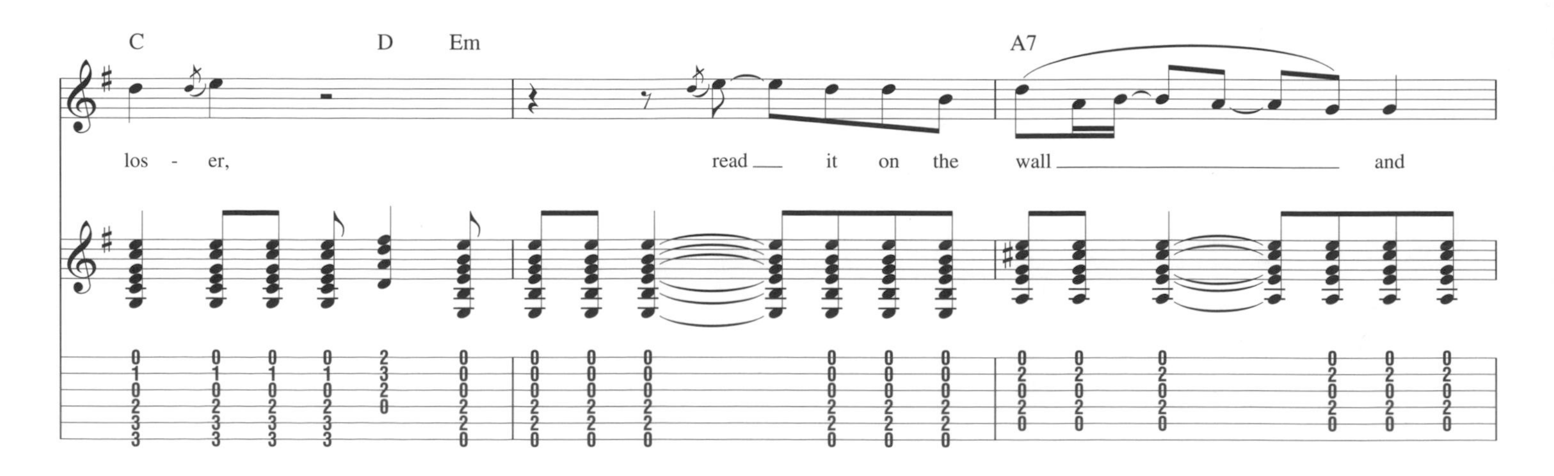
C
D
Em
A7
los - er, read it on the wall and

G
Am
re - al - ize
you
just
can't
have
it
all,
and

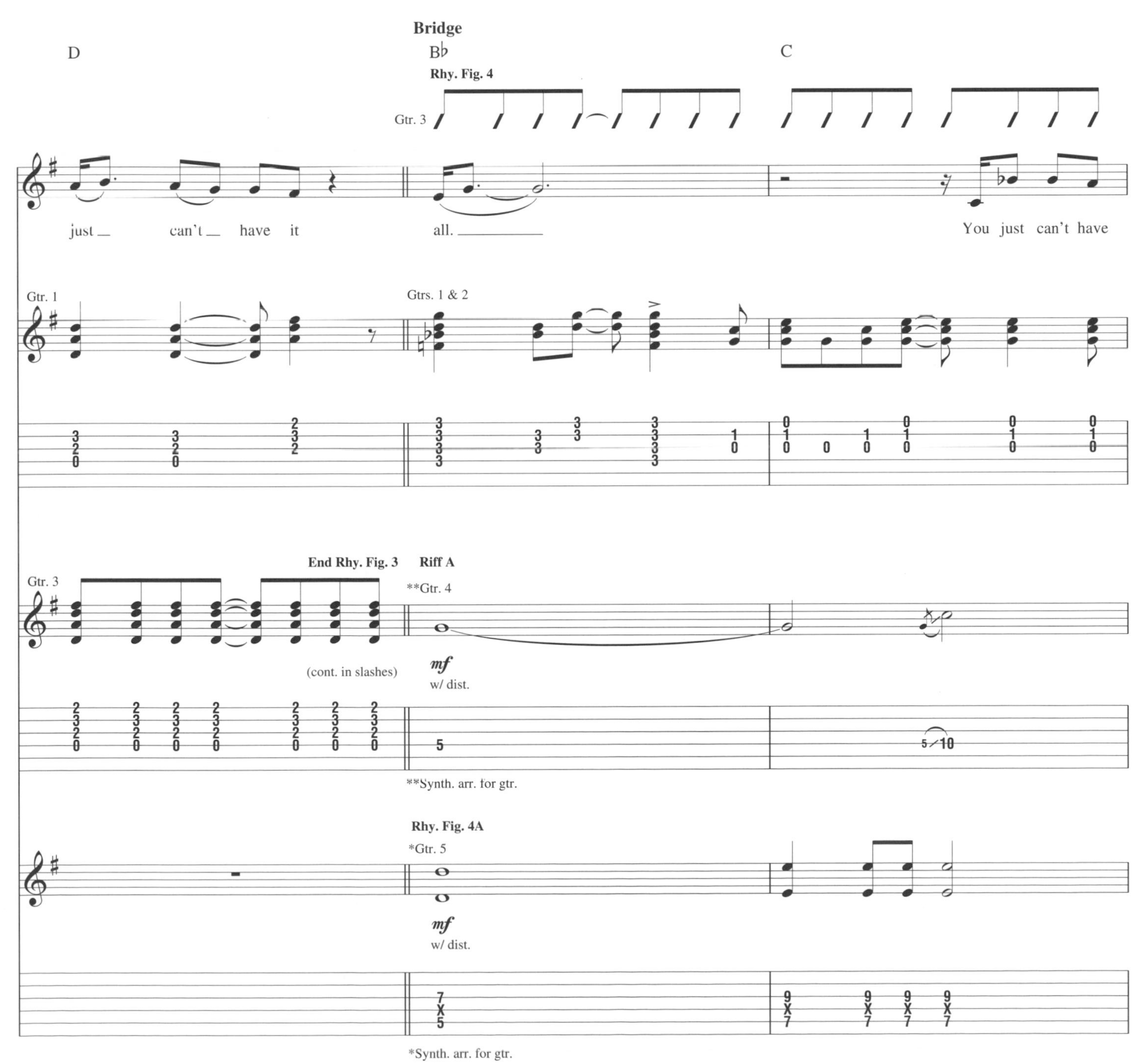
D
Bridge
B♭
C
Rhy. Fig. 4
Gtr. 3
just
can't
have
it
all.
You just can't have
Gtr. 1
Gtrs. 1 & 2
Gtr. 3
End Rhy. Fig. 3
Riff A
**Gtr. 4
(cont. in slashes)
mf
w/ dist.
**Synth. arr. for gtr.
Rhy. Fig. 4A
*Gtr. 5
mf
w/ dist.
*Synth. arr. for gtr.

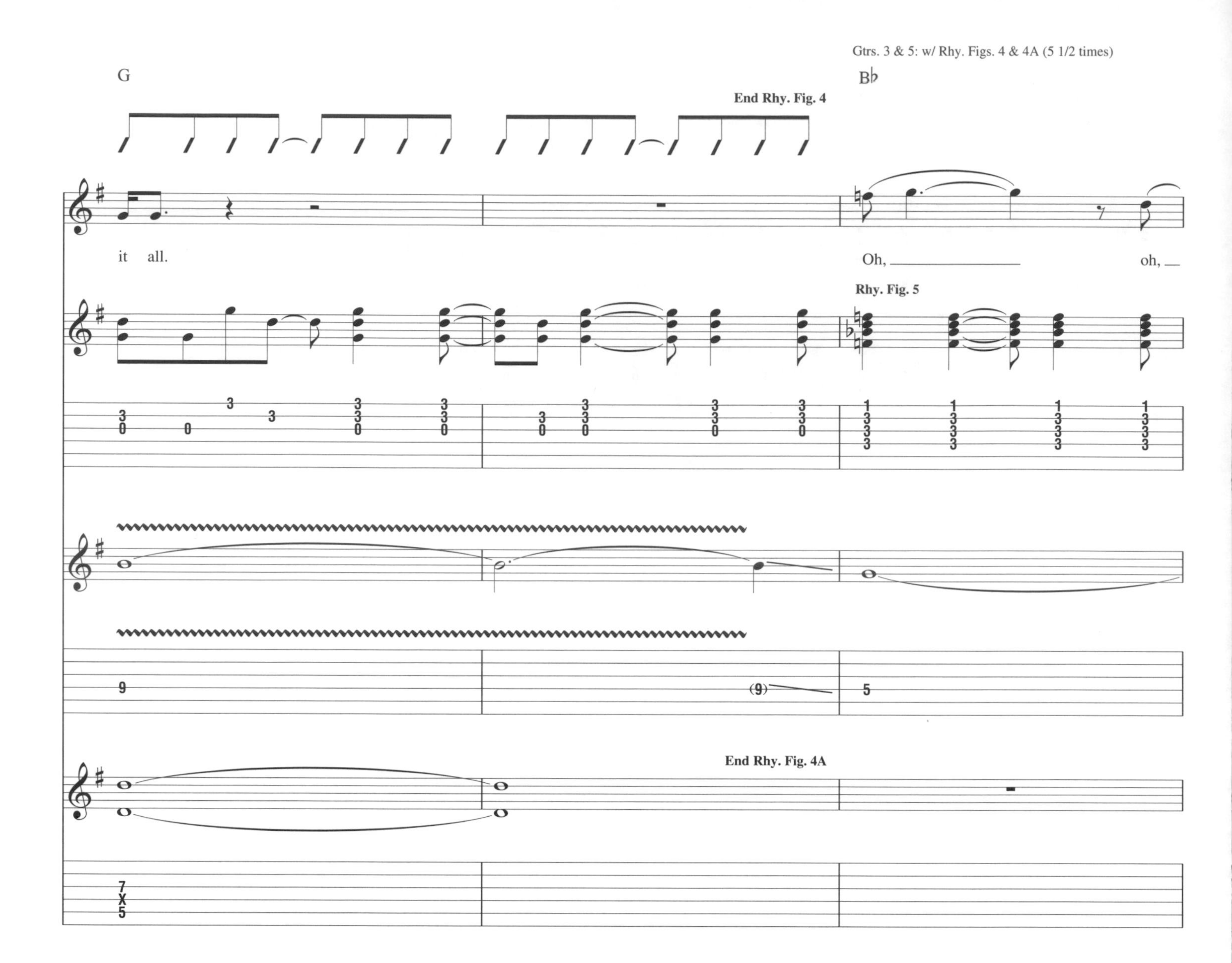
Gtrs. 3 & 5: w/ Rhy. Figs. 4 & 4A (5 1/2 times)
G
B♭
End Rhy. Fig. 4
it all.
Oh, oh,
Rhy. Fig. 5
End Rhy. Fig. 4A

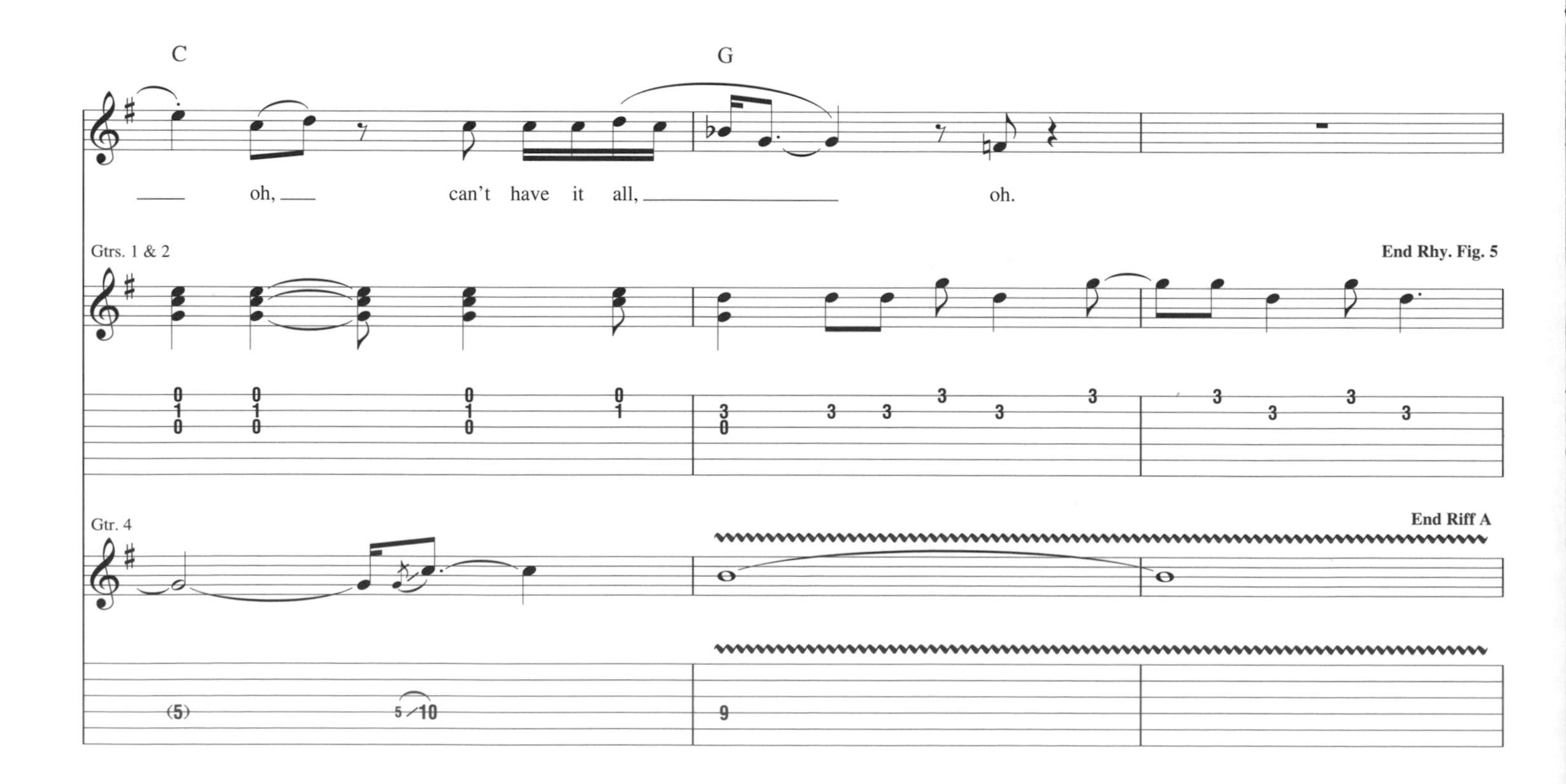
C
G
oh, can't have it all, oh.
Gtrs. 1 & 2
End Rhy. Fig. 5
Gtr. 4
End Riff A

Gtrs. 1 & 2: w/ Rhy. Fig. 5 (4 1/2 times)
Gtr. 4: w/ Riff A (1 1/2 times)
B♭
C
G
You can try, you can try but you can't have it all,
whoa.
B♭
C
G
Ah, yeah.
B♭
C
G
He'll nev - er make an - y en - e - mies, en - e - mies, no.
B♭
C
G
He won't com - plain if he's caught in a freeze.
Gtr. 4
5
5 10
9
B♭
C
He'll al - ways ask, he'll al - ways say please.
steady gliss.
(9)
5
0 2 9 13 20

Piano Solo

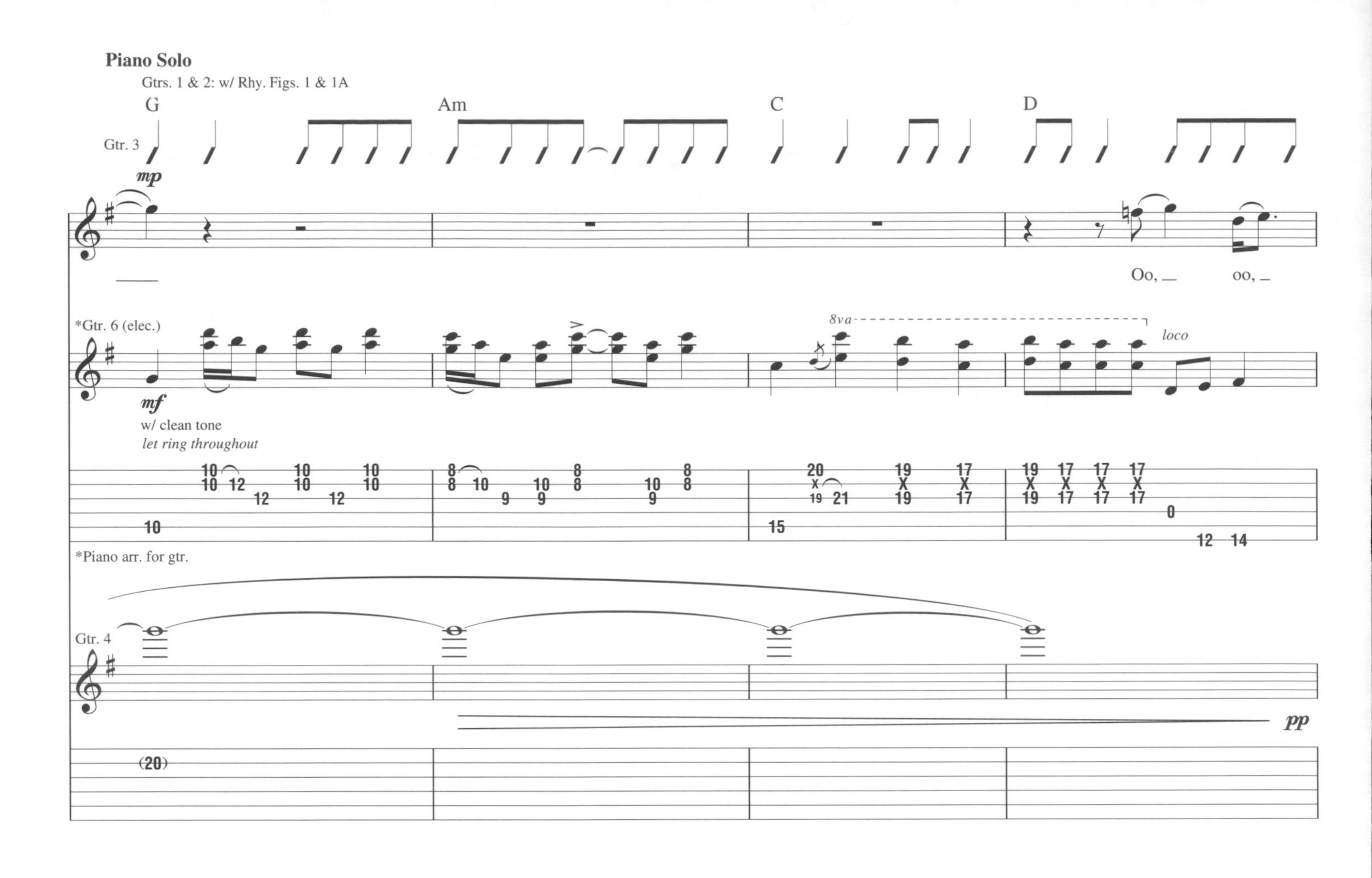

Chorus

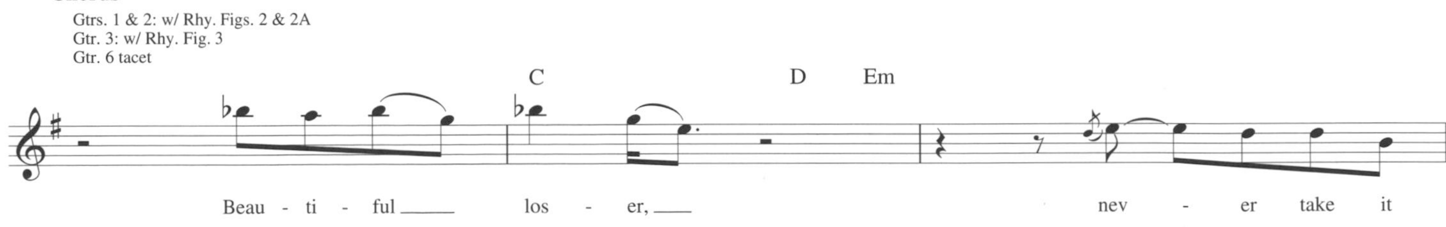

Am
D
fast - er when you fall, you just don't need it
C
Em
Am
Gtr. 3
all, oh. Oh, you
Gtr. 1
D
Outro
G
just don't need it all.

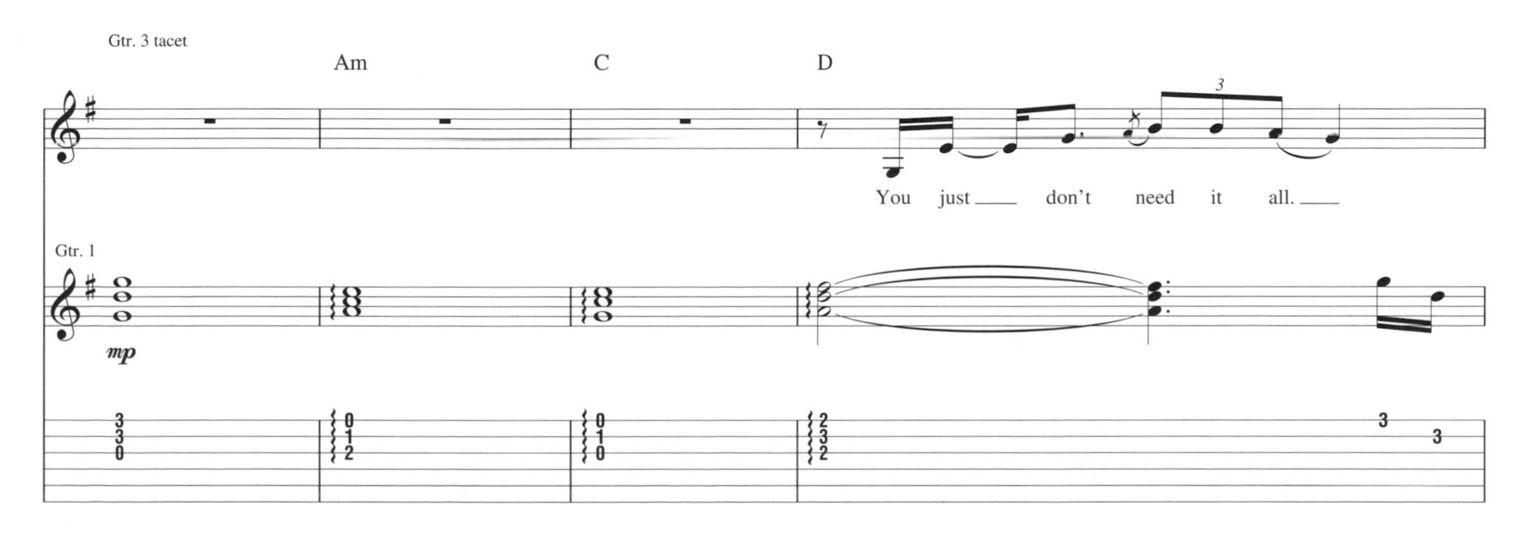
Gtr. 3 tacet
Am
C
D
You just don't need it all.
Gtr. 1
mp

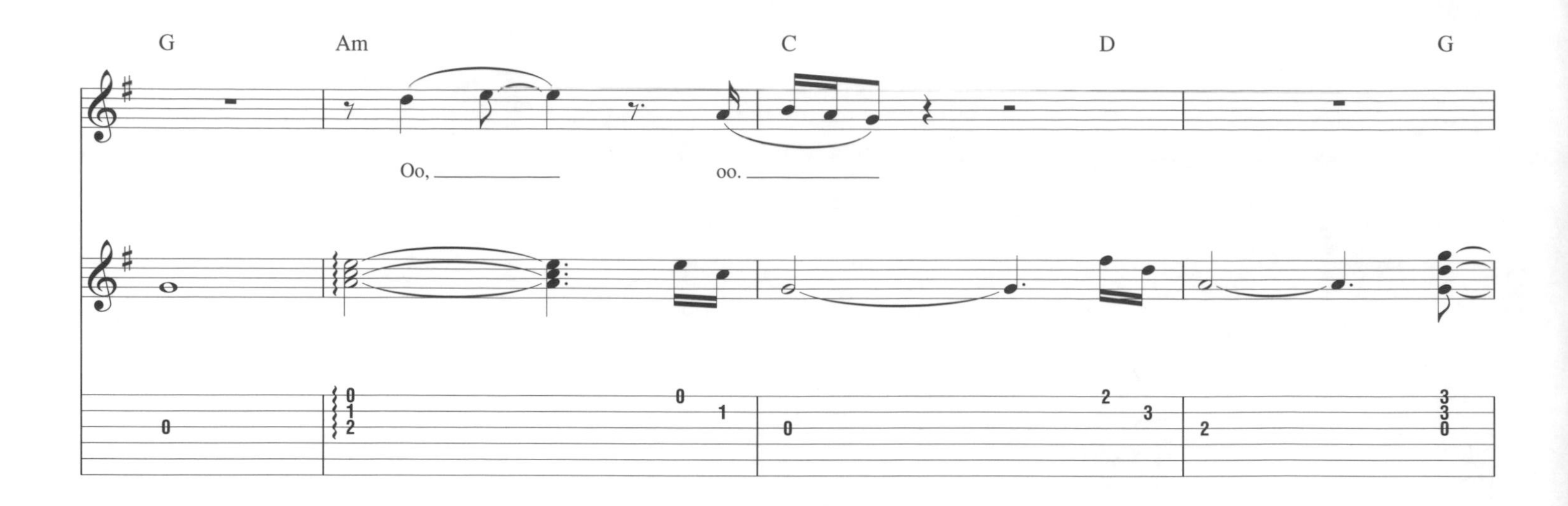

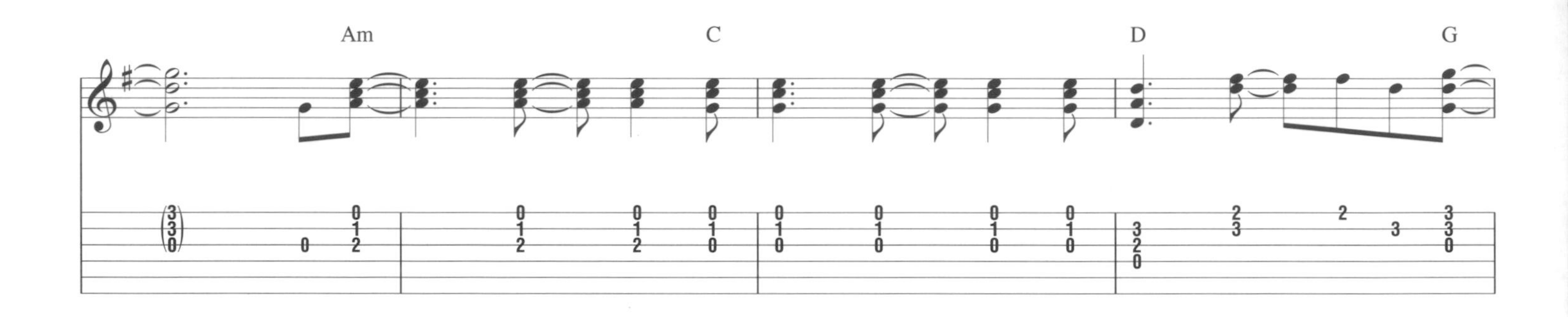

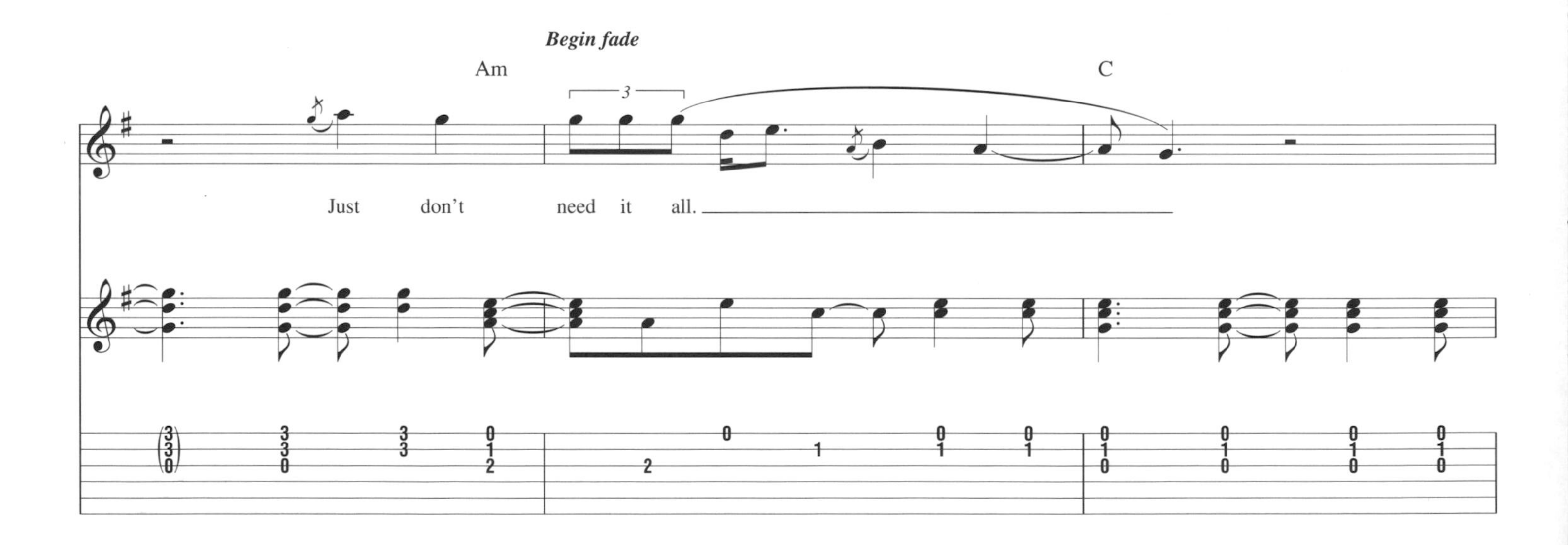

Fade out

D G Am C

Sunspot Baby

Words and Music by Bob Seger

B
5
2fr
E5
P.M.
with the bills she owed.
She
slight P.M.
A5
E5
A5
B
5
2fr
P.M.
gave me a false ad - dress,
took off with my A - mer - i - can Ex - press.
slight P.M.
E5
B5
A5
B
5
2fr
P.M.
Sun - spot Ba - by, she sure had me way out - guessed.
slight P.M.

E5
End Rhy. Fig. 1
P.M.
slight P.M.
Verse
Gtr. 2: w/ Rhy. Fig. 1
E
A
P.M.
2. She left me here strand - ed like a dog out in the yard,
packed up her bags, she took off down the road;
packed up her bags and she took off down the road;
slight P.M.
slight P.M.
E
A
charged up a for - tune
she said she was go - ing to vis -
she left me here strand - ed,
P.M. P.M.
P.M. P.M.
slight P.M.

E
on my cred - it card. She
it sis - ter, Flo. Well, she
with the bills she owed. She
slight P.M.

To Coda 2
A7
E7
A7
used my ad - dress and my name, man, that was sure un - kind.
used my ad - dress and my name, and man, that was sure un - kind.
used my ad - dress and my name, put my cred - it to shame.
slight P.M.

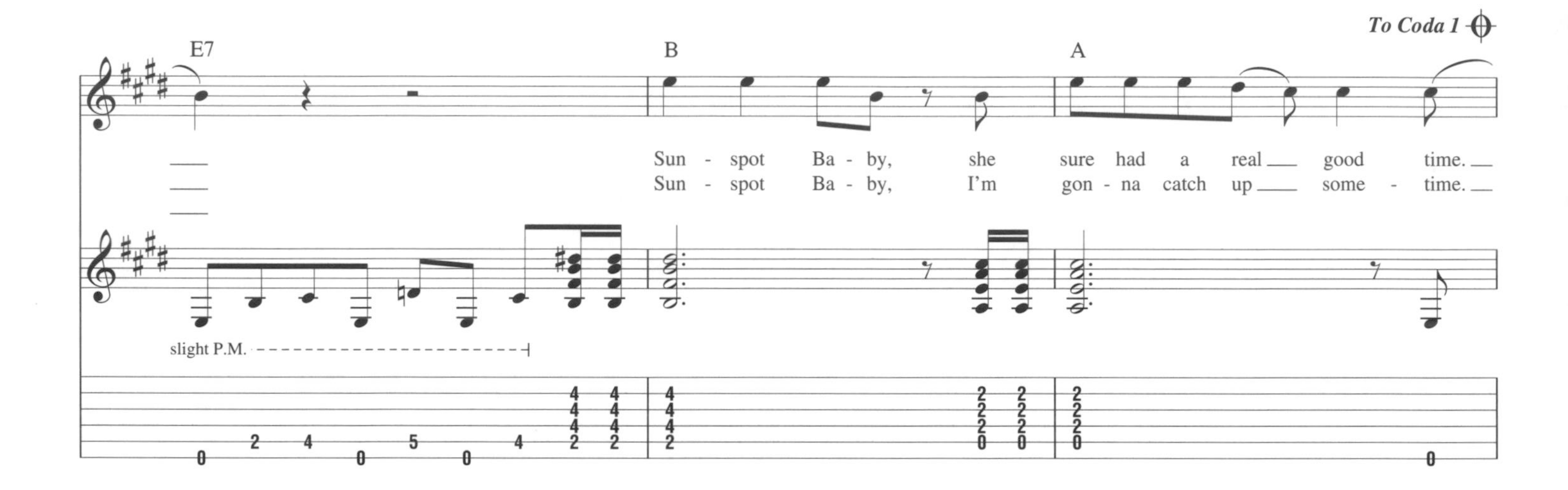
To Coda 1
E7
B
A
Sun - spot Ba - by, she sure had a real good time.
Sun - spot Ba - by, I'm gon - na catch up some - time.
slight P.M.

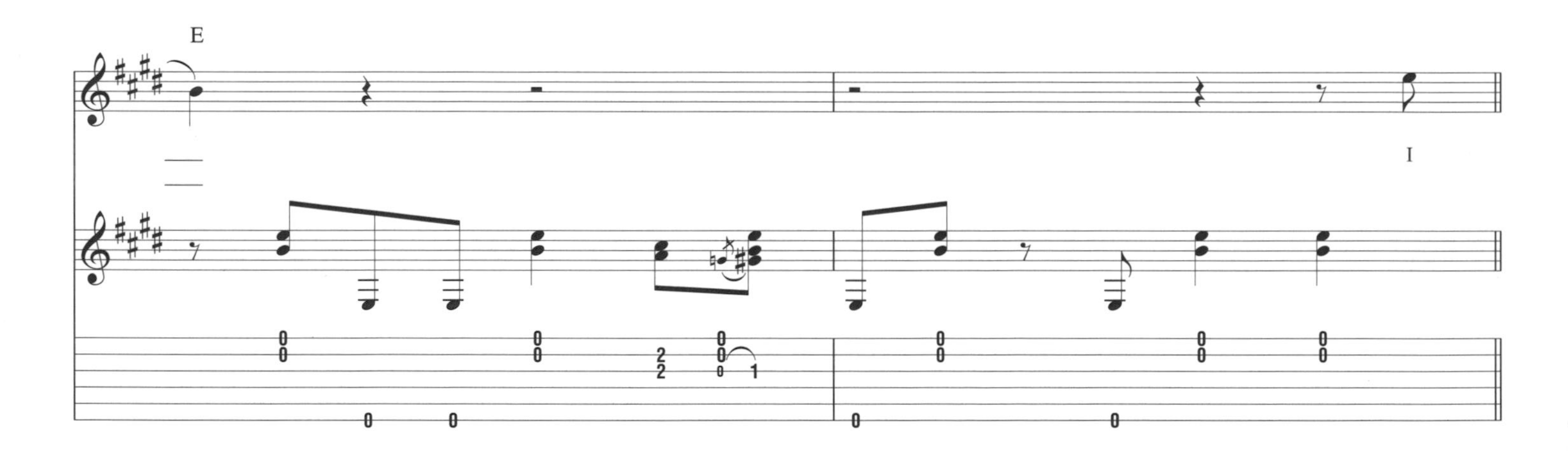
E
I

Chorus
A5
Rhy. Fig. 2
E5
A5
Gtr. 2
looked in Mi - am - i, I looked in Ne - gril. The clos - est I came was a month -
Gtr. 1

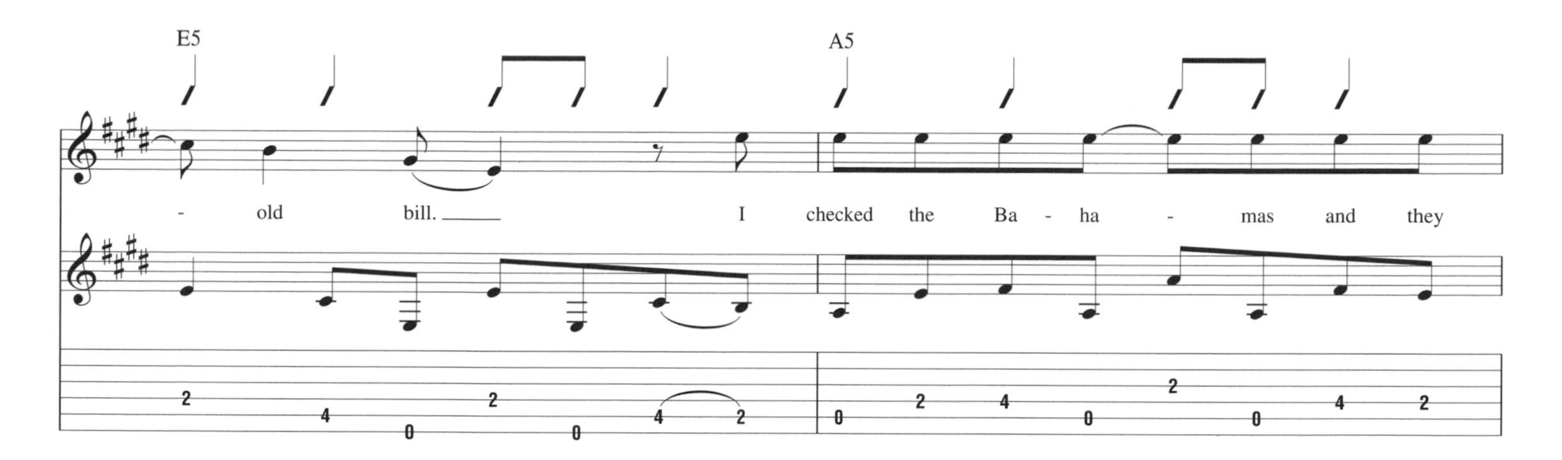
E5
A5
- old bill. I checked the Ba - ha - mas and they

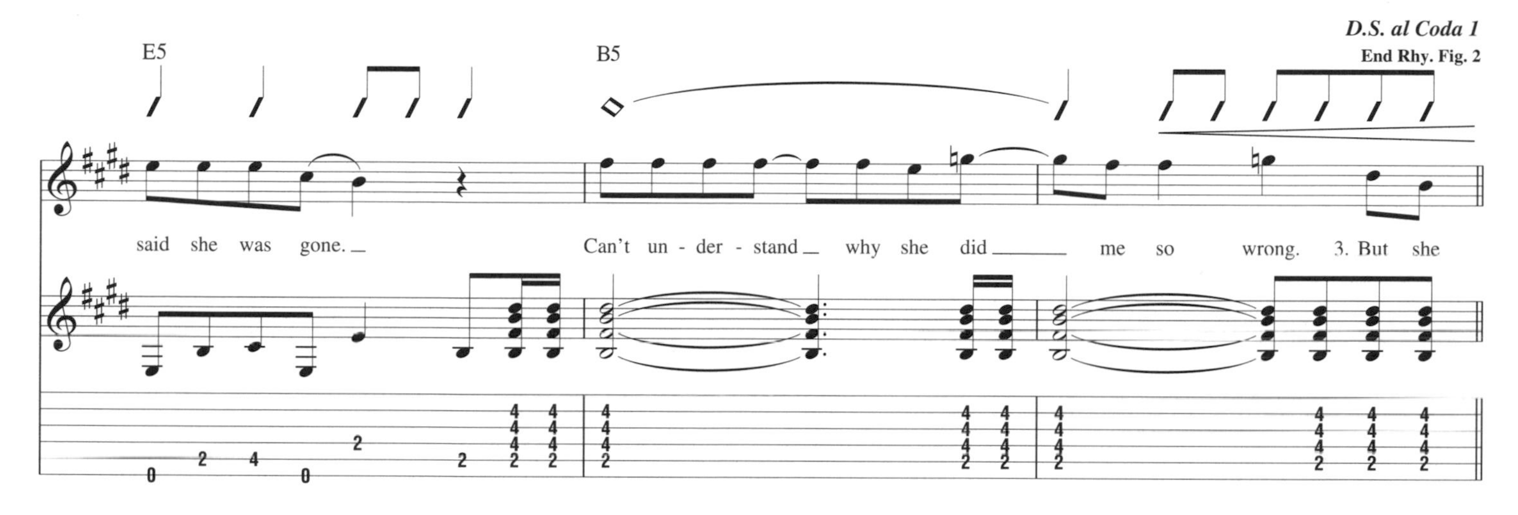
D.S. al Coda 1
End Rhy. Fig. 2
E5
B5
said she was gone. Can't un - der - stand why she did me so wrong. 3. But she

Coda 1
E
Guitar Solo
E5 E6 E5 E6
Rhy. Fig. 3
Gtr. 2
P.M.
Sure had a real good time. Oh!
grad. bend
hold bend
A5 A6 A5 A6 E5 E6 E5 E6 E5 E6 E5 E6
Yeah. Oh.

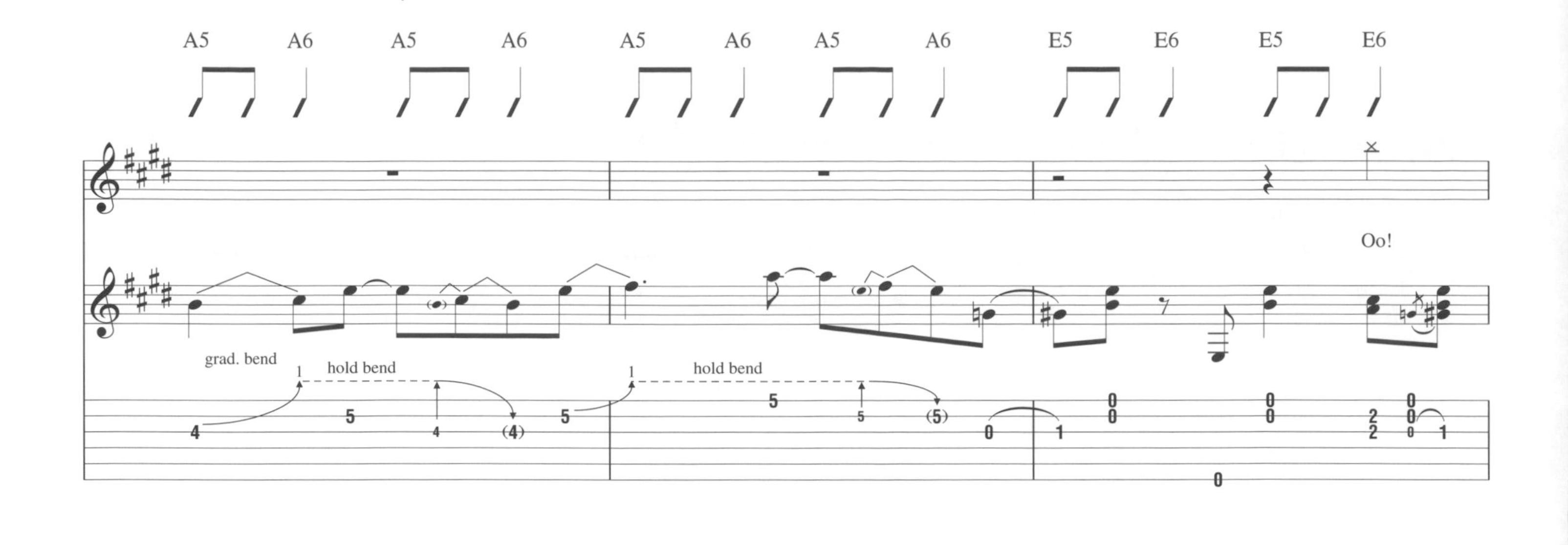
A5 A6 A5 A6 A5 A6 A5 A6 E5 E6 E5 E6
Oo!
grad. bend
hold bend
hold bend

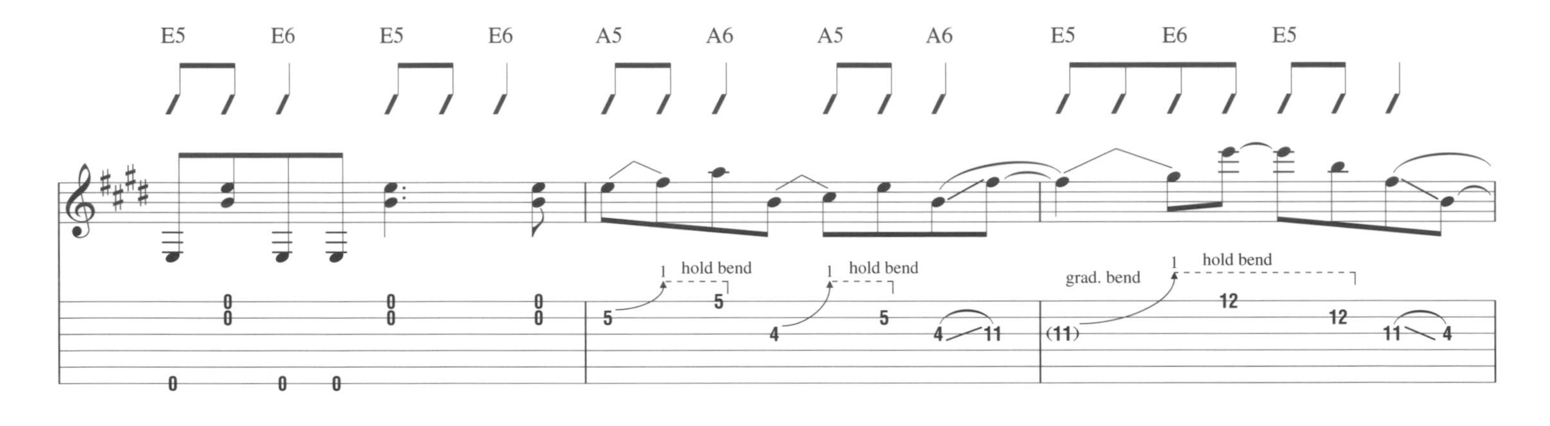
E5 E6 E5 E6 A5 A6 A5 A6 E5 E6 E5
hold bend
hold bend
grad. bend
hold bend

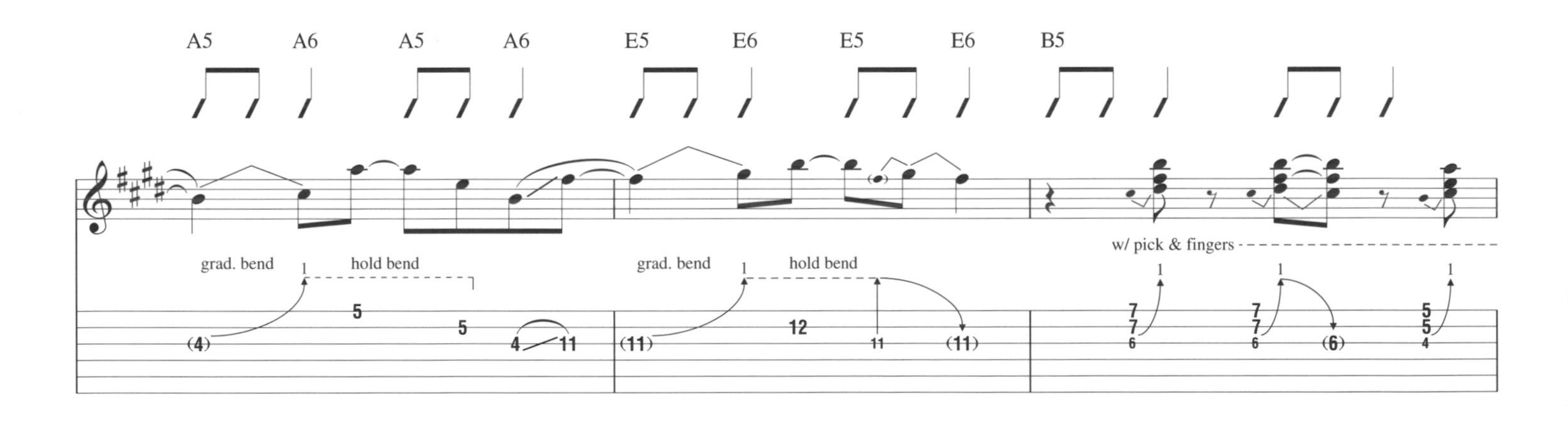
A5 A6 A5 A6 E5 E6 E5 E6 B5
grad. bend
hold bend
grad. bend
hold bend
w/ pick & fingers

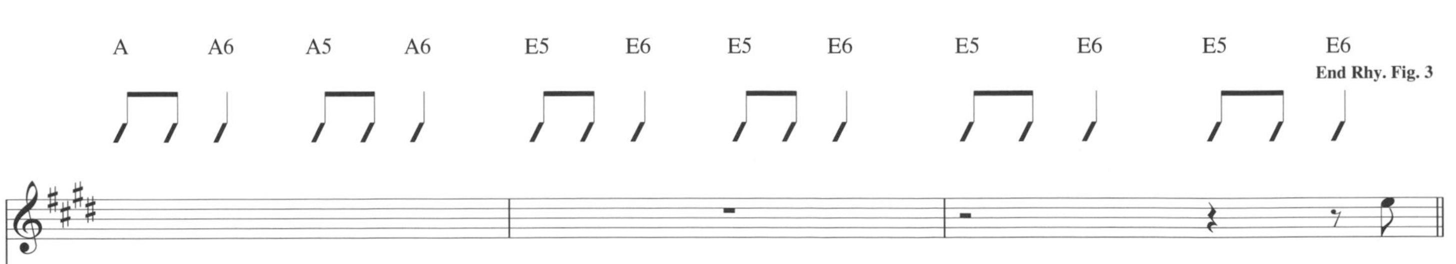
A A6 A5 A6 E5 E6 E5 E6 E5 E6 E5 E6
End Rhy. Fig. 3
I

w/ pick & fingers
P.M.
P.M.

Chorus

Gtr. 2: w/ Rhy. Fig. 2

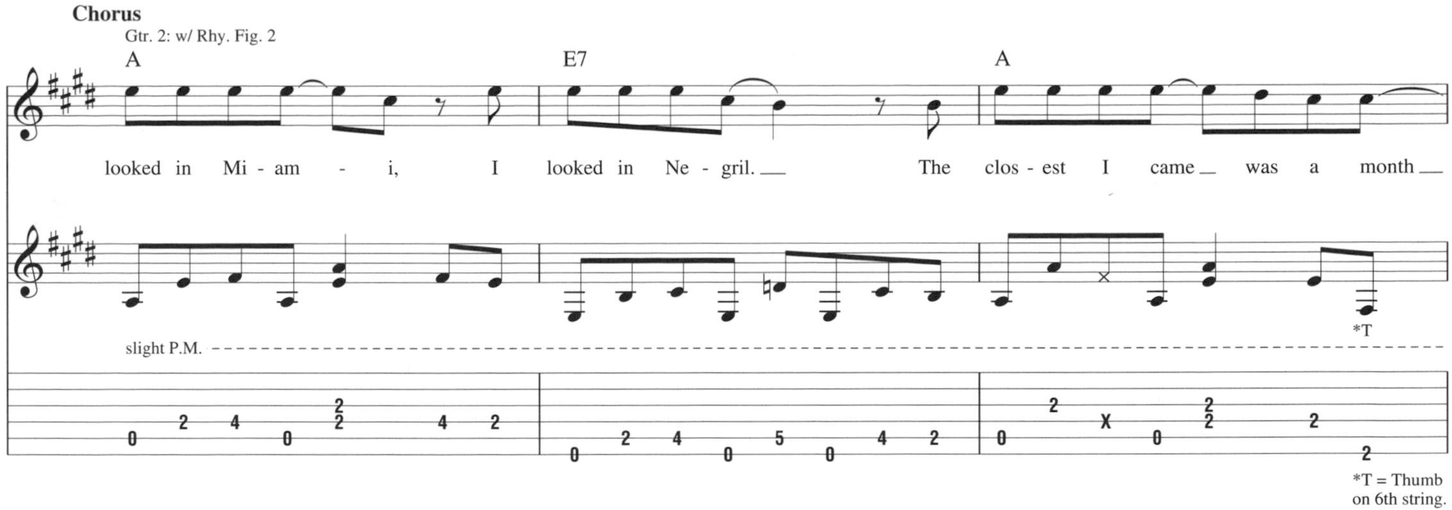
A
E7
A
looked in Mi - am - i, I looked in Ne - gril. The clos - est I came was a month
slight P.M.
*T
*T = Thumb on 6th string.

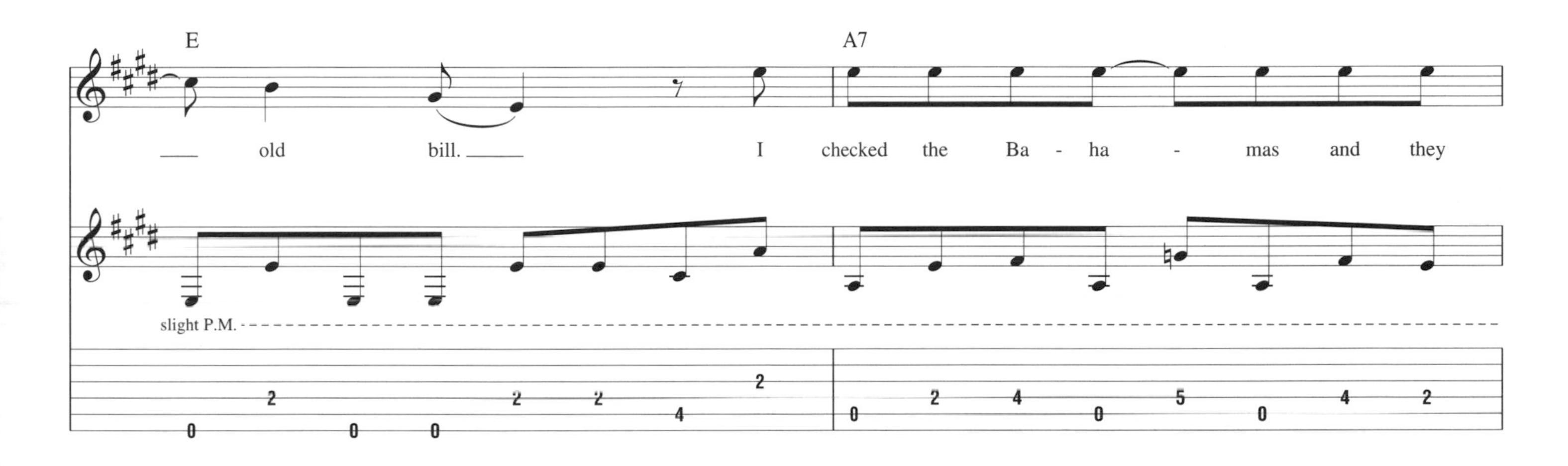
E
A7
old bill. I checked the Ba - ha - mas and they
slight P.M.

D.S. al Coda 2

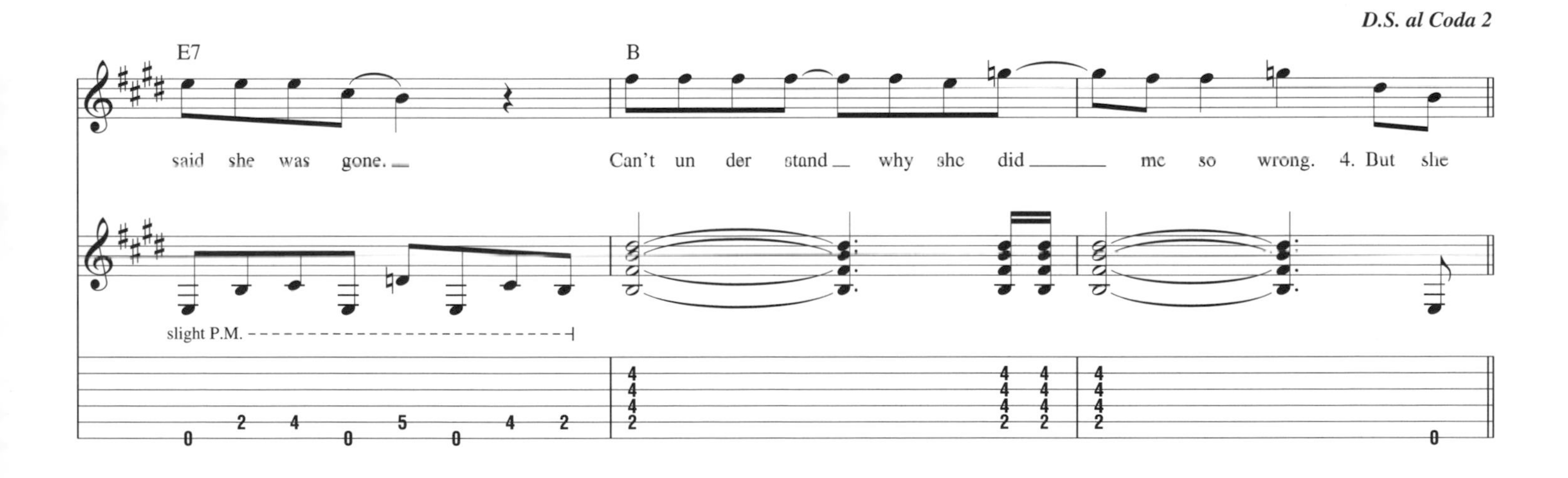
E7
B
said she was gone. Can't un der stand why she did me so wrong. 4. But she
slight P.M.

Coda 2

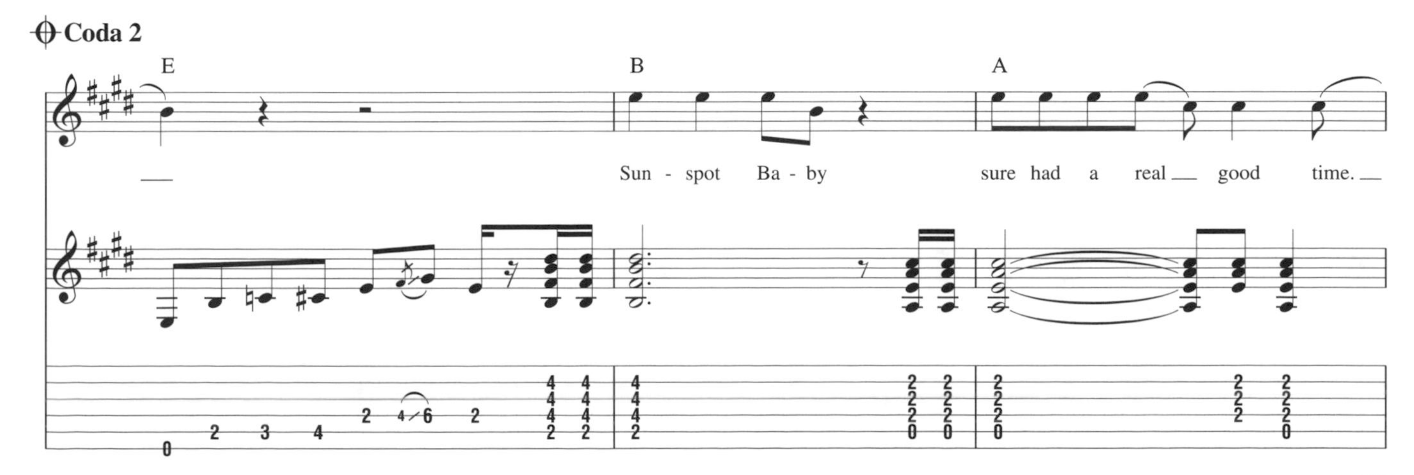
E
B
A
Sun - spot Ba - by sure had a real good time.

Gtr. 2: w/ Rhy. Fig. 1 (last 4 meas.)
E
B
Oh, Sun - spot Ba - by, she
P.M.
P.M.

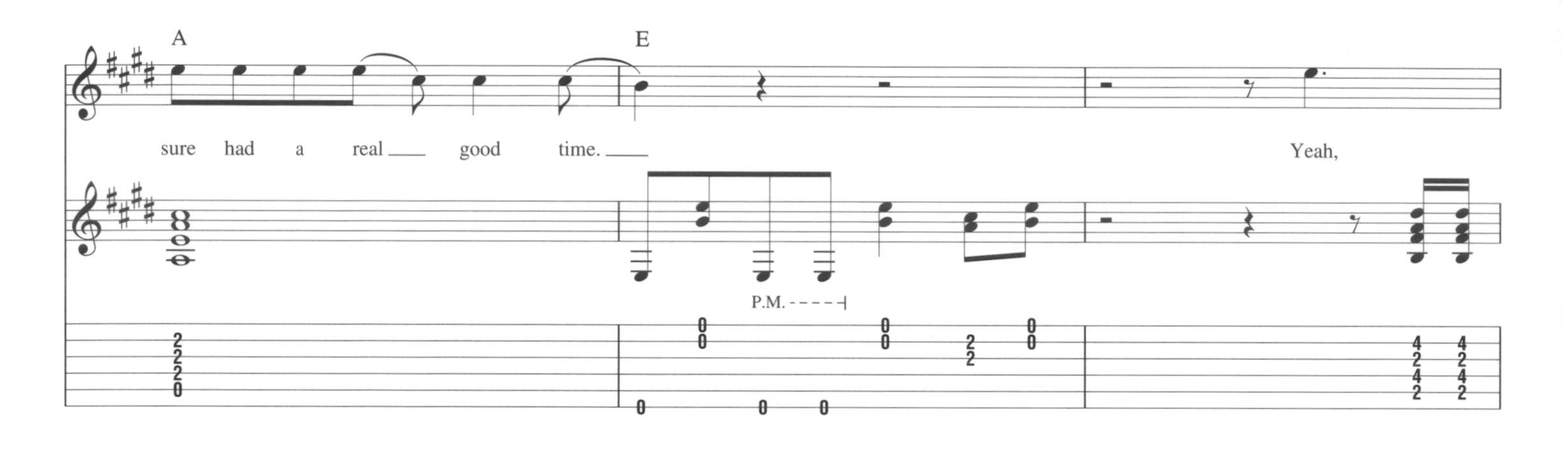
A
E
sure had a real good time.
Yeah,
P.M.

B5
A7
E5
Gtr. 2
P.M.
p cresc.
Sun - spot Ba - by, I'm gon - na catch up some - time, some - time.

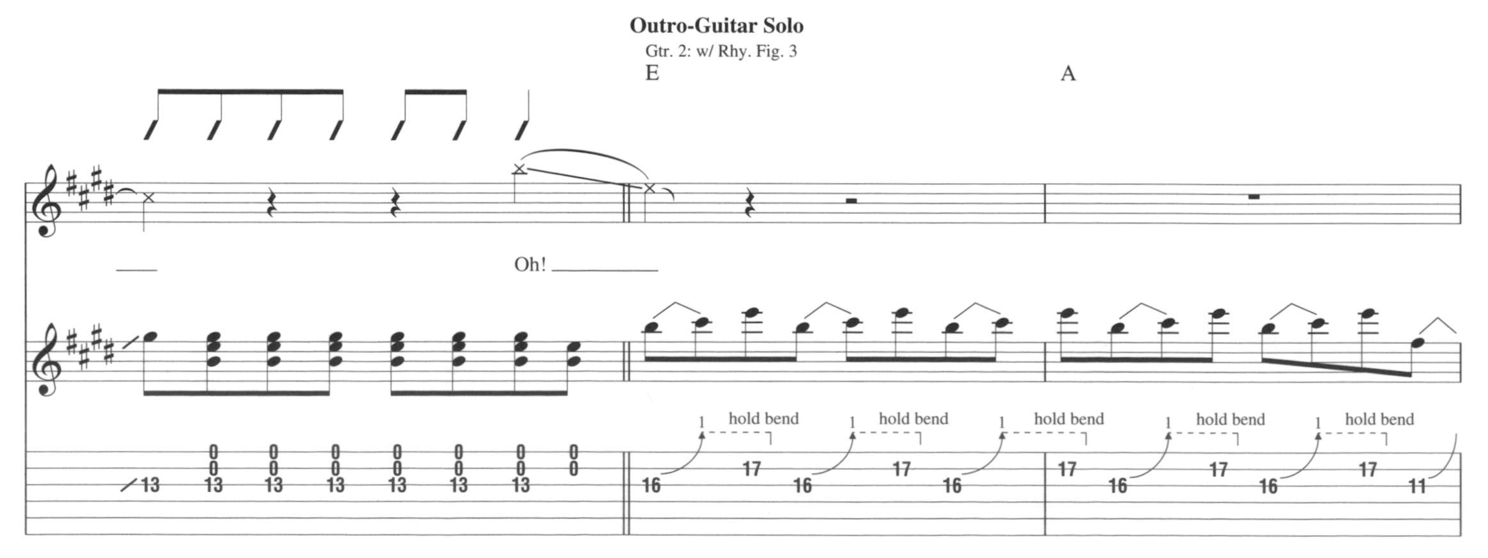
Outro-Guitar Solo
Gtr. 2: w/ Rhy. Fig. 3
E
A
Oh!
hold bend
hold bend
hold bend
hold bend
hold bend

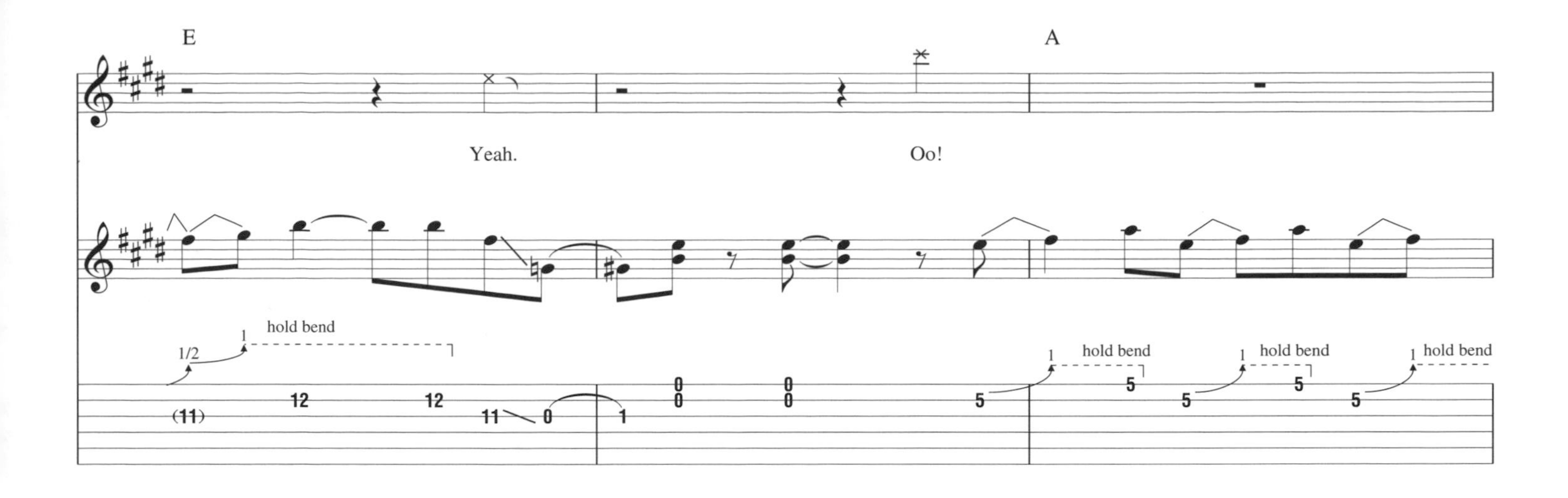
E
A
Yeah.
Oo!
hold bend
hold bend
hold bend
hold bend

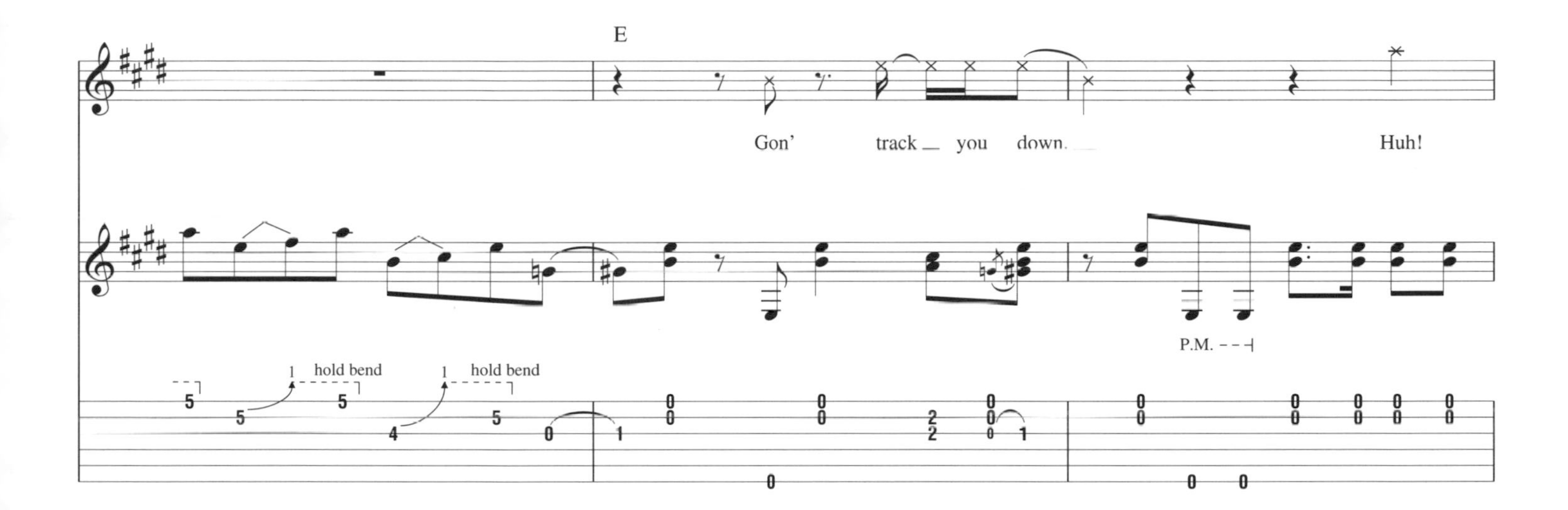
E
Gon' track _ you down. _
Huh!
hold bend
hold bend
P.M.

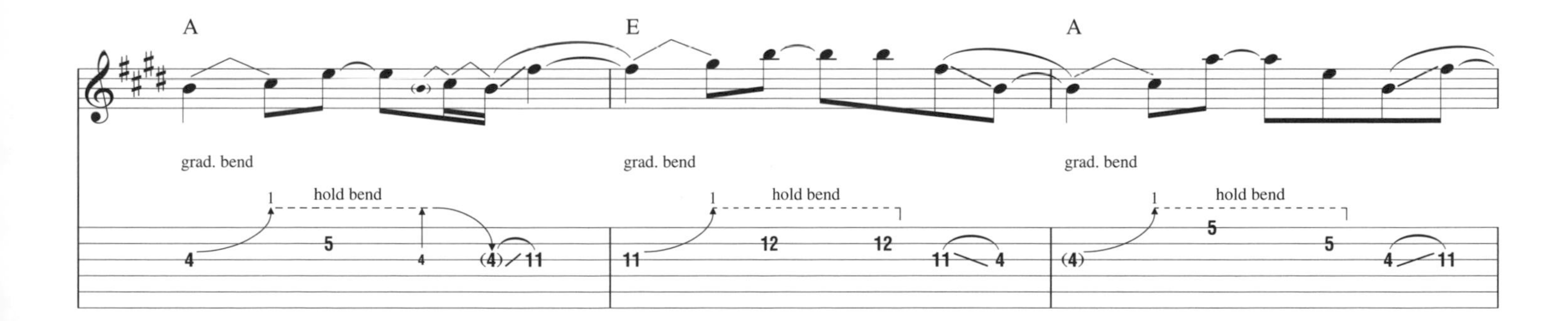
A
E
A
grad. bend
grad. bend
grad. bend
hold bend
hold bend
hold bend

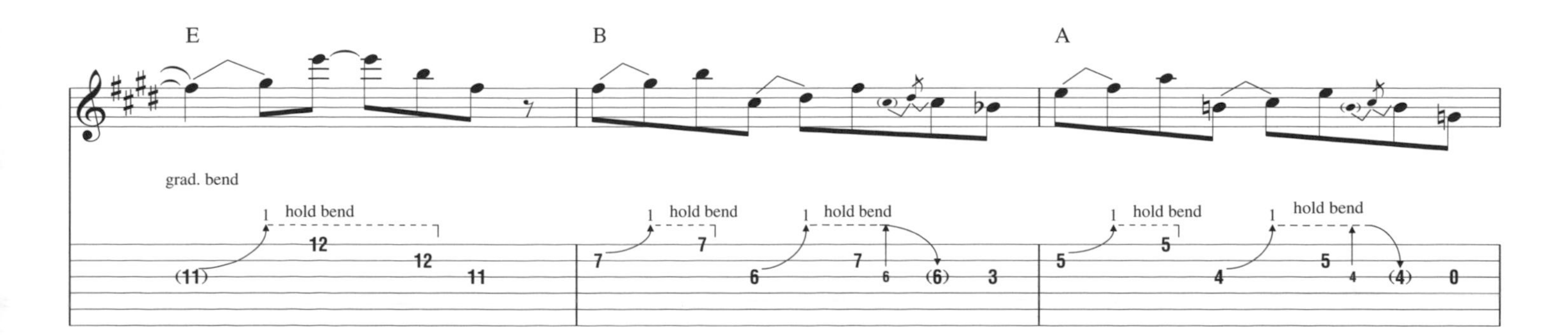
E
B
A
grad. bend
hold bend
hold bend
hold bend
hold bend
hold bend

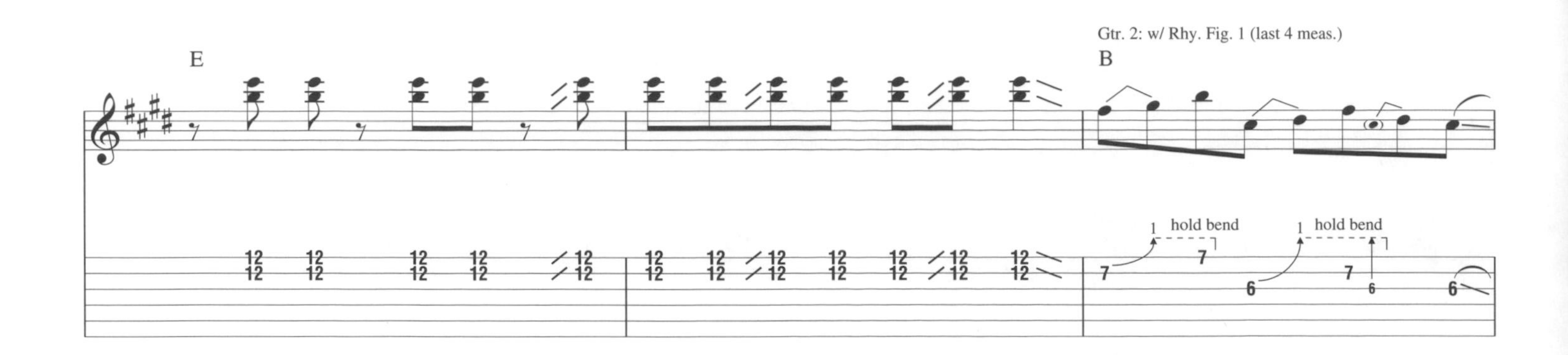
Gtr. 2: w/ Rhy. Fig. 1 (last 4 meas.)
E
B
hold bend
hold bend

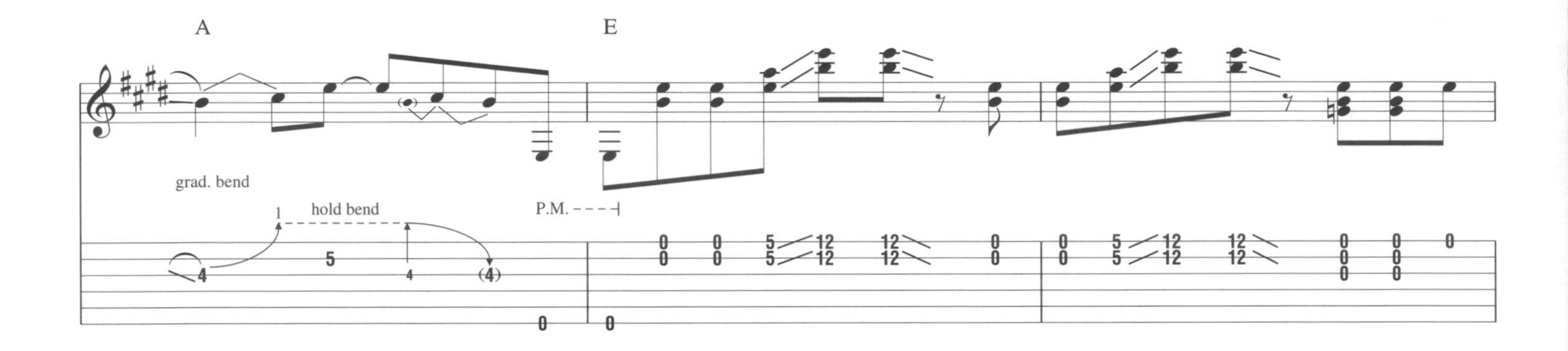
A
E
grad. bend
hold bend
P.M.

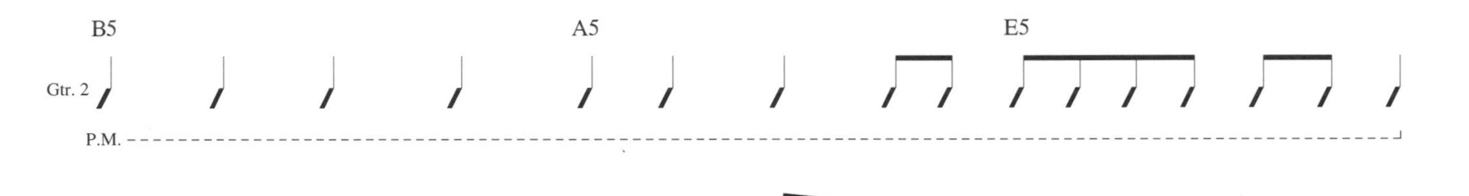
B5
A5
E5
Gtr. 2
P.M.

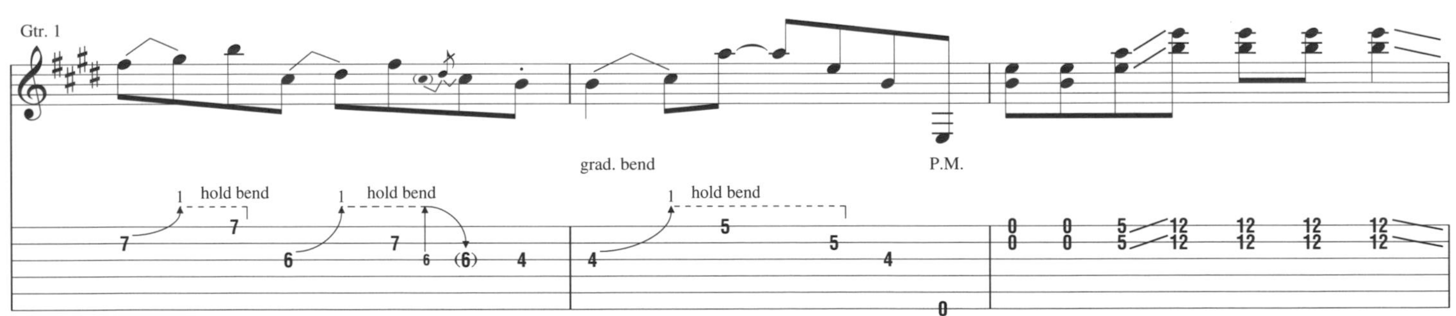
Gtr. 1
hold bend
hold bend
grad. bend
hold bend
P.M.

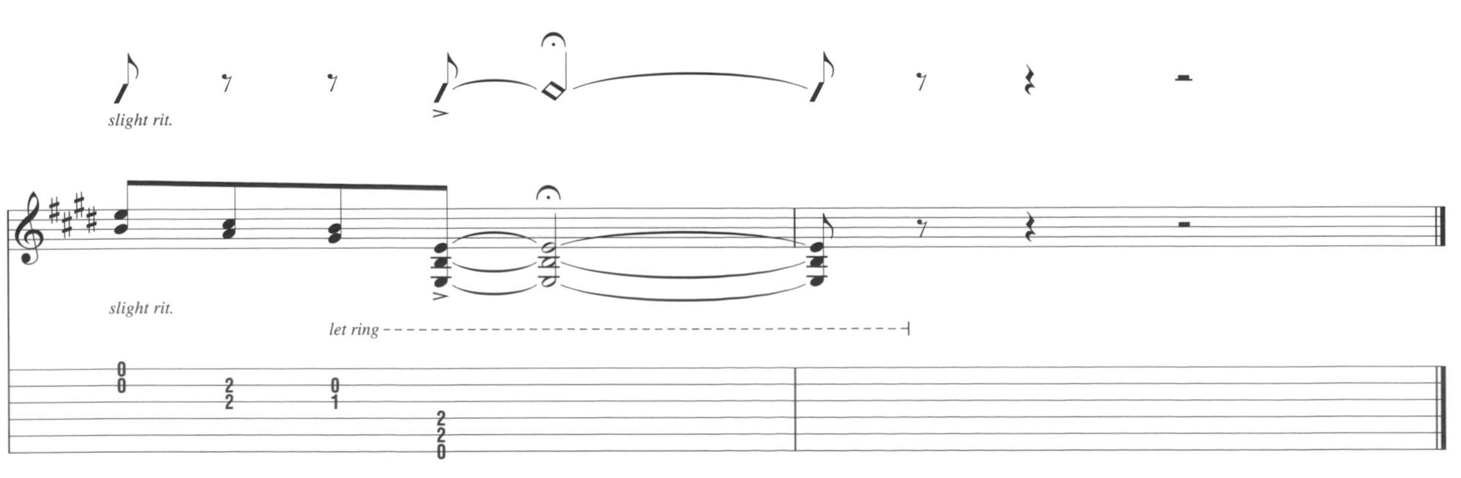
slight rit.
slight rit.
let ring

Katmandu

Words and Music by Bob Seger

E
man - du,
I think it's real - ly where I'm go - in' to.
Gtrs. 1 & 2
slight P.M.

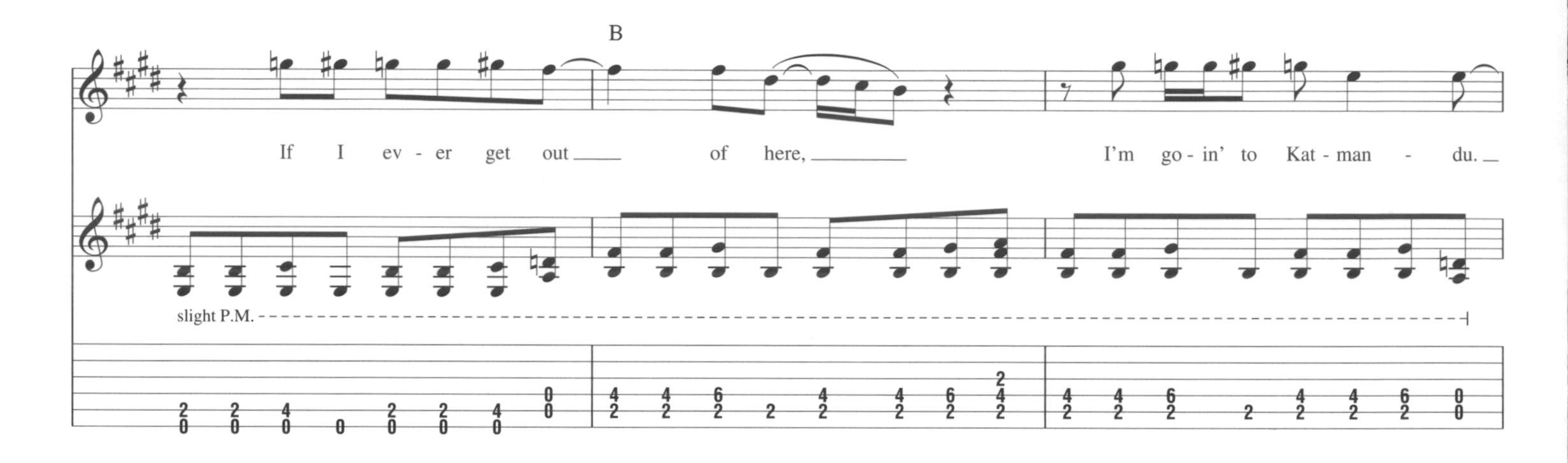
B
If I ev - er get out of here,
I'm go - in' to Kat - man - du.
slight P.M.

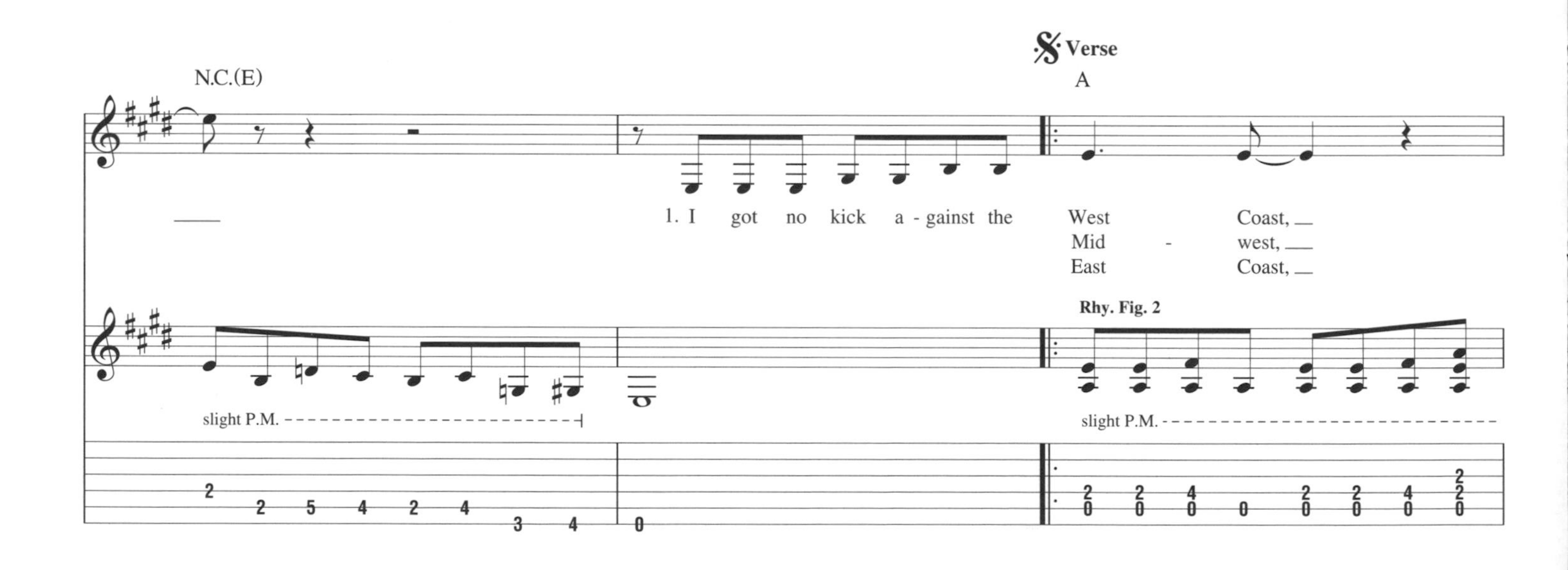
N.C.(E)
Verse
A
1. I got no kick a - gainst the West Coast,
Mid - west,
East Coast,
Rhy. Fig. 2
slight P.M.
slight P.M.

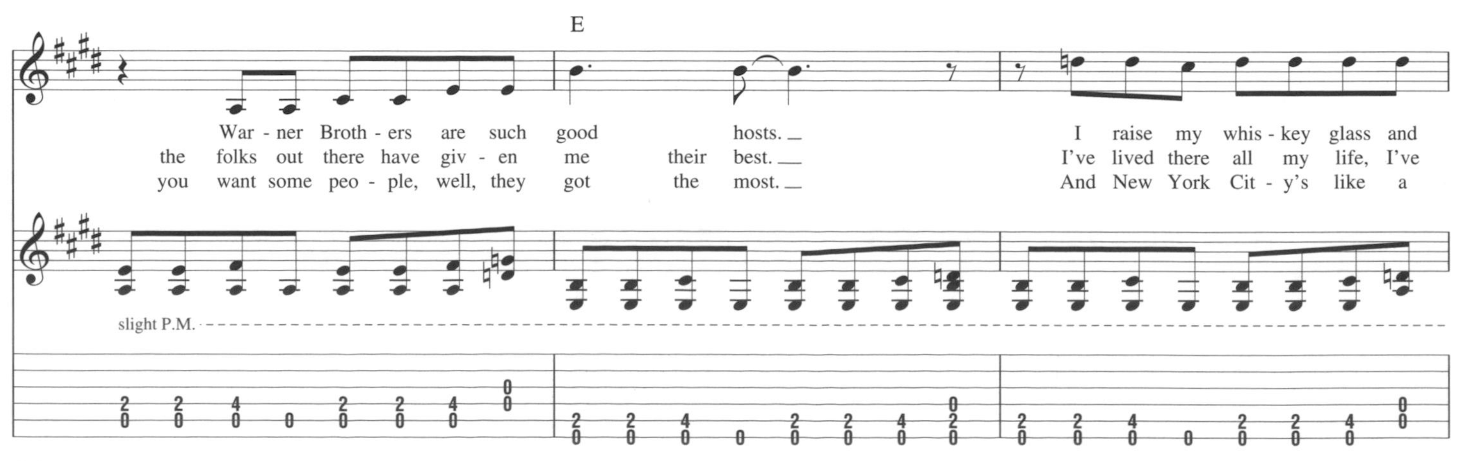
E
War - ner Broth - ers are such good hosts.
I raise my whis - key glass and
the folks out there have giv - en me their best.
I've lived there all my life, I've
you want some peo - ple, well, they got the most.
And New York Cit - y's like a
slight P.M.

B
E
give 'em a toast,
been their guest,
friend - ly ghost,
I'm sure they know it's true.
I sure have loved it, too.
you seem to pass right through.
slight P.M.
A
I got no rap a - gainst the South - ern states,
I'm tired of look - in' at the T V news,
I know I'm gon - na miss the U. S. A.,
ev - 'ry - time I've been there,
I'm tired of driv - in' hard and
I guess I'll miss it ev - 'ry
slight P.M.
E
B
it's been great.
pay - in' dues.
sin - gle day.
But now I'm leav - in' and I can't be late,
I fig - ure, ba - by, I got noth - in' to lose,
But no one loves me here an - y - way,
End Rhy. Fig. 2
slight P.M.
E
N.C.
A
and to my - self be true.
I'm tired of be - ing blue.
I know my plane is due.
Ow,
That's why I'm go - in' to Kat -
that's why I'm go - in' to Kat -
The one that's go - in' to Kat -
slight P.M.

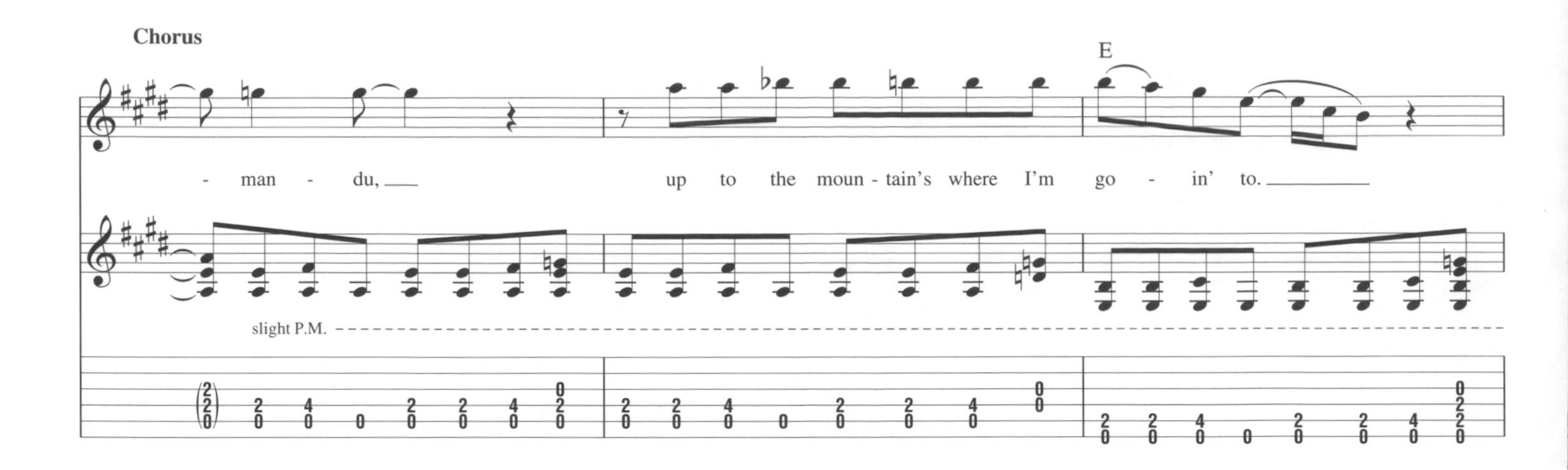
Chorus
E
- man - du,
up to the moun - tain's where I'm go - in' to.
slight P.M.

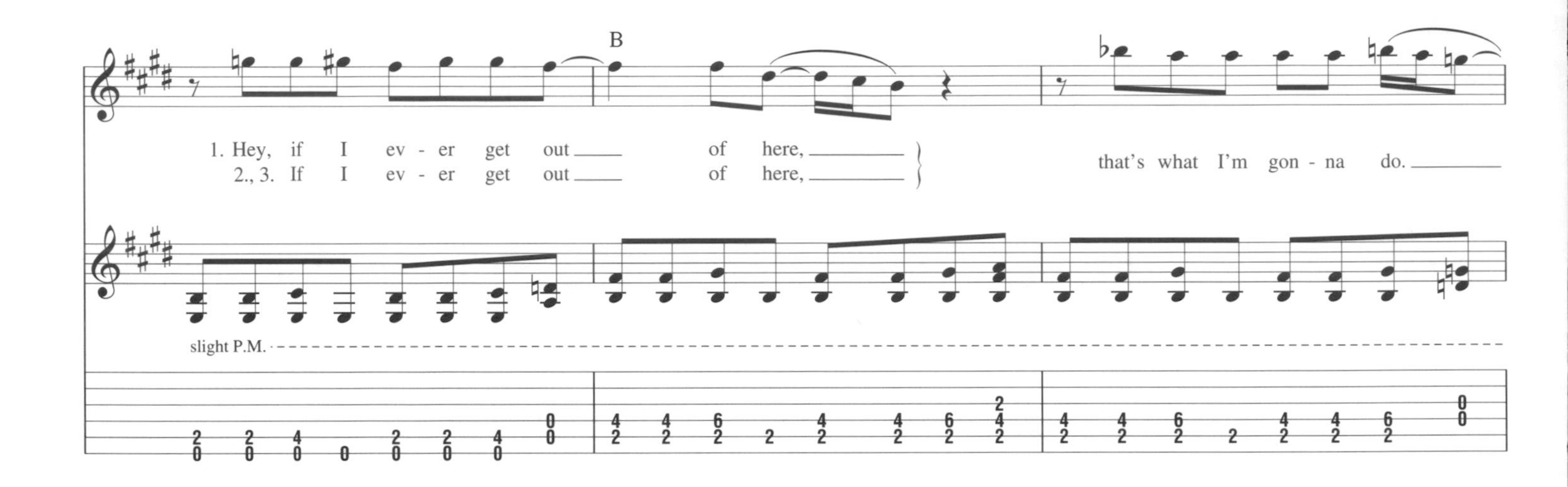
B
1. Hey, if I ev - er get out of here,
2., 3. If I ev - er get out of here,
that's what I'm gon - na do.
slight P.M.

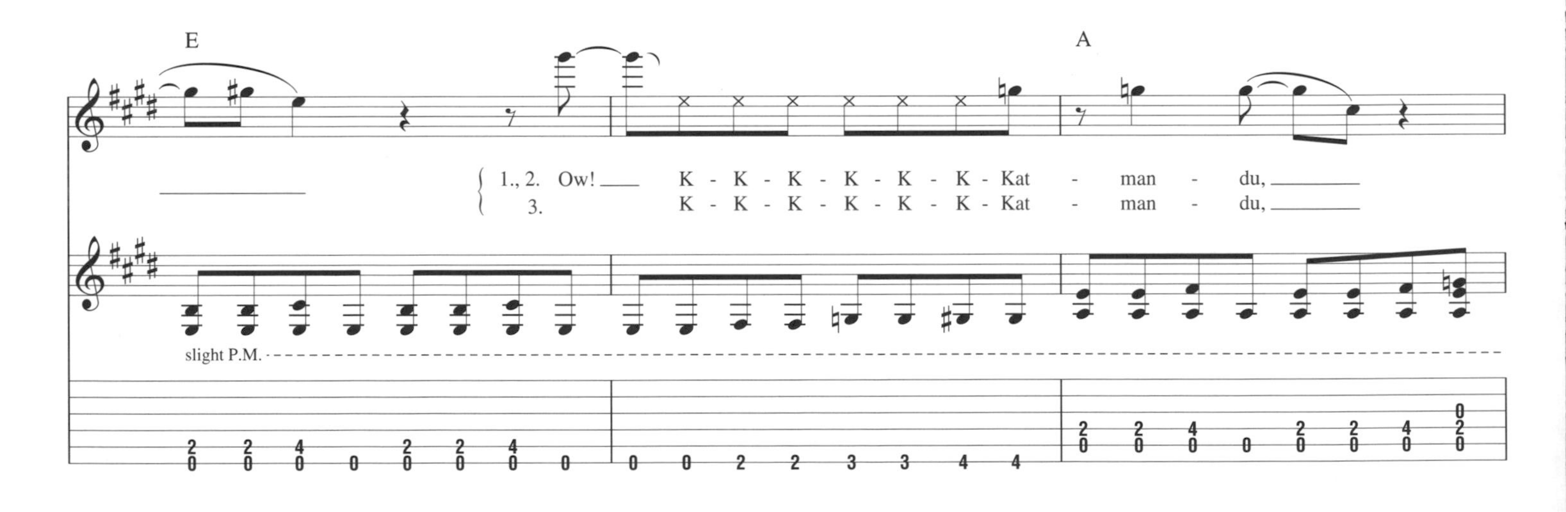
E
A
1., 2. Ow! K - K - K - K - K - K - Kat - man - du,
3. K - K - K - K - K - K - Kat - man - du,
slight P.M.

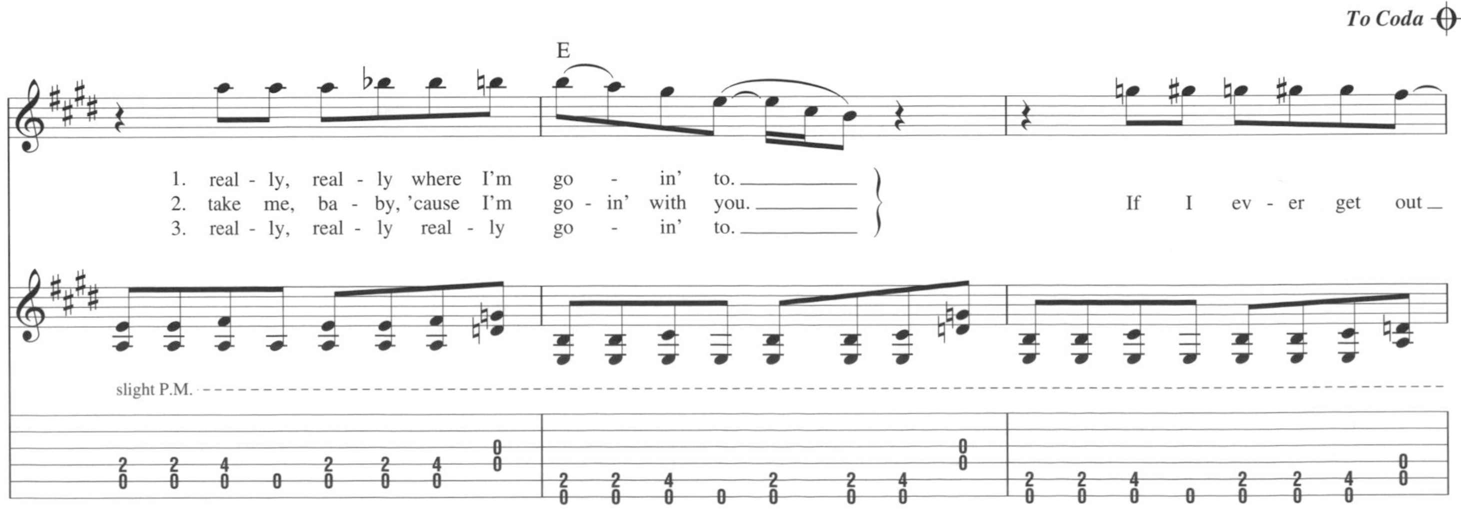
To Coda
E
1. real - ly, real - ly where I'm go - in' to.
2. take me, ba - by, 'cause I'm go - in' with you.
3. real - ly, real - ly real - ly go - in' to.
If I ev - er get out
slight P.M.

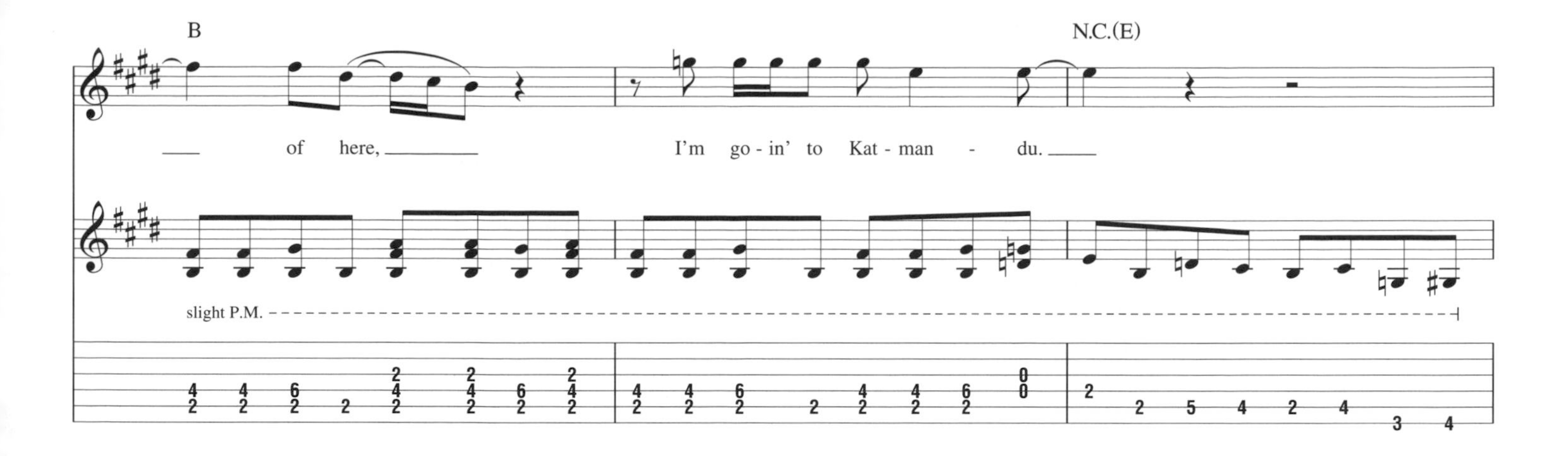
B
N.C.(E)
of here,
I'm go - in' to Kat - man - du.
slight P.M.

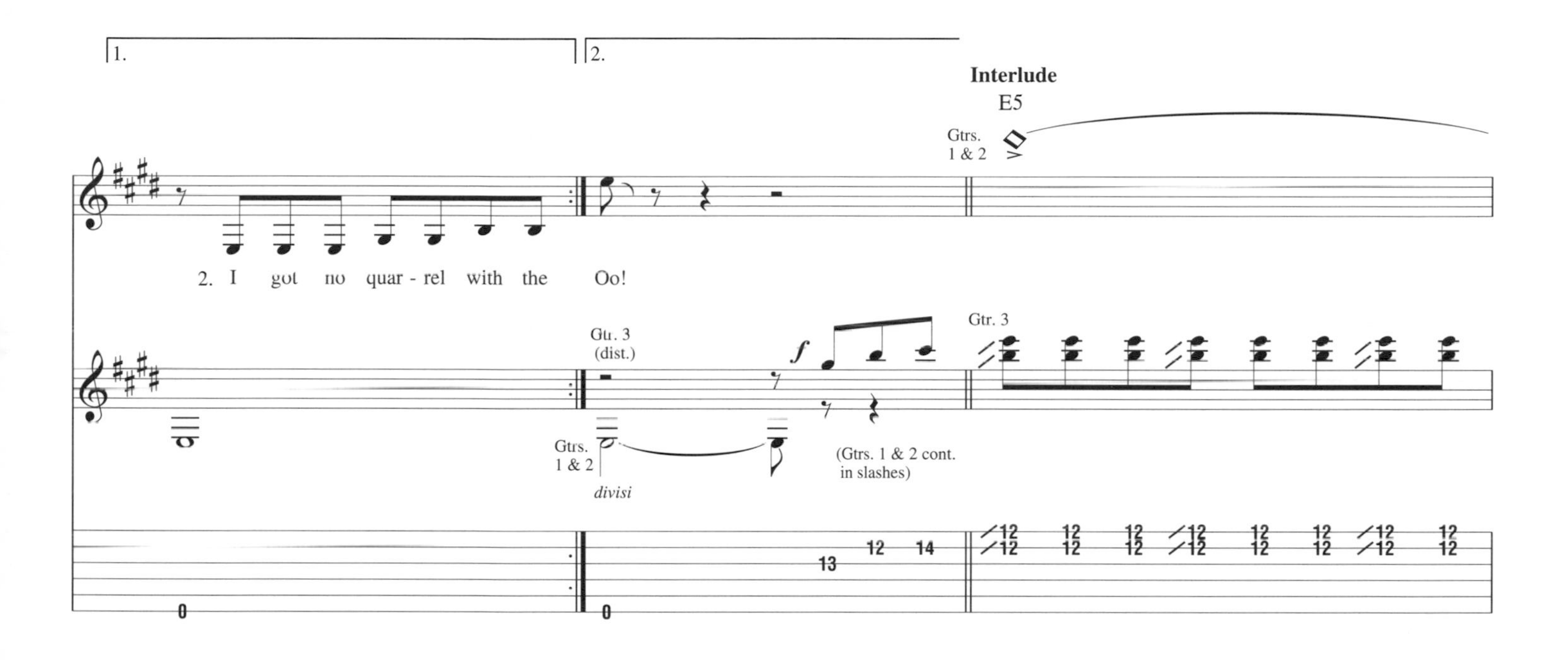
1.
2.
Interlude
E5
Gtrs. 1 & 2
2. I got no quar - rel with the
Oo!
Gtr. 3 (dist.)
Gtr. 3
Gtrs. 1 & 2
divisi
(Gtrs. 1 & 2 cont. in slashes)

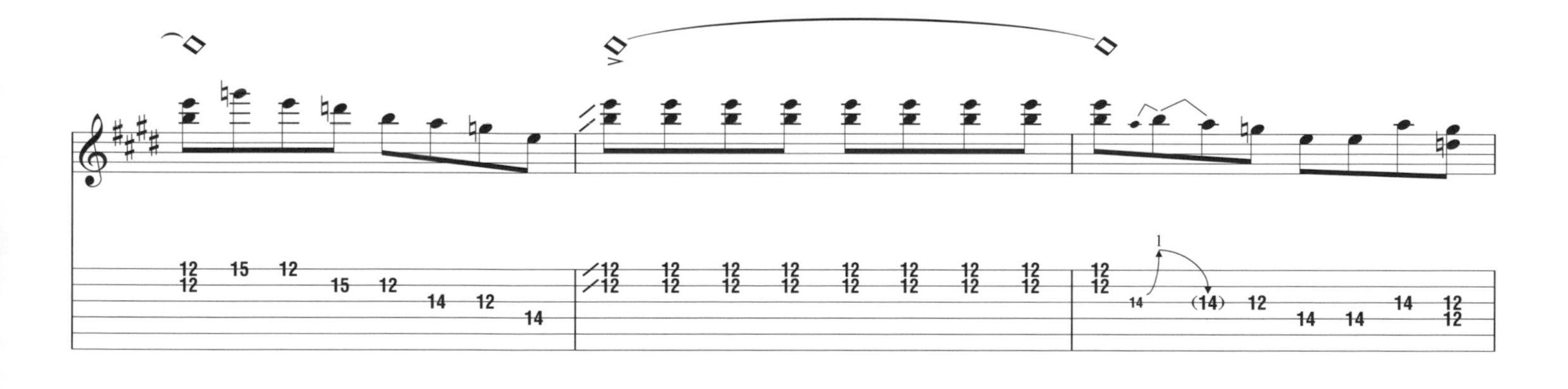

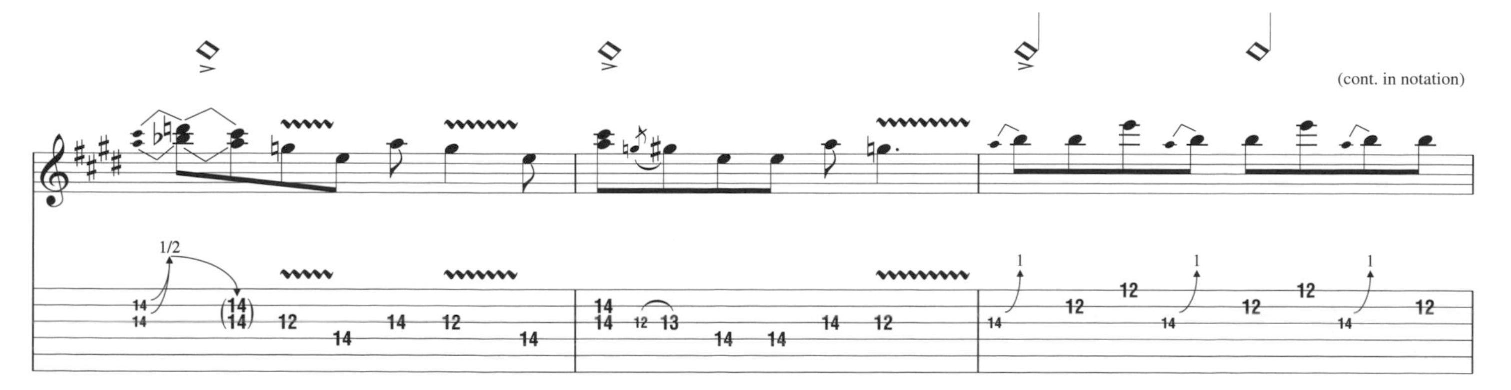
(cont. in notation)

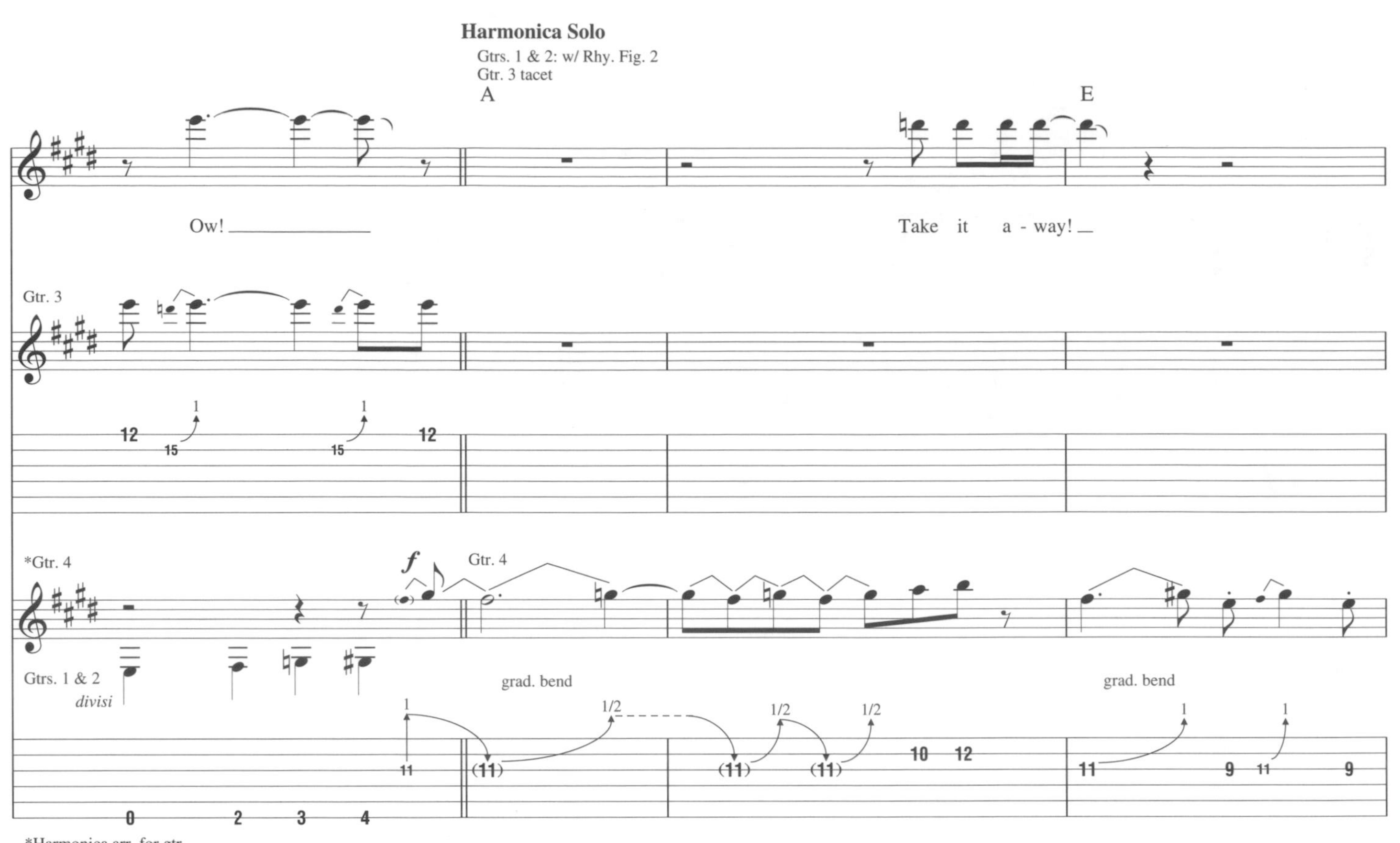

Harmonica Solo
Gtrs. 1 & 2: w/ Rhy. Fig. 2
Gtr. 3 tacet
A
E
Ow!
Take it a - way!
Gtr. 3
*Gtr. 4
Gtr. 4
Gtrs. 1 & 2
divisi
grad. bend
grad. bend
*Harmonica arr. for gtr.

Gtr. 4
B

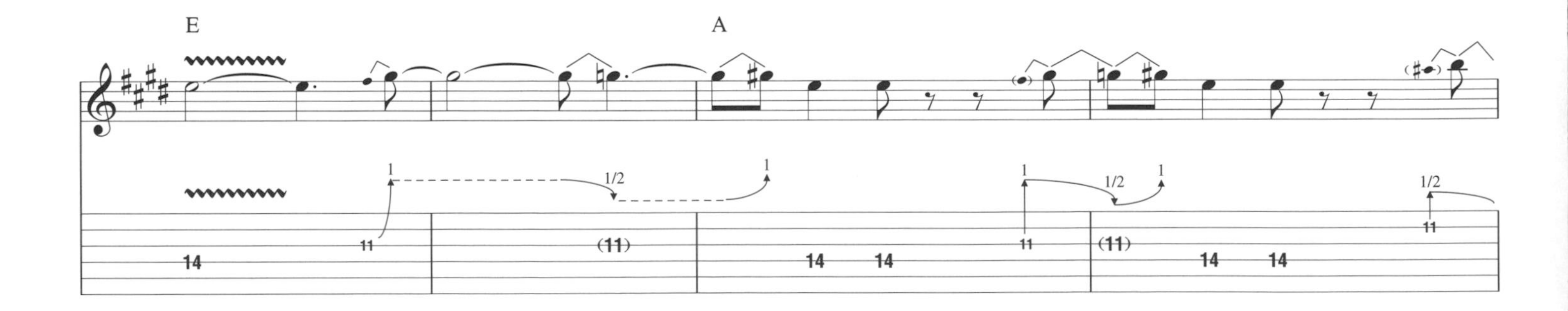

E
A

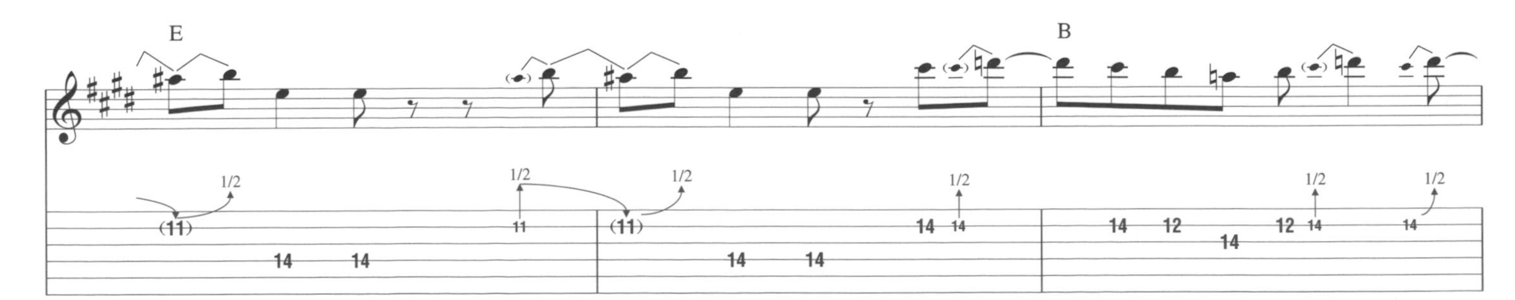

E
B

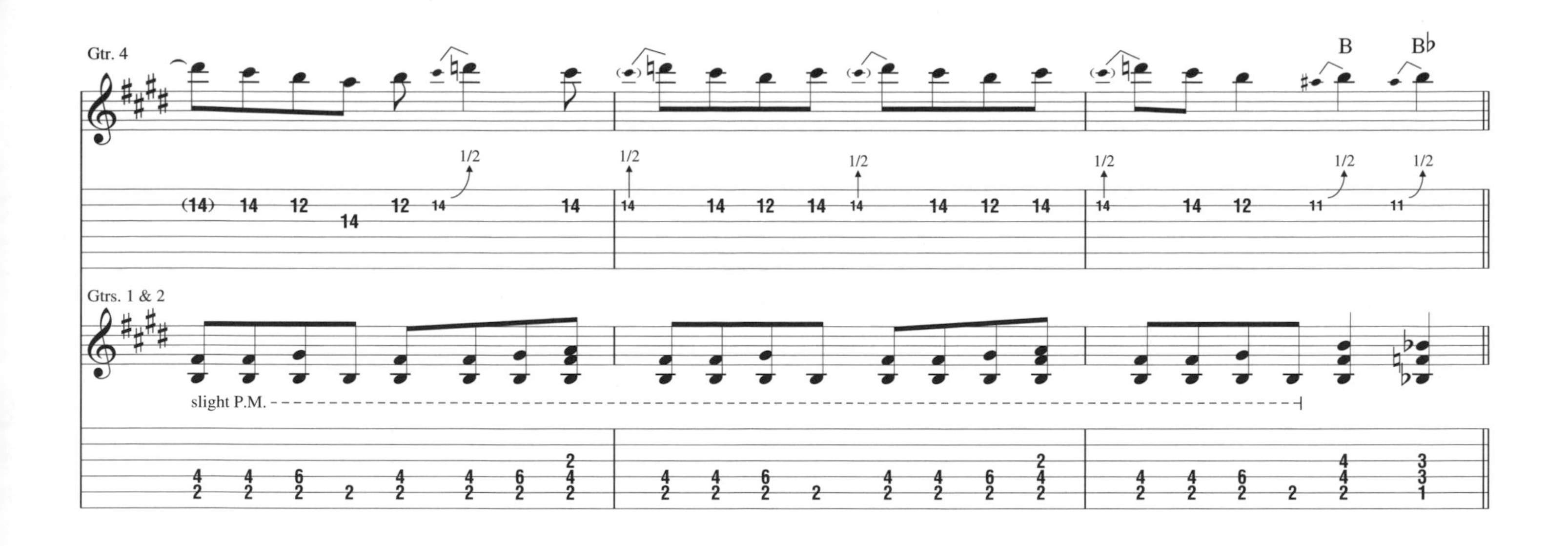

Saxophone Solo

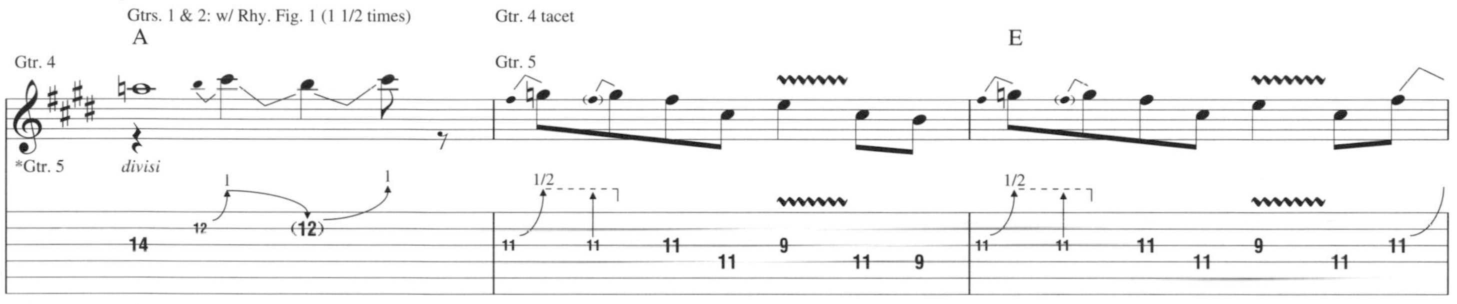

*Tenor sax. arr. for gtr.

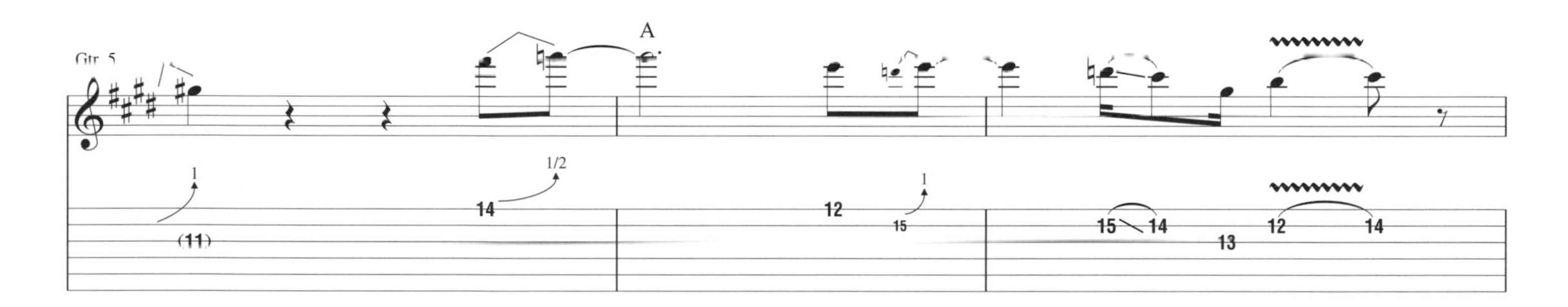

D.S. al Coda

Gtrs. 1 & 2: w/ Riff A

N.C.(E)

3. I ain't got noth - in' 'gainst the

Gtr. 5

*Gtr. 6

f

*Horns arr. for gtr.

Coda

B
of here,
if I ev - er get out
of here,
slight P.M.

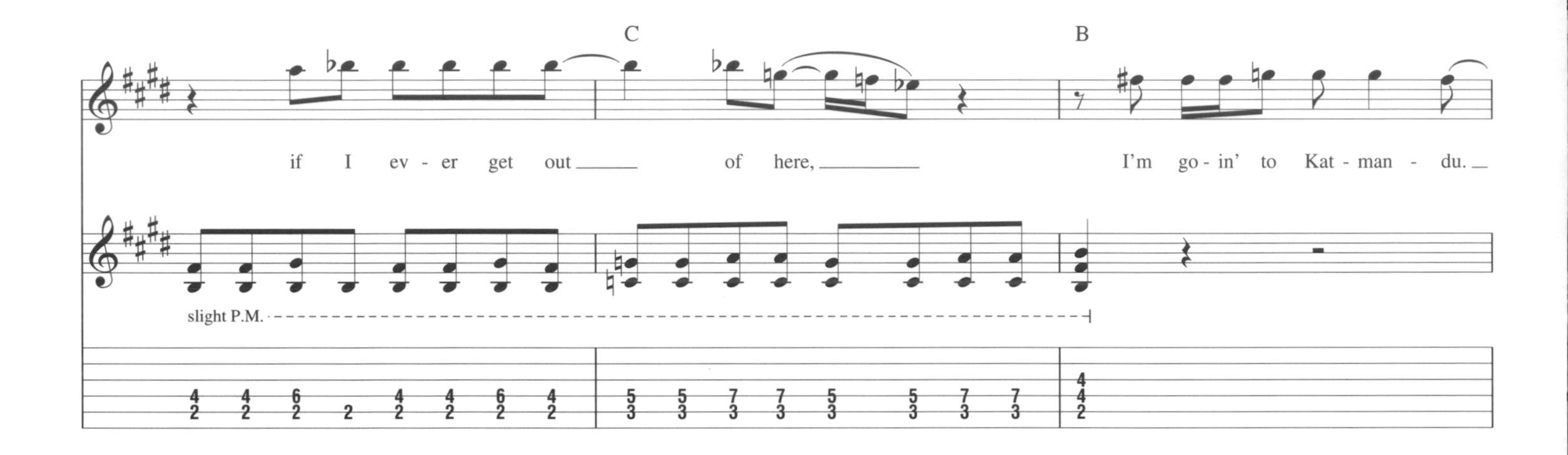
C
B
if I ev - er get out
of here,
I'm go - in' to Kat - man - du.
slight P.M.

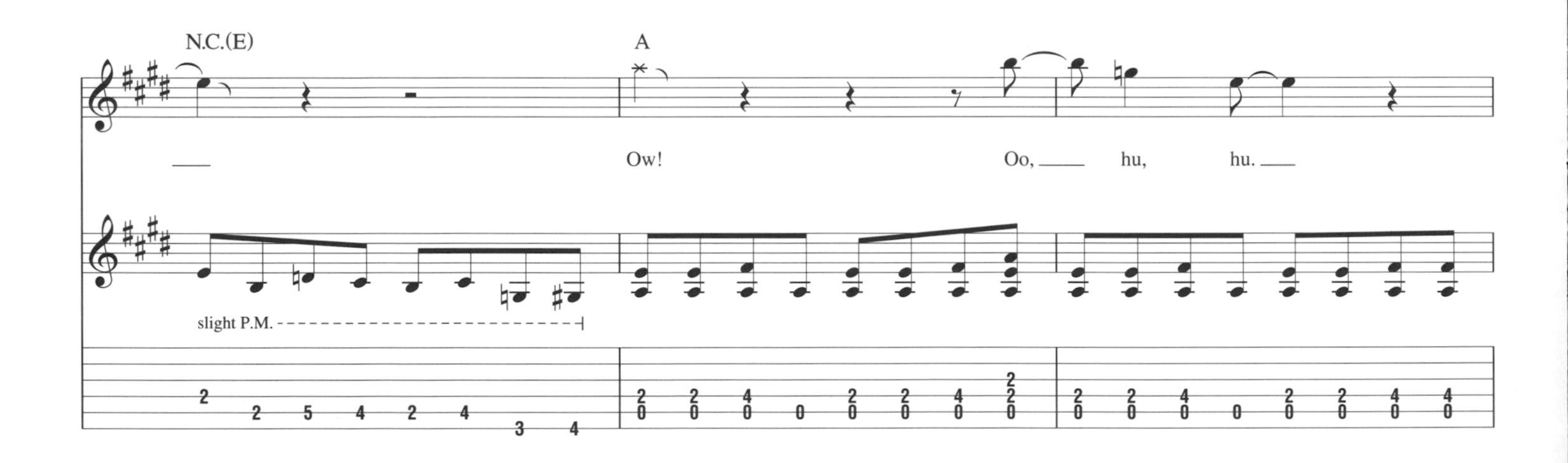
N.C.(E)
A
Ow!
Oo, hu, hu.
slight P.M.

G
F♯
Oo, hu, hu.
Oo, yeah,

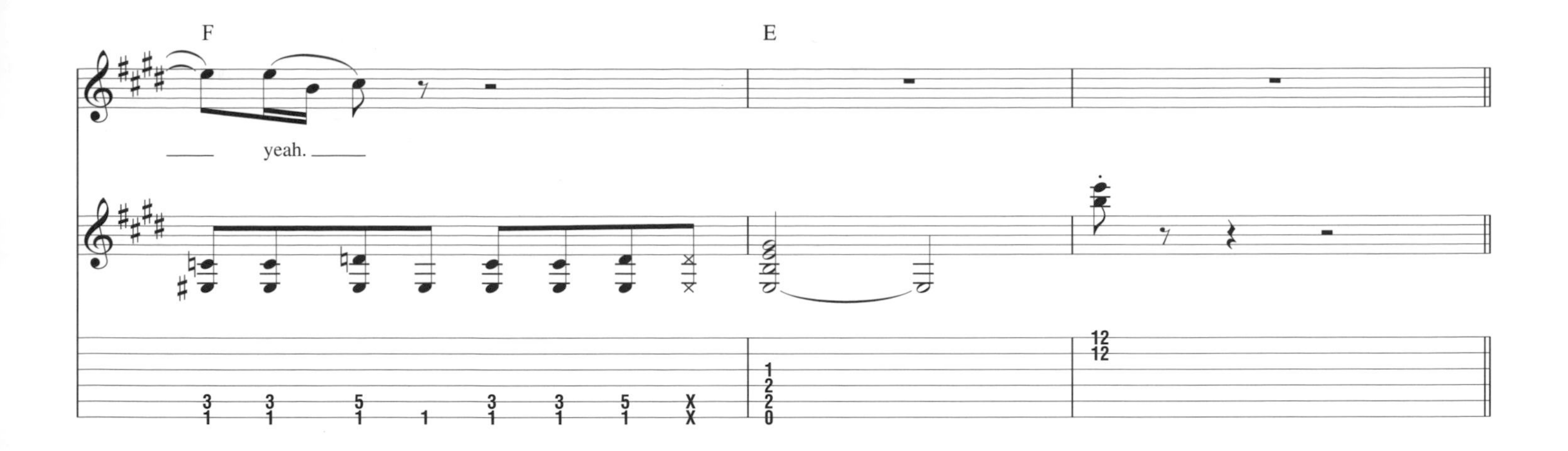

Outro-Guitar Solo

Gtrs. 1 & 2: w/ Rhy. Fig. 1 (till fade)

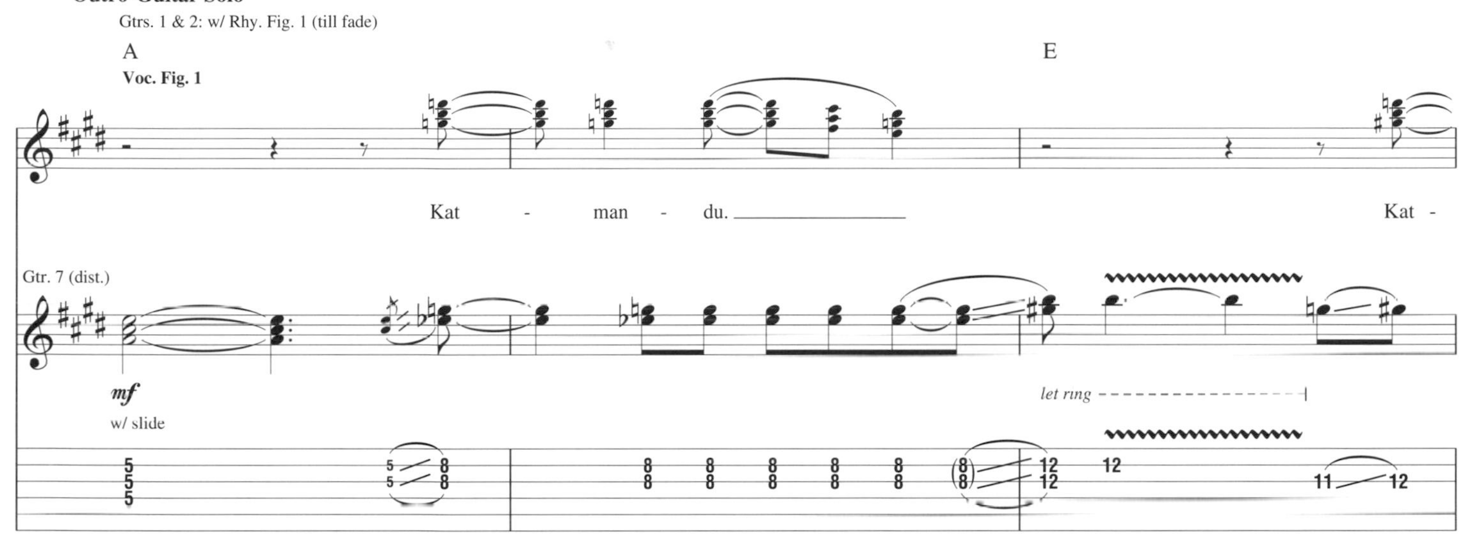

Bkgd. Voc.: w/ Voc. Fig. 1 (5 times)

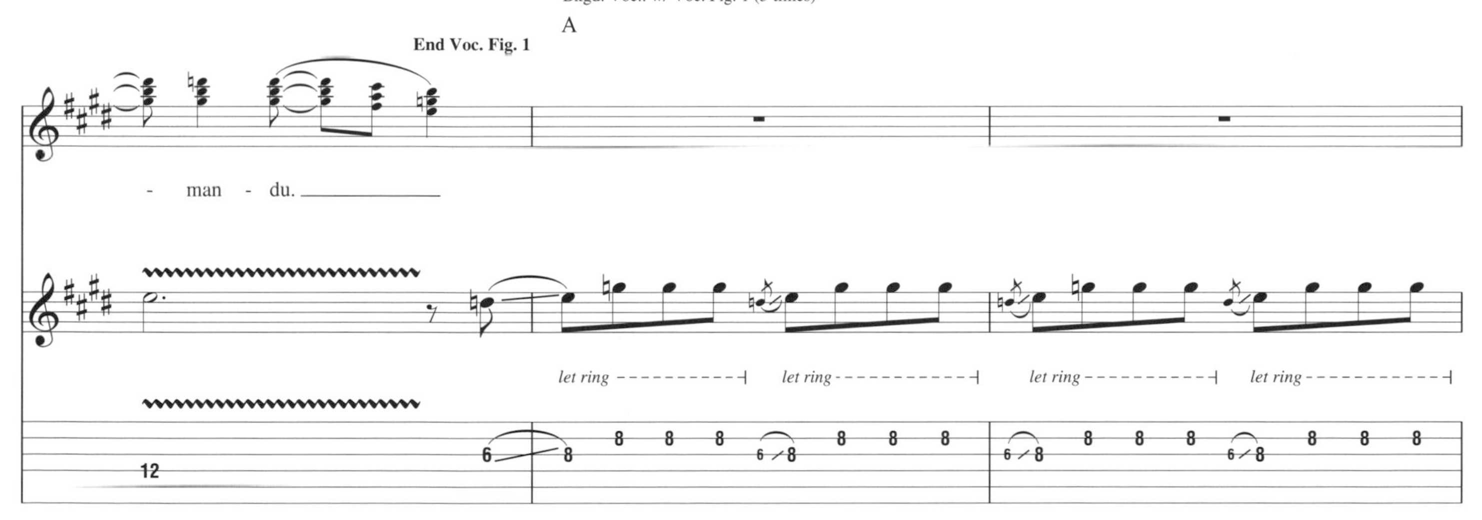

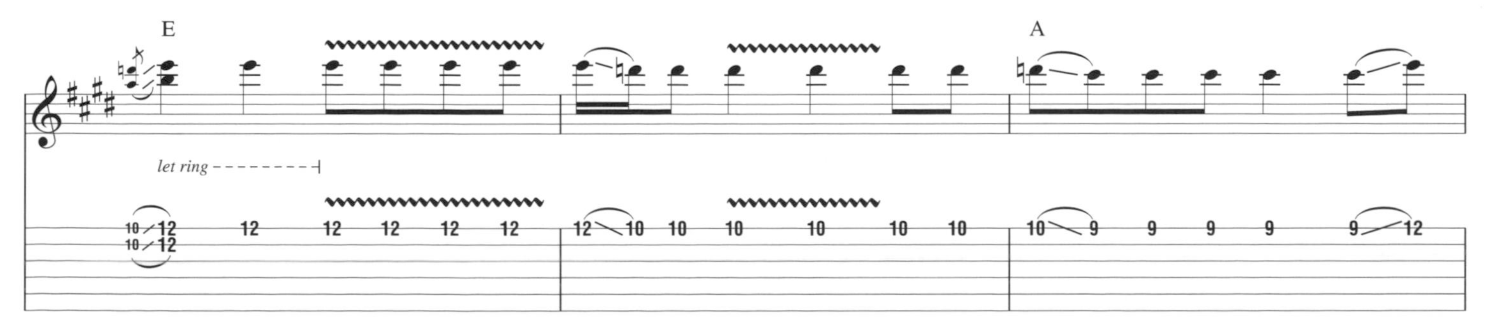

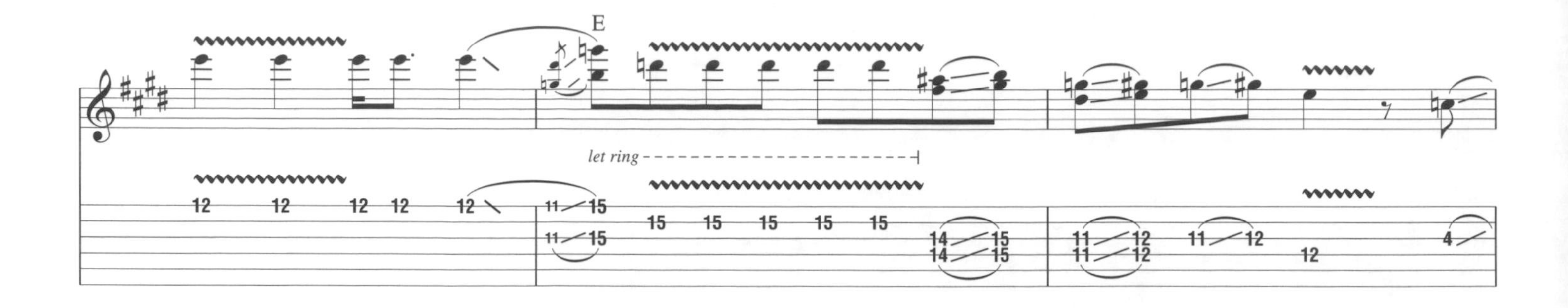
E
let ring

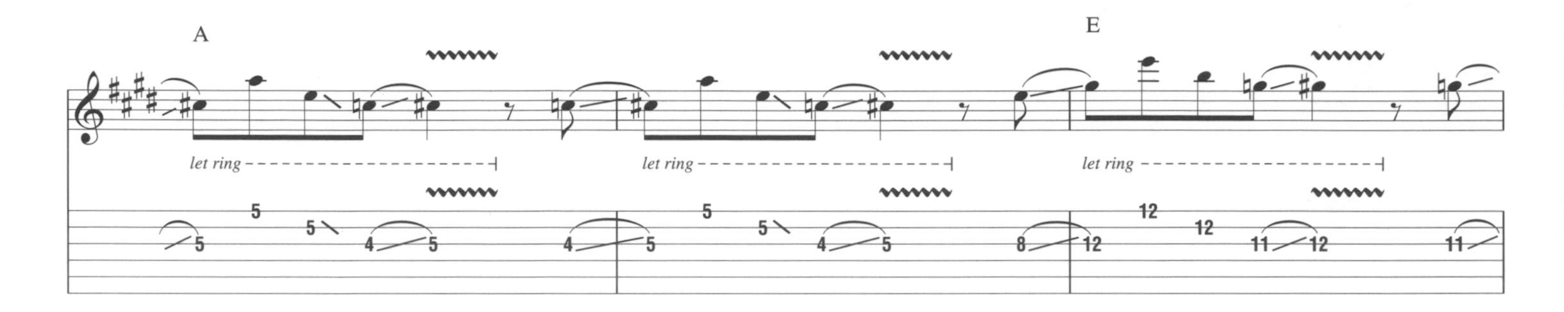
A
E
let ring
let ring
let ring

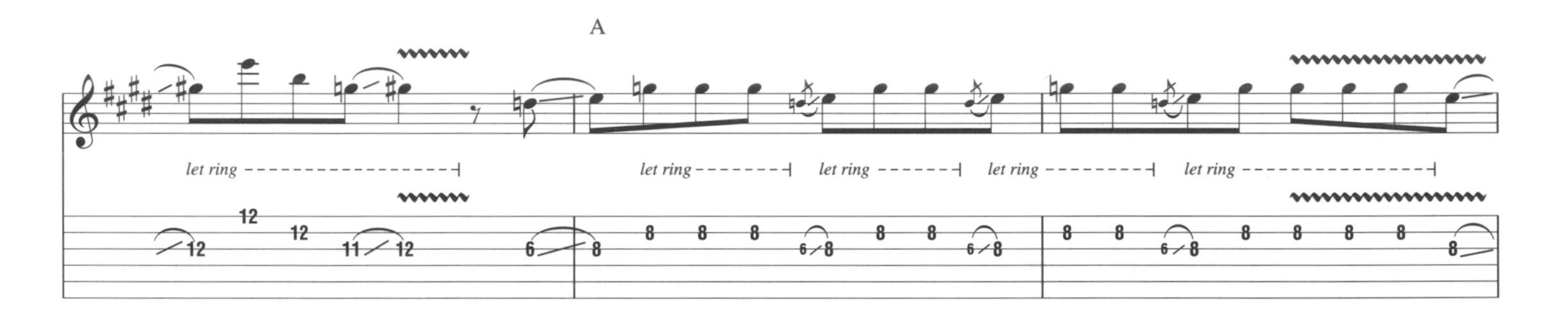
A
let ring
let ring
let ring
let ring
let ring

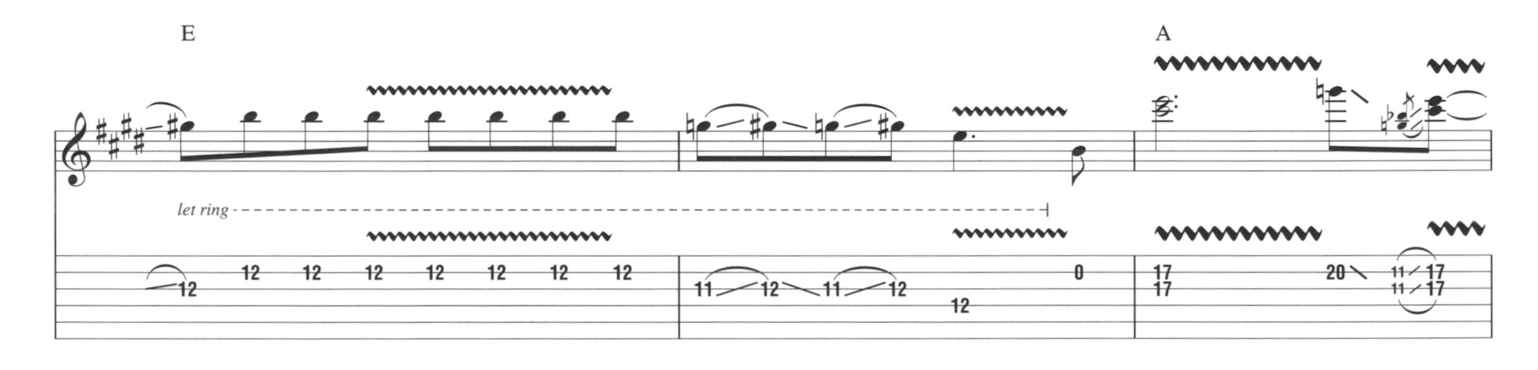
E
A
let ring

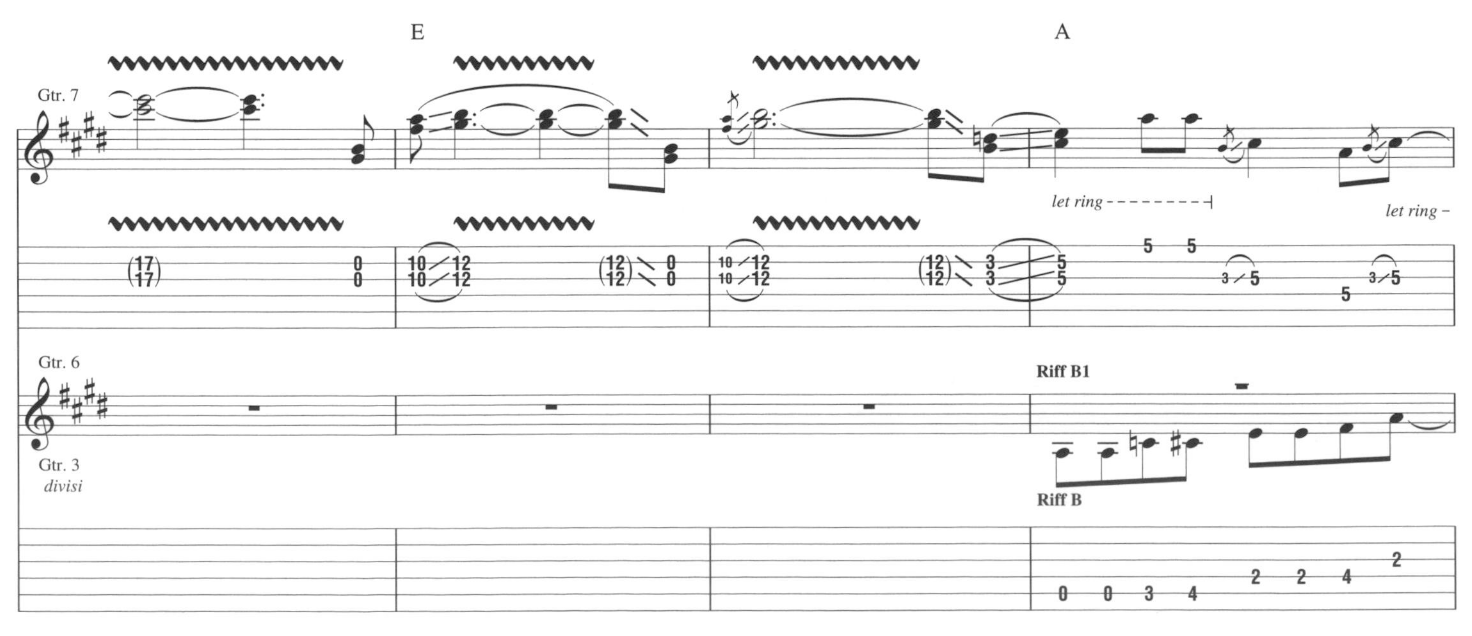
E
A
Gtr. 7
let ring
let ring
Gtr. 6
Riff B1
Gtr. 3
divisi
Riff B

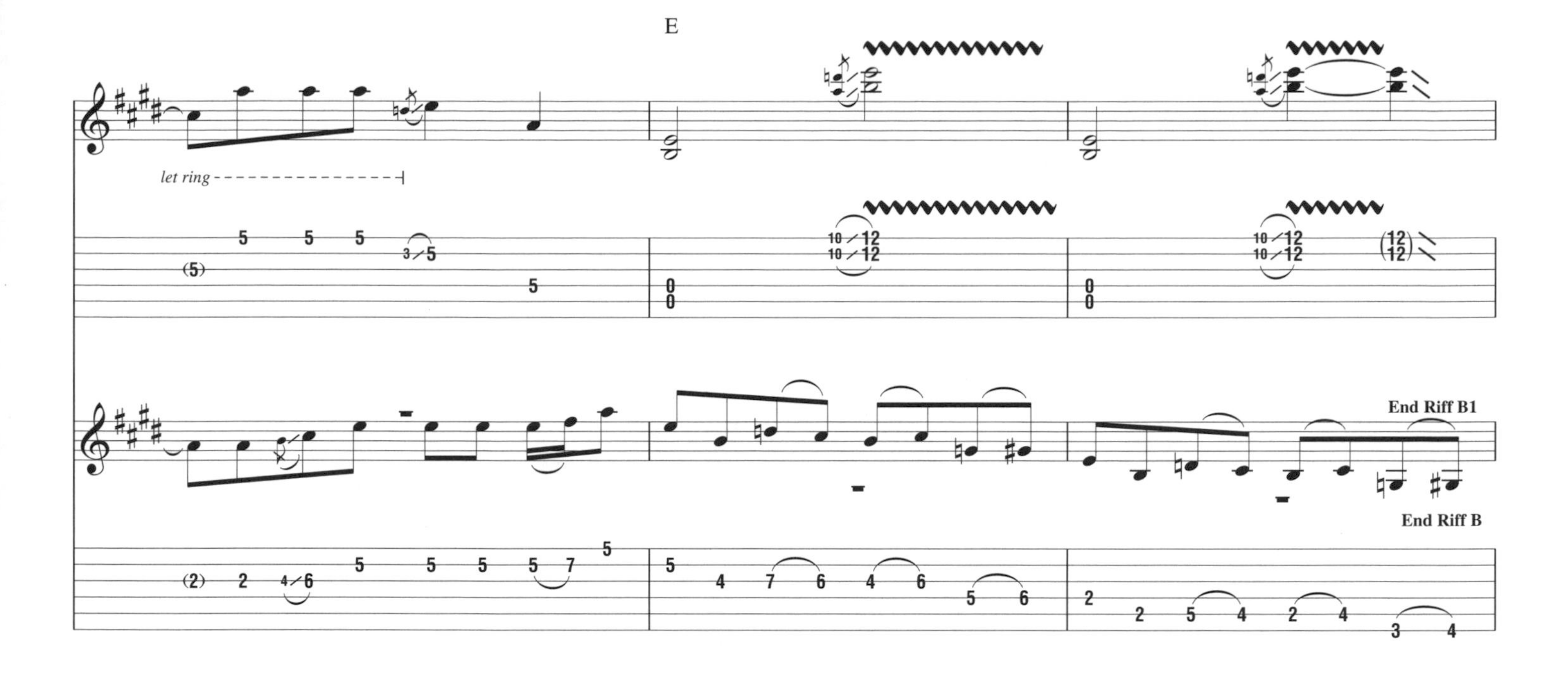
E
let ring
End Riff B1
End Riff B

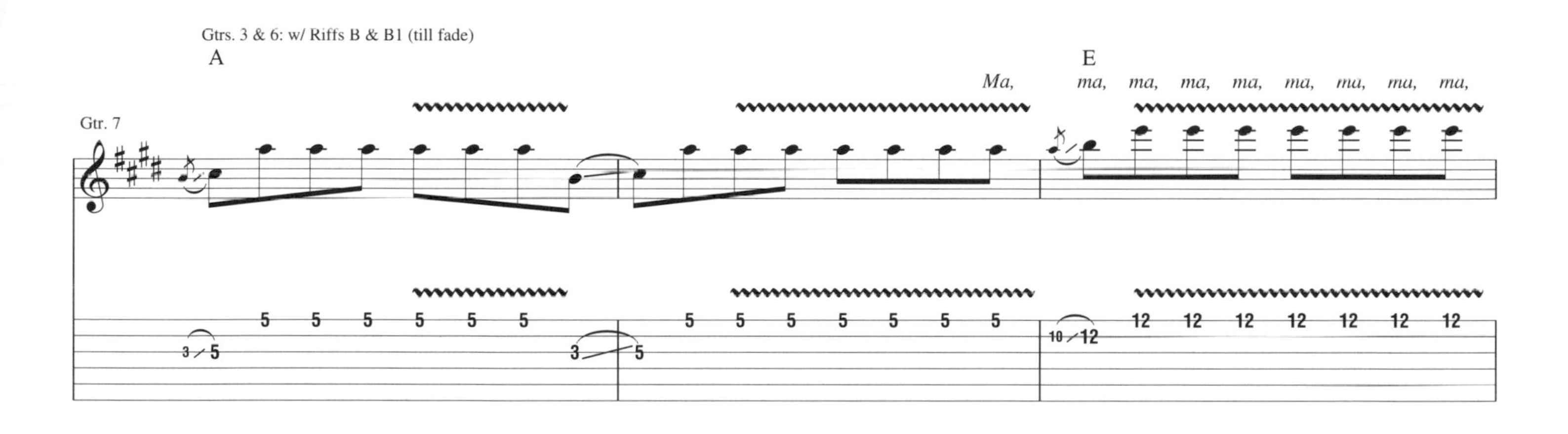
Gtrs. 3 & 6: w/ Riffs B & B1 (till fade)
A
Gtr. 7
Ma,
E
ma, ma, ma, ma, ma, ma, ma, ma,

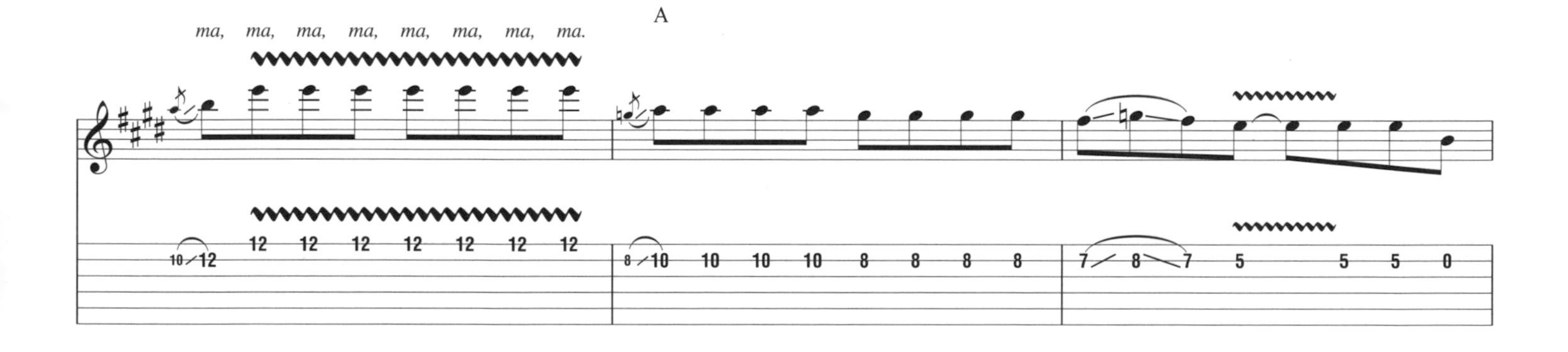
ma, ma, ma, ma, ma, ma, ma, ma.
A

E
Ow, ow, ow, yeah, yeah!
A

E
La, da, da, da, da, na, no, no, no. Ow, ow, ow!
let ring

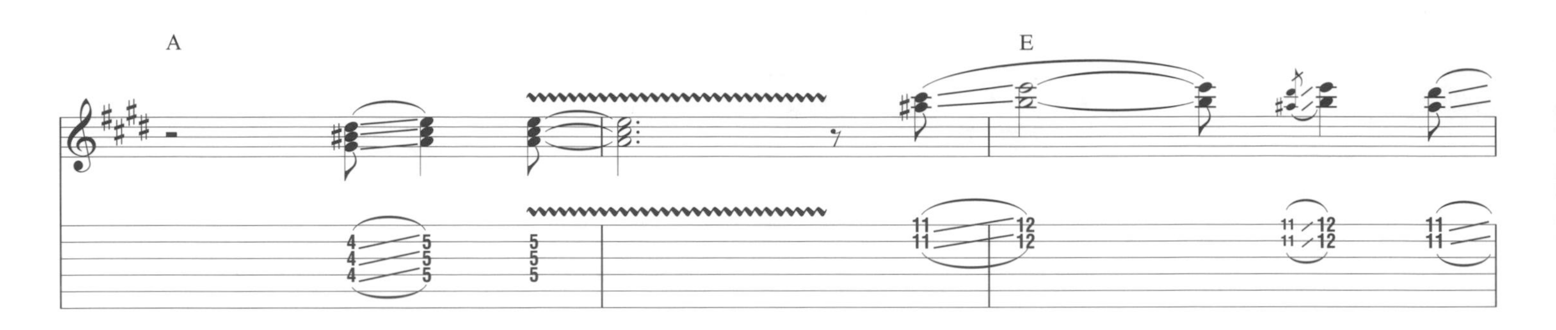
A
E

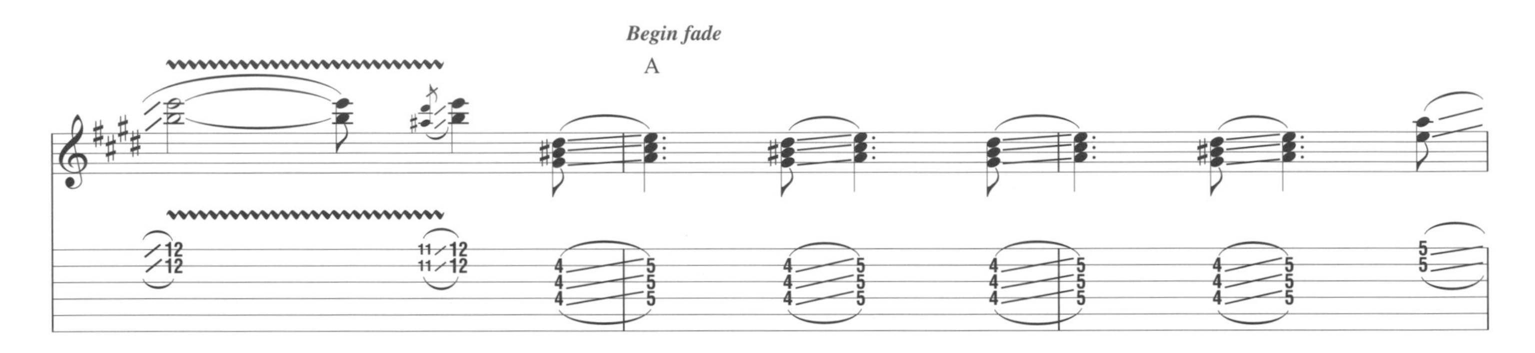
Begin fade
A

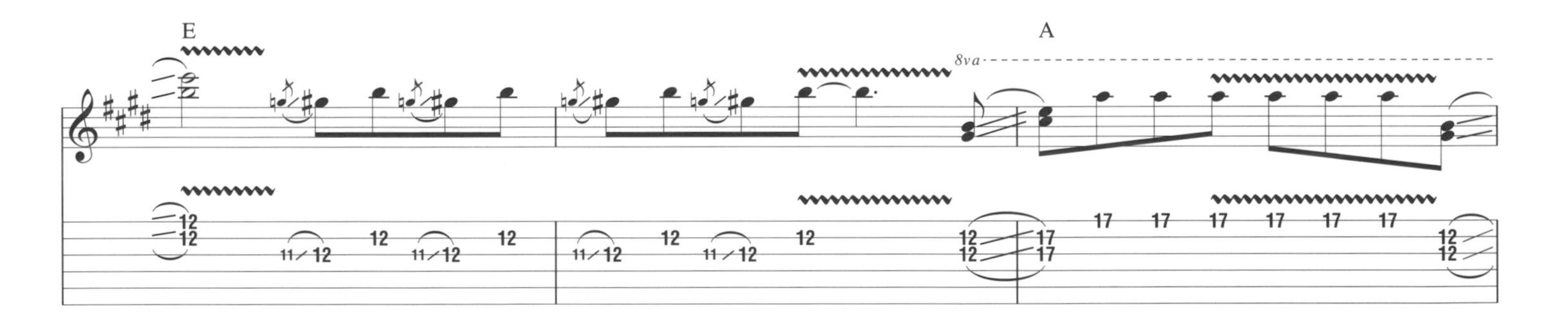
E
A
8va

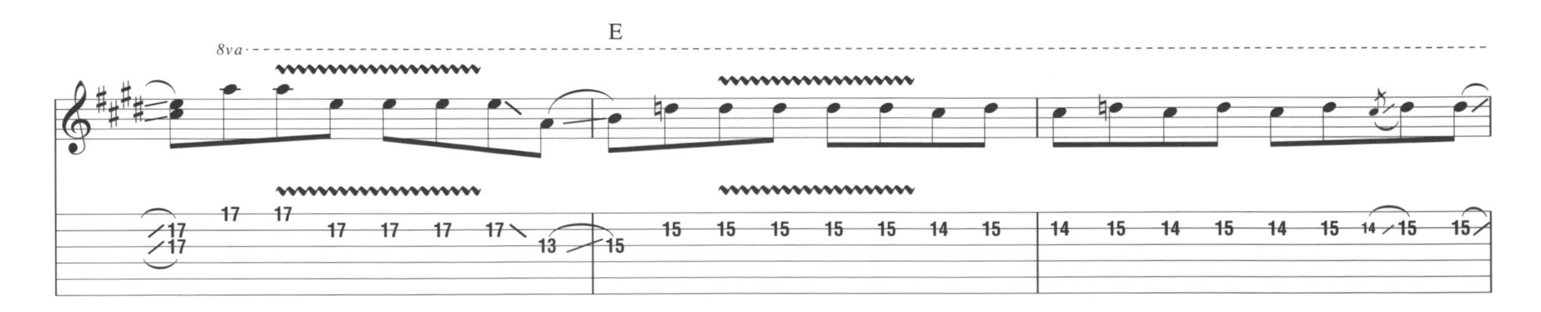
8va
E

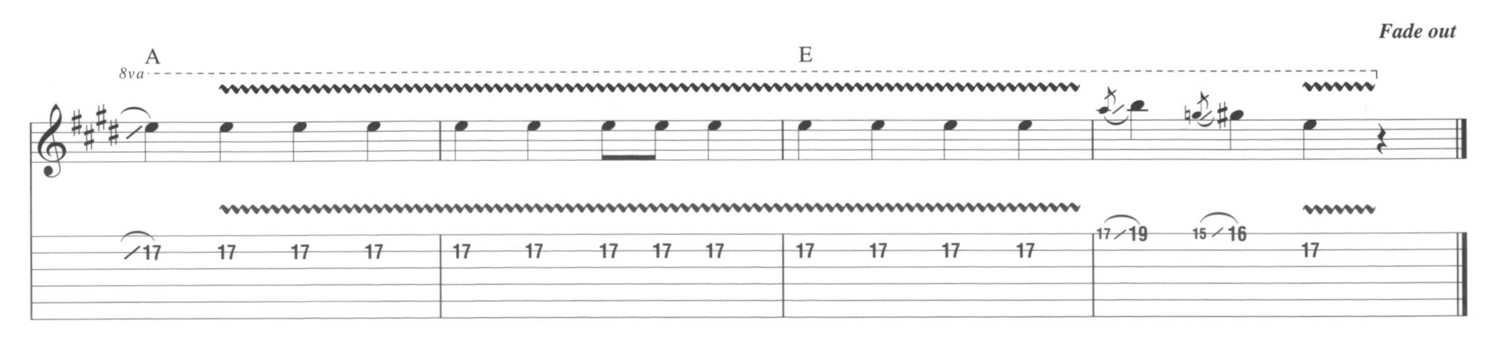
Fade out
A
E
8va

Shame on the Moon

Words and Music by Rodney Crowell

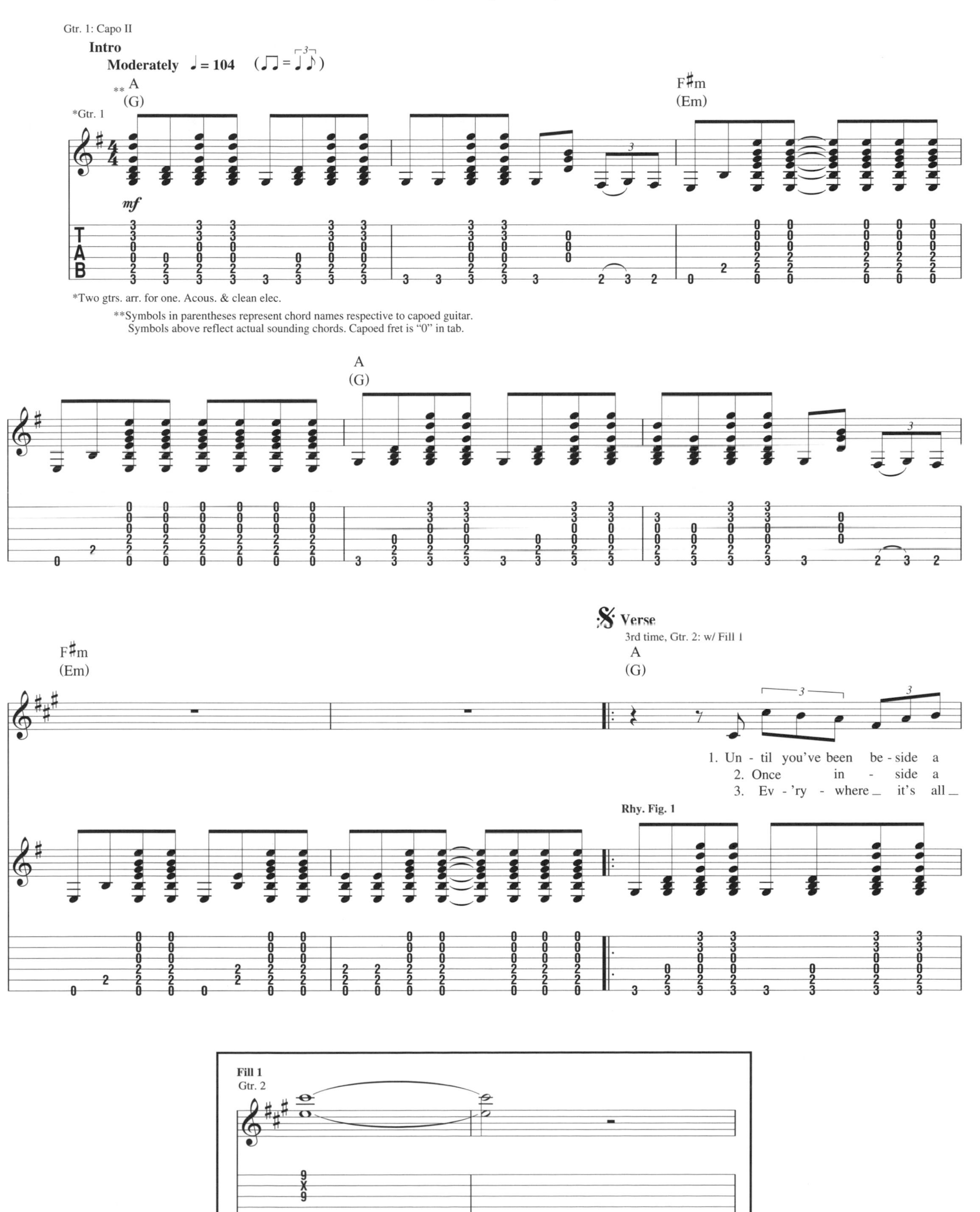

F♯m
(Em)
man
wom - an's heart
a - round,
you don't know what he wants.
a man must keep his head.
com - fort in a crowd.

A
(G)
F♯m
(Em)
You don't know if he cries at night,
Heav - en o-pens up the door
Strang - er's fac - es all a - round;
you don't know if he
where an - gels fear to
laugh - in' right out

Bridge

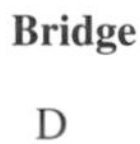
E5
(D5)

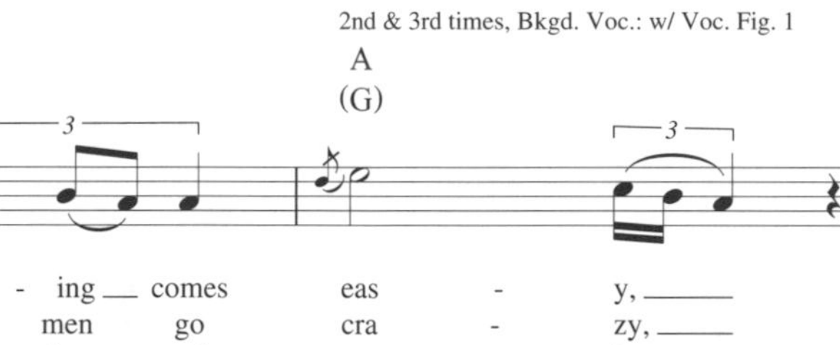
2nd & 3rd times, Bkgd. Voc.: w/ Voc. Fig. 1
A
(G)

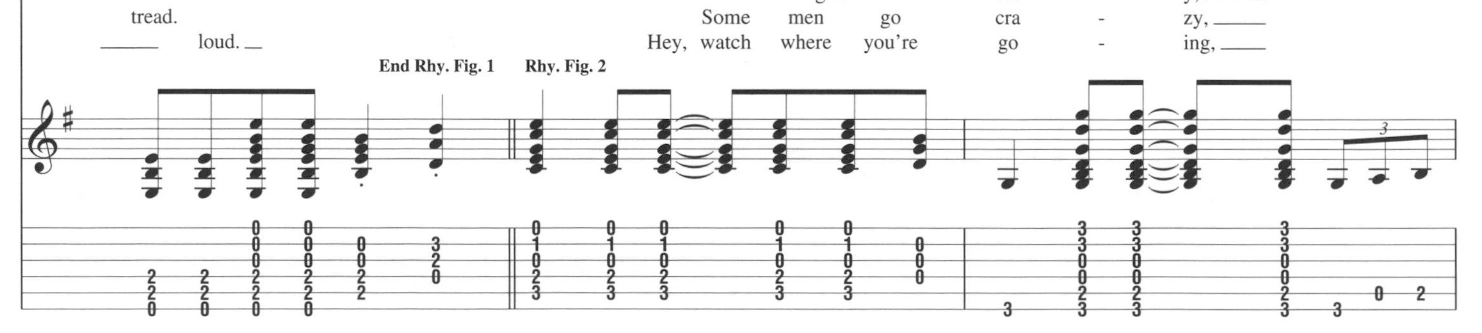
D
(C)
don't.
tread.
loud.
When noth - ing comes eas - y,
Some men go cra - zy,
Hey, watch where you're go - ing,
End Rhy. Fig. 1
Rhy. Fig. 2

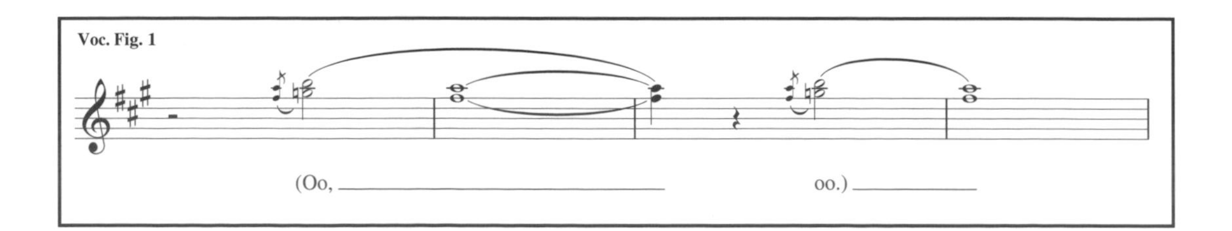
Voc. Fig. 1
(Oo, oo.)

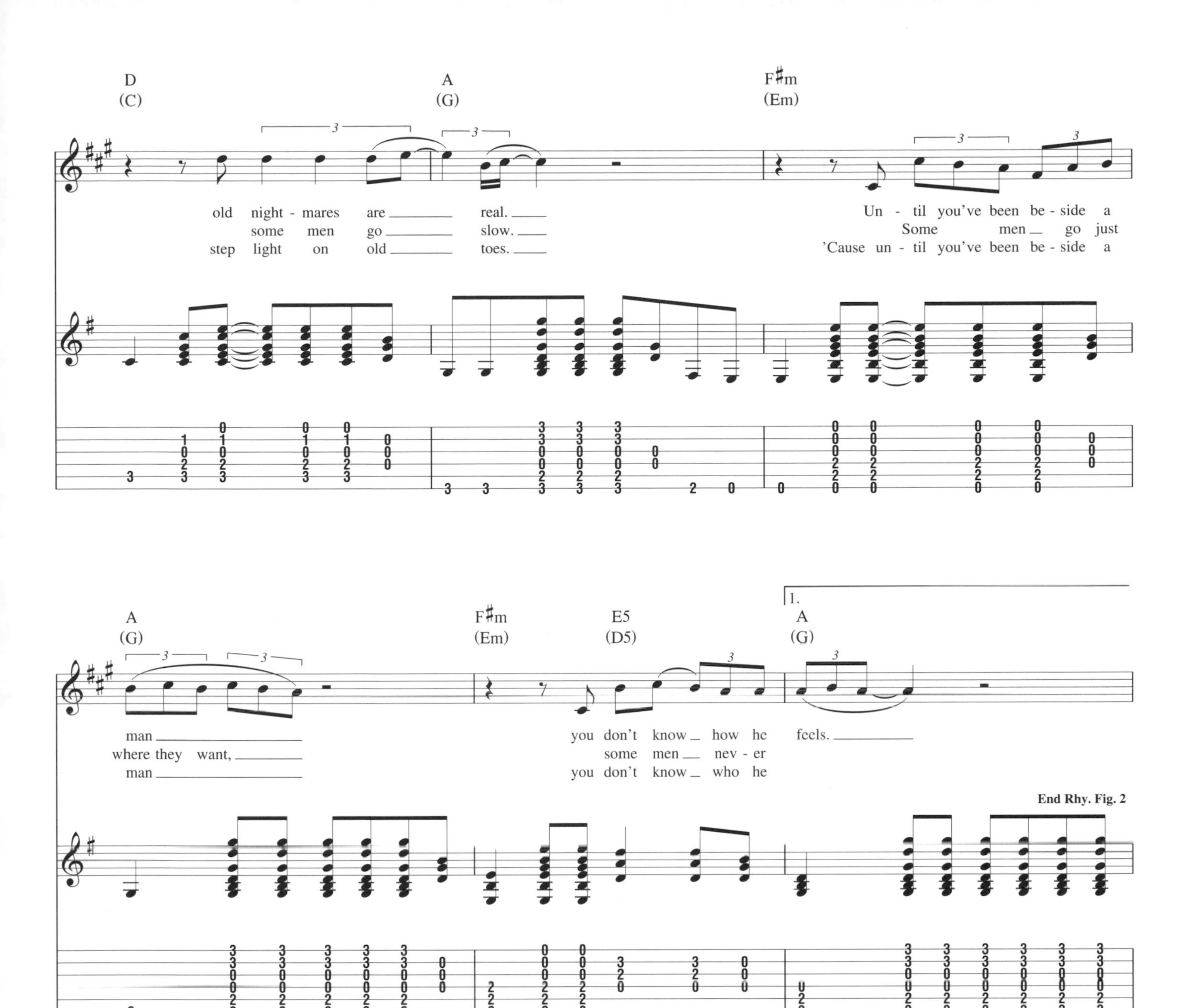
D
(C)
A
(G)
F♯m
(Em)
old night - mares are real.
some men go slow.
step light on old toes.
Un - til you've been be - side a
Some men go just
'Cause un - til you've been be - side a
A
(G)
F♯m
(Em)
E5
(D5)
1.
A
(G)
man
where they want,
man
you don't know how he feels.
some men nev - er
you don't know who he
End Rhy. Fig. 2

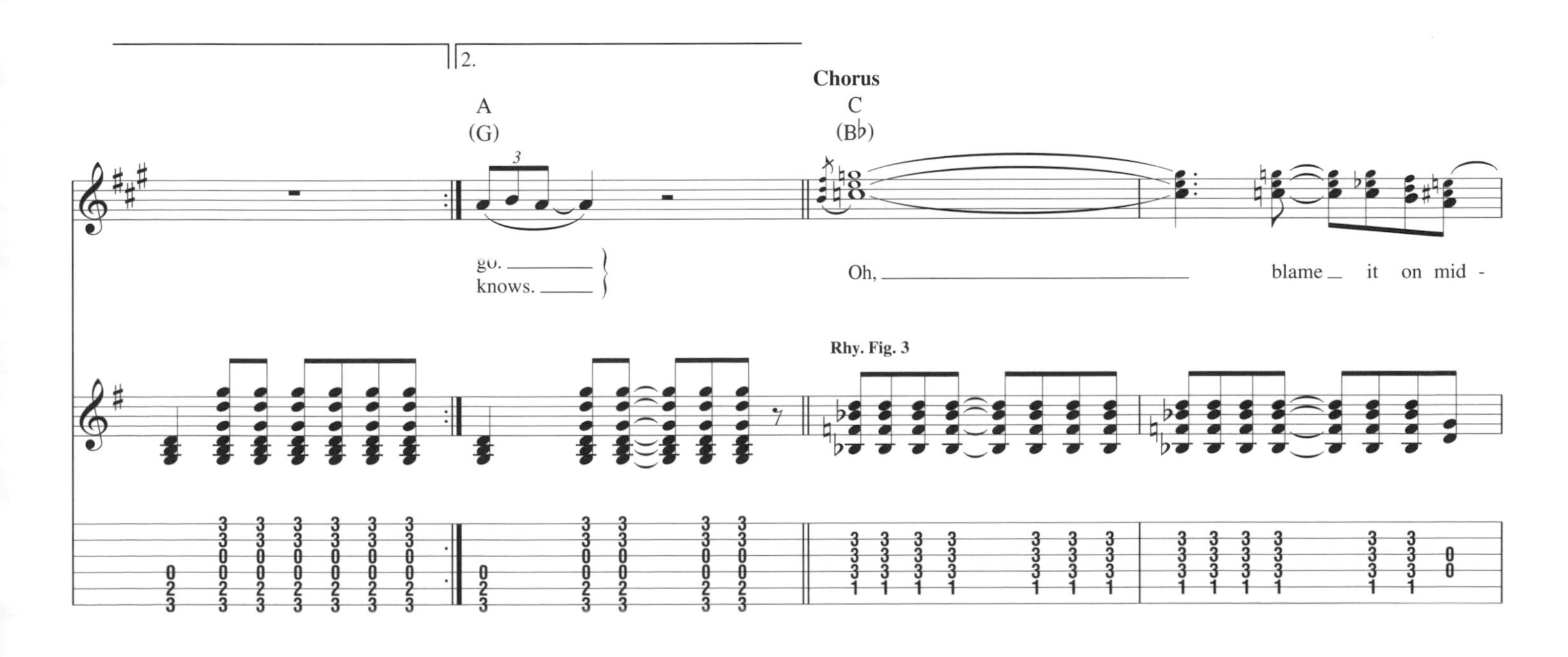
2.
Chorus
A
(G)
C
(B♭)
go.
knows.
Oh, blame it on mid -
Rhy. Fig. 3

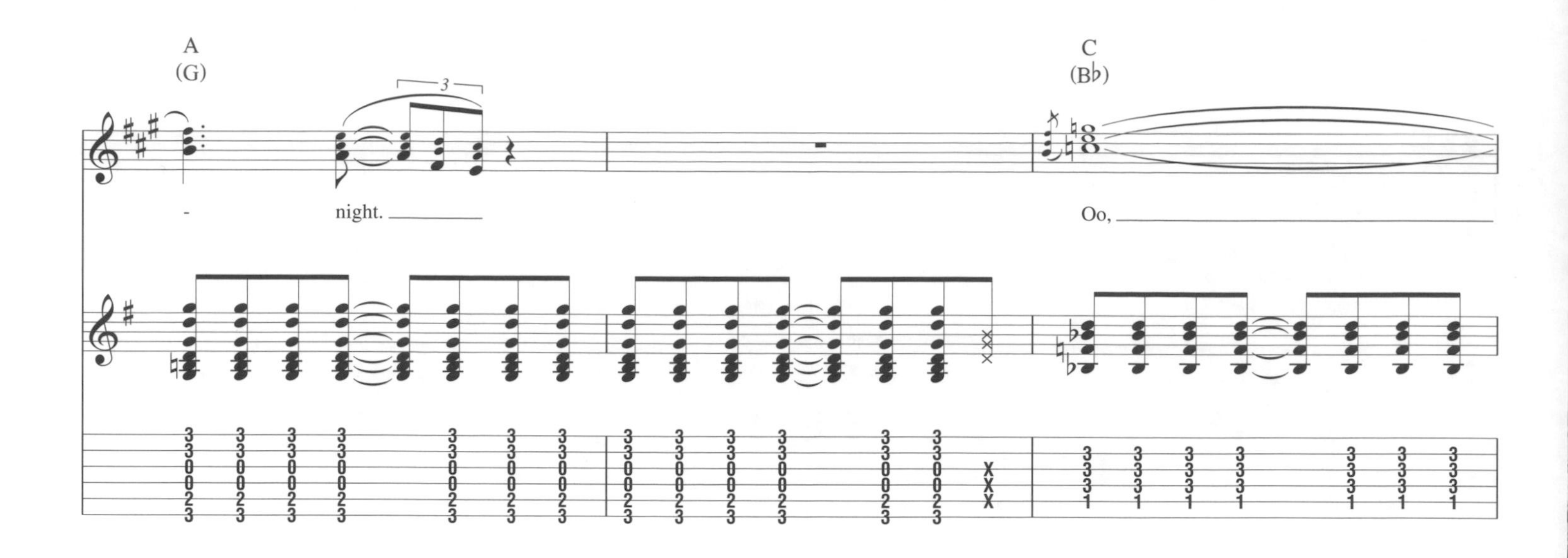
A
(G)
C
(B♭)
night.
Oo,

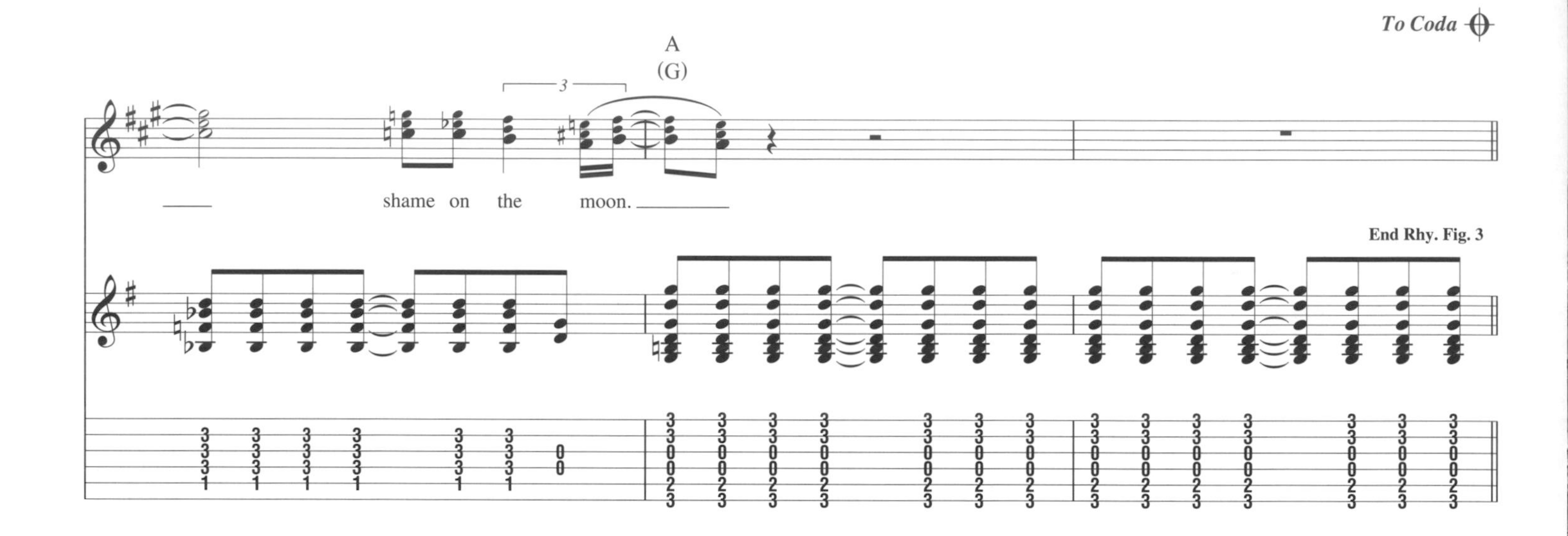
To Coda
A
(G)
shame on the moon.
End Rhy. Fig. 3

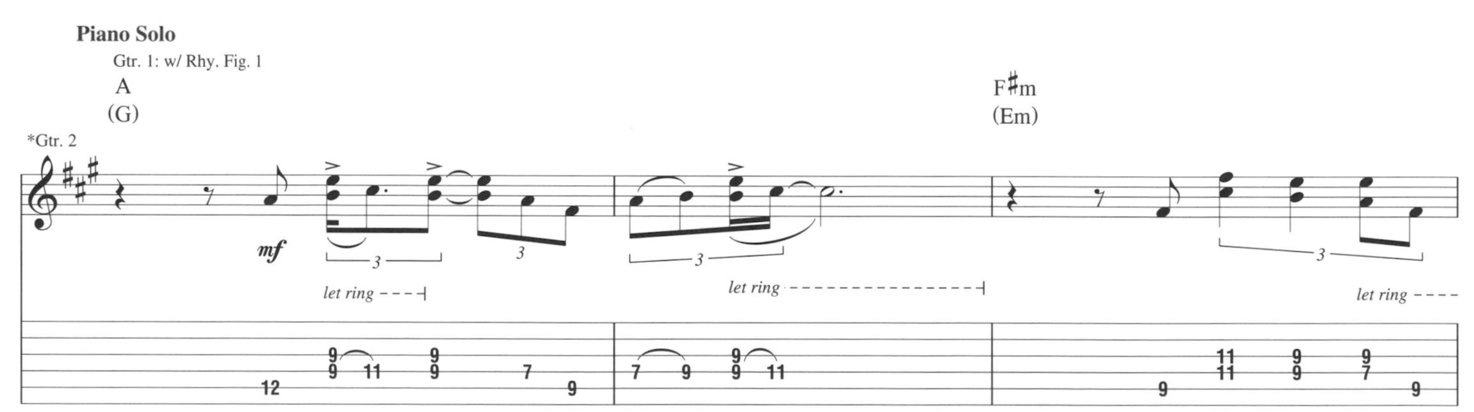
Piano Solo
Gtr. 1: w/ Rhy. Fig. 1
A
(G)
F♯m
(Em)
*Gtr. 2
mf
let ring
*Piano arr. for. gtr.

A
(G)
let ring

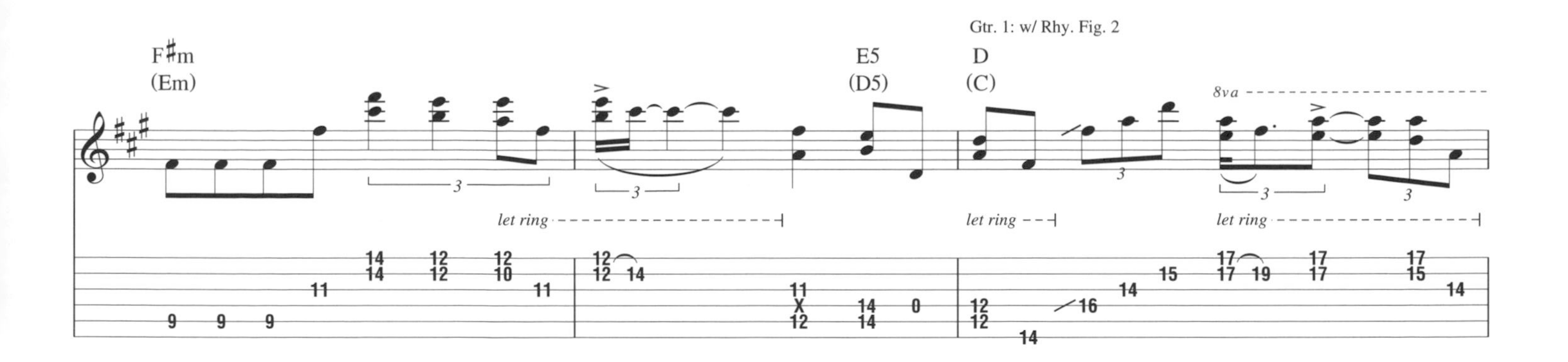

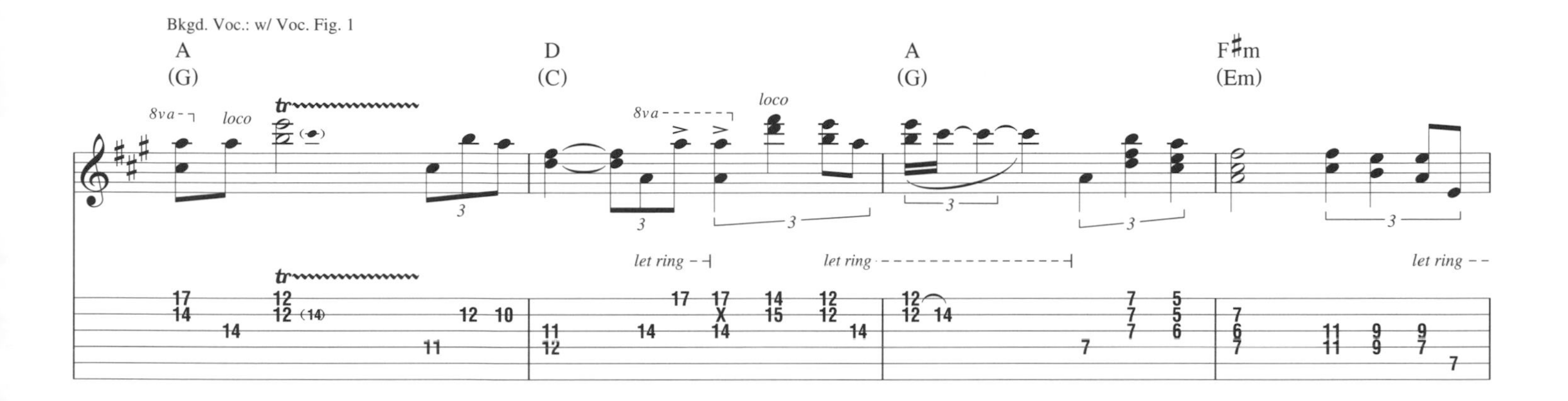

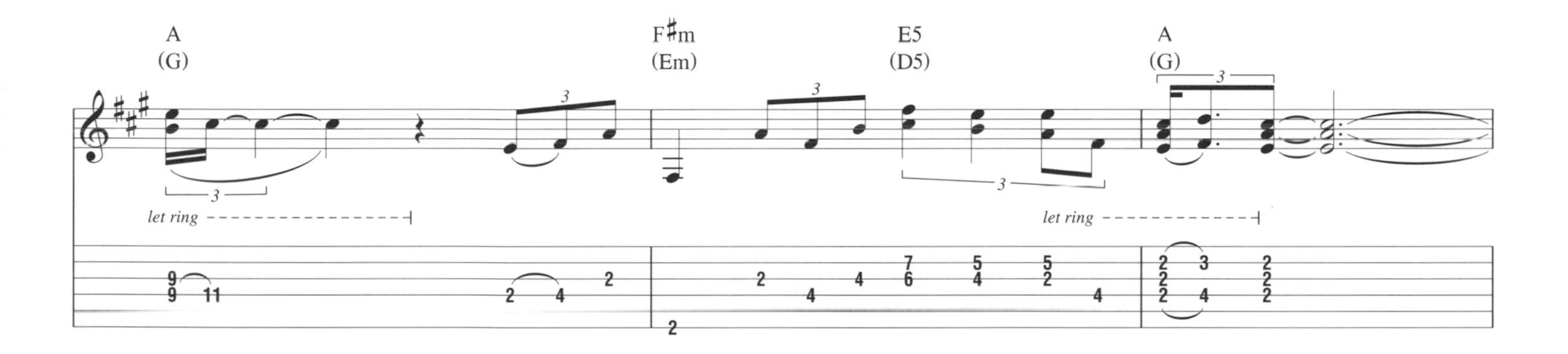

D.S. al Coda
(take 2nd ending)

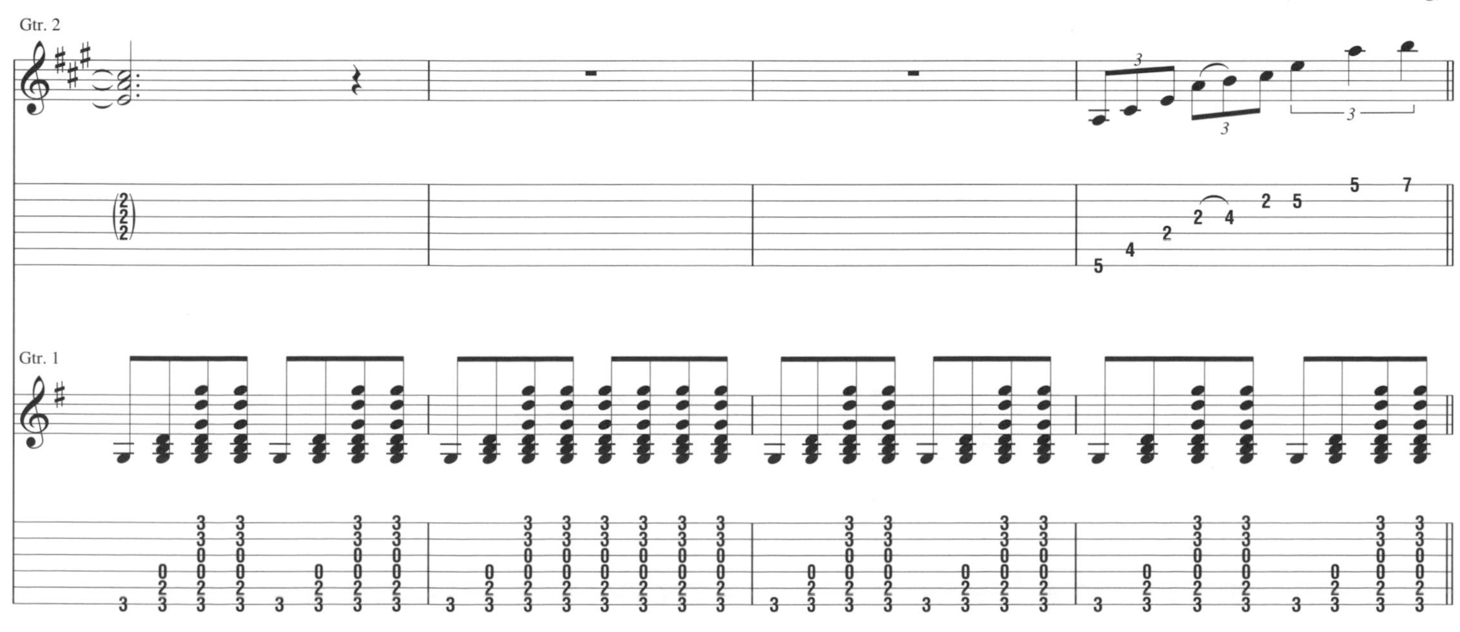

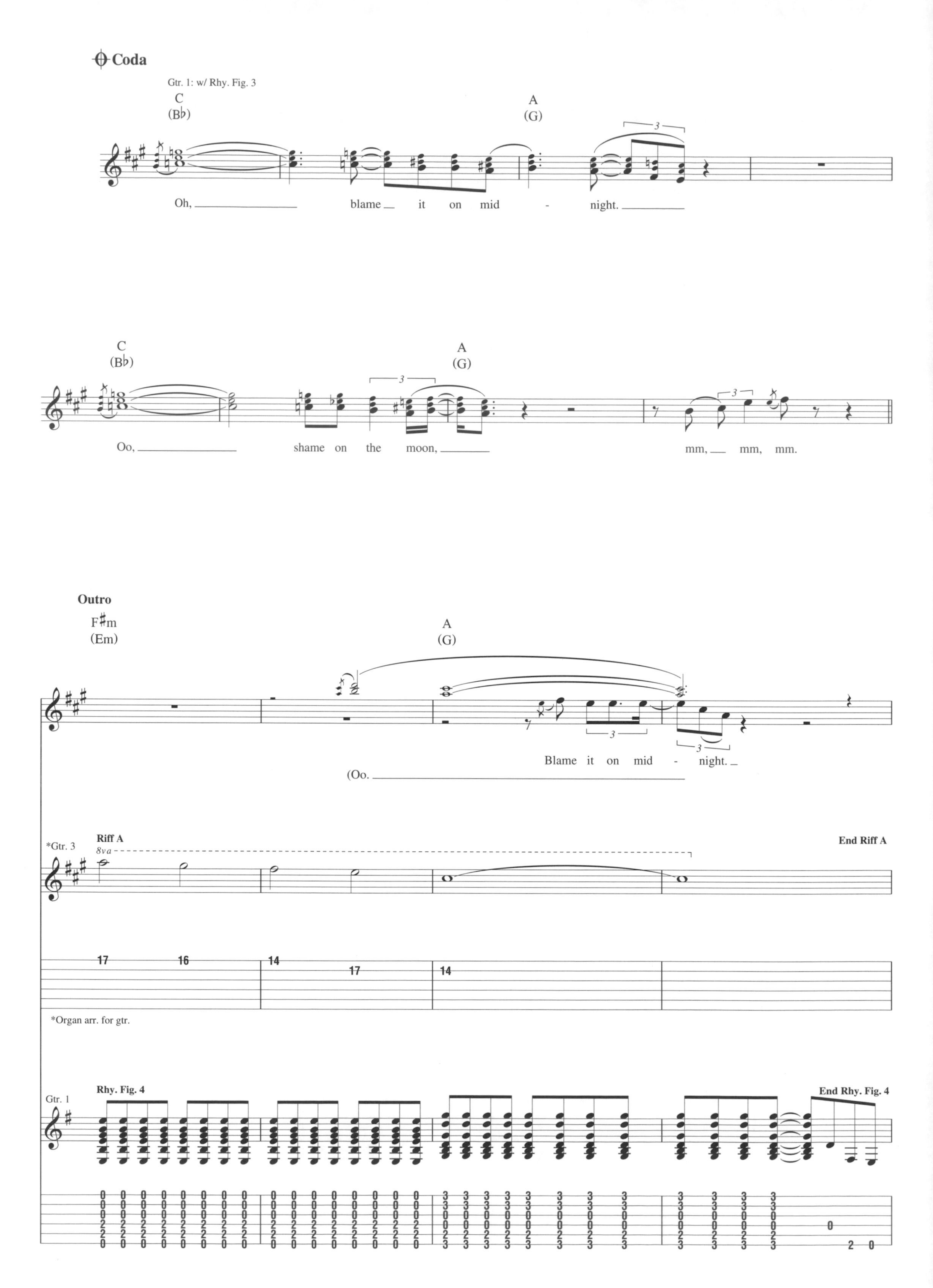
Coda
Gtr. 1: w/ Rhy. Fig. 3
C
(B♭)
A
(G)
Oh,
blame it on mid - night.
C
(B♭)
A
(G)
Oo,
shame on the moon,
mm, mm, mm.
Outro
F♯m
(Em)
A
(G)
Blame it on mid - night.
(Oo.
*Gtr. 3
Riff A
8va
End Riff A
*Organ arr. for gtr.
Gtr. 1
Rhy. Fig. 4
End Rhy. Fig. 4

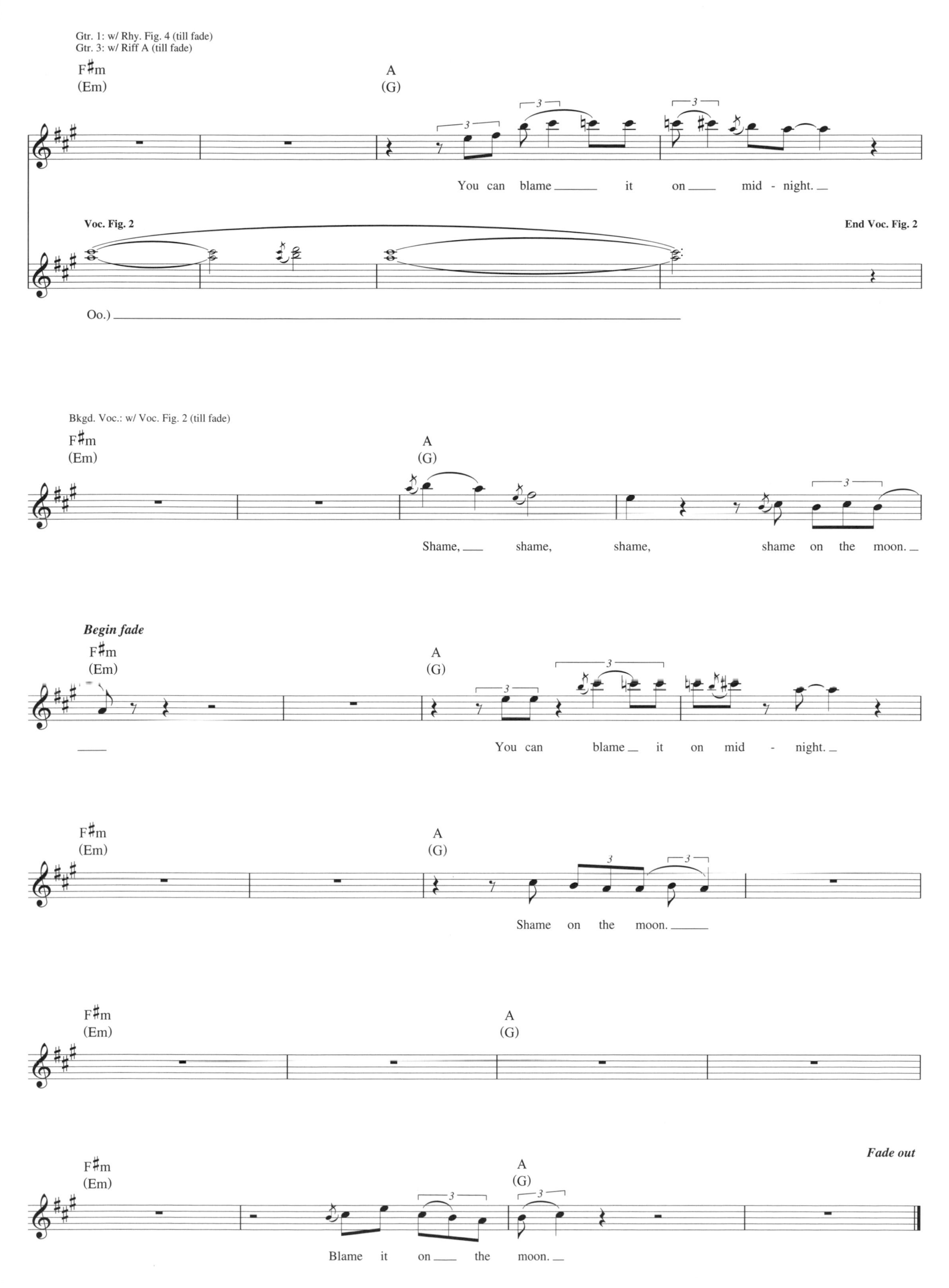
Gtr. 1: w/ Rhy. Fig. 4 (till fade)
Gtr. 3: w/ Riff A (till fade)
F♯m
(Em)
A
(G)
You can blame it on mid - night.
Voc. Fig. 2
End Voc. Fig. 2
Oo.)
Bkgd. Voc.: w/ Voc. Fig. 2 (till fade)
F♯m
(Em)
A
(G)
Shame, shame, shame, shame on the moon.
Begin fade
F♯m
(Em)
A
(G)
You can blame it on mid - night.
F♯m
(Em)
A
(G)
Shame on the moon.
F♯m
(Em)
A
(G)
F♯m
(Em)
A
(G)
Fade out
Blame it on the moon.

Fire Lake

Words and Music by Bob Seger

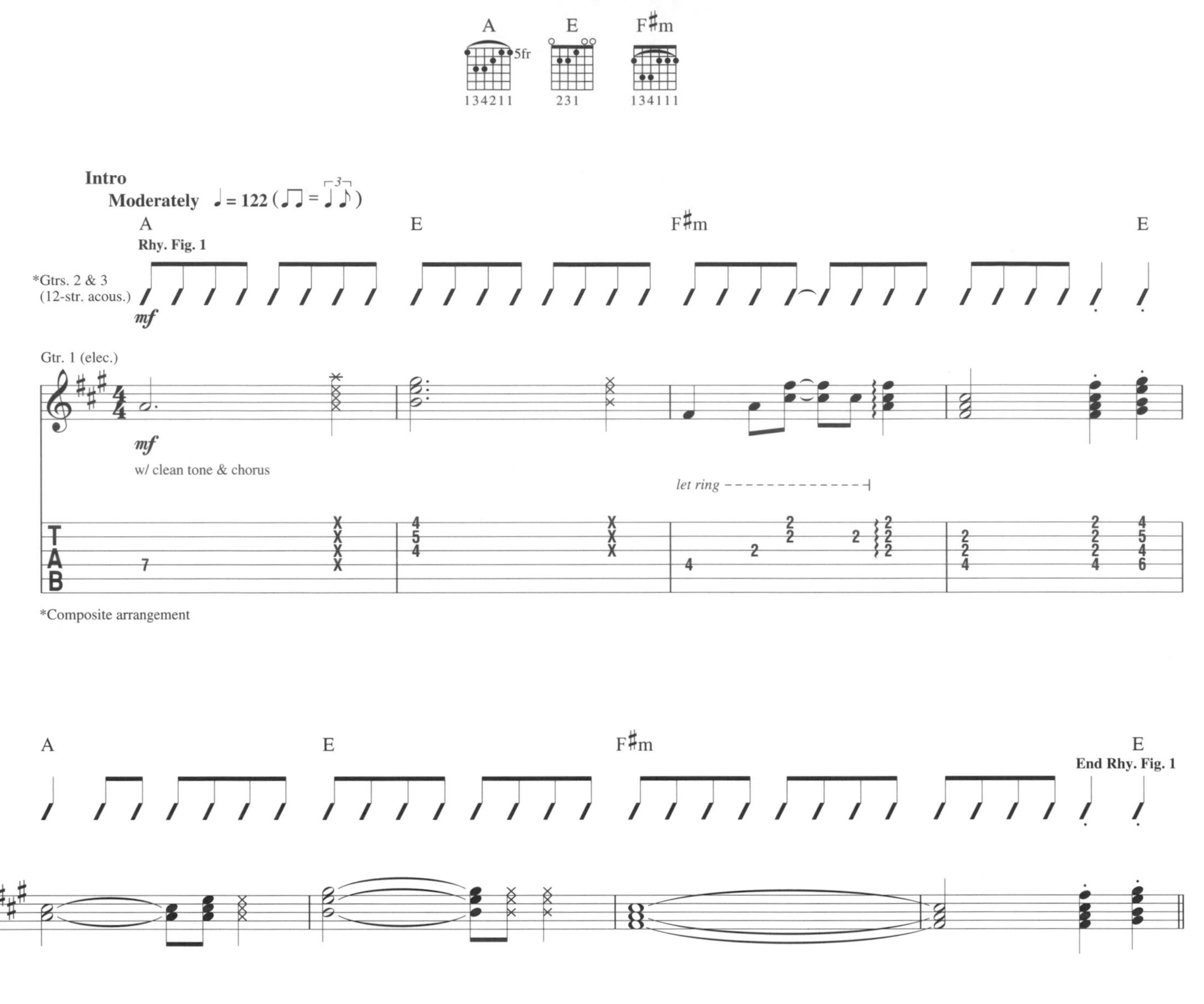

*Composite arrangement

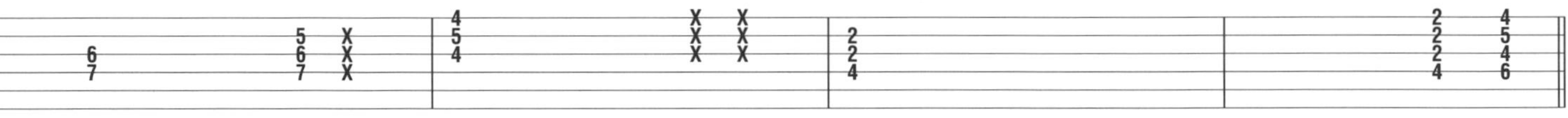

*Chord symbols reflect overall harmony.

E/G♯
A
E
Who's gon - na make that first mis - take?
let ring
let ring

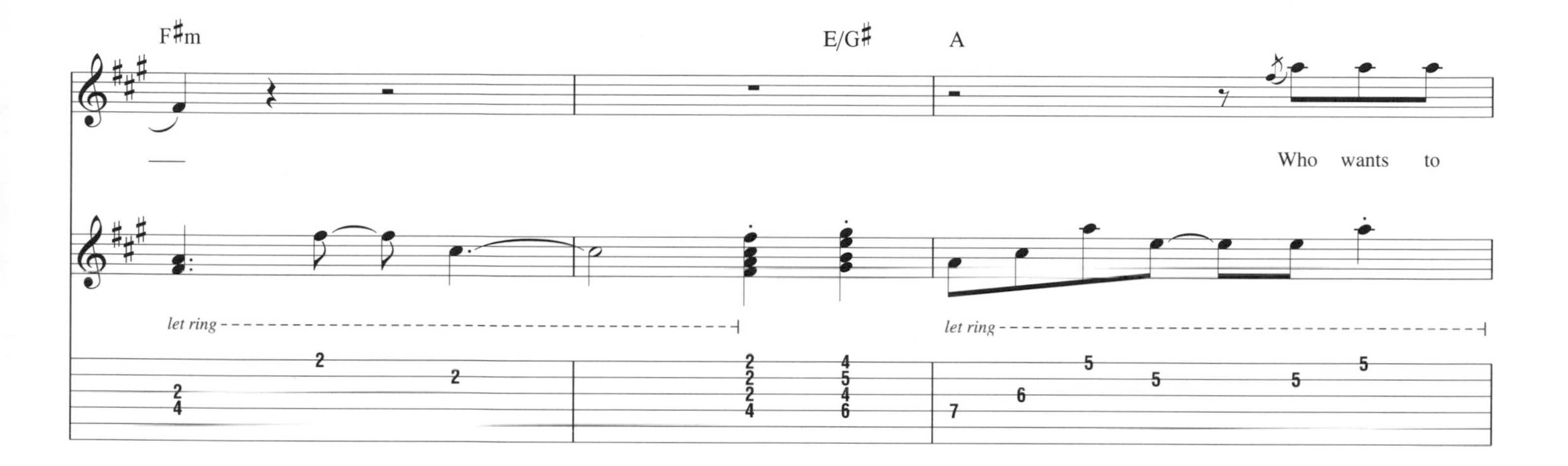
F♯m
E/G♯
A
Who wants to
let ring
let ring

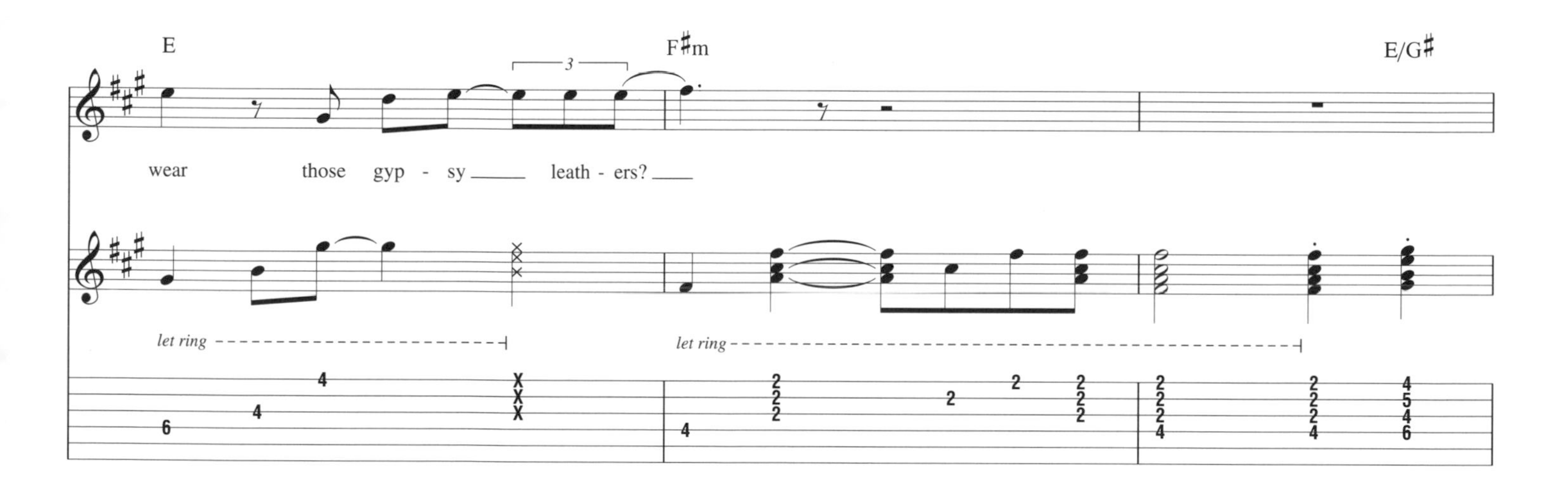
E
F♯m
E/G♯
wear those gyp - sy leath - ers?
let ring
let ring

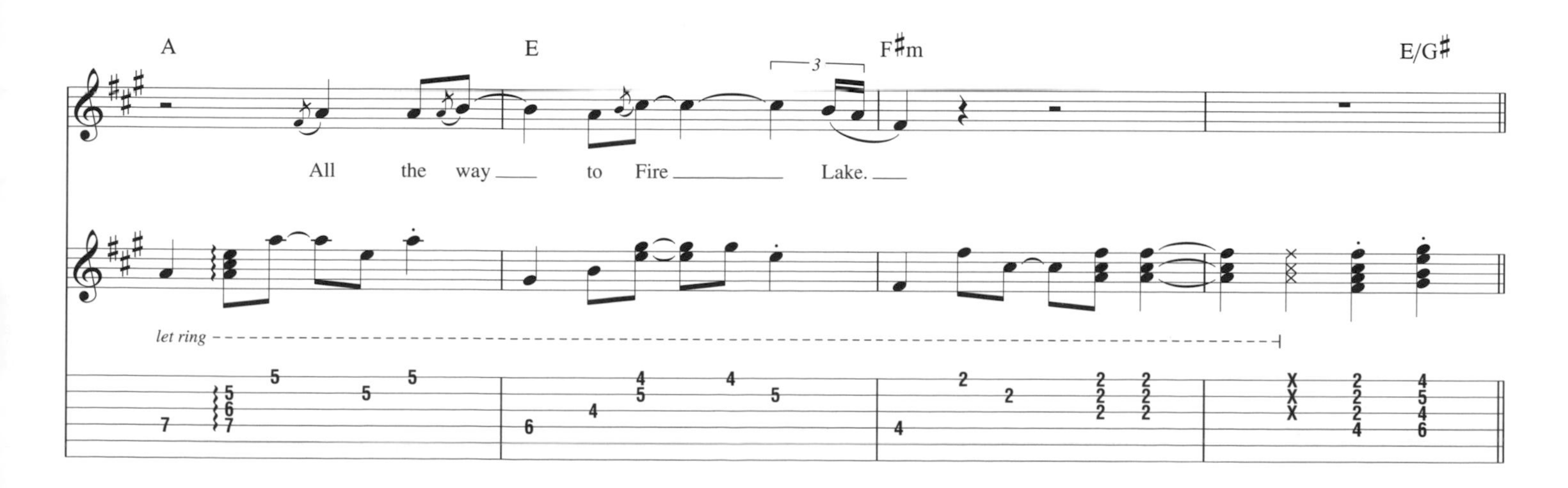
A
E
F♯m
E/G♯
All the way to Fire Lake.
let ring

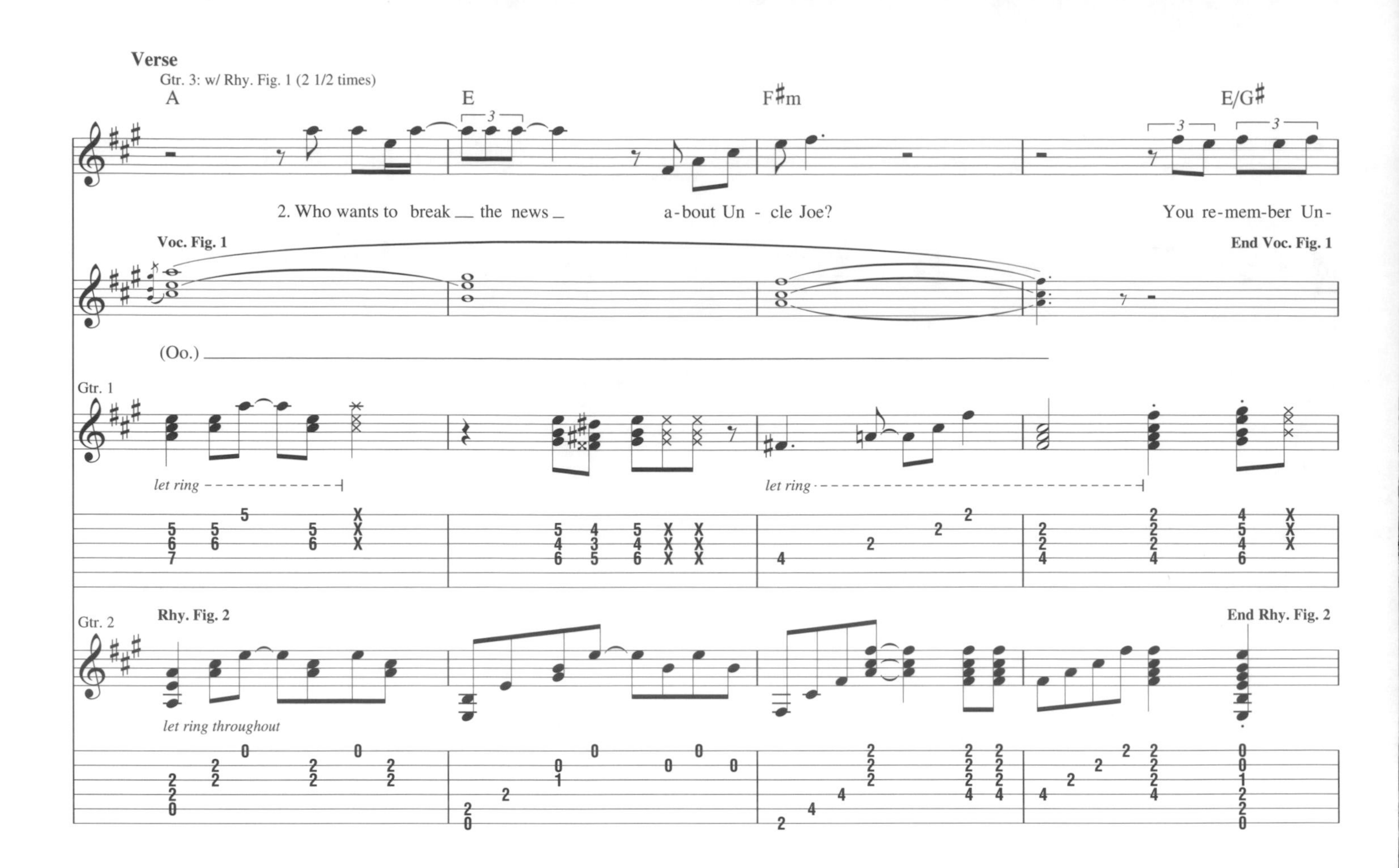
Verse
Gtr. 3: w/ Rhy. Fig. 1 (2 1/2 times)
A
E
F#m
E/G#
2. Who wants to break the news a-bout Un - cle Joe? You re-mem-ber Un-
Voc. Fig. 1
End Voc. Fig. 1
(Oo.)
Gtr. 1
let ring
Gtr. 2
Rhy. Fig. 2
End Rhy. Fig. 2
let ring throughout

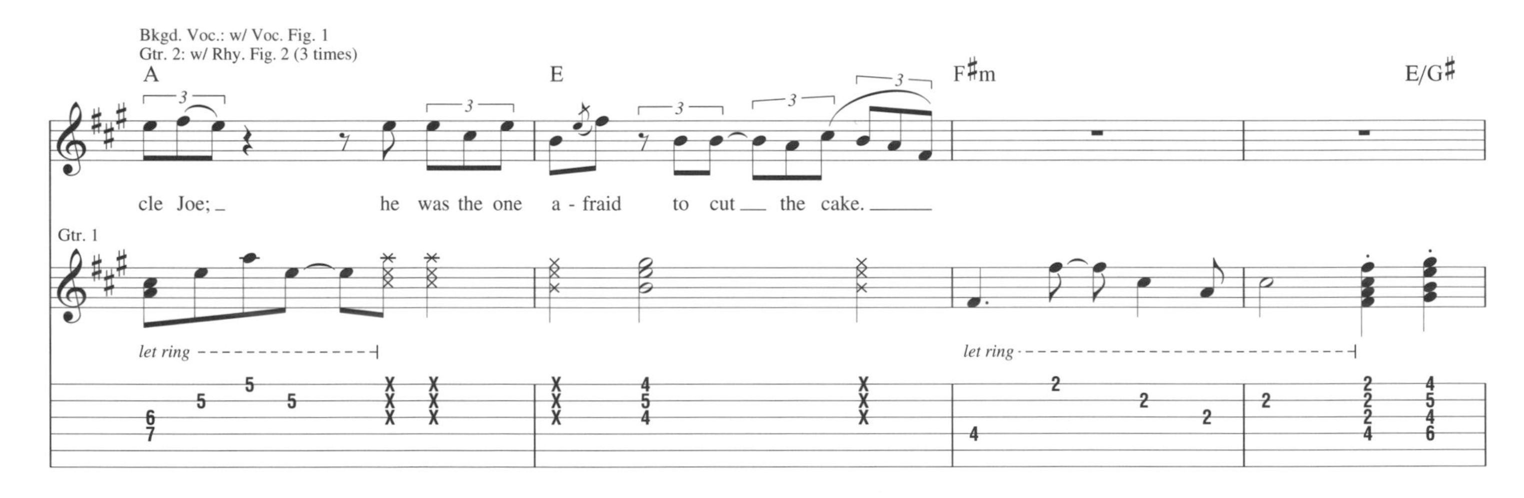
Bkgd. Voc.: w/ Voc. Fig. 1
Gtr. 2: w/ Rhy. Fig. 2 (3 times)
A
E
F#m
E/G#
cle Joe; he was the one a - fraid to cut the cake.
Gtr. 1
let ring

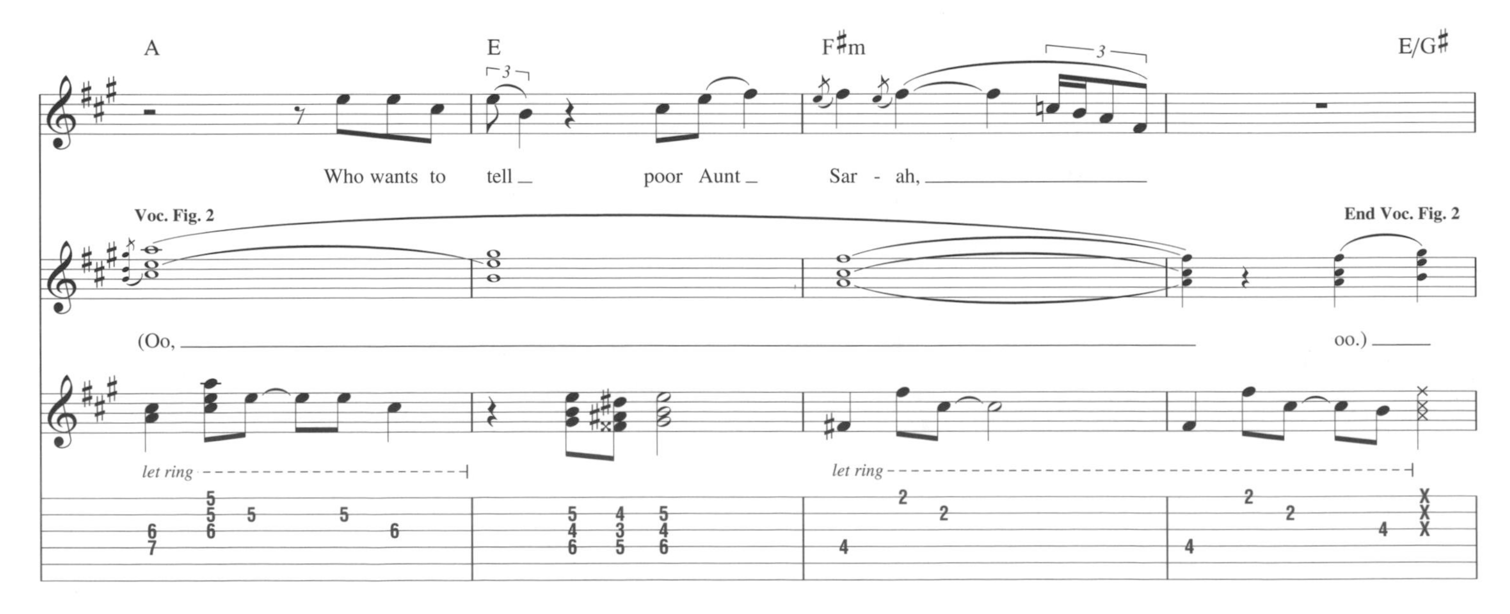
A
E
F#m
E/G#
Who wants to tell poor Aunt Sar - ah,
Voc. Fig. 2
End Voc. Fig. 2
(Oo, oo.)
let ring

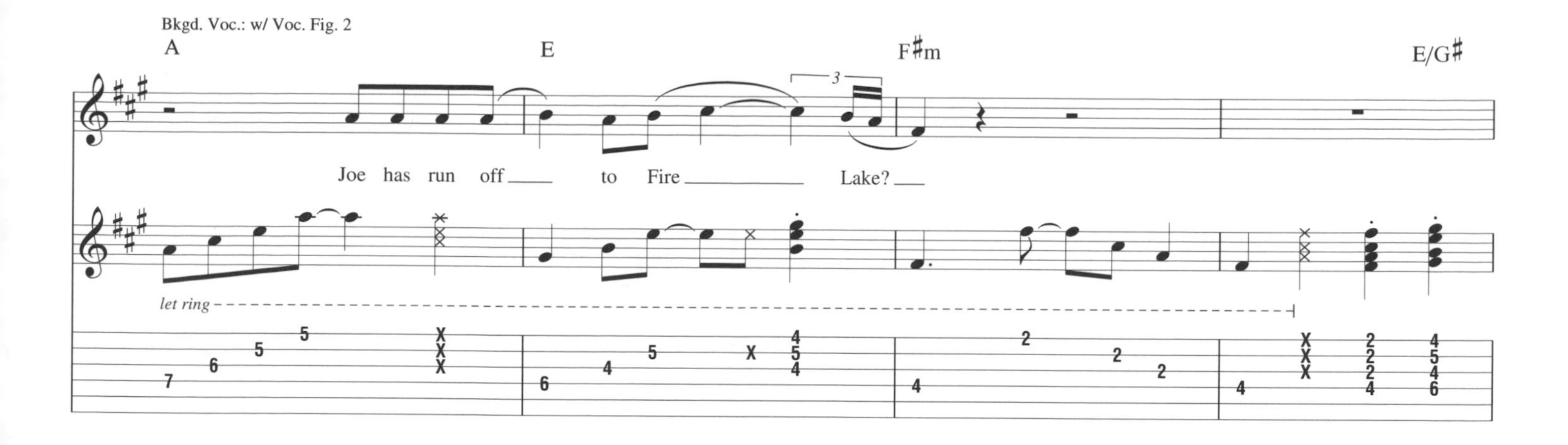
Bkgd. Voc.: w/ Voc. Fig. 2
A
E
F#m
E/G#
Joe has run off to Fire Lake?
let ring

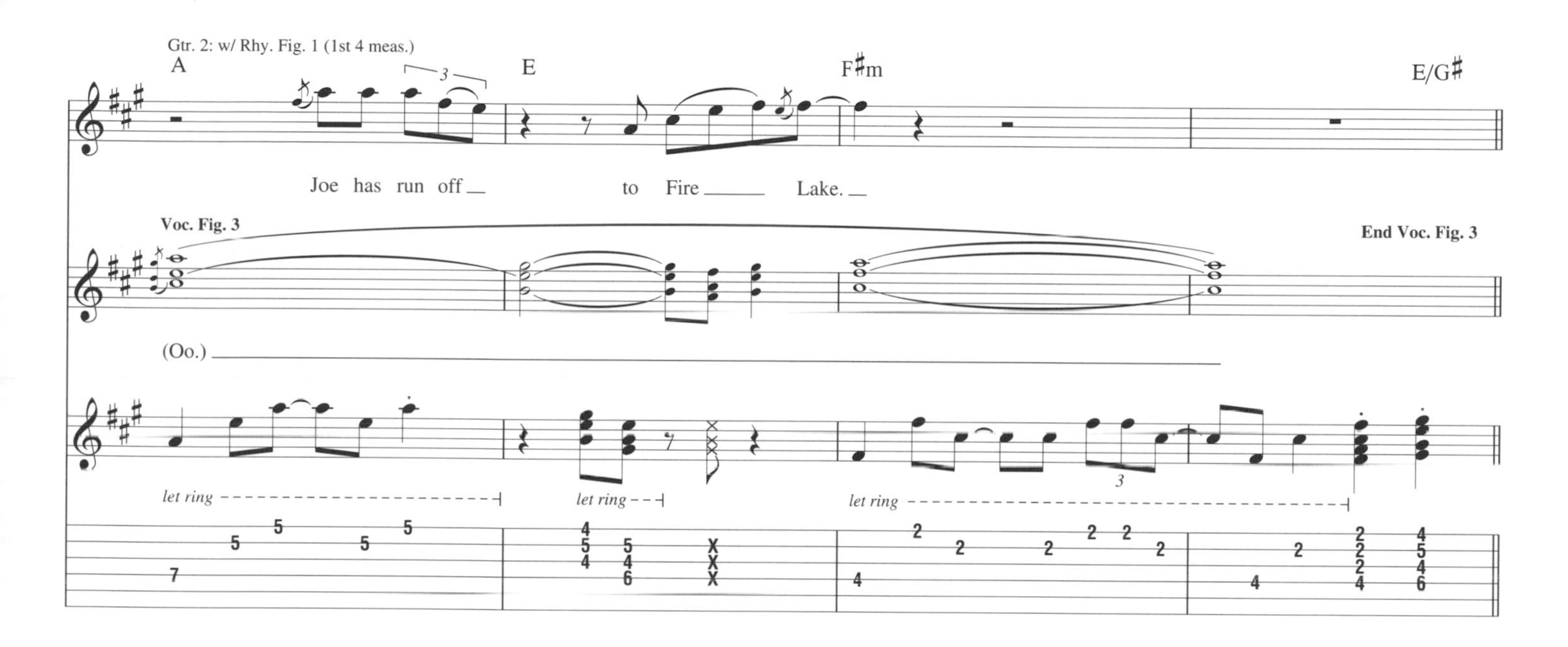
Gtr. 2: w/ Rhy. Fig. 1 (1st 4 meas.)
A
E
F#m
E/G#
Joe has run off to Fire Lake.
Voc. Fig. 3
End Voc. Fig. 3
(Oo.)
let ring

Interlude
D
C#m
F#m
Who wants to brave those bronze beau - ties ly - ing in the sun, with their
Gtr. 1
let ring throughout
Gtr. 2
let ring throughout
Gtr. 3
let ring throughout

C♯m
C♯m7
Bm
Bm7
long soft hair fall - ing, fly - in' as they run? Oh, they
D
Dmaj7
A
smile so shy and they flirt so well and they lay you down so fast. Till you

E
Gtr. 1 tacet
look straight up and say...
"Oh Lord,
am I real-
Gtr. 1
Gtrs. 2 & 3
- ly here at last?"
Verse
Bkgd. Voc.: w/ Voc. Fig. 1 (2 times)
Gtr. 2: w/ Rhy. Fig. 1 (1st 4 meas.)
Gtr. 3: w/ Rhy. Fig. 1 (2 times)
A
Gtr. 3
3. Who wants to
Gtrs. 1 & 2
(Gtr. 3, cont. in slashes)
F♯m
E/G♯
play those eights and ac - es?

Gtr. 2: w/ Rhy. Fig. 2 (3 times)
A
E
F♯m
Who wants a raise, who needs a stake?
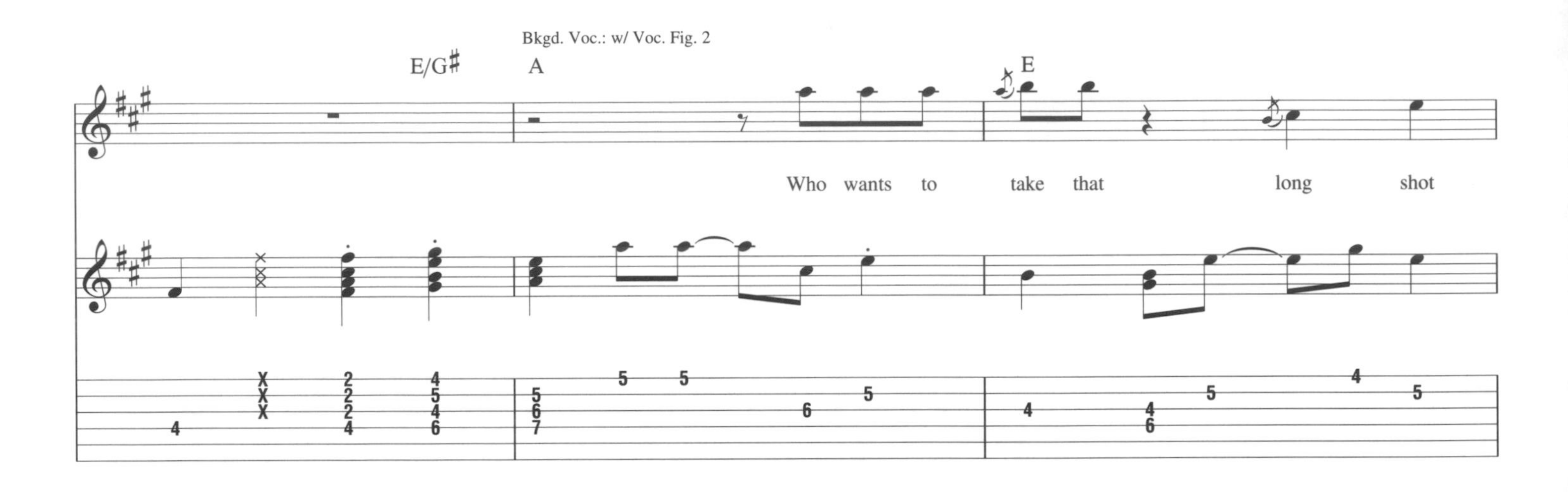
E/G♯
Bkgd. Voc.: w/ Voc. Fig. 2
A
E
Who wants to take that long shot
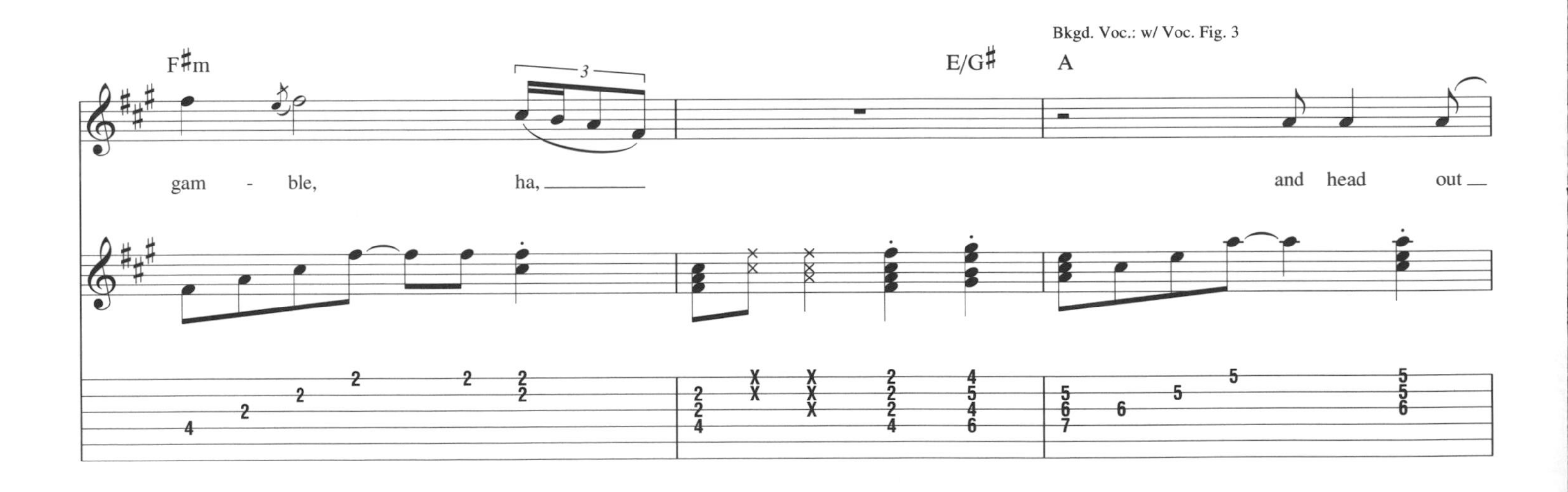
F♯m
E/G♯
Bkgd. Voc.: w/ Voc. Fig. 3
A
gam - ble, ha,
and head out
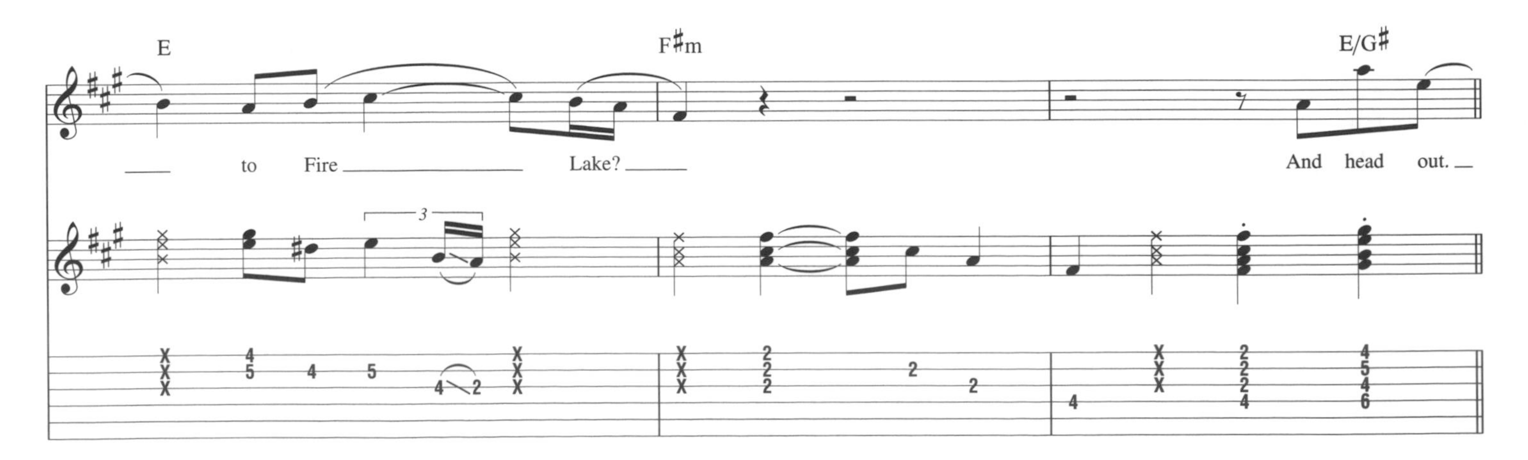
E
F♯m
E/G♯
to Fire Lake?
And head out.

Outro
Gtr. 2: w/ Rhy. Fig. 2 (till end)
Gtr. 3: w/ Rhy. Fig. 1 (till end)
2nd, 3rd & 4th times, Lead. Voc., ad lib.
A
E
F♯m
(Who wants to go to Fire Lake?

E/G♯
A
And head out,
Who wants to

Play 4 times & fade
E
F♯m
E/G♯
hey.
And head out.
go to Fire Lake?)

Tryin' to Live My Life Without You

Words and Music by Eugene Williams

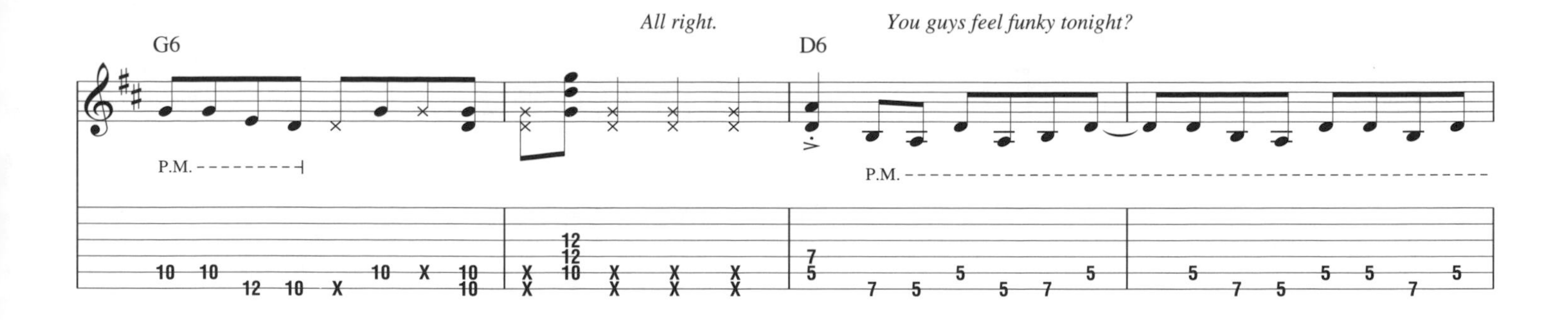
All right.
You guys feel funky tonight?
G6
D6
P.M.
10 10 12 10 X 10 X 10 10
X X 10 12 12 X X X X X X
7 5 7 5 5 5 7 5
5 7 5 5 5 7 5

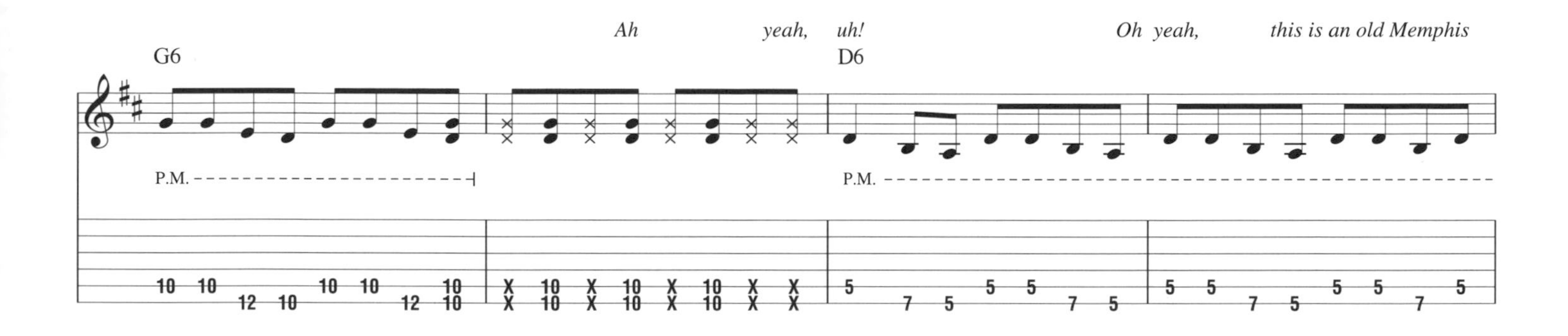
Ah
yeah,
uh!
Oh yeah,
this is an old Memphis
G6
D6
P.M.
10 10 12 10 10 10 12 10 10
X X 10 10 X X 10 10 X X 10 10 X X X X
5 7 5 5 5 7 5
5 5 7 5 5 5 7 5

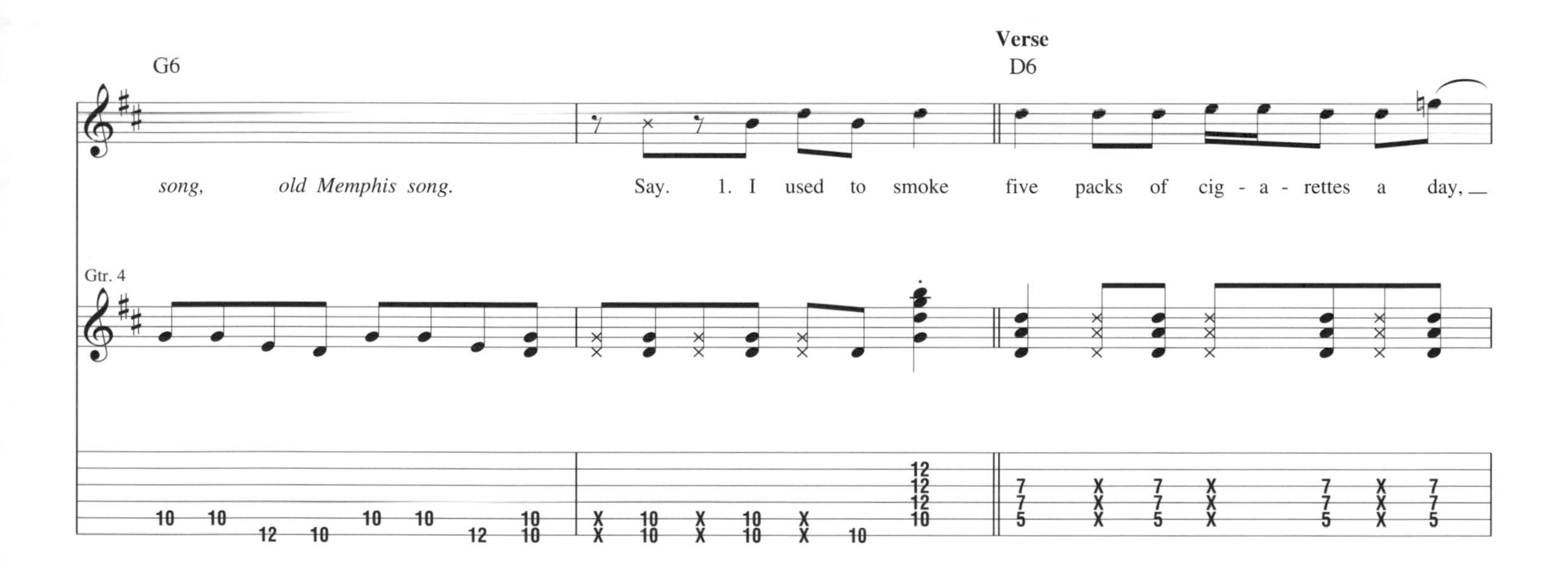
Verse
G6
D6
song,
old Memphis song.
Say.
1. I used to smoke five packs of cig - a - rettes a day,
Gtr. 4
10 10 12 10 10 10 12 10 10
X X 10 10 X X 10 10 X X 10 12 12 12 10
7 7 5 X X X 7 7 5 X X X 7 7 5 X X X 7 7 5

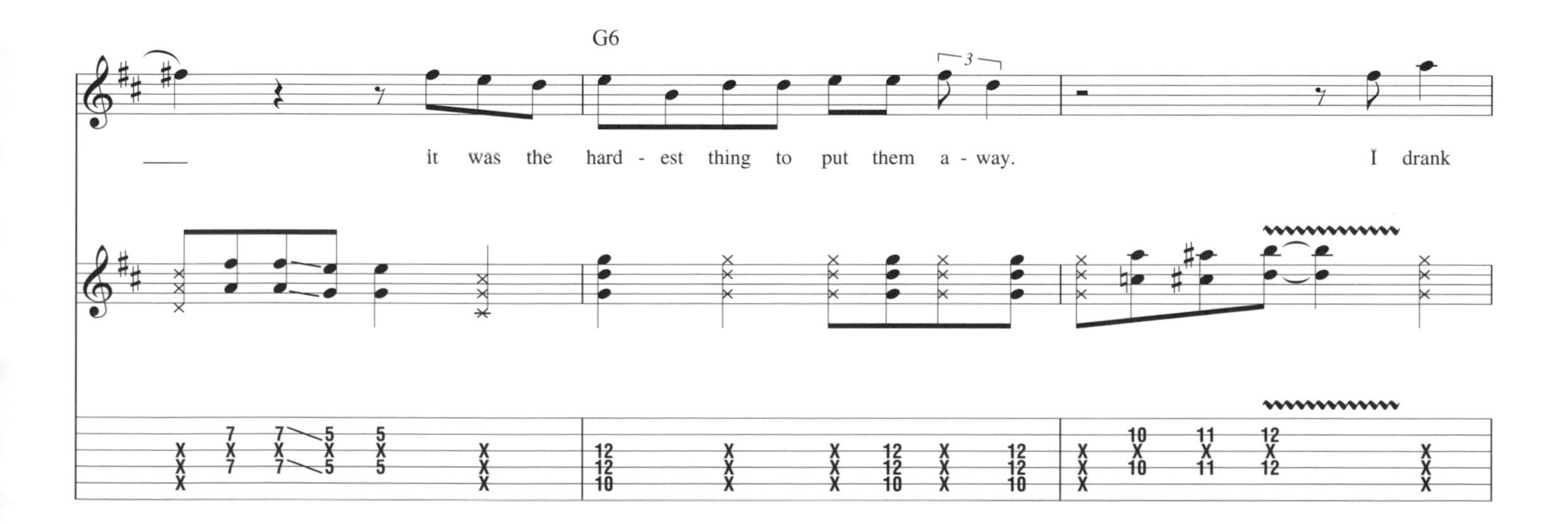
G6
it was the hard - est thing to put them a - way.
I drank
3
X X X 7 X 7 7 X 7 5 X 5 5 X 5 X X X
12 12 10 X X X X X X 12 12 10 X X X 12 12 10
X X X 10 10 11 11 12 X 12 X X X

D6
G6
four or five bot - tles of wine,
I kept a glass in my hand all the time.
Pre-Chorus
B5
Gtr. 4
Break - in' those hab - its was hard to do, but
Gtr. 2
A.H.
T T
(cont. in slashes)
Gtr. 3
divisi
G5
A5
Chorus
Gtrs. 2 & 3 tacet
D6
(cont. in notation)
noth - in' com - pared to the chang - es that you put me through.
Try - in' to live my life with - out you,
Voc. Fig. 1
Female: (Try - in' to live my life with - out you,
Gtr. 4

Gtrs. 2 & 3 tacet
G6
babe, it's the hard - est thing I'll ev - er do.
babe, hard - est thing I'll ev - er do.
Riff B
End Riff B
Gtr. 2
Riff B1
End Riff B1
Gtr. 3
divisi
Gtr. 4

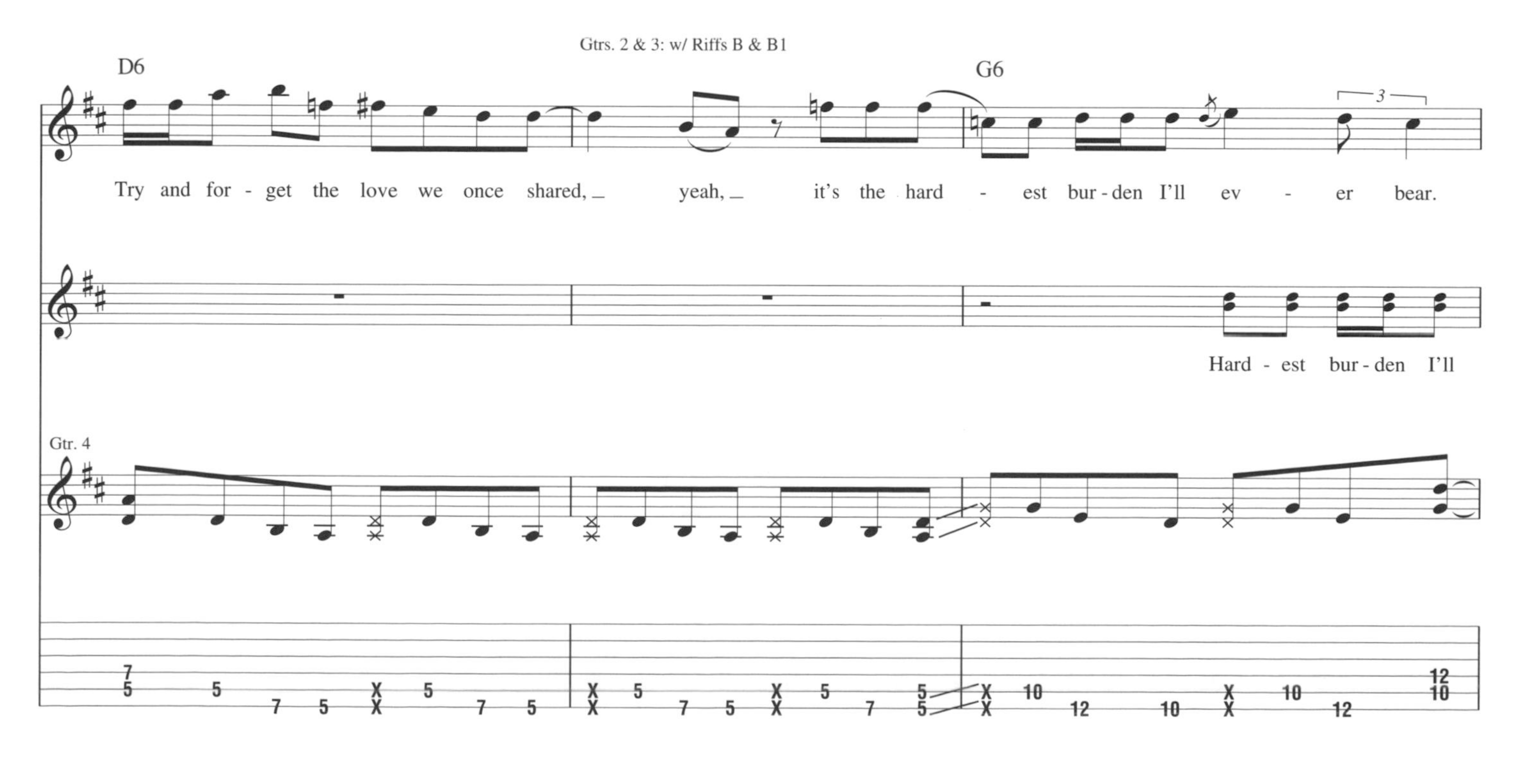

Gtrs. 2 & 3: w/ Riffs B & B1
D6
G6
Try and for - get the love we once shared, yeah, it's the hard - est bur - den I'll ev - er bear.
Hard - est bur - den I'll
Gtr. 4

Interlude
B5
Rhy. Fig. 1
Gtr. 4
A5
G5
A5
Al - right!
Box, Stax!
End Voc. Fig. 1
ev - er bear.)
Riff C
Gtr. 2
(cont. in slashes)
Gtr. 3
divisi
Riff C1
Verse
Gtrs. 2 & 3 tacet
B5
G5
A5
End Rhy. Fig. 1
D6
(cont. in notation)
I had the worst rep - u - ta - tion in town
End Riff C
Gtr. 4
End Riff C1
G6
for chas - in' all the wom - en a - round.
I thought
let ring

D6
chang - in' my way of liv - in' was hard to do, but it's
G6
noth - in' com - pared to the chang - es that you put me through.
(cont. in slashes)
Pre-Chorus
B5
Gtr. 4
I've done ev - 'ry - thing I've tried to do, but it's
Gtr. 2
Gtr. 3
divisi
G5
A5
(cont. in notation)
gon - na take a mir - a - cle to get me o - ver you.

Chorus
Bkgd. Voc.: w/ Voc. Fig. 1
D6
G6
Try - in' to live my life with - out you, __ babe, it's the hard - est thing I'll ev - er do.
Gtr. 2
Gtr. 3
Gtr. 4
Rhy. Fig. 2
End Rhy. Fig. 2
D6
G6
Try and for - get the love we once shared, __ yeah, _ it's the hard - est bur - den I'll ev - er bear. Sil - ver Bul - let!
Rhy. Fig. 3
End Rhy. Fig. 3
Interlude
Gtrs. 2 & 3: w/ Riffs C & C1
Gtr. 4: w/ Rhy. Fig. 1
Bm
A G
Bm
G A
Oh, yeah.

Chorus
Bkgd. Voc.: w/ Voc. Fig. 1 (2 times)
D6
G6
Try-in' to live my life with-out you, babe, it's the hard - est thing I'll ev - er do.
Gtr. 2
Gtr. 3
divisi
Gtr. 4
Gtr. 4: w/ Rhy. Fig. 2 (2 times)
D6
G6
Try and for-get the love we shared, it's the hard - est bur-den I'll ev - er bear. Lis-ten.
Gtr. 2
Gtr. 3
D6
G6
Try - in' to live my life with-out you, babe, oh, hard - est thing I'll ev - er do.

Gtr. 4: w/ Rhy. Fig. 3
D6
G6
Try and for-get the love we shared, it's the hard - est bur-den I'll ev-er bear. Hit me, babe.
Interlude
Gtr. 4: w/ Rhy. Fig. 1
Bm
A
G
Bm
G
A
Oo, yeah. Try -
Chorus
Bkgd. Voc.: w/ Voc. Fig. 1
Gtr. 4: w/ Rhy. Fig. 2
D6
- in' to live my life with - out you, babe, it's the hard -
G6
- est thing I'll ev - er do.

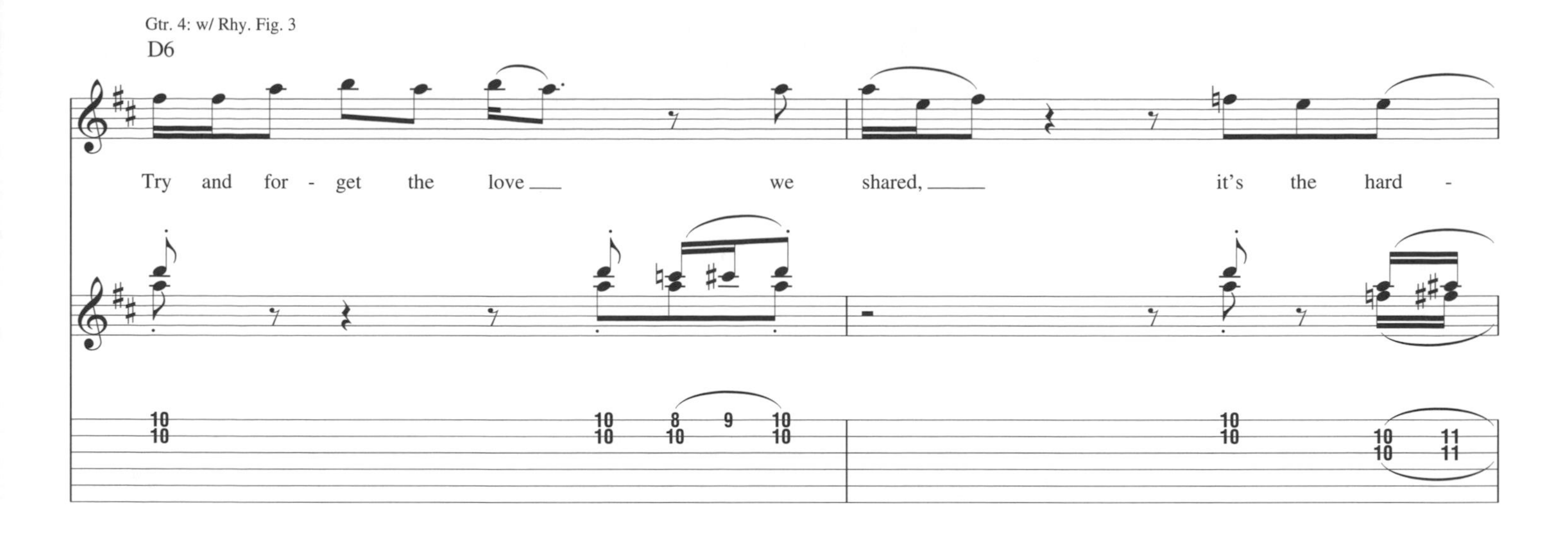
Gtr. 4: w/ Rhy. Fig. 3
D6
Try and for - get the love we shared, it's the hard -

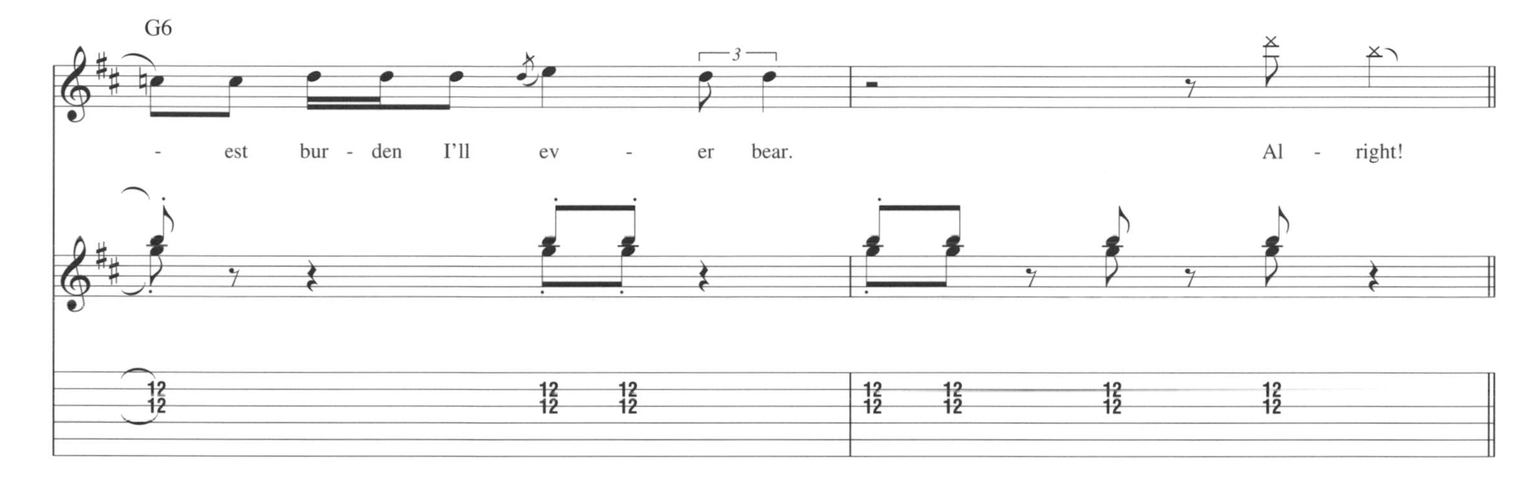
G6
- est bur - den I'll ev - er bear. Al - right!

Outro

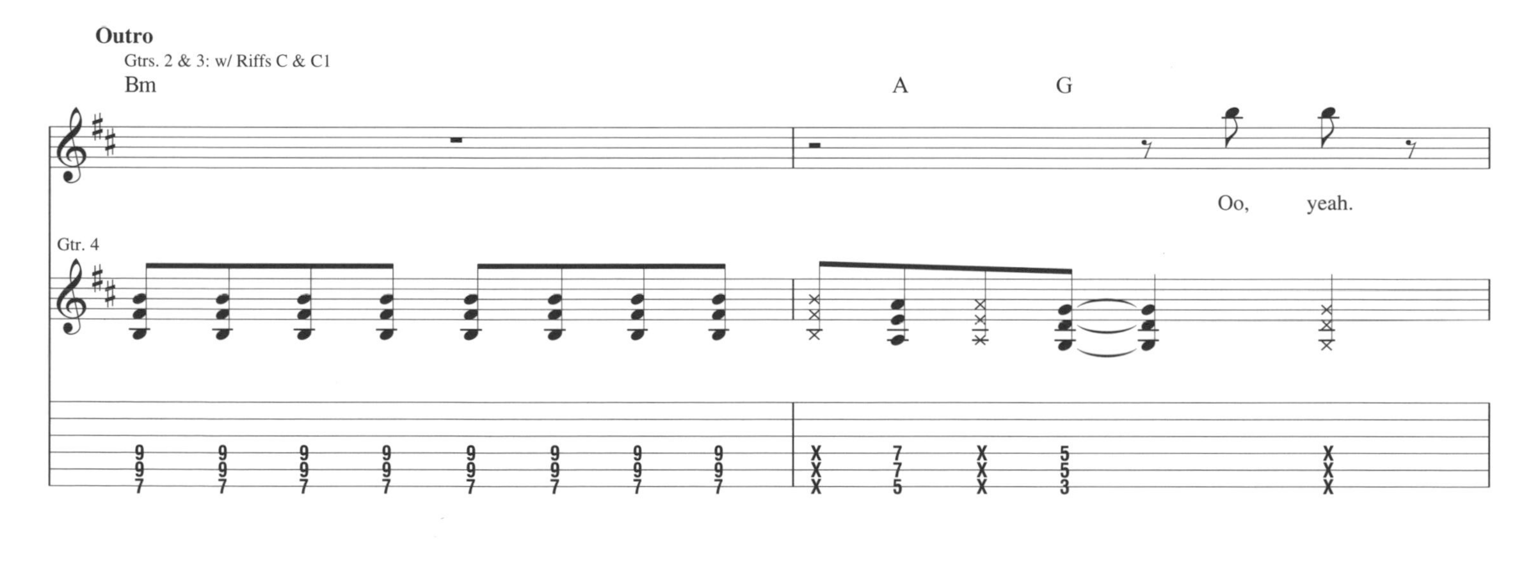
Gtrs. 2 & 3: w/ Riffs C & C1
Bm
A
G
Oo, yeah.
Gtr. 4

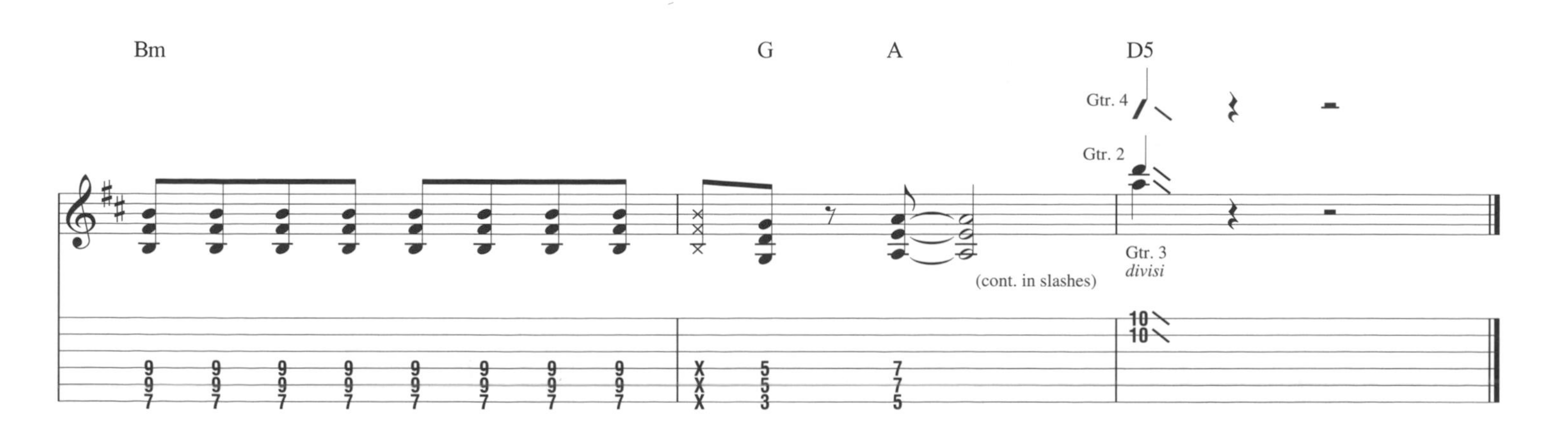
Bm
G
A
D5
Gtr. 4
Gtr. 2
(cont. in slashes)
Gtr. 3
divisi

Shakedown

from the Paramount Motion Picture BEVERLY HILLS COP II
Words and Music by Keith Forsey, Harold Faltermeyer and Bob Seger

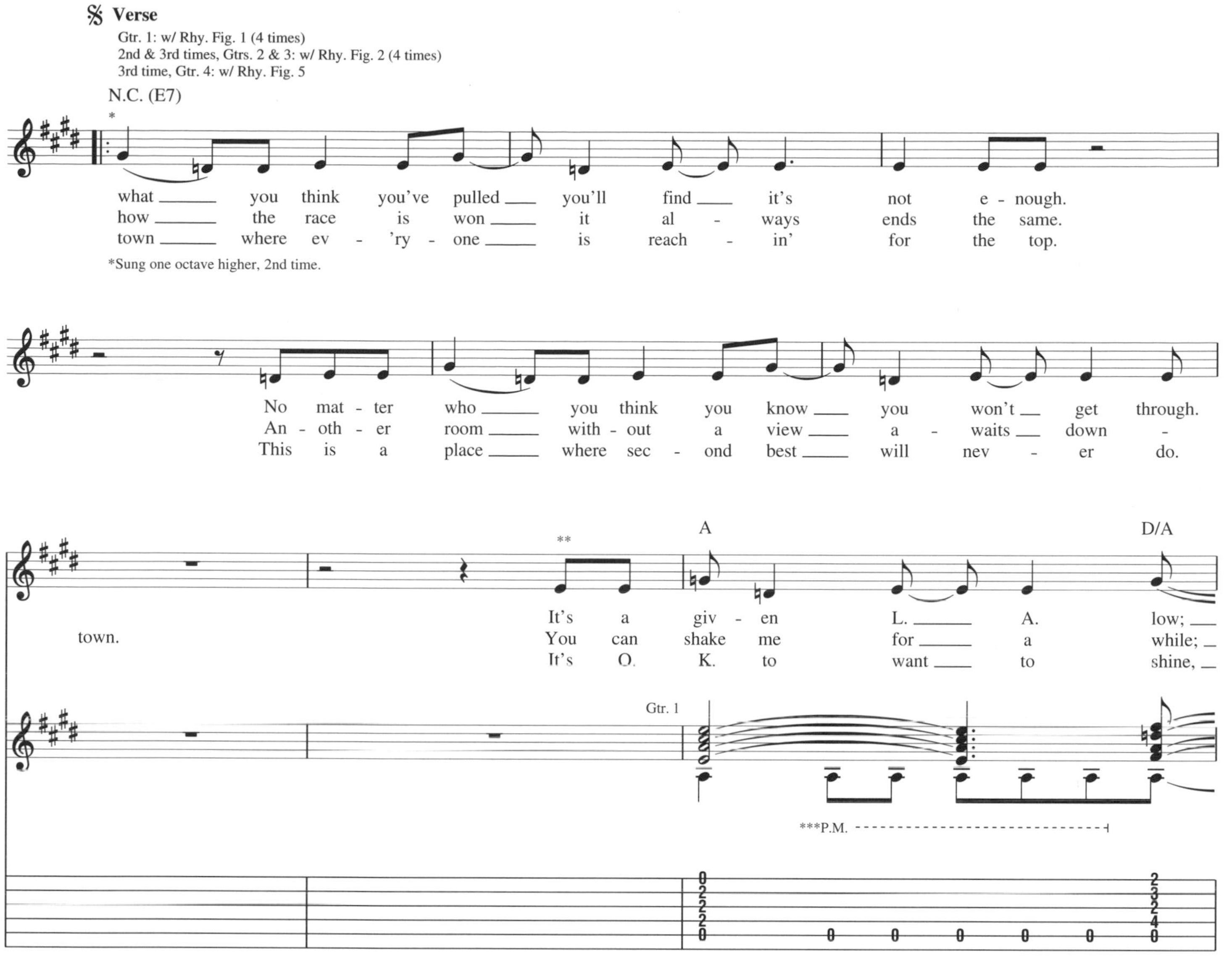

Verse
Gtr. 1: w/ Rhy. Fig. 1 (4 times)
2nd & 3rd times, Gtrs. 2 & 3: w/ Rhy. Fig. 2 (4 times)
3rd time, Gtr. 4: w/ Rhy. Fig. 5
N.C. (E7)
what you think you've pulled you'll find it's not e - nough.
how the race is won it al - ways ends the same.
town where ev - 'ry - one is reach - in' for the top.
*Sung one octave higher, 2nd time.
No mat - ter who you think you know you won't get through.
An - oth - er room with - out a view a - waits down -
This is a place where sec - ond best will nev - er do.
A
D/A
town.
It's a giv - en L. A. low;
You can shake me for a while;
It's O. K. to want to shine,
Gtr. 1
***P.M.
** Sung one octave higher, 3th time, next 8 meas.
***P.M. refers to downstem notes only, next 4 meas.

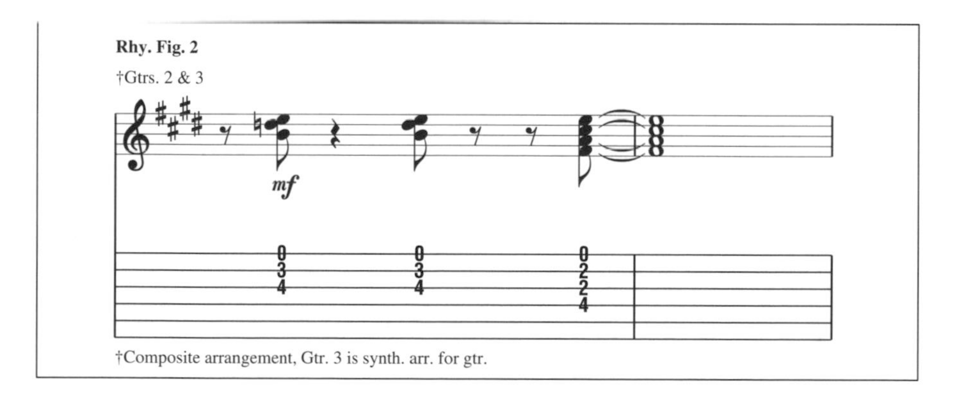

Rhy. Fig. 2
†Gtrs. 2 & 3
mf
†Composite arrangement, Gtr. 3 is synth. arr. for gtr.

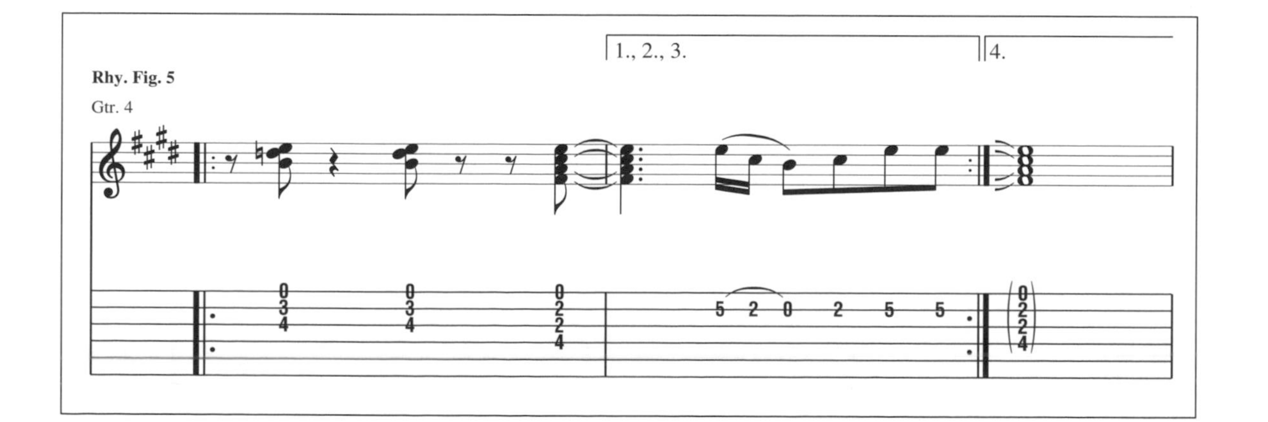

1., 2., 3.
4.
Rhy. Fig. 5
Gtr. 4

Em/A
G/A
D/A
E
some-one's
fast - er on
the draw.
No mat - ter
live it up
in style.
No mat - ter
but once you
step a - cross
that line,
no mat - ter
*Gtr. 2
mf
Gtr. 1
P.M.
*Horns arr. for gtr.
Gtr. 1: w/ Rhy. Fig. 1 (2 times)
1st time, Gtr. 2 tacet
2nd & 3rd times, Gtrs. 2 & 3: w/ Rhy. Fig. 2 (2 times)
3rd time, Gtr. 4: w/ Rhy. Fig. 3 (last 4 meas.)
N.C. (E7)
where you hide I'm com - in' af - ter you.
what you do I'm go - in' to take you down.
where you hide I'm com - in' af - ter you.
1.
Gtr. 1: w/ Riff A
Yup.
Gtr. 2
2.
2. No mat - ter

Chorus

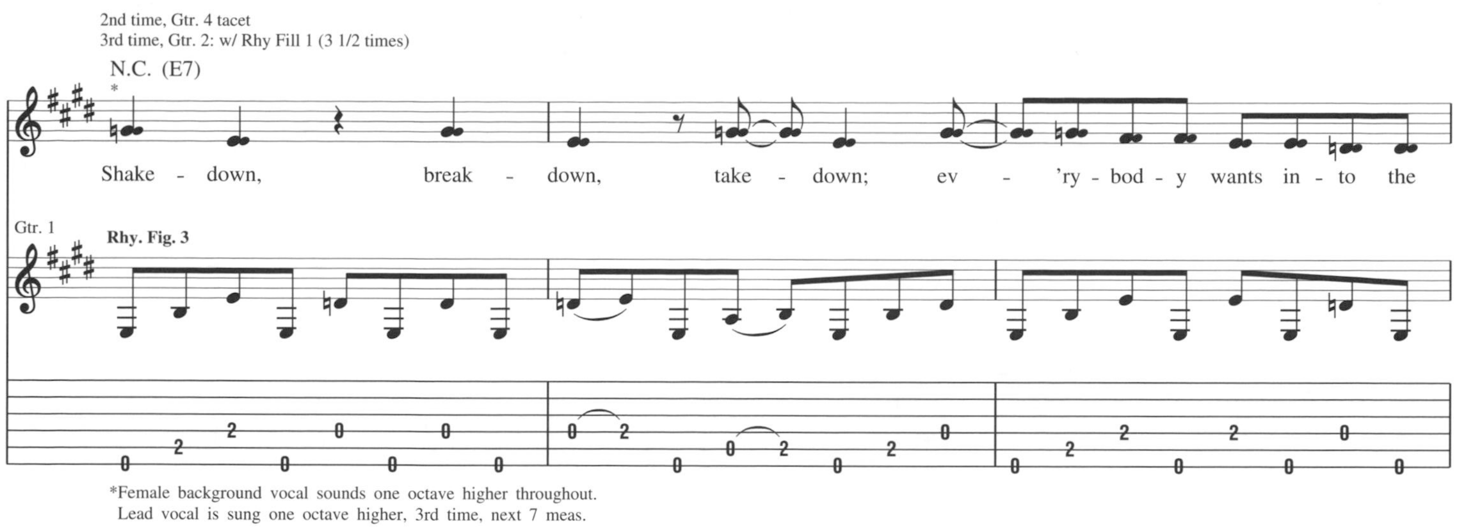
2nd time, Gtr. 4 tacet
3rd time, Gtr. 2: w/ Rhy Fill 1 (3 1/2 times)
N.C. (E7)
Shake - down, break - down, take - down; ev - 'ry - bod - y wants in - to the
Gtr. 1
Rhy. Fig. 3
*Female background vocal sounds one octave higher throughout.
Lead vocal is sung one octave higher, 3rd time, next 7 meas.

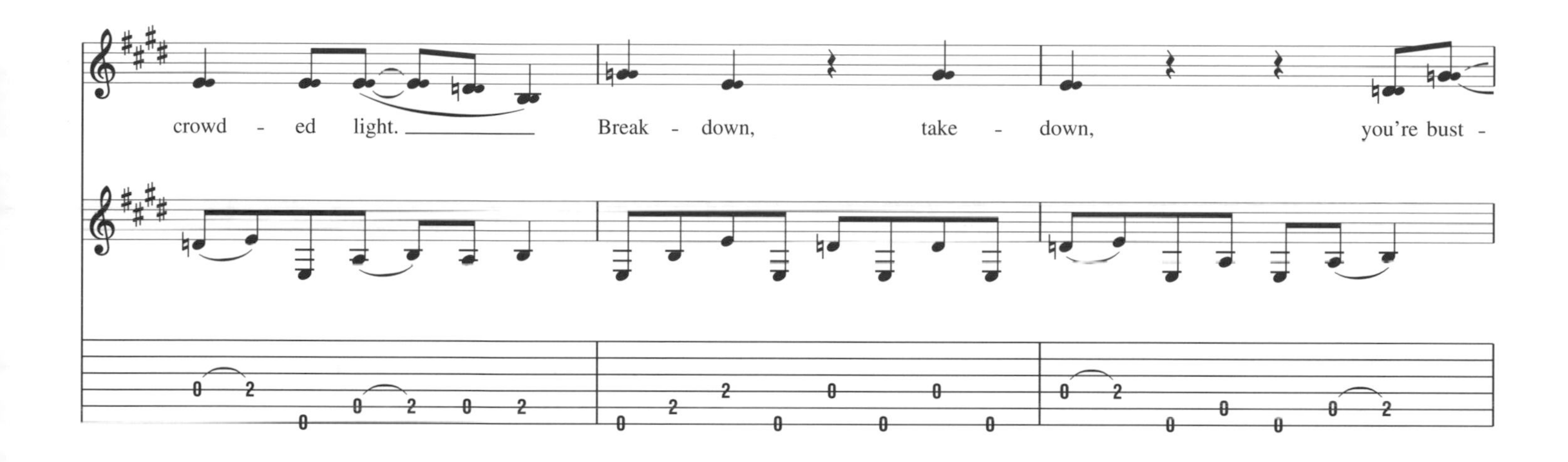
crowd - ed light. Break - down, take - down, you're bust -

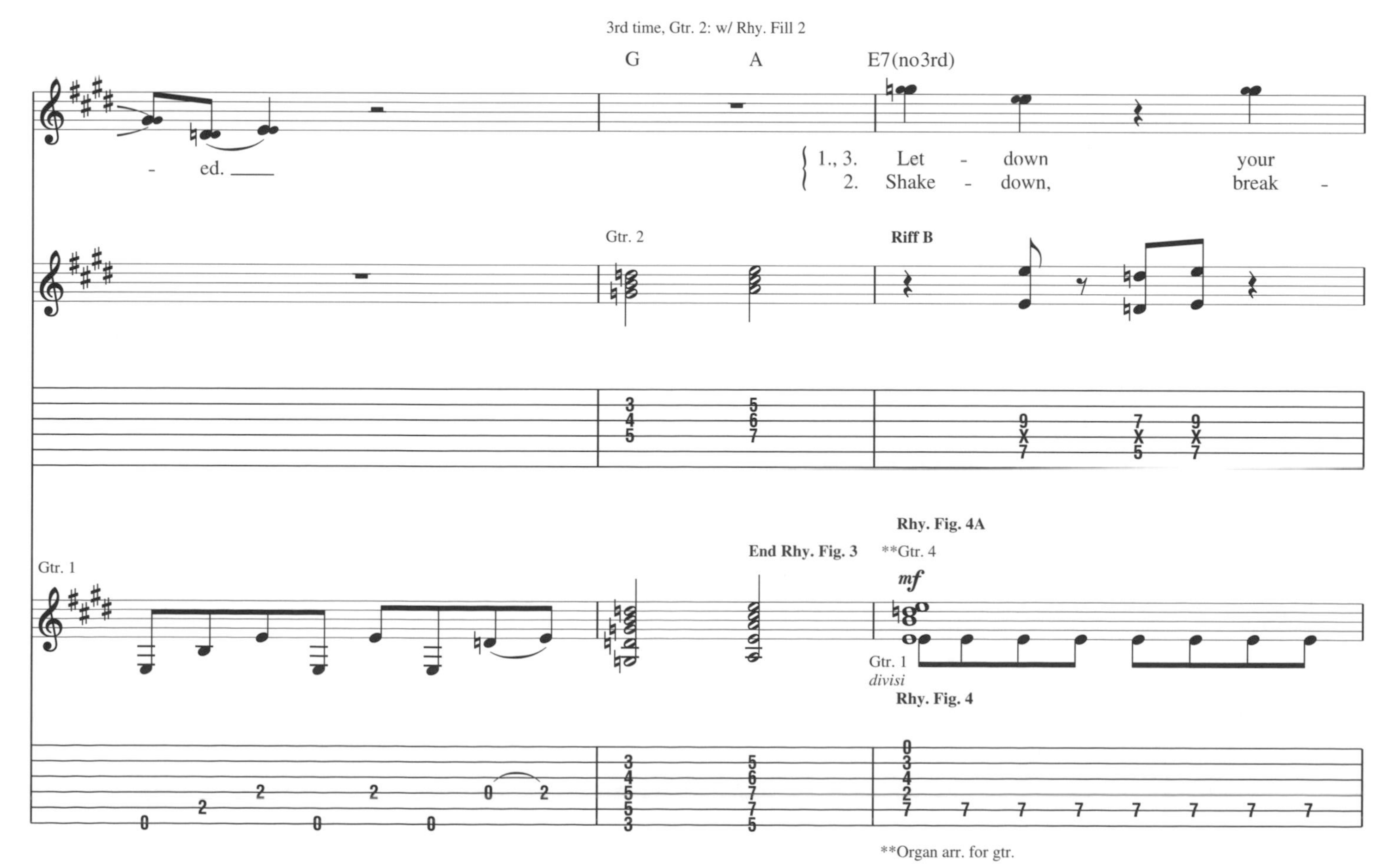
3rd time, Gtr. 2: w/ Rhy. Fill 2
G A E7(no3rd)
- ed.
1., 3. Let - down your
2. Shake - down, break -
Gtr. 2
Riff B
Gtr. 1
End Rhy. Fig. 3
Rhy. Fig. 4A
**Gtr. 4
mf
Gtr. 1
divisi
Rhy. Fig. 4
**Organ arr. for gtr.

Dsus2
E7(no3rd)
Dsus2
guard,
down,
hon - ey,
just
a - bout the time you think that
it's all
right.
End Riff B

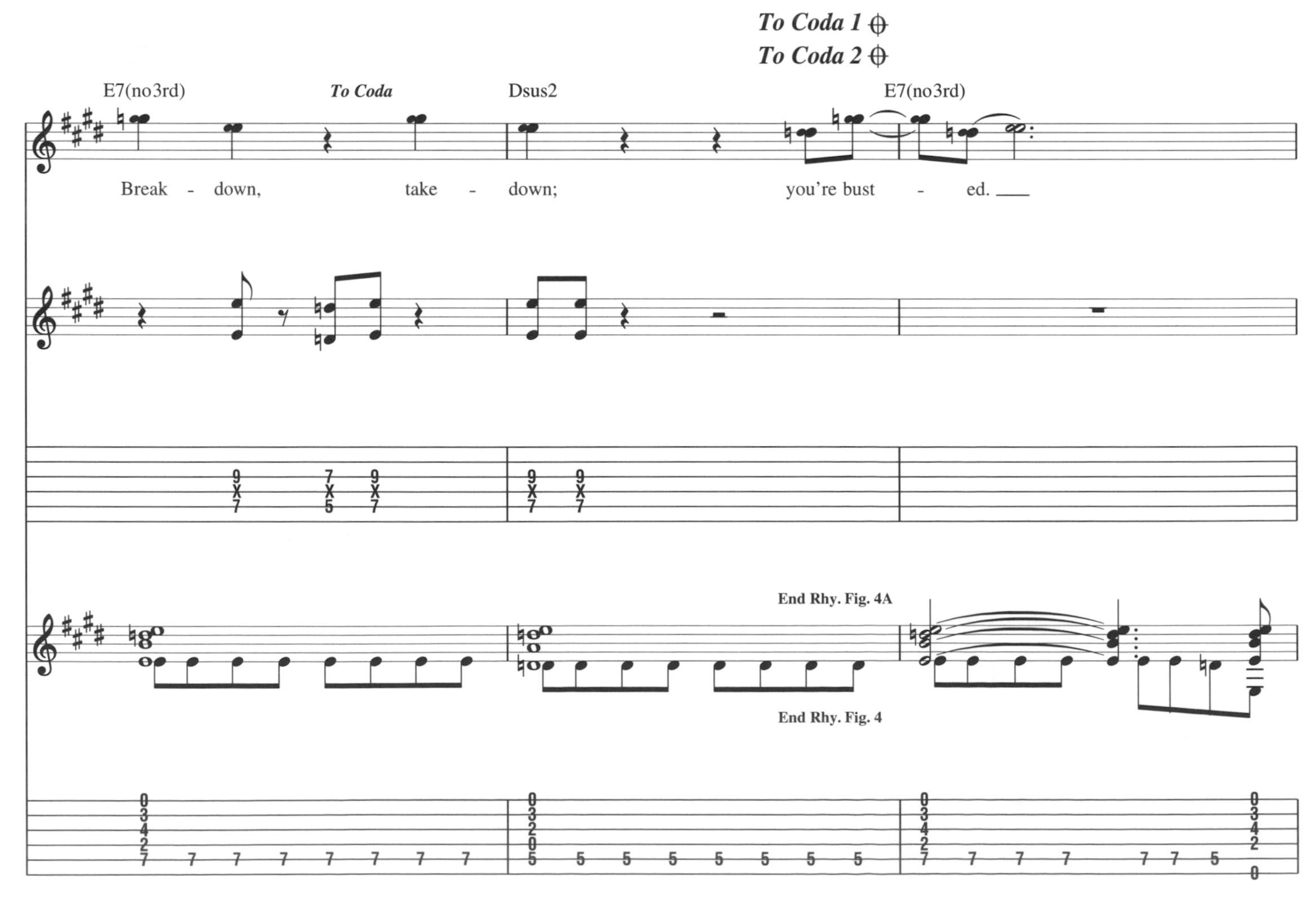
To Coda 1
To Coda 2
E7(no3rd)
To Coda
Dsus2
E7(no3rd)
Break - down,
take - down;
you're bust - ed.
End Rhy. Fig. 4A
End Rhy. Fig. 4

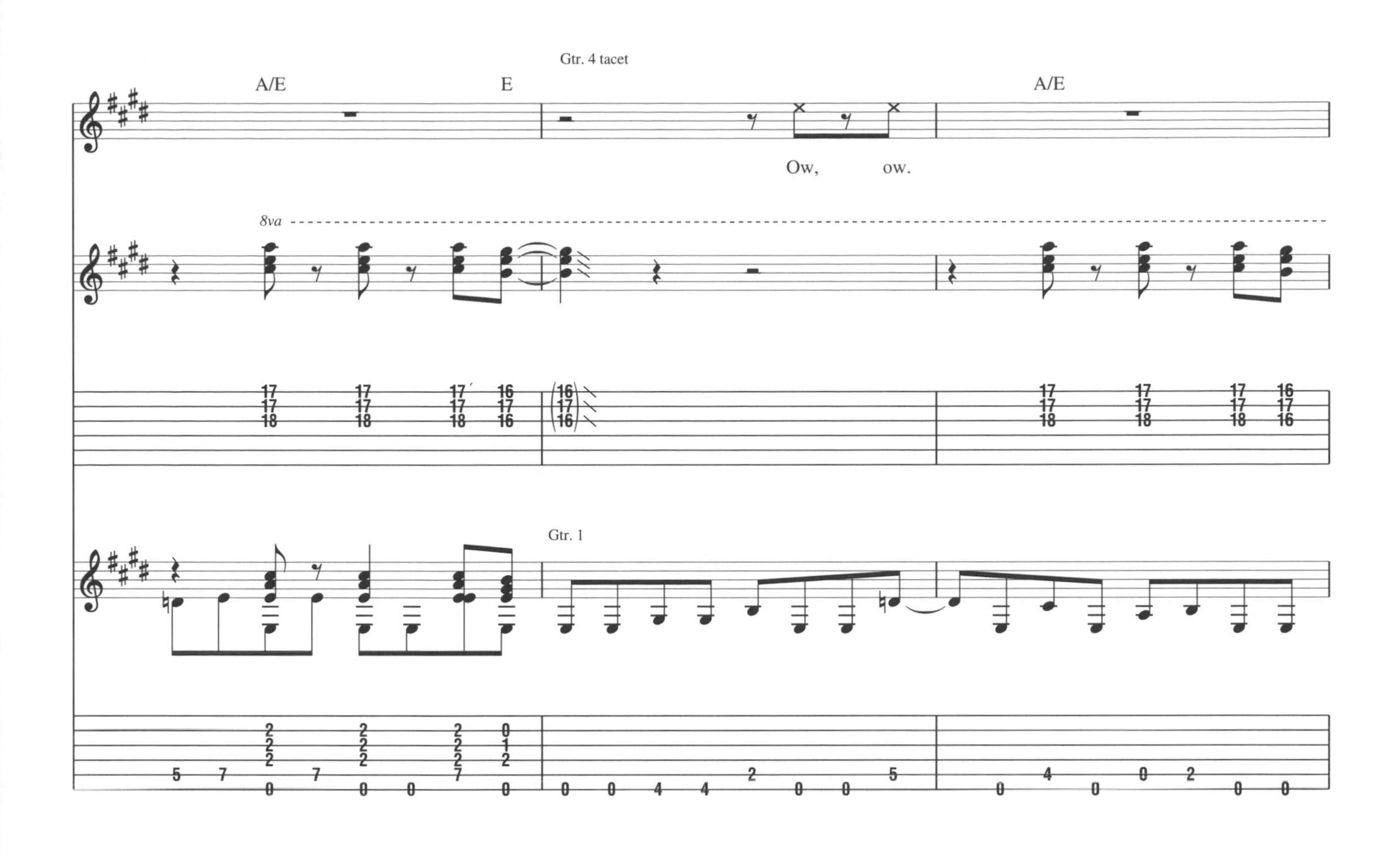
Gtr. 4 tacet
A/E
E
A/E
Ow, ow.
8va
Gtr. 1
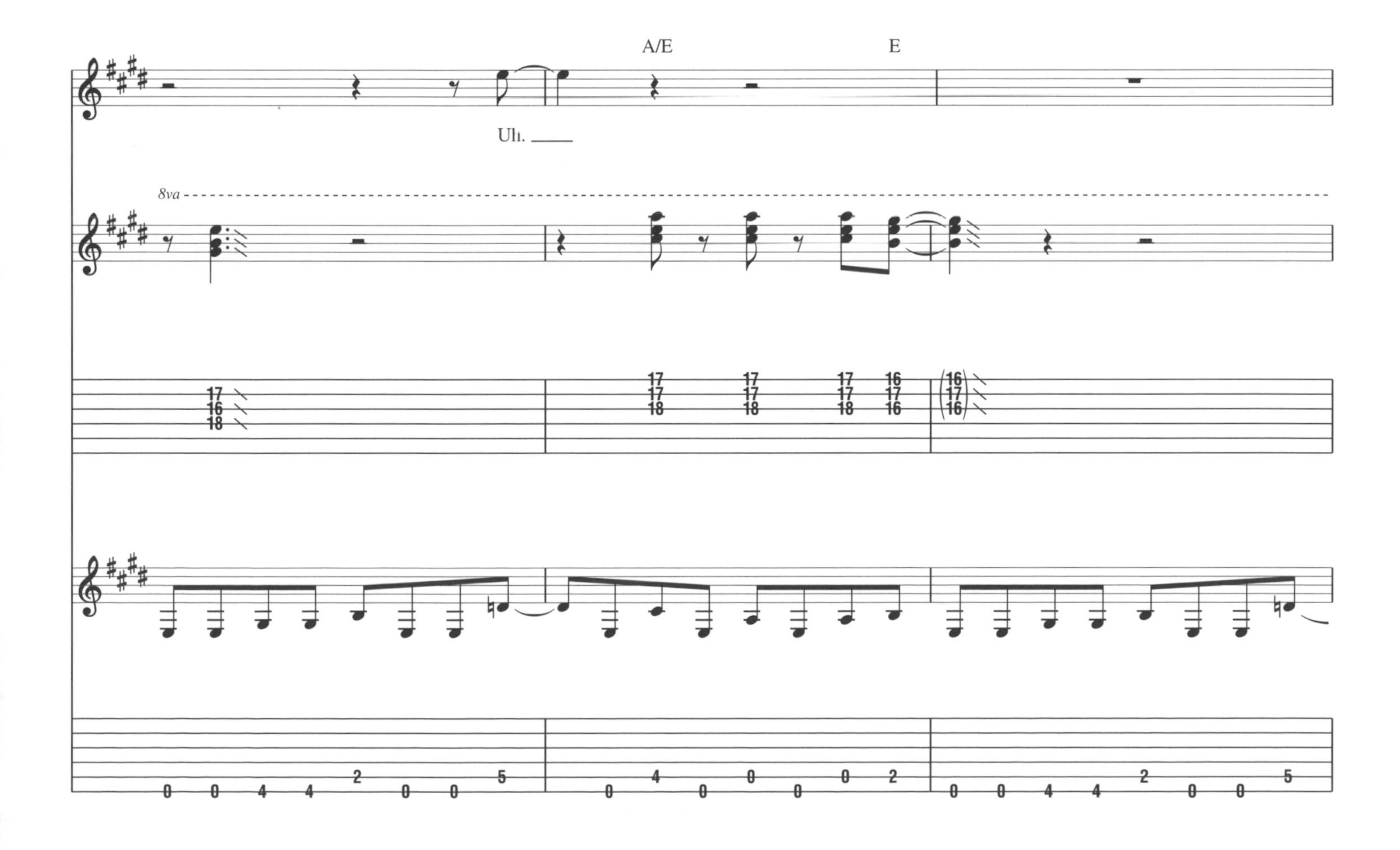
A/E
E
Uh.
8va

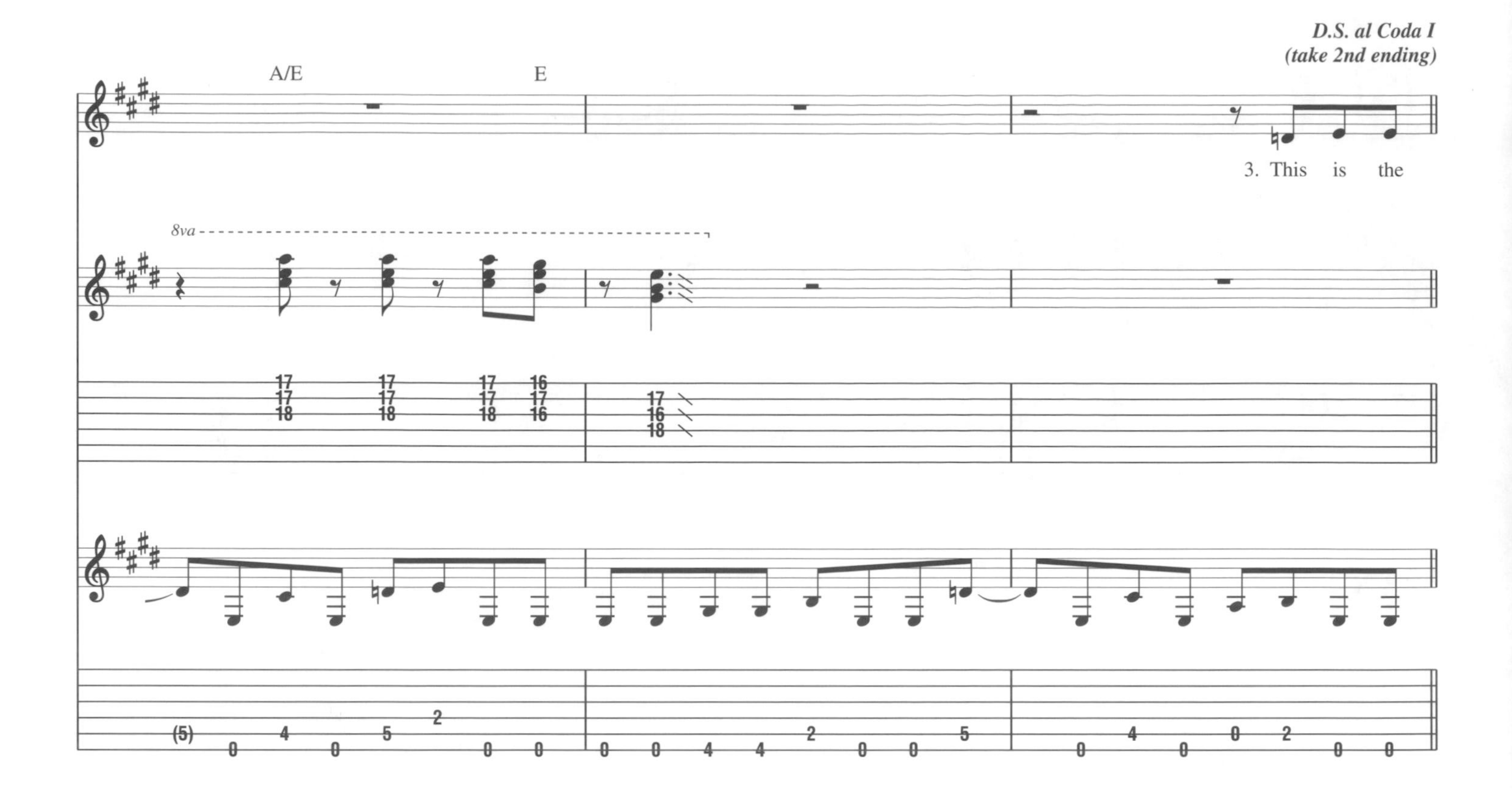
D.S. al Coda I
(take 2nd ending)
A/E
E
3. This is the
8va

Coda 1

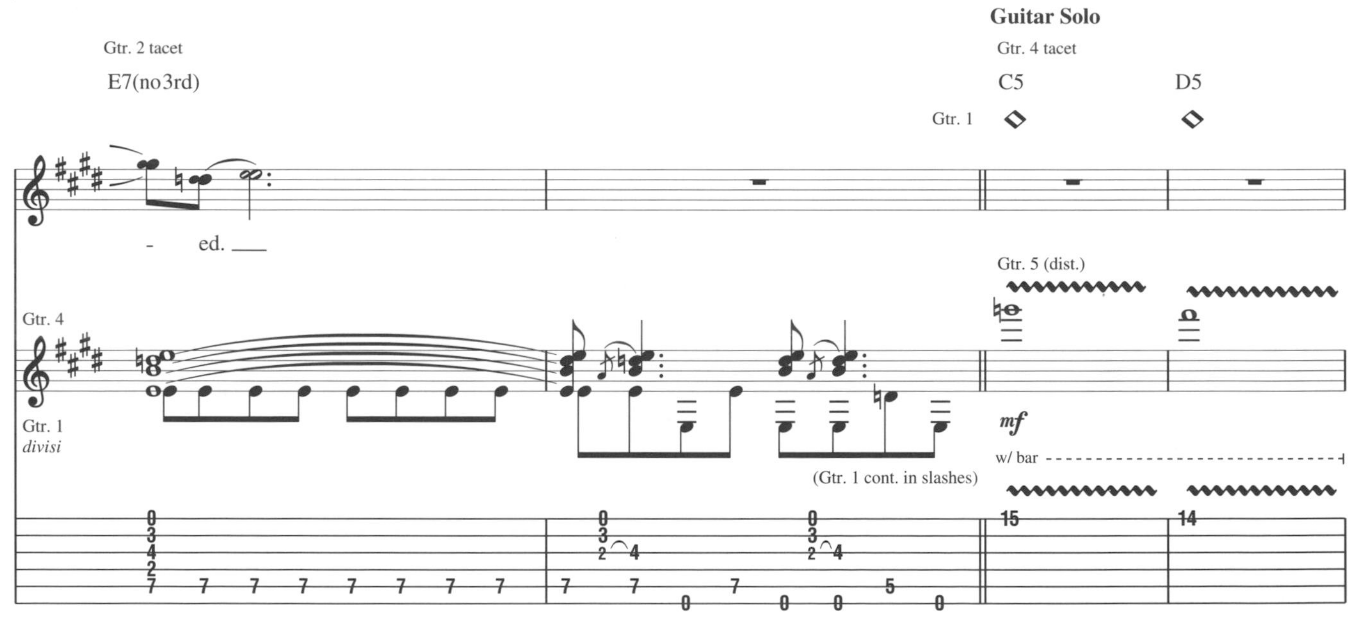
Guitar Solo
Gtr. 2 tacet
E7(no3rd)
Gtr. 4 tacet
C5
D5
Gtr. 1
- ed.
Gtr. 5 (dist.)
Gtr. 4
Gtr. 1
divisi
mf
w/ bar
(Gtr. 1 cont. in slashes)

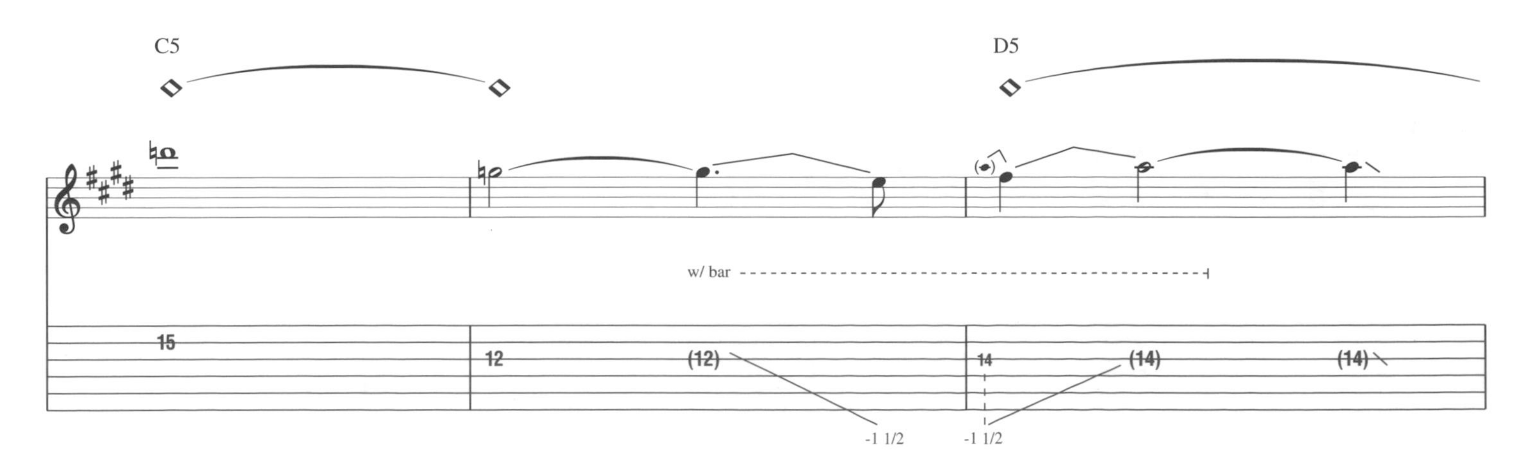
C5
D5
w/ bar
-1 1/2
-1 1/2

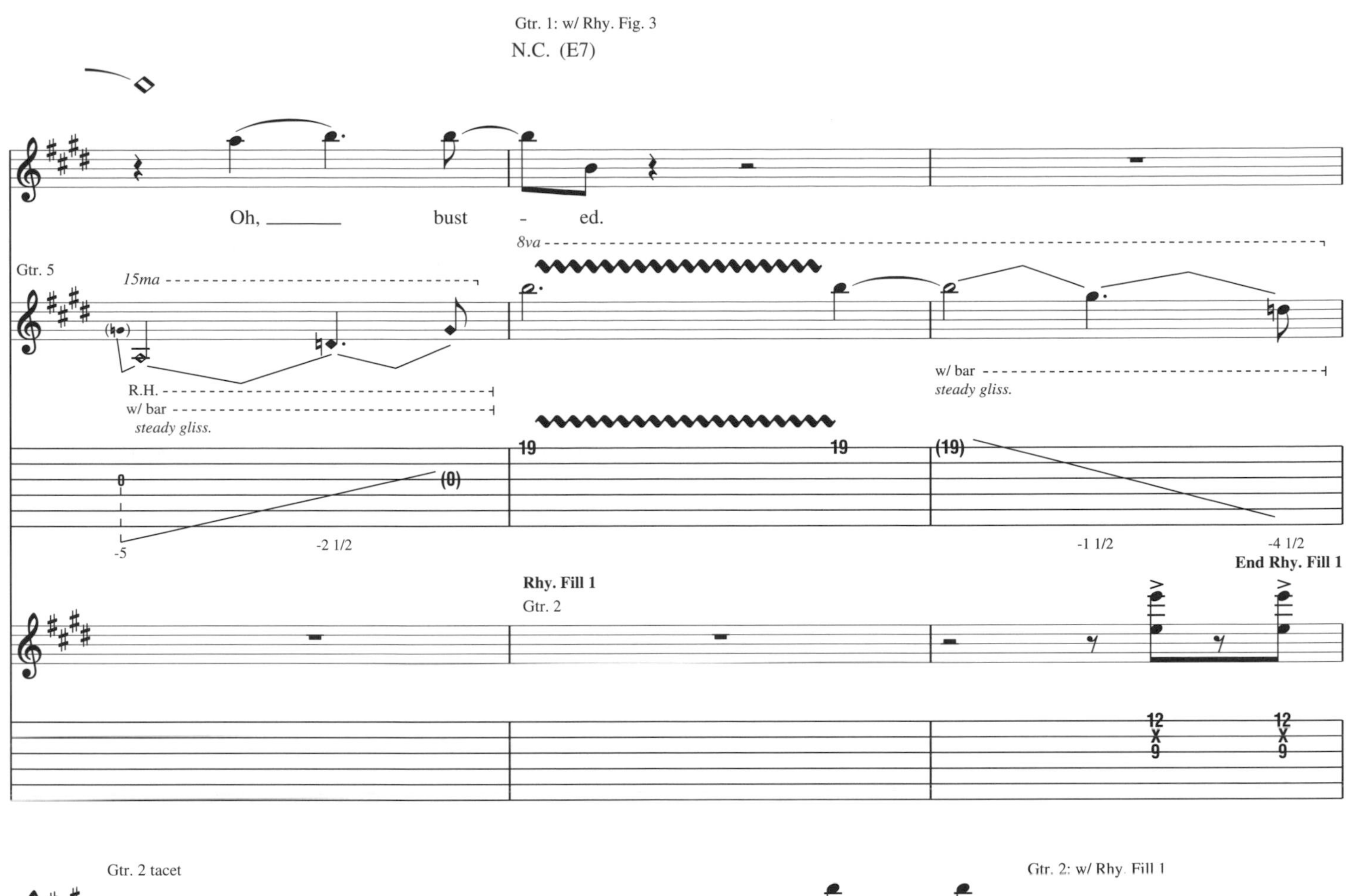

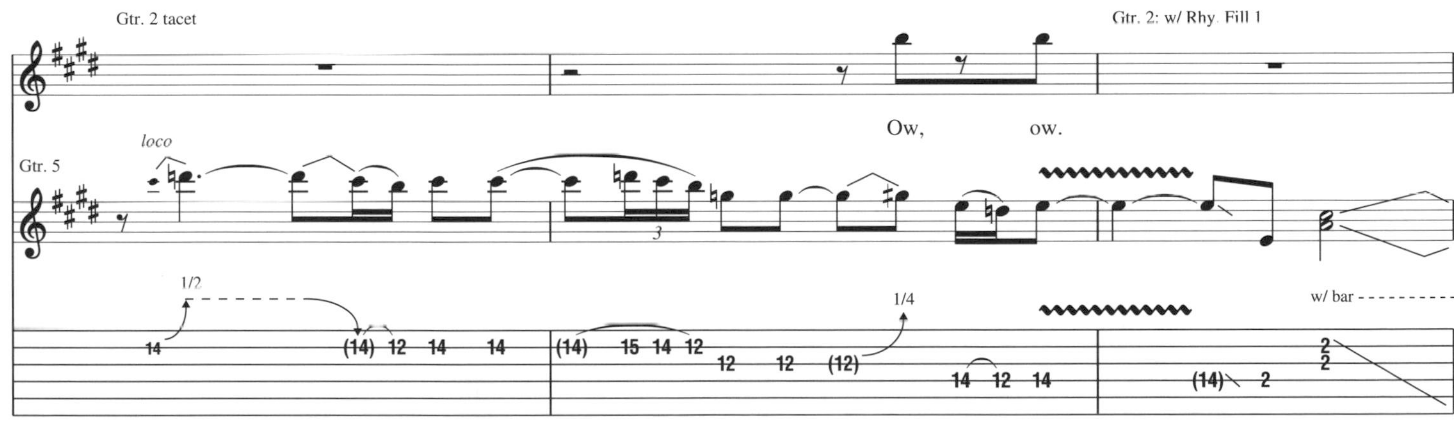

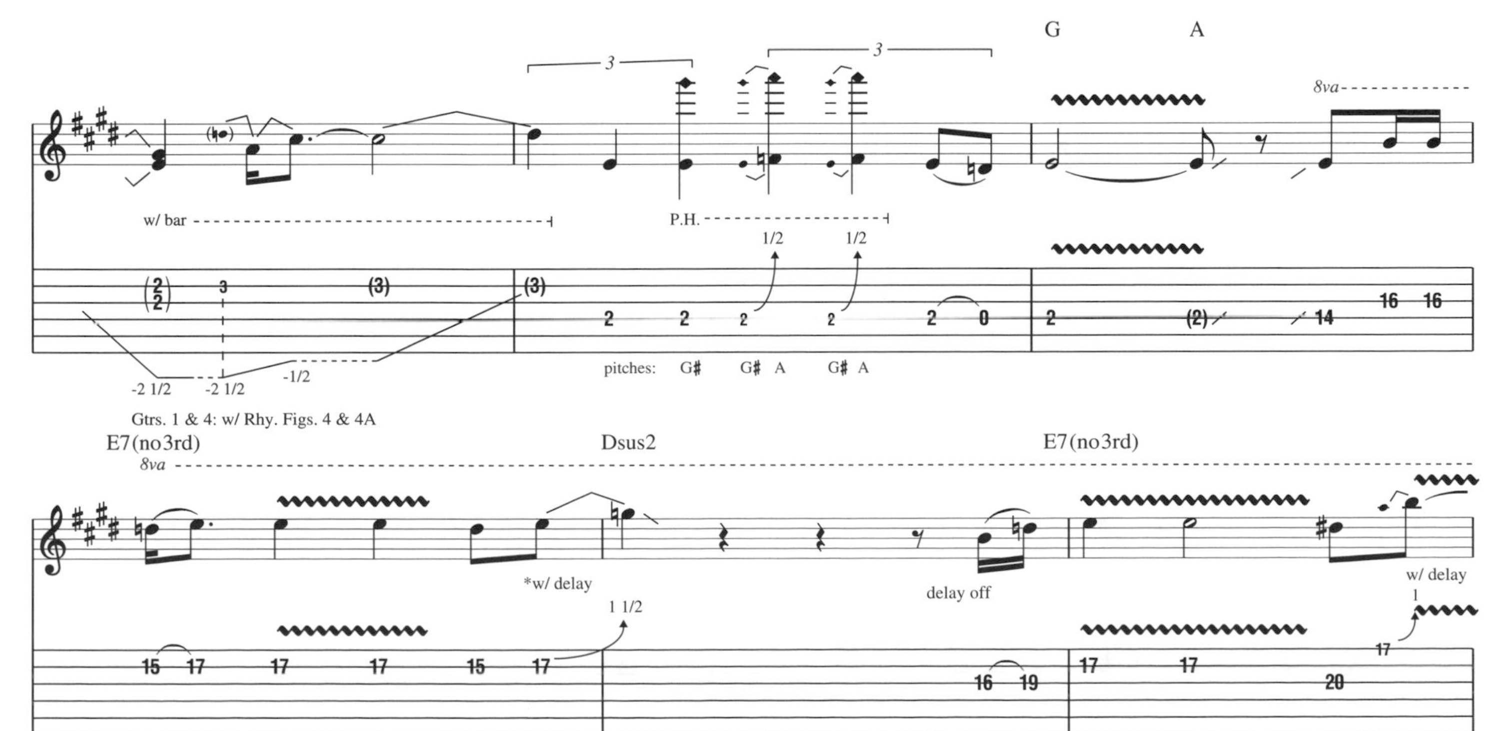

* Set for half-note regeneration, w/ 1 repeat.

Dsus2
E7(no3rd)
Dsus2
8va
delay off
1/2
1
E7(no3rd)
Chorus
Gtrs. 1 & 4 tacet
N.C.
Shake - down, break - down, take - down; ev - 'ry - bod - y wants in - to the crowd - ed light.
(Break - down, take - down.)
Gtr. 5
Gtr. 4
Gtr. 1
divisi
Break - down, take - down; you're bust - ed. (Bust - ed.)
(Take - down, shake - down, bust - ed.)
Gtr. 1: w/ Rhy. Fig. 3 (last meas.)
Gtr. 2: w/ Rhy. Fill 1 (3 1/2 times)
G
A
N.C. (E7)
Shake - down, break - down, hon - ey, just
(Break - down, take - down.)
Gtr. 2
Rhy. Fill 2
End Rhy. Fill 2

a - bout the time you think that it's all right.
Break - down, take - down;
(Take - down, shake - down.)
you're bust - ed.
D.S.S. al Coda 2
Gtr. 2: w/ Rhy. Fill 2
G
A
Coda 2
Gtr. 2 tacet
Em7(no3rd)
- ed.
Gtr. 2 w:/ Rhy. Fill 2
G
A
Gtr. 4
Gtr. 1
divisi
* Gtr. 4 to left of slash in tab
Outro Chorus
Gtr. 1: w/ Rhy. Fig. 3
Gtr. 2: w/ Rhy. Fill 1 (3 1/2 times)
Gtr. 4 tacet
N.C. (E7)
Begin fade
Shake - down, break - down, take - down; ev - 'ry - bod - y wants in - to the
crowd - ed light. Break - down, shake - down; you're bust -
Gtr. 2: w/ Rhy. Fill 2
G
A
Gtrs. 1 & 4: w/ Rhy. Figs. 4 & 4A (1st 4 meas.)
Gtr. 2: w/ Riff B
E7(no3rd)
- ed. Let down your
Dsus2
E7(no3rd)
Dsus2
Fade out
guard, hon - ey, just a - bout the time you think that it's all right.

Manhattan

Words and Music by Bob Seger

Gtr. 2: w/ Rhy. Fig. 1 (3 times)
E
B
Asus2
sawed off to the lim - it,
he's got a vague
plan.
E
B
There's this liq - uor store on Mad - i - son,
there's an - oth - er one down on Wash - ing - ton Square.
Asus2
E
He's pret - ty sure no one's ev - er seen him
B
Asus2
down a - round
there.
Gtr. 1
w/ bar
steady gliss.
*Vol. swell
Interlude
E
Esus4
B
E
Aadd9
8va
w/ bar
A.H.
E
B
A
2. The
loco
grad. bend
1 1/2
steady gliss.

Verse
Gtr. 1 tacet
Gtr. 2: w/ Rhy. Fig. 1 (4 times)
E B Asus2
first one's bird - shot, the next four are dou - ble aught buck. The
E B Asus2
last one's a slug just for good luck. He's got his
E B Asus2
works in his pock - et, he wants to score as soon as he's done. He can't wait
E B Asus2
to get straight, to get long gone.
Gtr. 1
P.S.

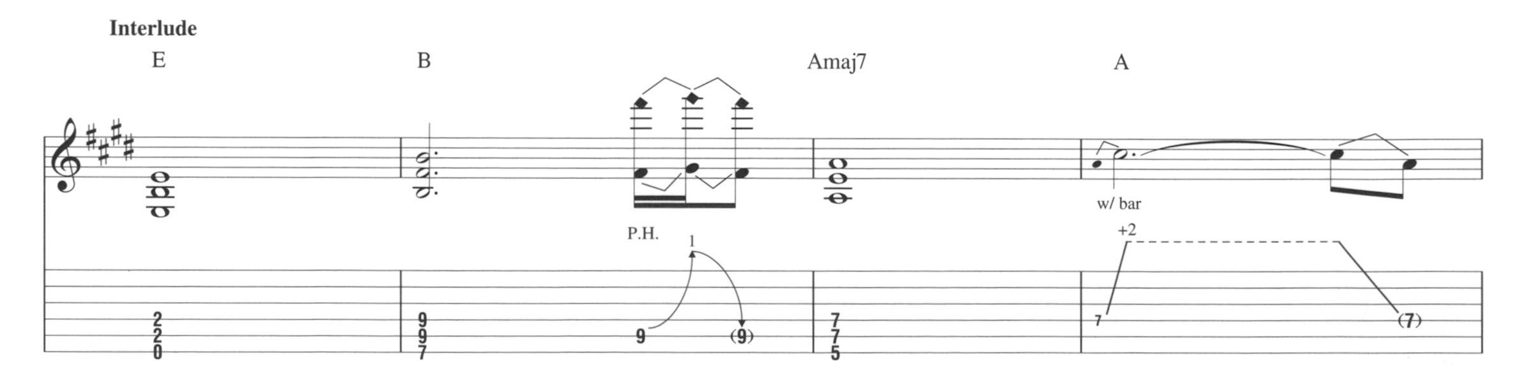

Interlude
E B Amaj7 A
P.H.
w/ bar
+2

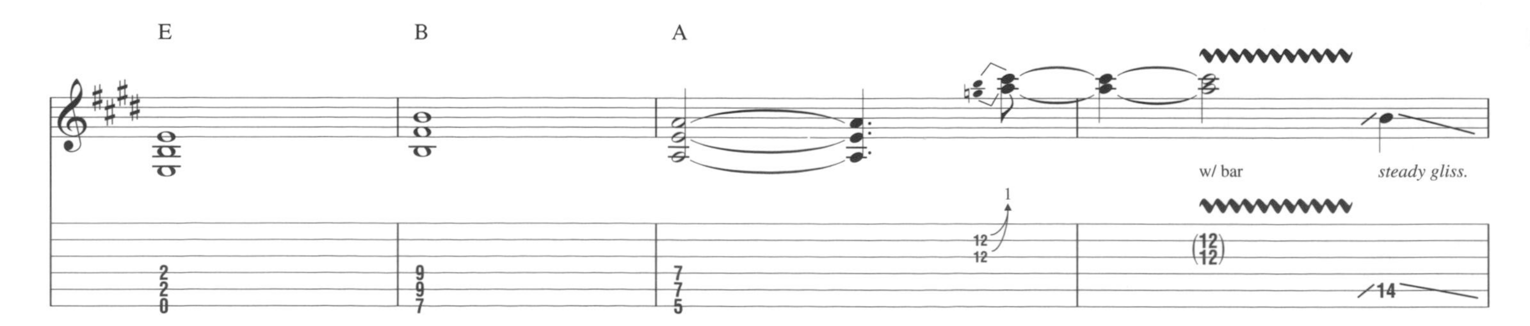

E B A
w/ bar
steady gliss.

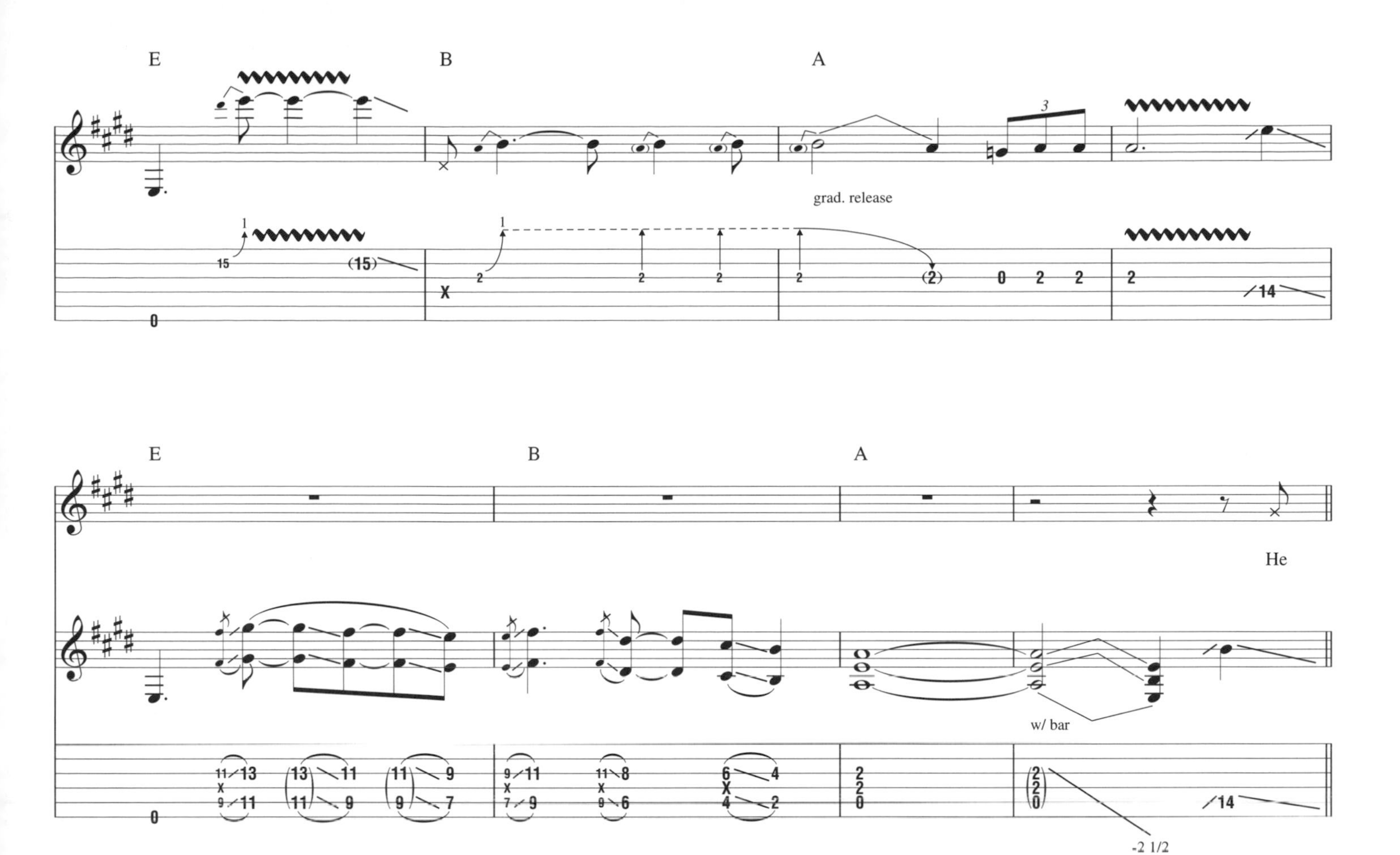
E
B
A
grad. release
E
B
A
He
w/ bar
-2 1/2

Bridge

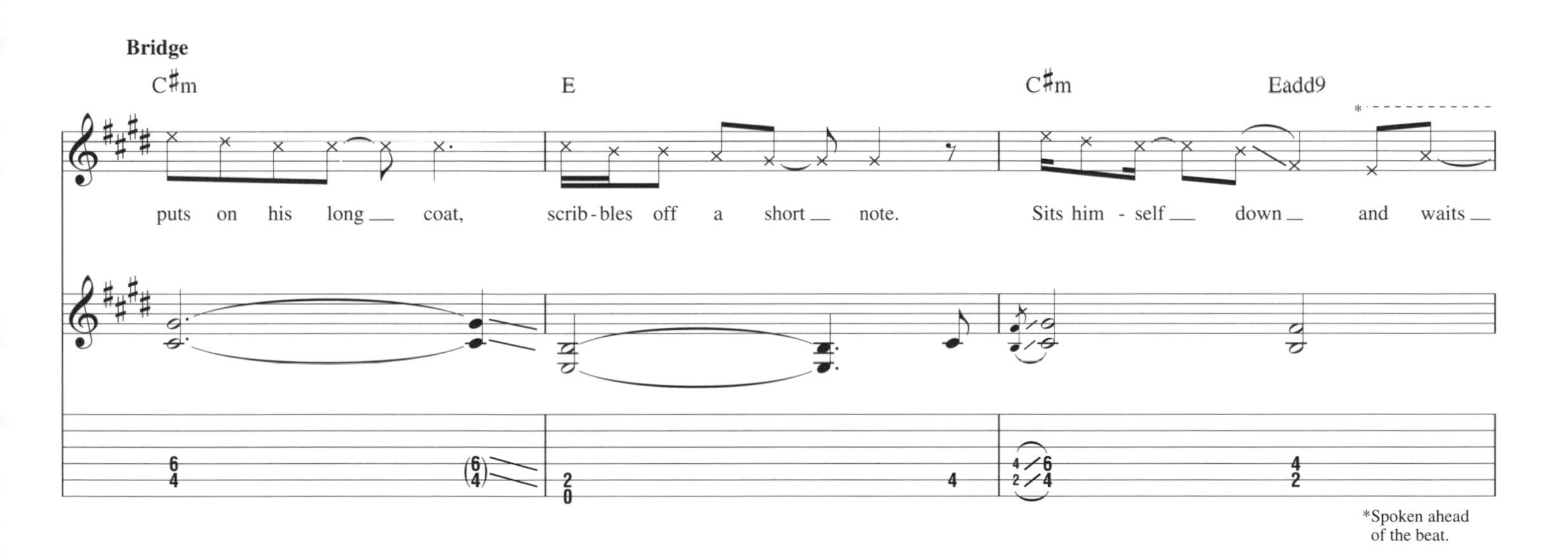
C♯m
E
C♯m
Eadd9
puts on his long coat, scrib-bles off a short note. Sits him-self down and waits
*Spoken ahead of the beat.

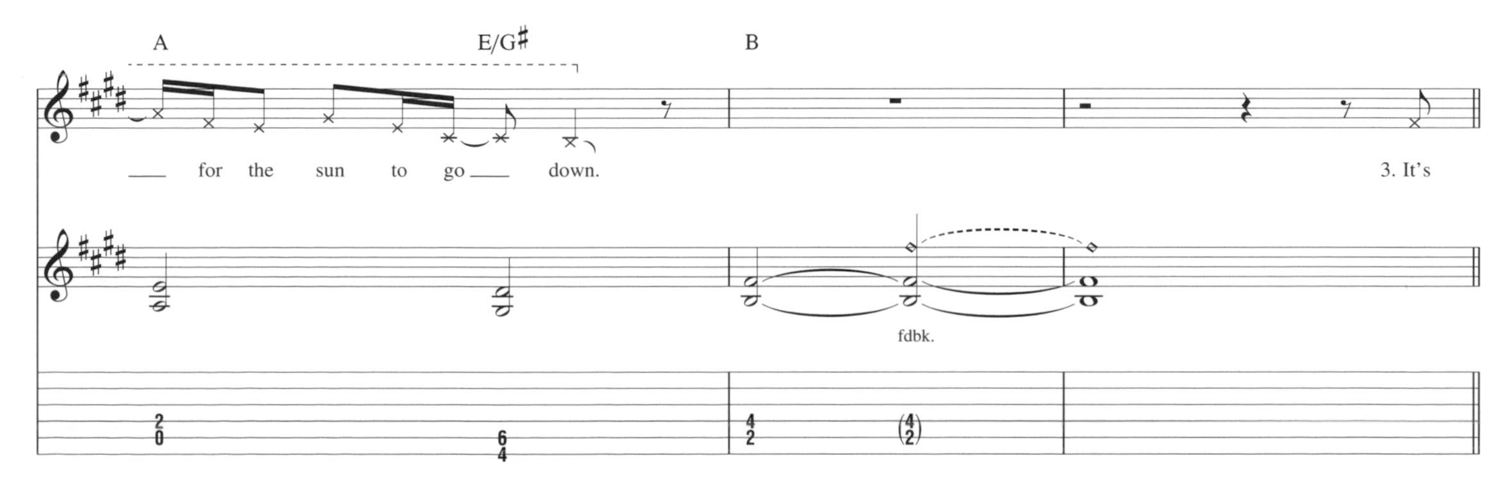
A
E/G♯
B
for the sun to go down. 3. It's
fdbk.

Verse
Gtr. 1 tacet
Gtr. 2: w/ Rhy. Fig. 1 (4 times)
E
B
Asus2
right a - round mid - night and there's still too damn man - y peo - ple on this street.
He's walked all the way from Bat - ter - y Park, he's got sweat - y hands and burn -
in' feet.
He's des - p'rate for a fix, his
Gtr. 1
P.S.
*Stop and restart pick scrape in rhythm of eighth-note triplets.
bod - y's scream - in', "Get me high."
He
8va
grad. bend and release
1 1/2
1/2
16
(16)
(16)
bursts through the door, and lets one fly.
loco
P.S.
14

Guitar Solo

E
B
Aadd9
P.M.
P.M.
P.M.
grad. release

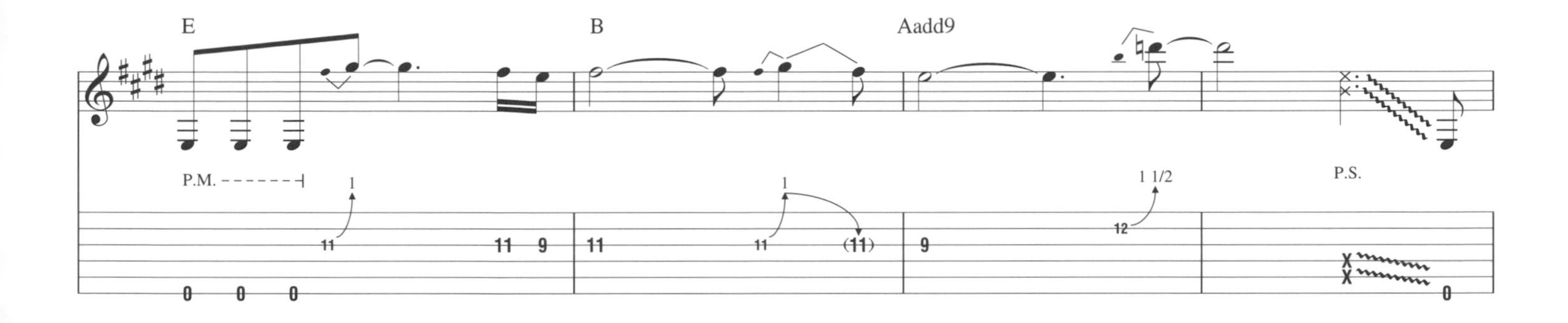
E
B
Aadd9
P.M.
1
1
1 1/2
P.S.

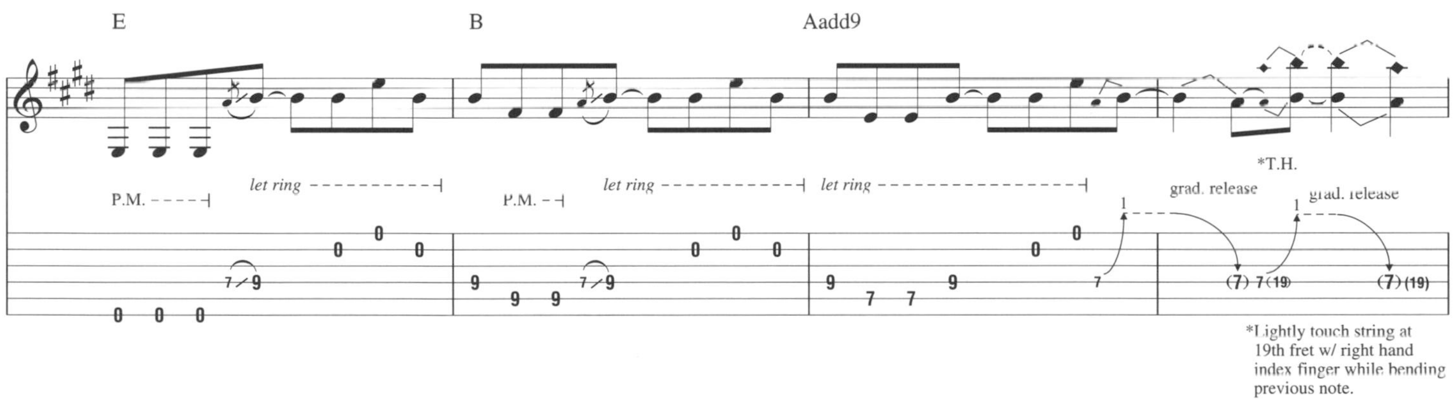
E
B
Aadd9
P.M.
let ring
P.M.
let ring
let ring
grad. release
grad. release
*T.H.
*Lightly touch string at 19th fret w/ right hand index finger while bending previous note.

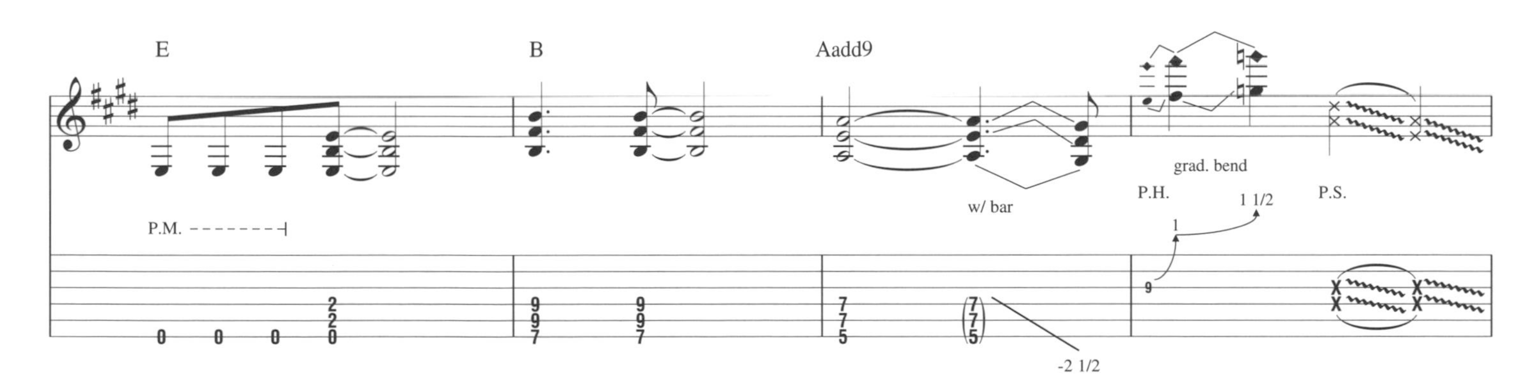
E
B
Aadd9
P.M.
w/ bar
grad. bend
P.H.
1 1/2
P.S.
-2 1/2

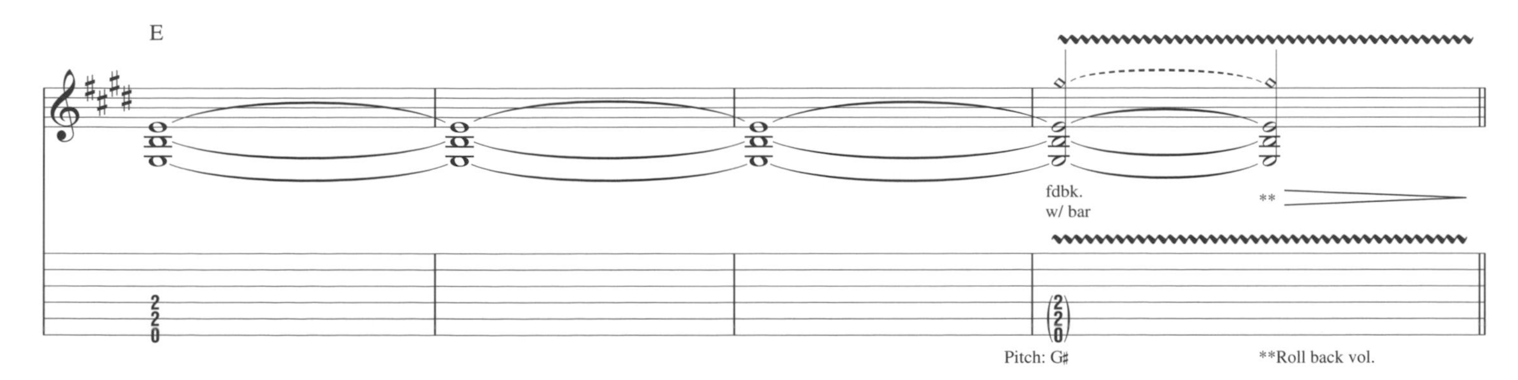
E
fdbk.
w/ bar
Pitch: G♯
**Roll back vol.

Verse
Gtr. 1 tacet
Gtr. 2: w/ Rhy. Fig. 1 (4 times)
E B Asus2
4. Sun - rise in the park, and Dav - ey's cold as stone.
E B
He got some bad mer - chan - dise, and he was all a - lone.
Asus2 E
Two more un - solved mys - t'ries, a lot of pa -
8va
Gtr. 1
Harm. w/ bar
*Vol. swell
-1
-1 1/2
-3 1/2
B Asus2
per pushed a - round. Most folks are
loco
P.S.
P.S.
E B Asus2
just wak - in' up in this great big town.
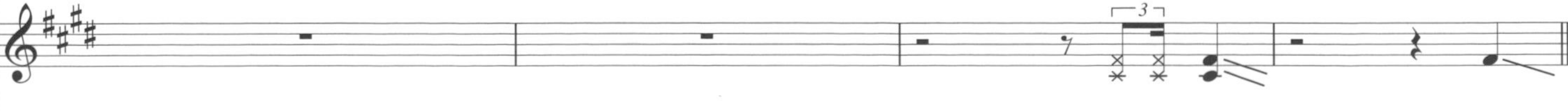

Outro-Guitar Solo

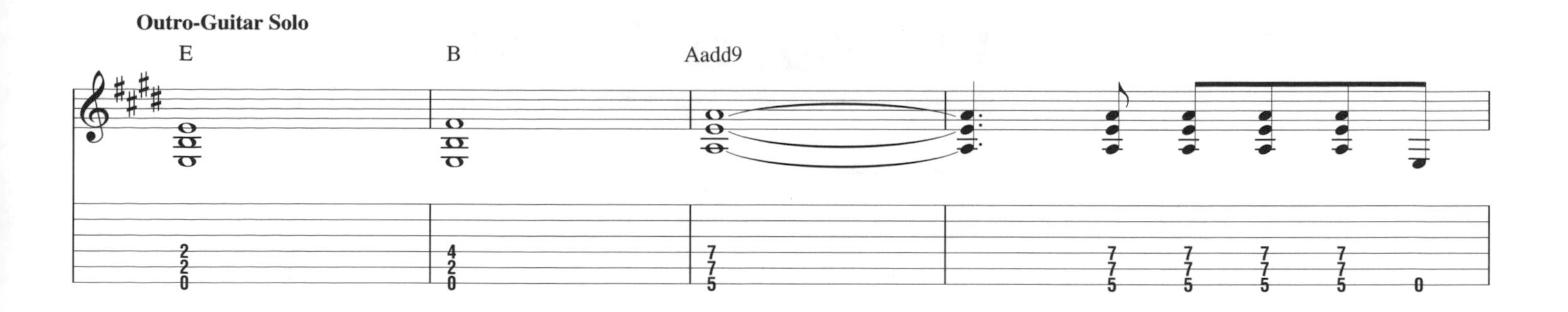

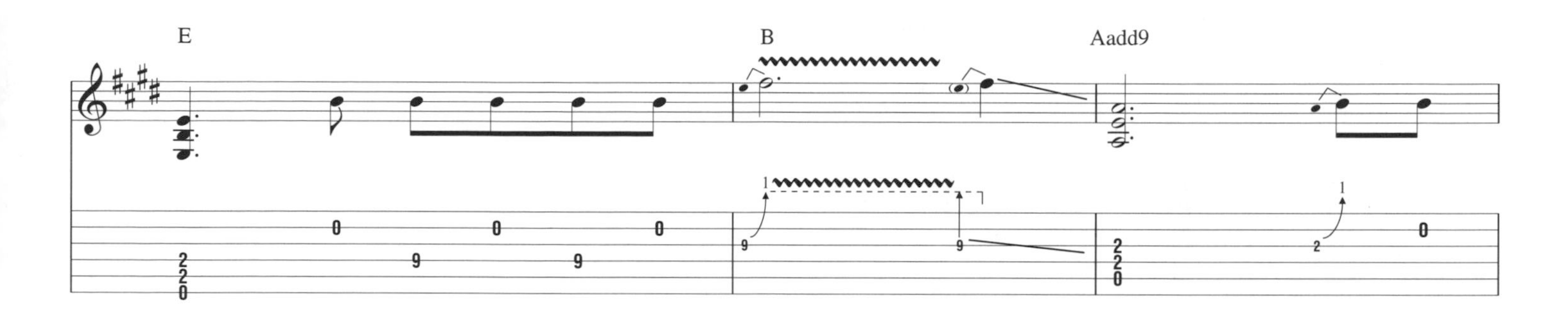

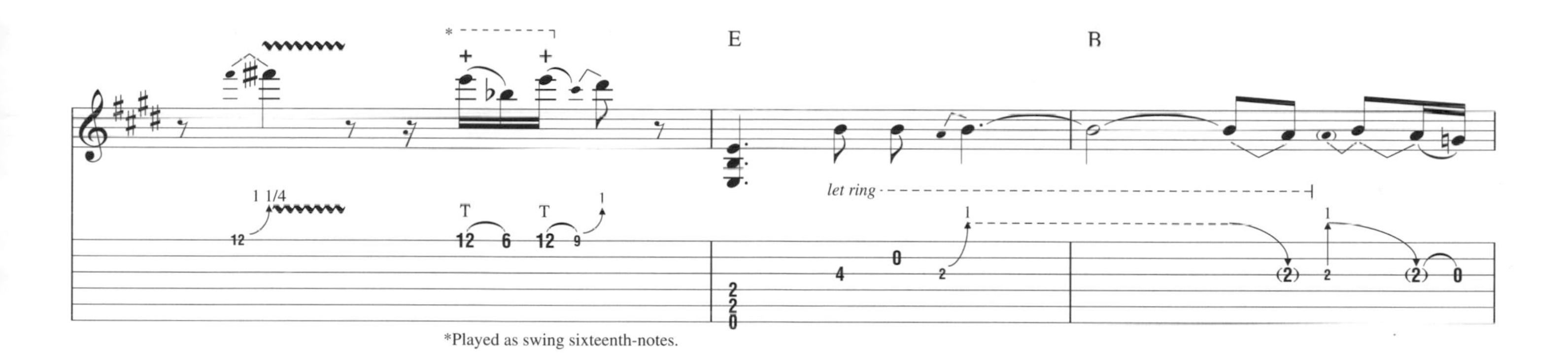

*Played as swing sixteenth-notes.

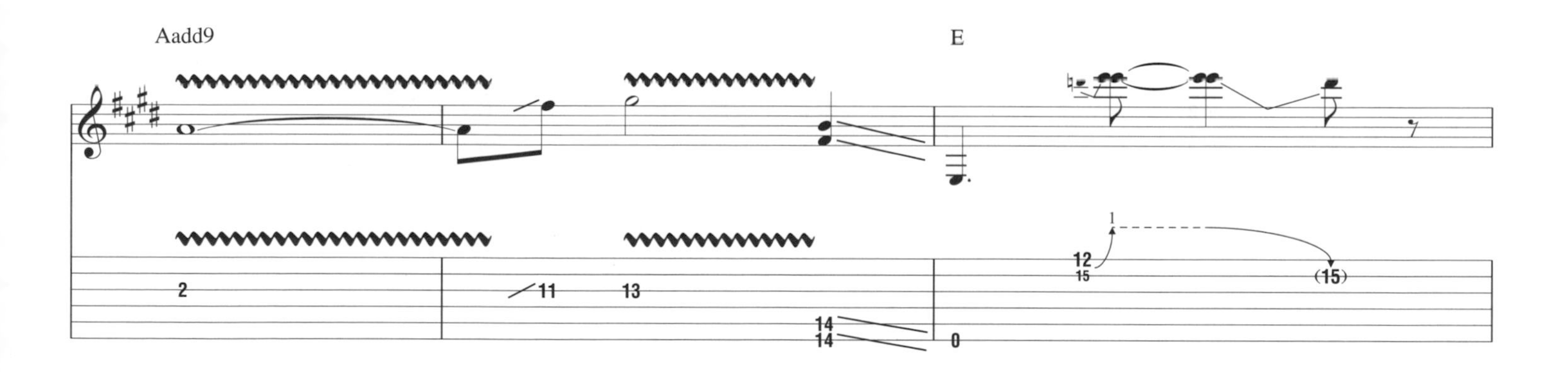

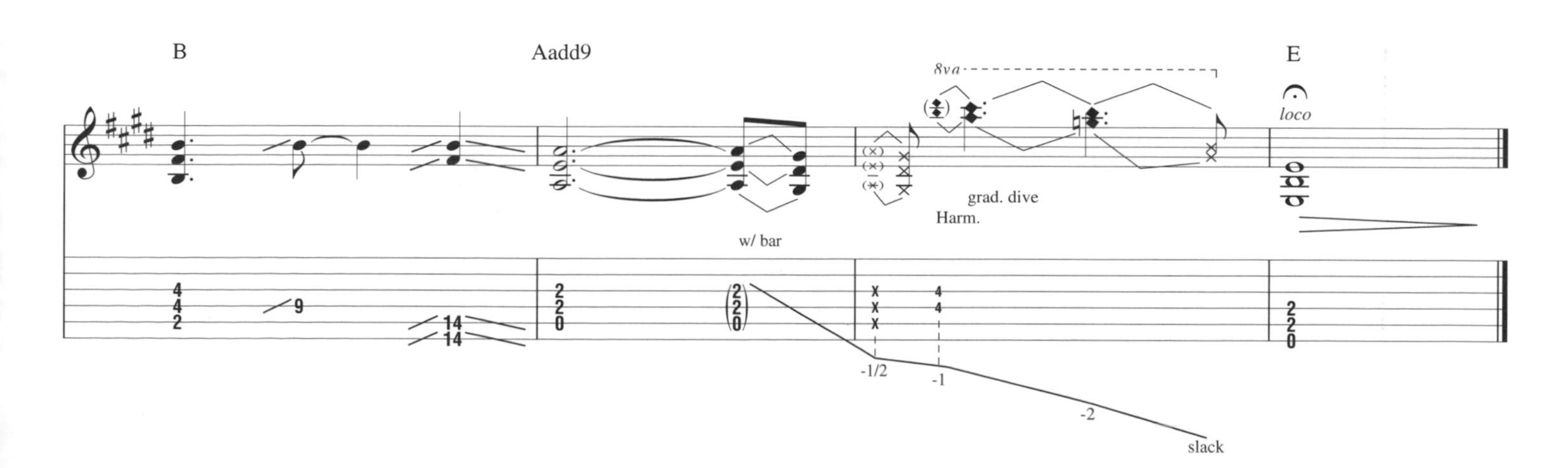

New Coat of Paint
Words and Music by Tom Waits
(Em7) (A7) (C7) (B7) (Em)
Capo I
Intro
Moderately ♩ = 77
Gtr. 1 (acous.)
Gtr. 2 (elec.)
(Drums)
mp
w/ clean tone
*Symbols in parentheses represent chord names respective to capoed guitar and do not reflect actual sounding chords. Capoed fret is "0" in tab.
w/ pick & fingers
let ring
w/ pick
(cont. in notation)
1. Let's put a

Verse
Fm7
*(Em7)
B♭7
(A7)
D♭7
(C7)
C7
(B7)
Fm7
(Em7)
B♭7
(A7)
new __ coat of paint on this lone-some old town. __ Set 'em up, set 'em up, __ we'll be
Gtr. 2
p
Gtr. 1
Rhy. Fig. 1
sim.

*Symbols in parentheses represent chord names repective to capoed guitar.
Symbols above reflect actual sounding chords.
Chord symbols reflect overall harmony.

D♭7
(C7)
C7
(B7)
Fm7
(Em7)
B♭7
(A7)
D♭7
(C7)
C7
(B7)
knock-in' 'em down. __ You __ wear a dress, babe, __ I'll wear a tie. __ We'll laugh at that
sim.

Fm7
(Em7)
B♭7
(A7)
D♭7
(C7)
C7
(B7)
Fm7
(Em7)
old blood - shot moon in that bur - gun - dy sky.
let ring
End Rhy. Fig. 1
(cont. in slashes)

Piano Solo

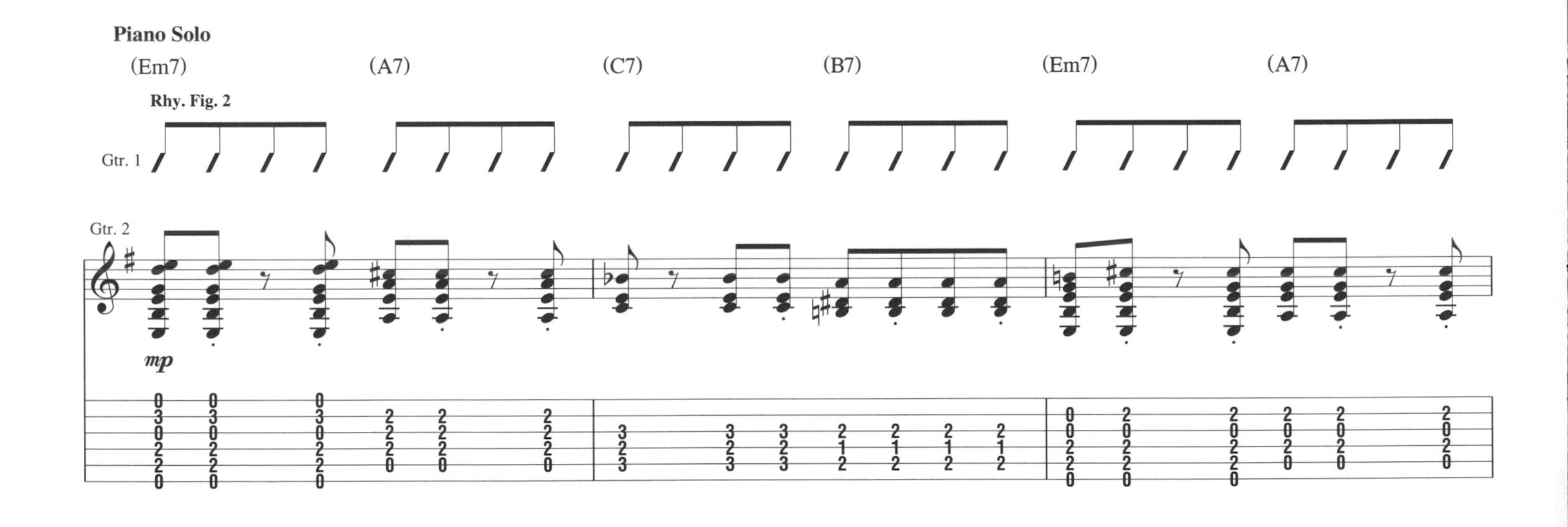
(Em7)
(A7)
(C7)
(B7)
(Em7)
(A7)
Rhy. Fig. 2
Gtr. 1
Gtr. 2
mp

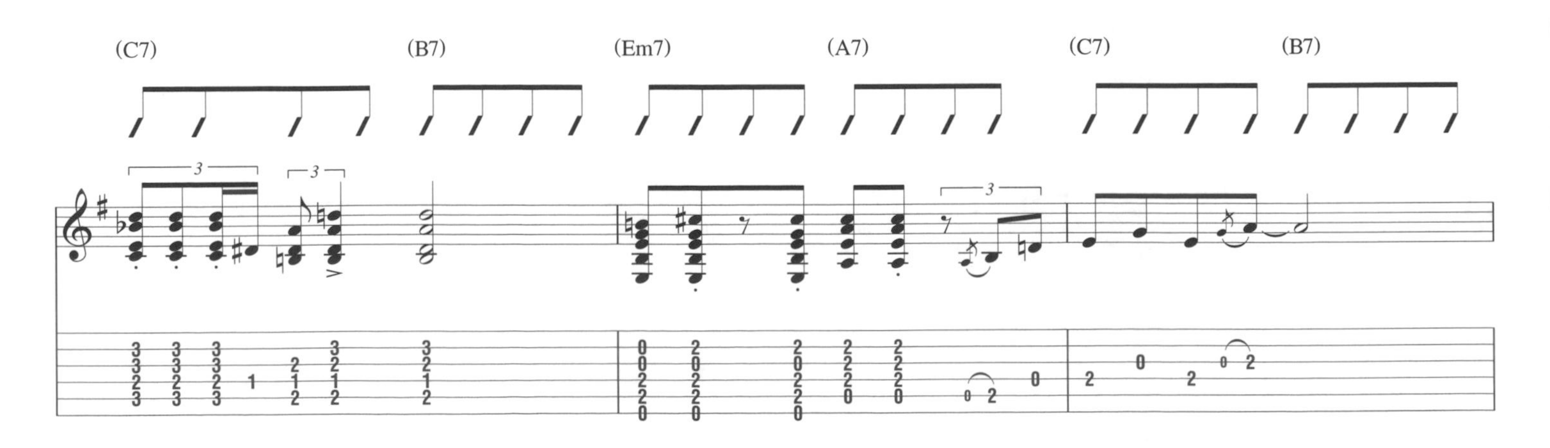
(C7)
(B7)
(Em7)
(A7)
(C7)
(B7)

(Em7) (A7) (C7) (B7) (Em)
End Rhy. Fig. 2
w/ pick & fingers
let ring
Verse
Gtr. 1: w/ Rhy. Fig. 1
Fm7 (Em7) B♭7 (A7) D♭7 (C7) C7 (B7) Fm7 (Em7) B♭7 (A7)
2. All our scrib-bled love dreams, lost or thrown a - way. Nev - er miss the shuf - fle on an o -
Gtr. 2
let ring
let ring
*Sung behind the beat.
D♭7 (C7) C7 (B7) Fm7 (Em7) B♭7 (A7) D♭7 (C7) C7 (B7)
ver - flow - in' day. When love needs a trans - fu - sion, shoot it full of wine.

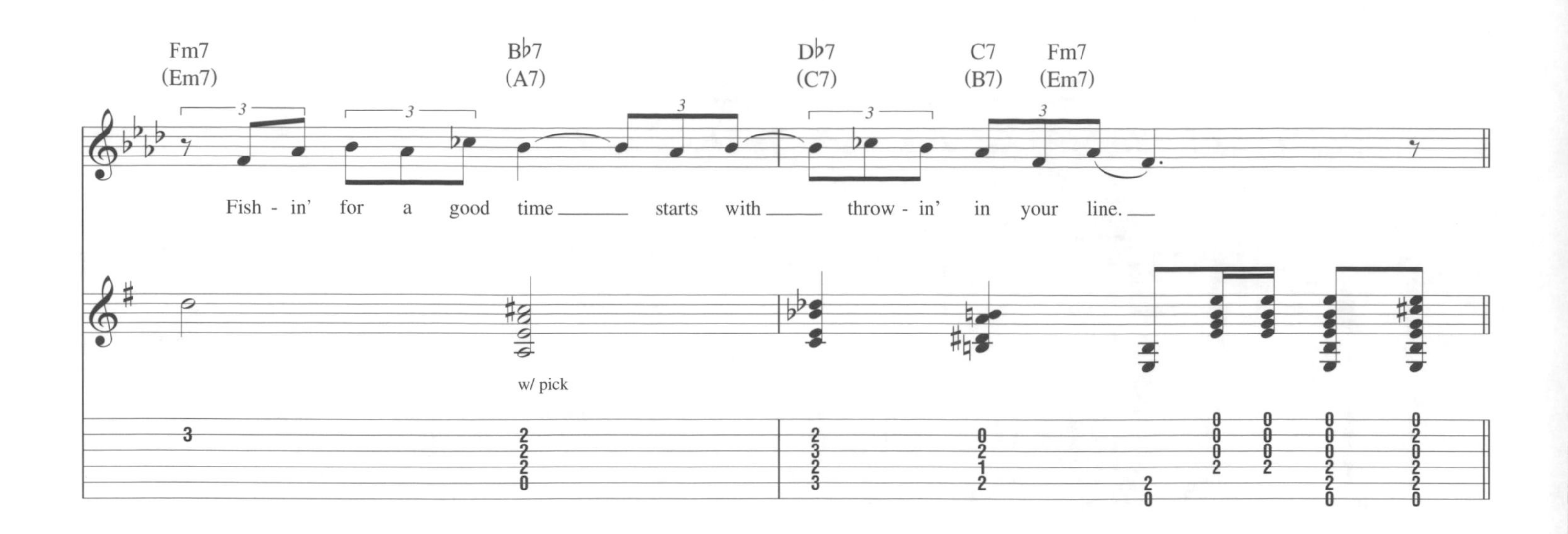

Piano Solo

Gtr. 1: w/ Rhy. Fig. 2

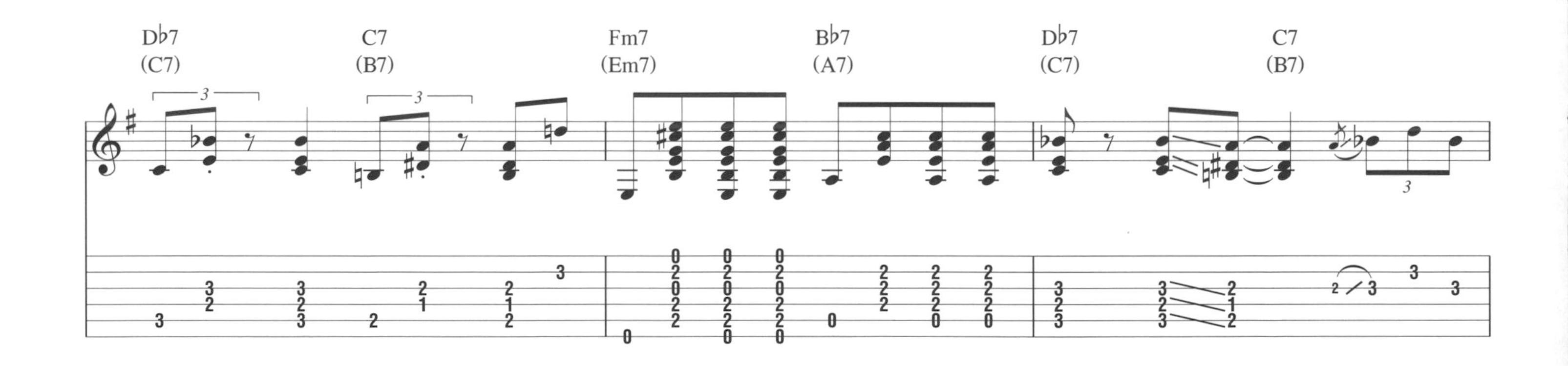

Db7 (C7) C7 (B7) Fm7 (Em7) Bb7 (A7) Db7 (C7) C7 (B7)

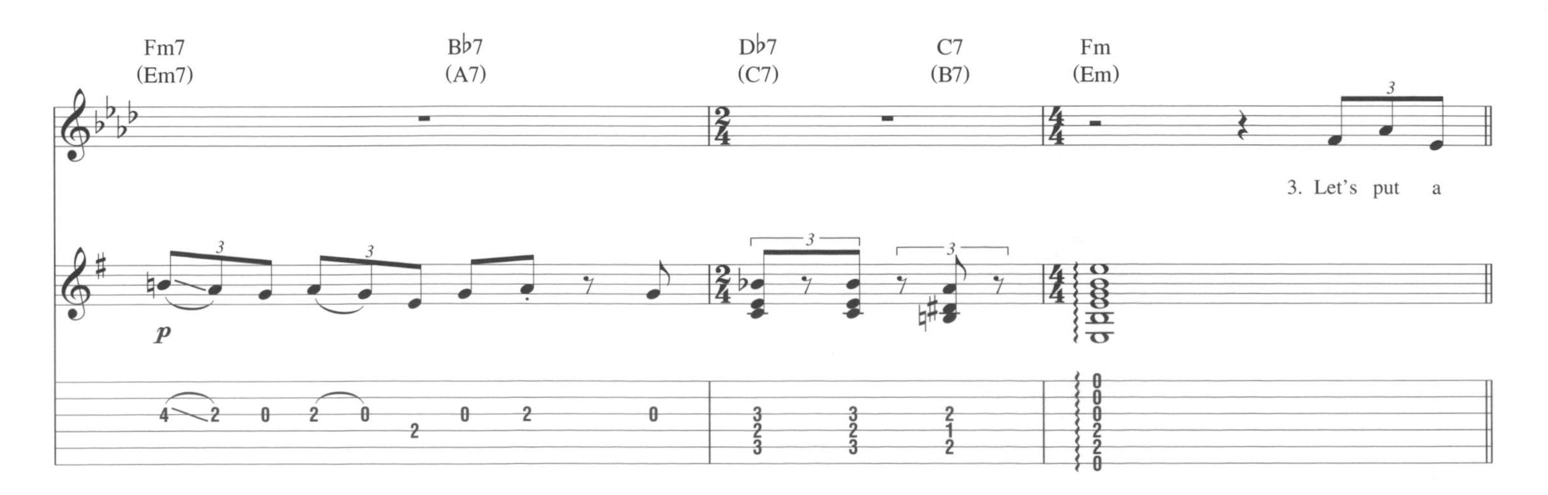

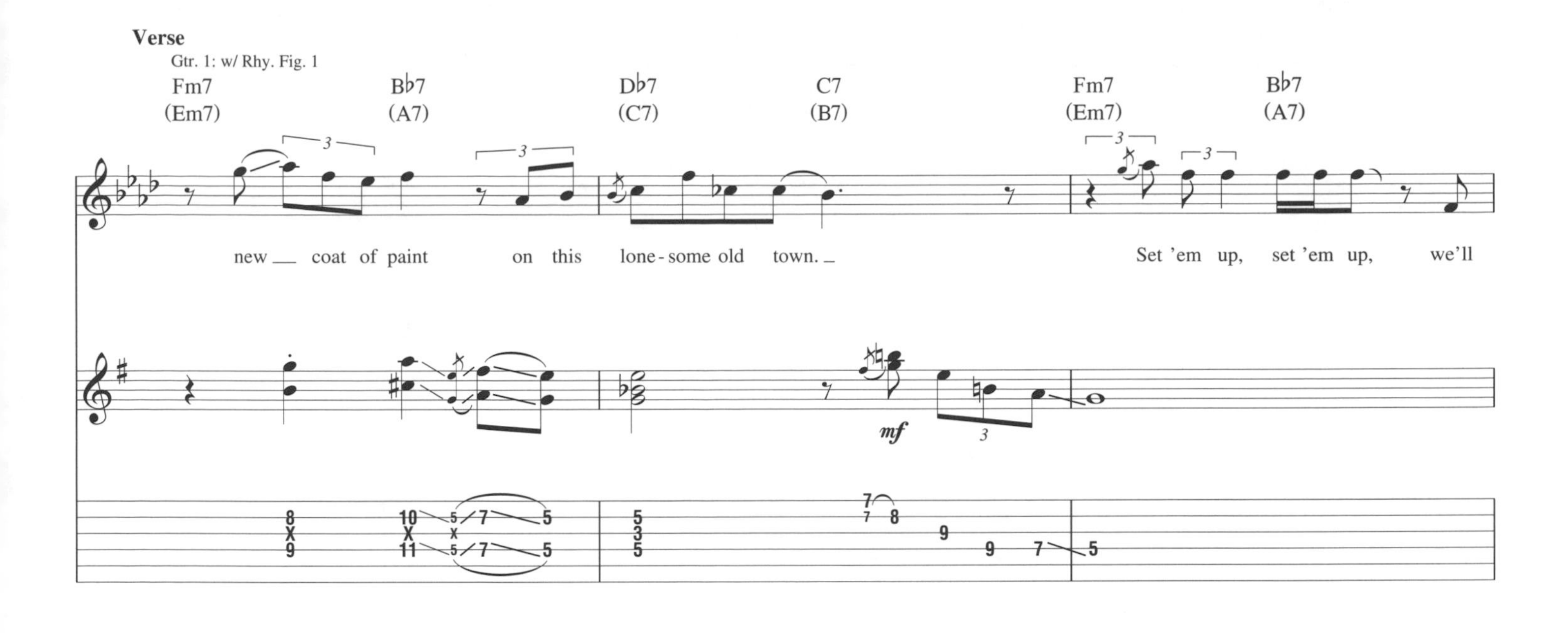

Verse
Gtr. 1: w/ Rhy. Fig. 1
Fm7 (Em7) B♭7 (A7) D♭7 (C7) C7 (B7) Fm7 (Em7) B♭7 (A7)
new coat of paint on this lone-some old town.
Set 'em up, set 'em up, we'll
mf

D♭7 (C7) C7 (B7) Fm7 (Em7) B♭7 (A7) D♭7 (C7) C7 (B7)
knock 'em all down.
You wear a dress, babe,
I'll wear a tie. We'll laugh at that
p
mp

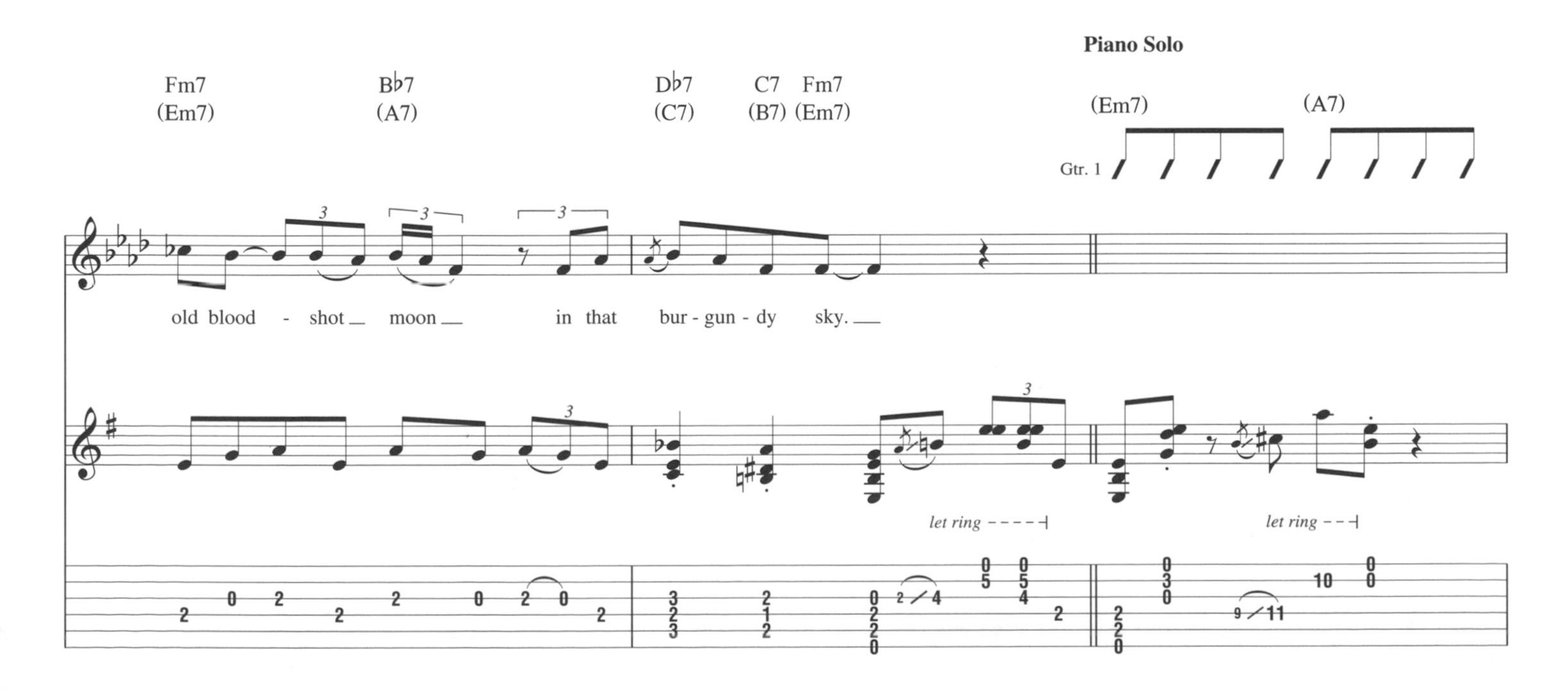

Piano Solo
Fm7 (Em7) B♭7 (A7) D♭7 (C7) C7 (B7) Fm7 (Em7)
(Em7) (A7)
Gtr. 1
old blood - shot moon in that bur-gun-dy sky.
let ring
let ring

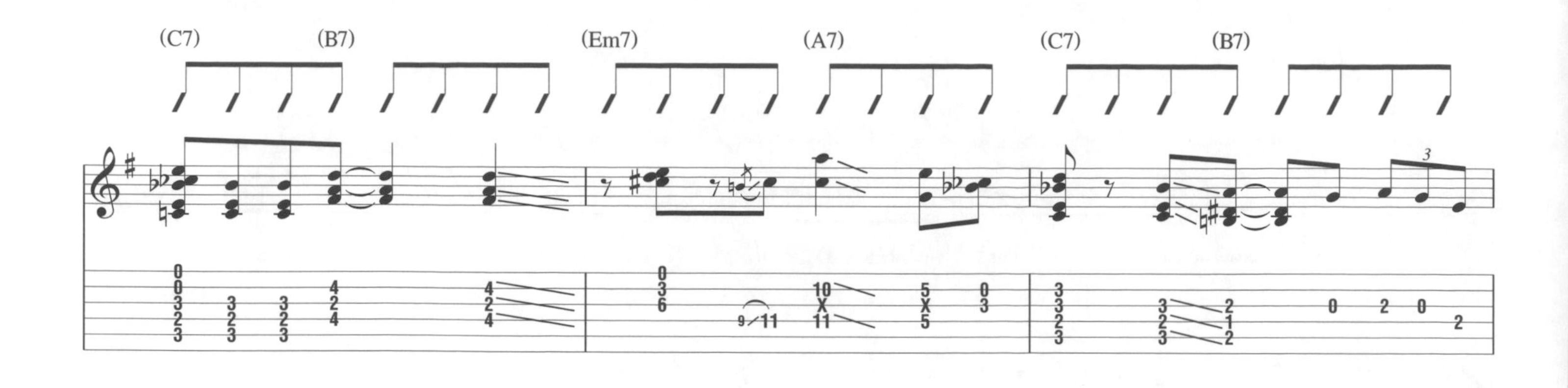
(C7)
(B7)
(Em7)
(A7)
(C7)
(B7)

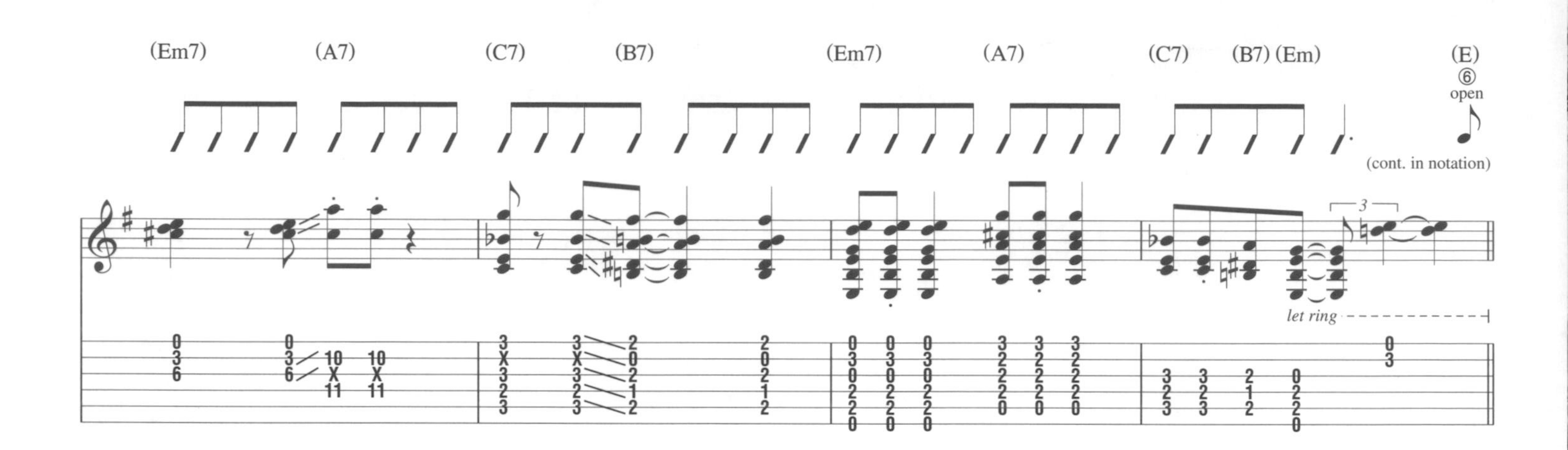
(Em7)
(A7)
(C7)
(B7)
(Em7)
(A7)
(C7)
(B7) (Em)
(E)
⑥ open
(cont. in notation)
let ring

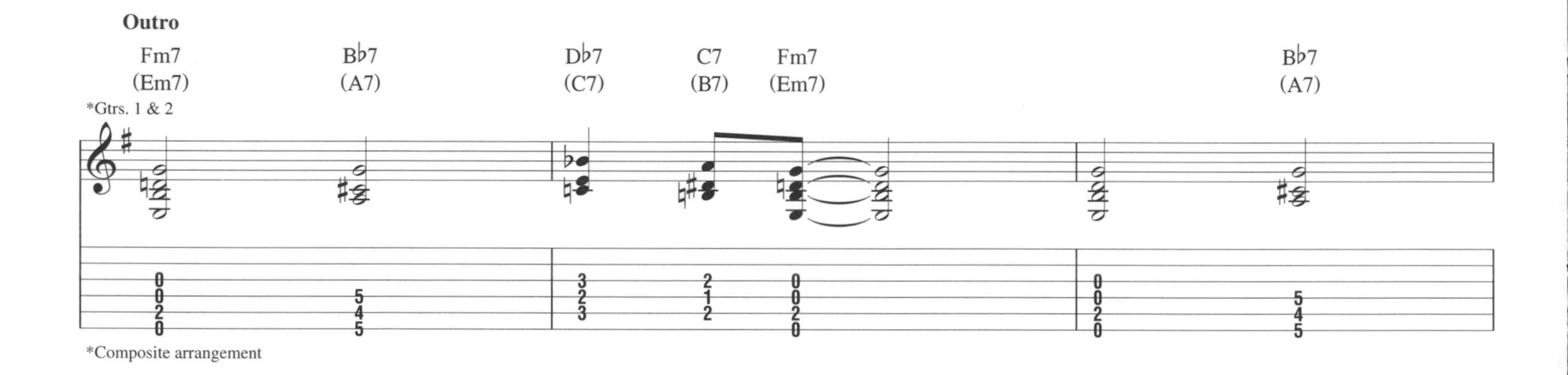
Outro
Fm7 (Em7)
B♭7 (A7)
D♭7 (C7)
C7 (B7)
Fm7 (Em7)
B♭7 (A7)
*Gtrs. 1 & 2
*Composite arrangement

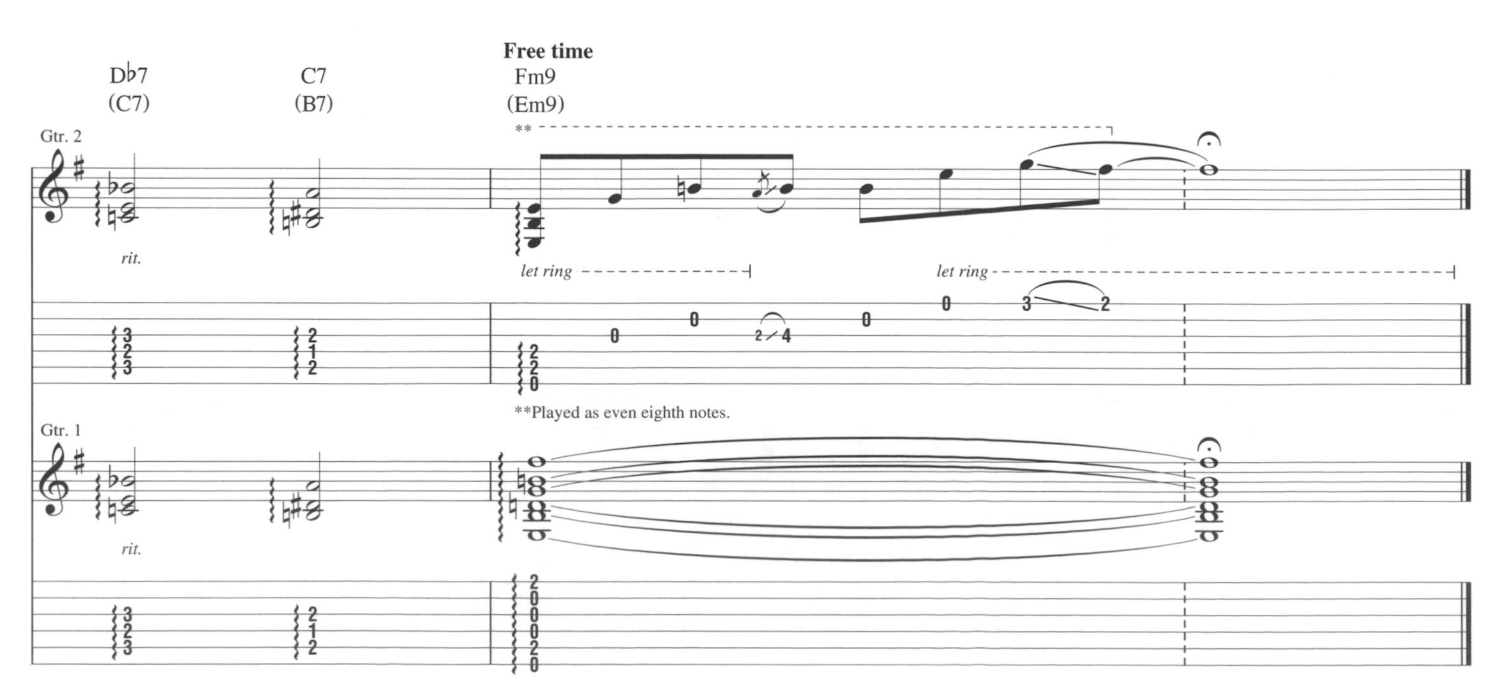
D♭7 (C7)
C7 (B7)
Free time
Fm9 (Em9)
Gtr. 2
rit.
let ring
let ring
**Played as even eighth notes.
Gtr. 1
rit.

Chances Are

Words and Music by Bob Seger

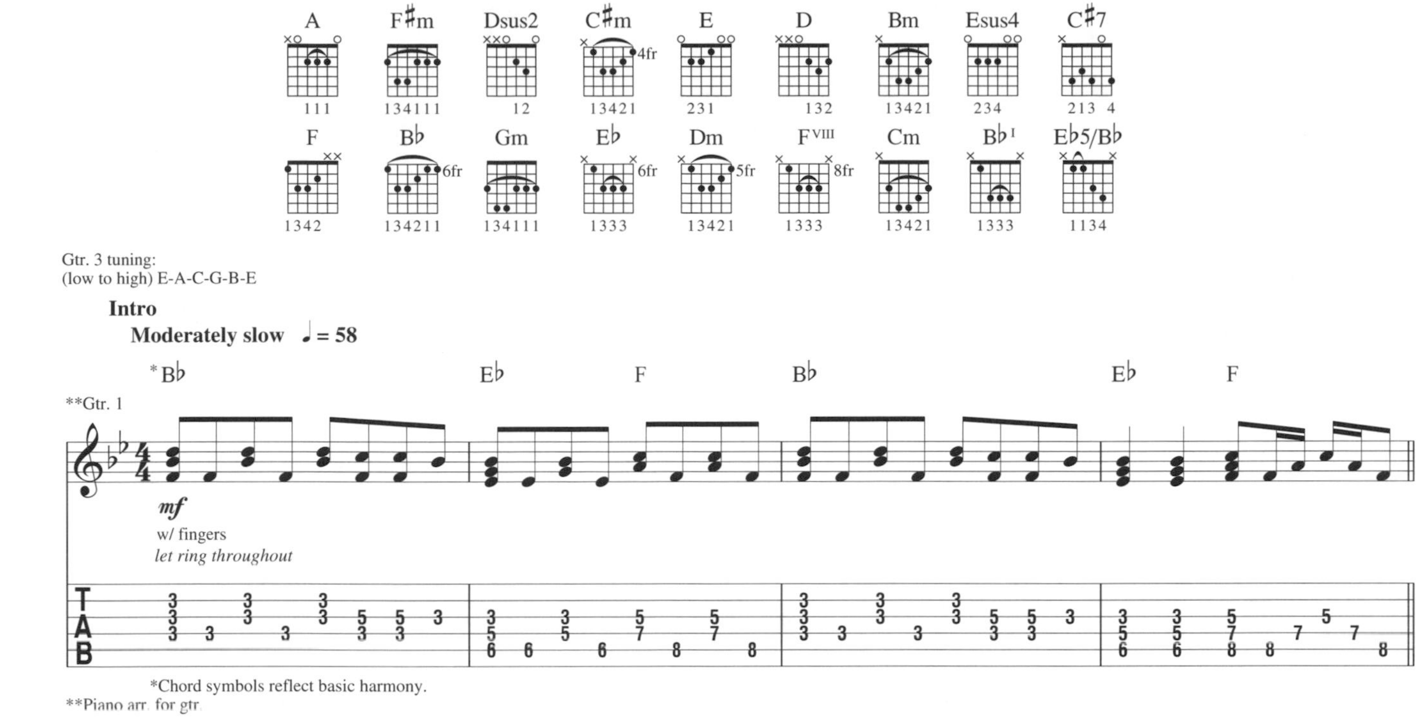

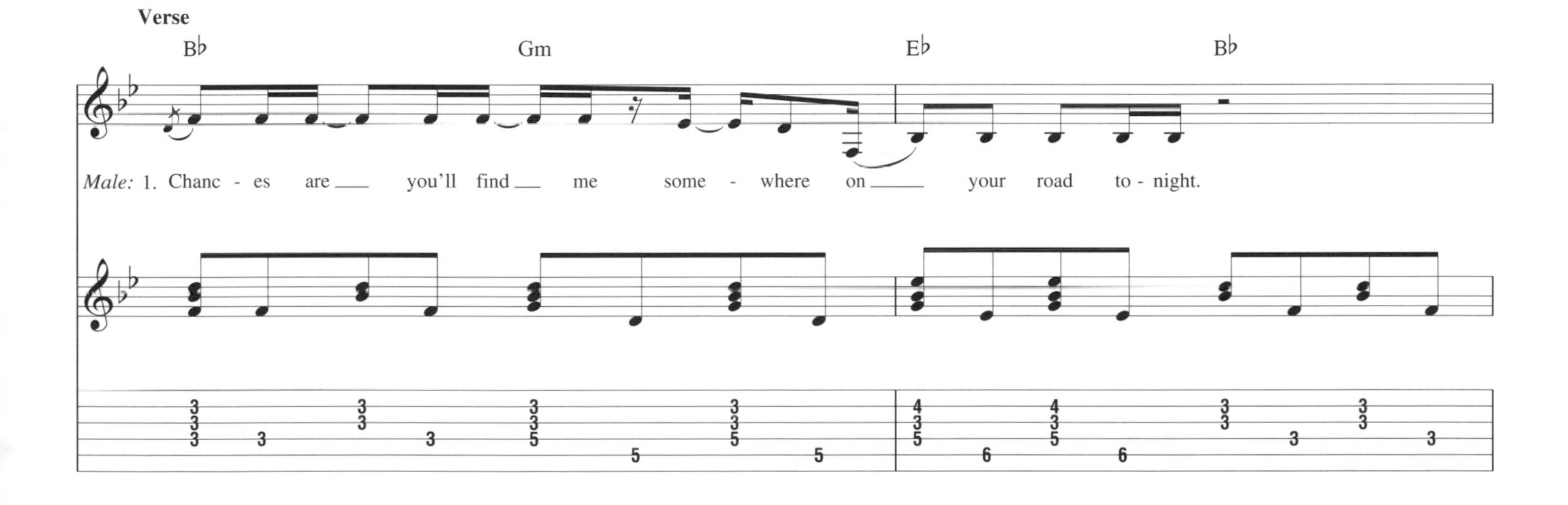

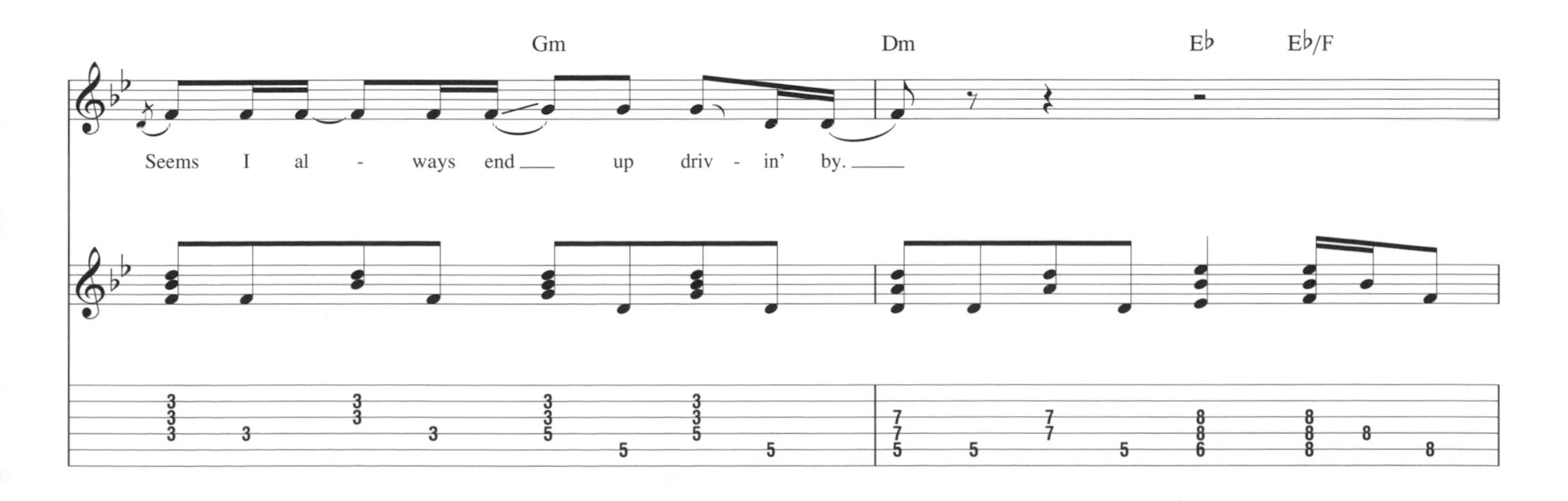

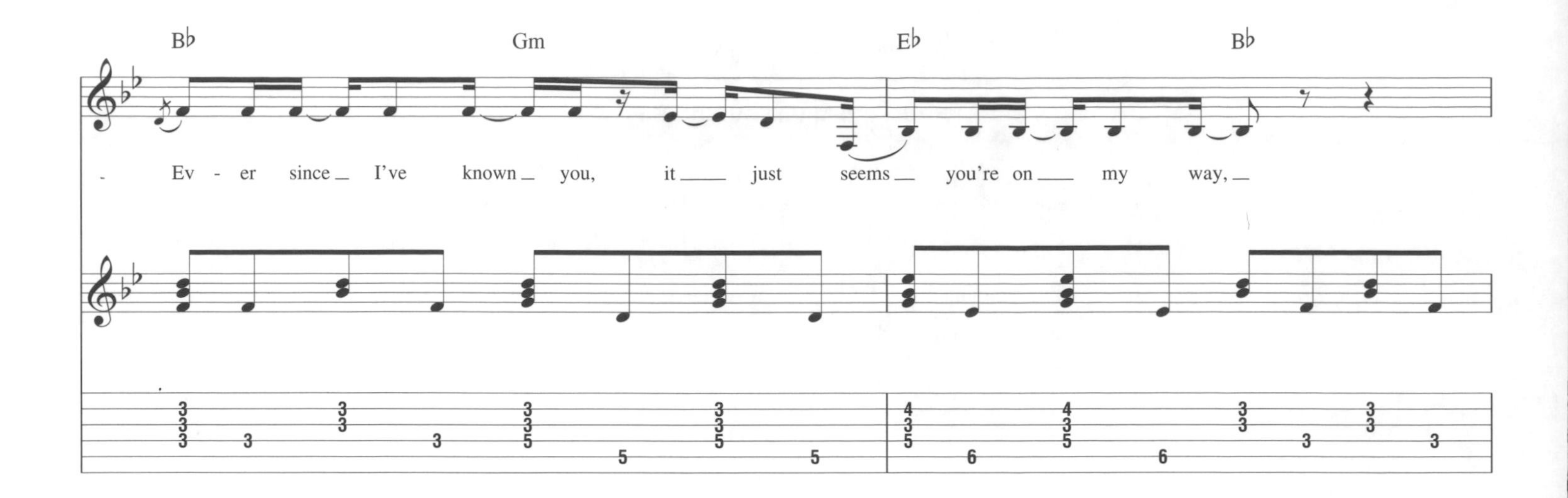
B♭
Gm
E♭
B♭
Ev - er since I've known you, it just seems you're on my way,

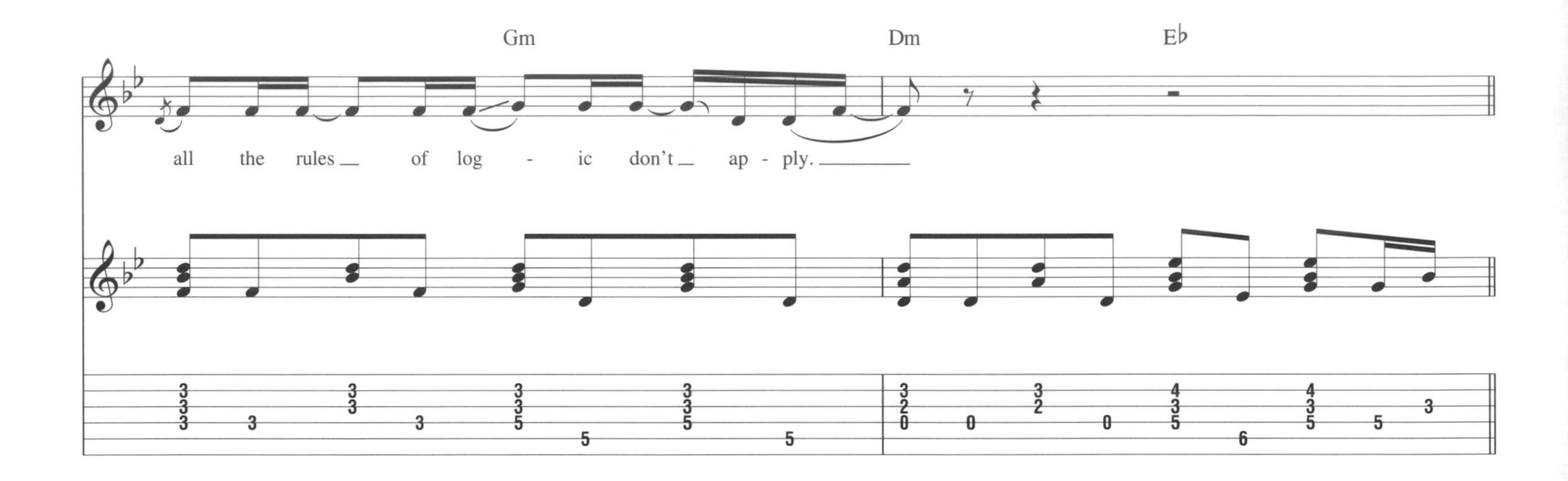
Gm
Dm
E♭
all the rules of log - ic don't ap - ply.

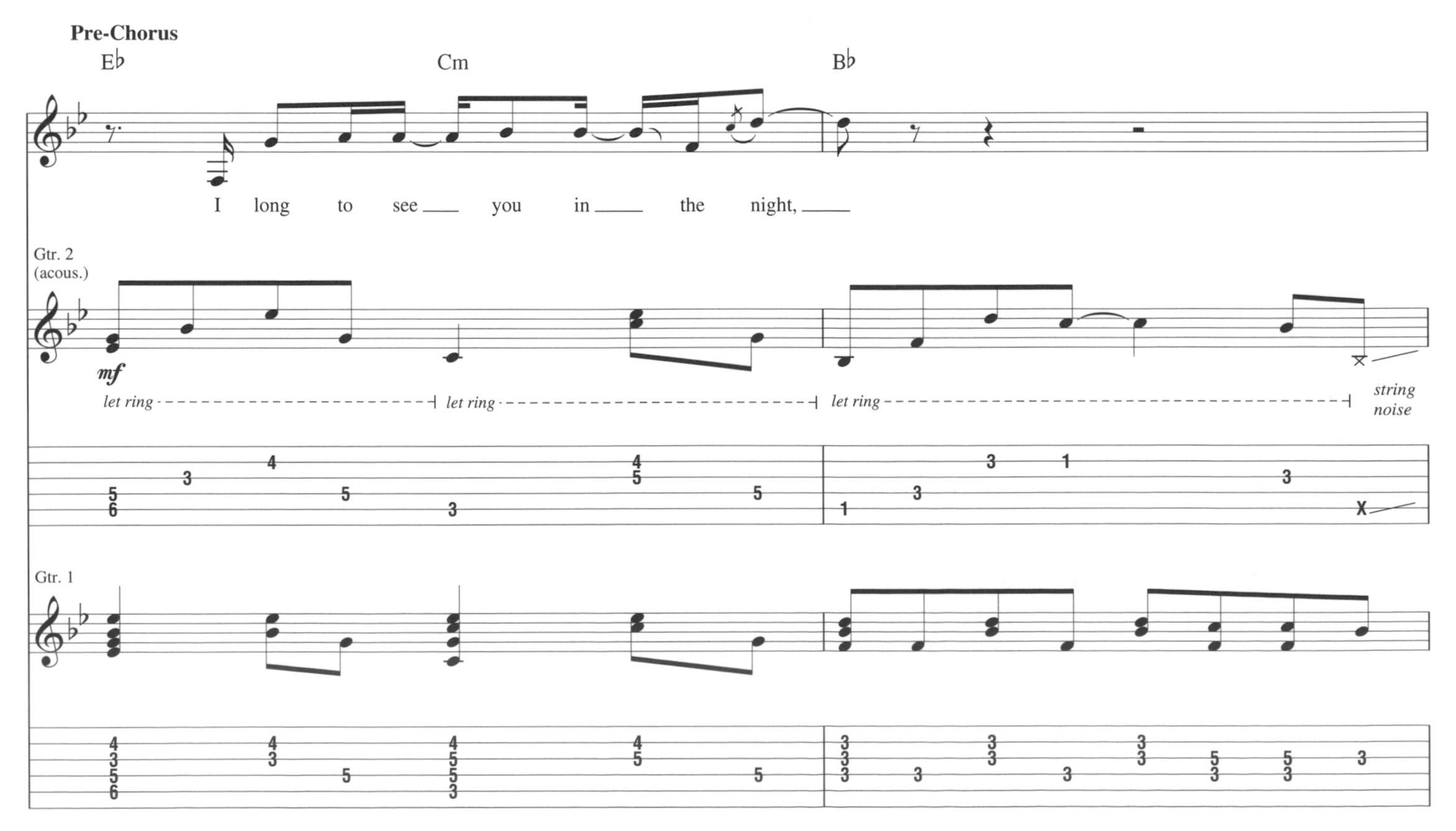
Pre-Chorus
E♭
Cm
B♭
I long to see you in the night,
Gtr. 2
(acous.)
mf
let ring
string noise
Gtr. 1

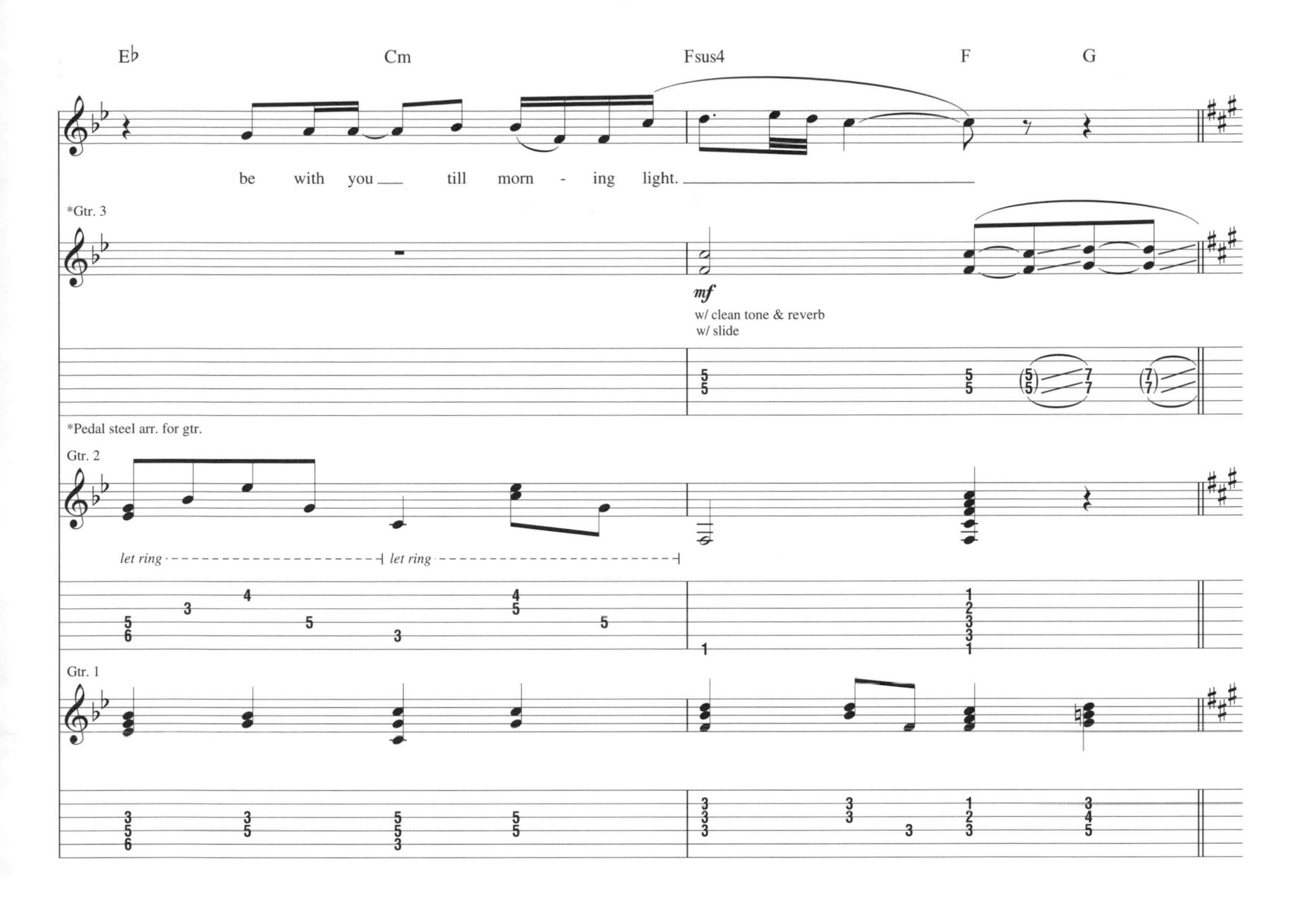
E♭
Cm
Fsus4
F
G
be with you till morn - ing light.
*Gtr. 3
mf
w/ clean tone & reverb
w/ slide
*Pedal steel arr. for gtr.
Gtr. 2
let ring
let ring
Gtr. 1

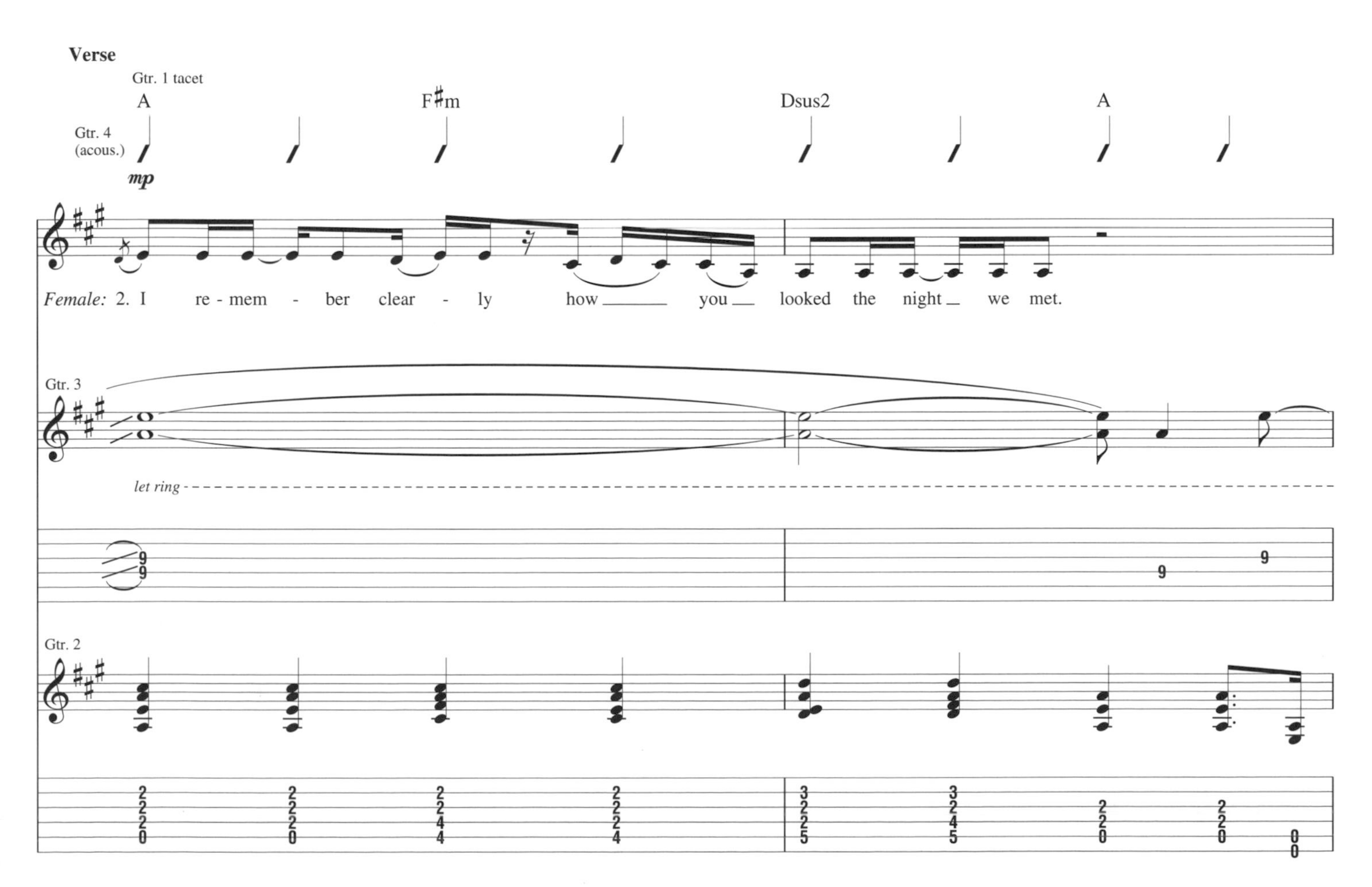
Verse
Gtr. 1 tacet
A
F♯m
Dsus2
A
Gtr. 4
(acous.)
mp
Female: 2. I re - mem - ber clear - ly how you looked the night we met.
Gtr. 3
let ring
Gtr. 2

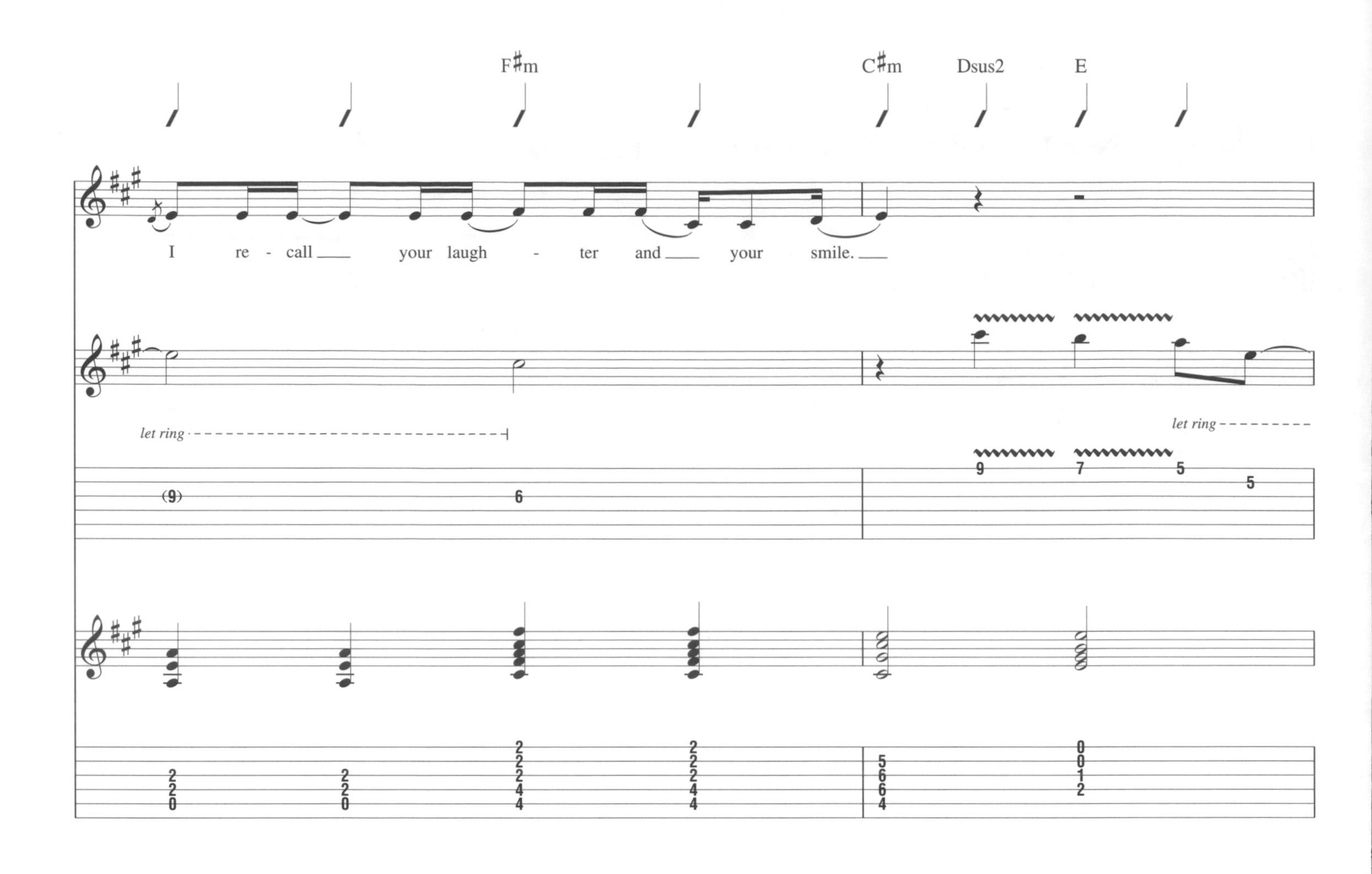
F♯m
C♯m
Dsus2
E
I re - call your laugh - ter and your smile.
let ring
let ring

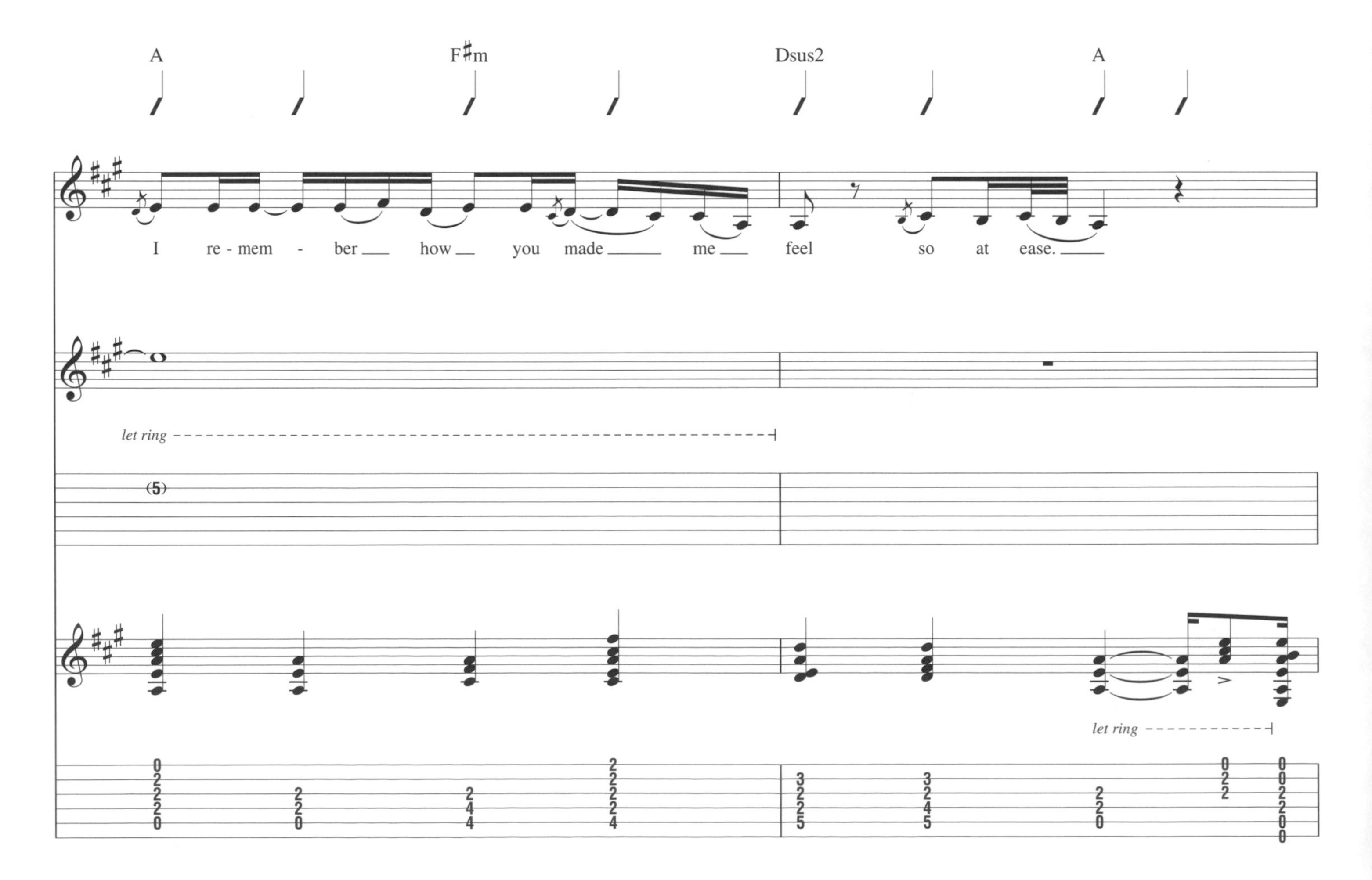
A
F♯m
Dsus2
A
I re - mem - ber how you made me feel so at ease.
let ring
let ring

F#m
C#m
Dsus2
I re - mem - ber all ___ your grace, your style.
let ring
Pre-Chorus
D
Bm
A
And now you're all ___ I long ___ to see. ______
Gtr. 3
let ring
Gtr. 5 (elec.)
mp
w/ clean tone & amp tremolo
let ring
let ring
Gtr. 2
let ring

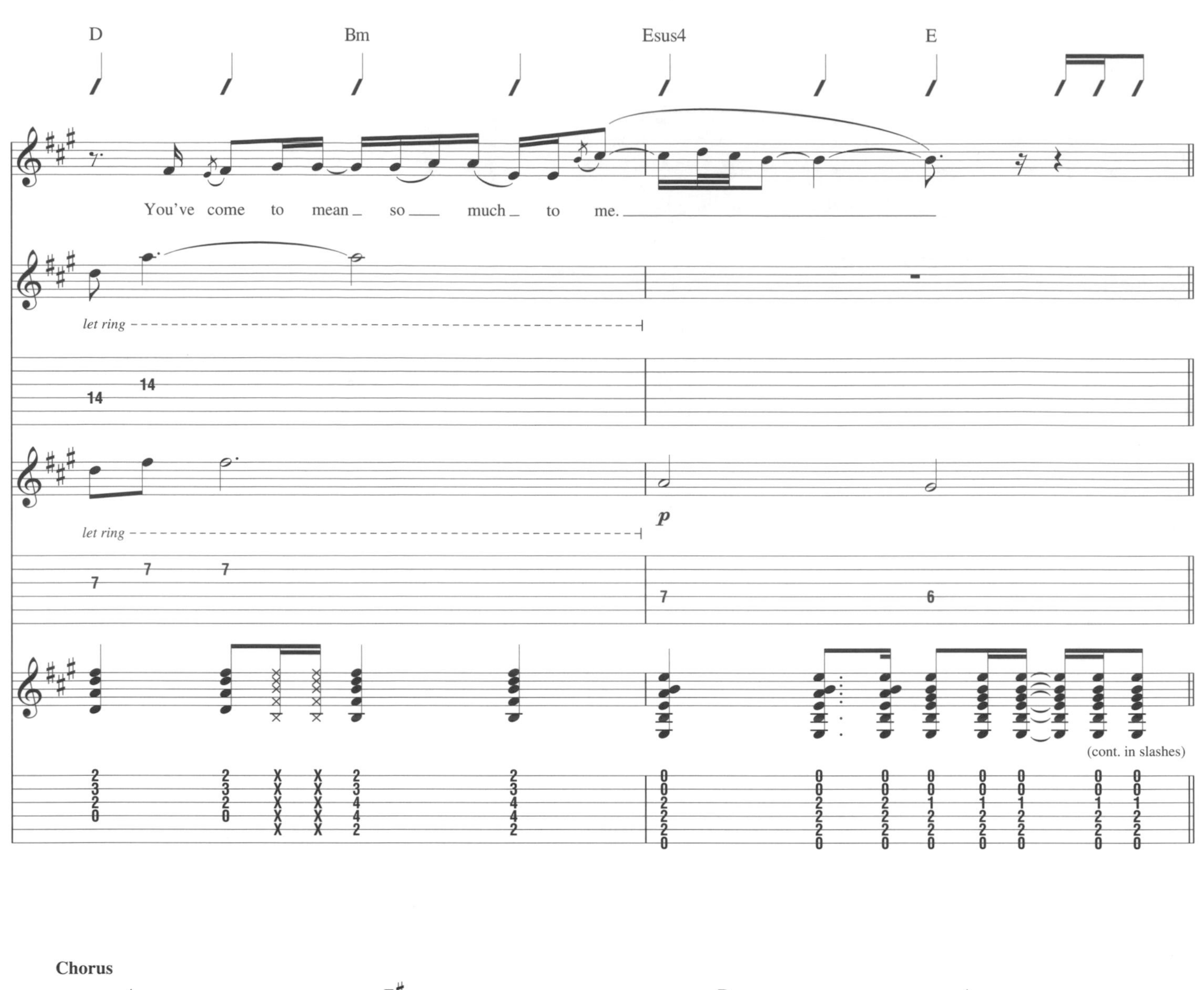

*Composite arrangement
**Male is the upper voice on the staff throughout.

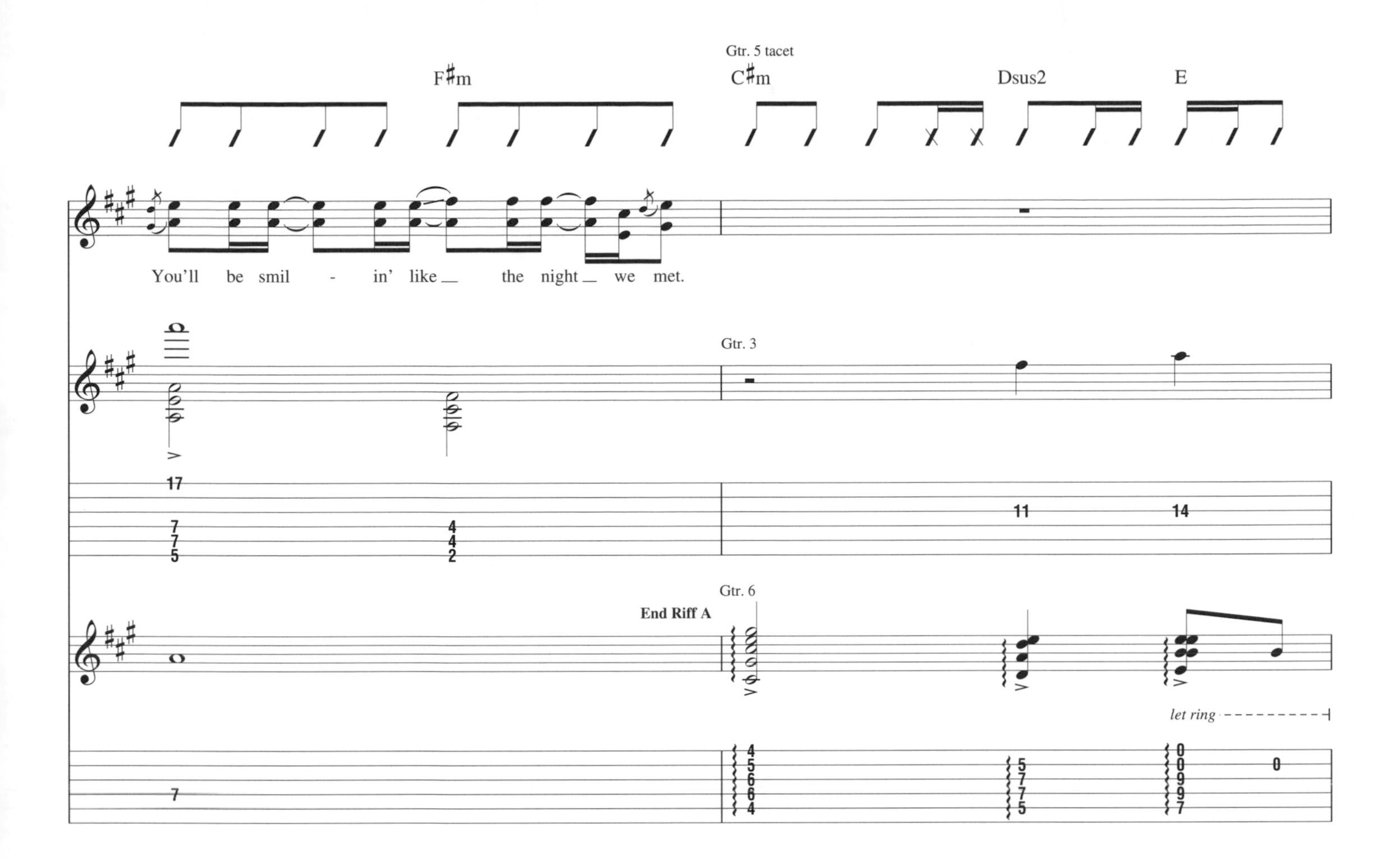
Gtr. 5 tacet
F♯m
C♯m
Dsus2
E
You'll be smil - in' like the night we met.
Gtr. 3
17
7 7 5
4 4 2
11
14
Gtr. 6
End Riff A
let ring
4 5 6 6 4
5 7 7 5
0 0 9 9 7
0
7

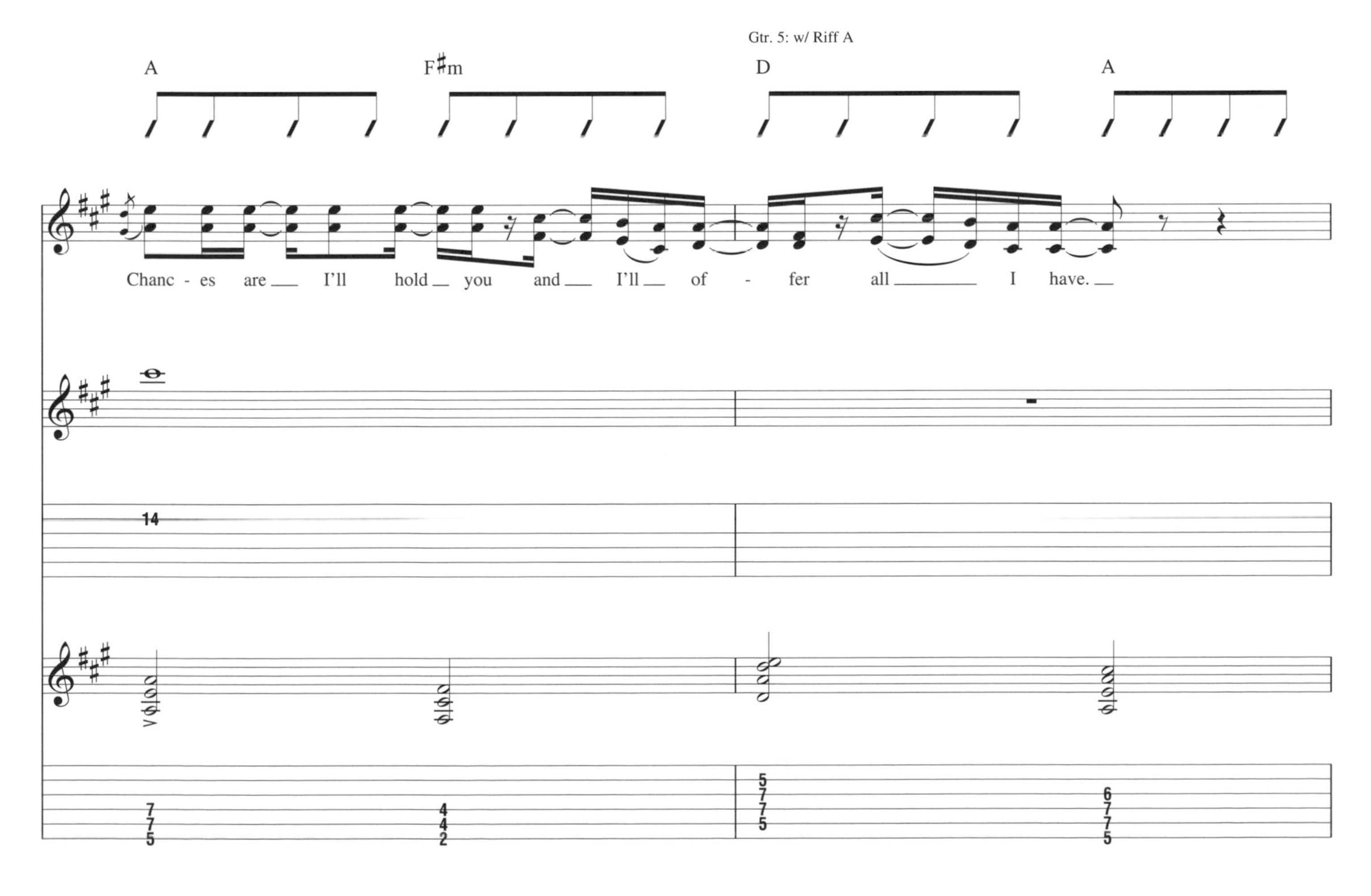
Gtr. 5: w/ Riff A
A
F♯m
D
A
Chanc - es are I'll hold you and I'll of - fer all I have.
14
7 7 5
4 4 2
5 7 7 5
6 7 7 5

D
C♯m
Bm
A
E
You're the on - ly one I can't for - get.
A
Male: Ba - by, you're the best I've ev - er met.
steady gliss.
let ring
Bridge
Gtr. 6 tacet
C♯7
F♯m
Male & Female: And I'll be dream - in' of the fu - ture,
Gtr. 3

C♯7
F♯m
and hop - in' you'll be by ___ my ___ side. ___
let ring

Bm
A
D
A
Male: And in the morn - ing I'll ___ be long - ing
Male & Female: for ___ the ___

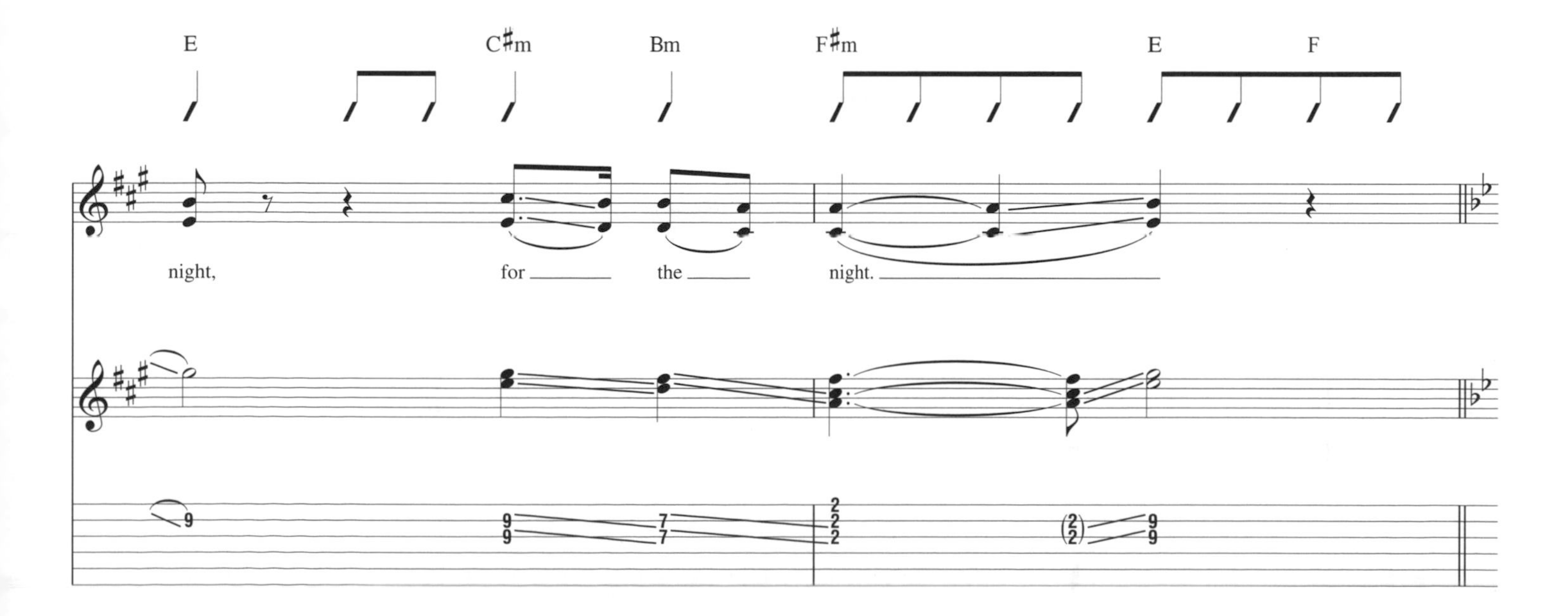
E
C♯m
Bm
F♯m
E
F
night,
for ___ the ___ night. ___

Chorus
B♭
Gm
E♭
B♭
Gtrs. 2 & 4
Chanc - es are I'll see you some - where in my dreams to - night.
Gtr. 3
Gtr. 6
Gm
Dm
E♭
F VIII
You'll be smil - in' like the night we met.
Female: Oh.

B♭
Gm
E♭
B♭
Male & Female:
Chanc - es are ___ I'll hold ___ you and ___ I'll ___ of - fer all ___ I have. ___
Gtr. 3
Gtr. 5
divisi
E♭
Dm
Cm
B♭ 1
Gtr. 5 tacet
F
You're the on - ly one ___ I can't ___ for - get.
Gtr. 3

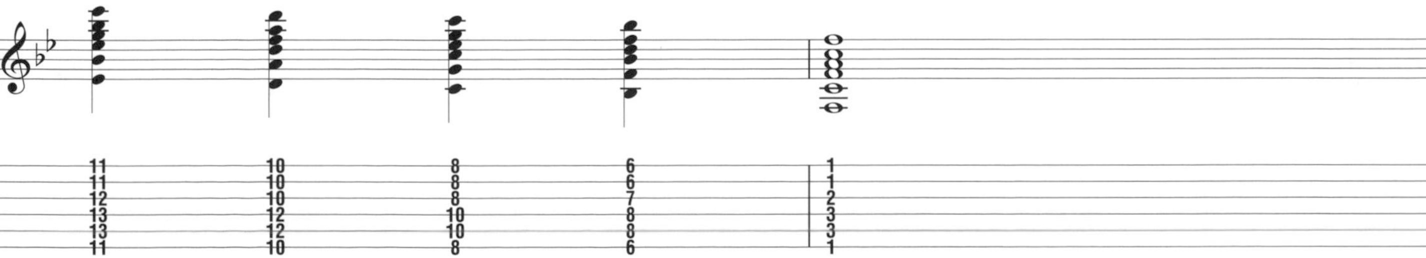

Outro
E♭5/B♭
B♭
Ba - by, you're the best I've ev - er met.
E♭
F VIII
B♭
Male: Oo, hoo.
Gtr. 5
let ring
Gtr. 3
divisi
Gtr. 6
Gtrs. 5 & 6 tacet
poco rit.
Female: Oo, hoo.

Rock and Roll Never Forgets

Words and Music by Bob Seger

E
F♯
lot less bold - er than you used to be.
down to the con - cert or the lo - cal bar.
So you
Check the
P.M.
F♯m
E
used to shake 'em down, but now you stop and think a - bout your
lo - cal news - pa - pers, chanc - es are you won't have to go
P.M.

dig - ni - ty.
too far.
So, now
Yeah, the
End Rhy. Fig. 2A
(cont. in slashes)
End Rhy. Fig. 2
P.M.
P.M.
Pre-Chorus
A
E
A
Rhy. Fig. 3
Gtr. 3
sweet six - teen's turned thir - ty - one, you
raf - ters will be ring - ing 'cause the beat's so strong, the
sweet six - teen's turned thir - ty - one,
Gtr. 1
P.M.
Gtr. 2

E
A
get to feel - in' wear - y when the work day's done. Well, all
crowd will be sway - ing and sing - ing a - long. And all
feel a lit - tle ti - red, feel - ing un - der the gun. Well, all
P.M.
E
End Rhy. Fig. 3
you got to do is get up and in - to your kicks
you got to do is get in, in - to the mix
of Chuck's chil - dren are out there, play - ing his licks.
P.M.

B
Rhy. Fig. 4
End Rhy. Fig. 4
if you're in a fix.
if you need a fix.
Get in - to your kicks,
F♯
(cont. in notation)

Come
You can come
then come

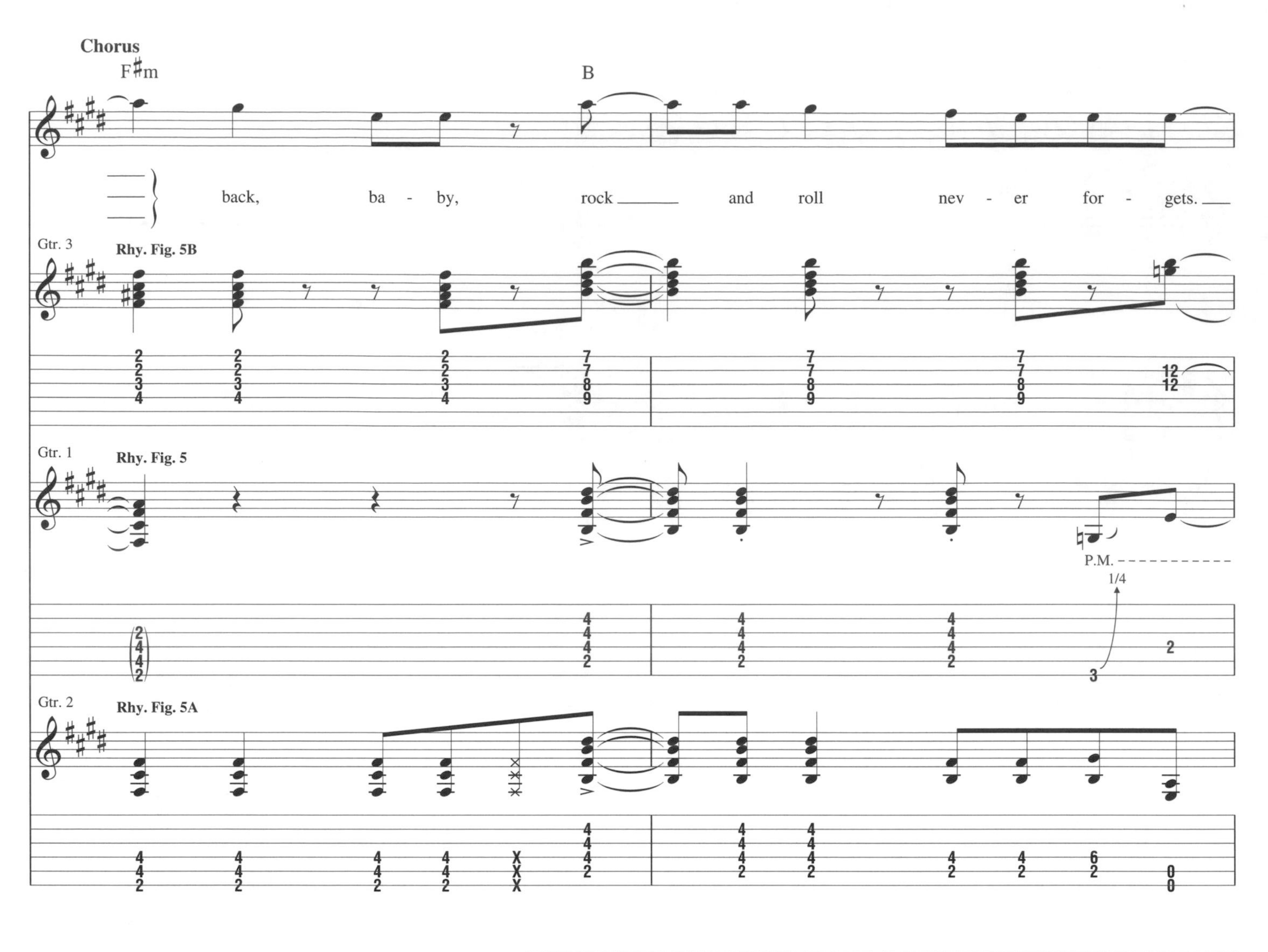
Chorus
F♯m
B
back, ba - by, rock and roll nev - er for - gets.
Gtr. 3
Rhy. Fig. 5B
Gtr. 1
Rhy. Fig. 5
P.M.
1/4
Gtr. 2
Rhy. Fig. 5A

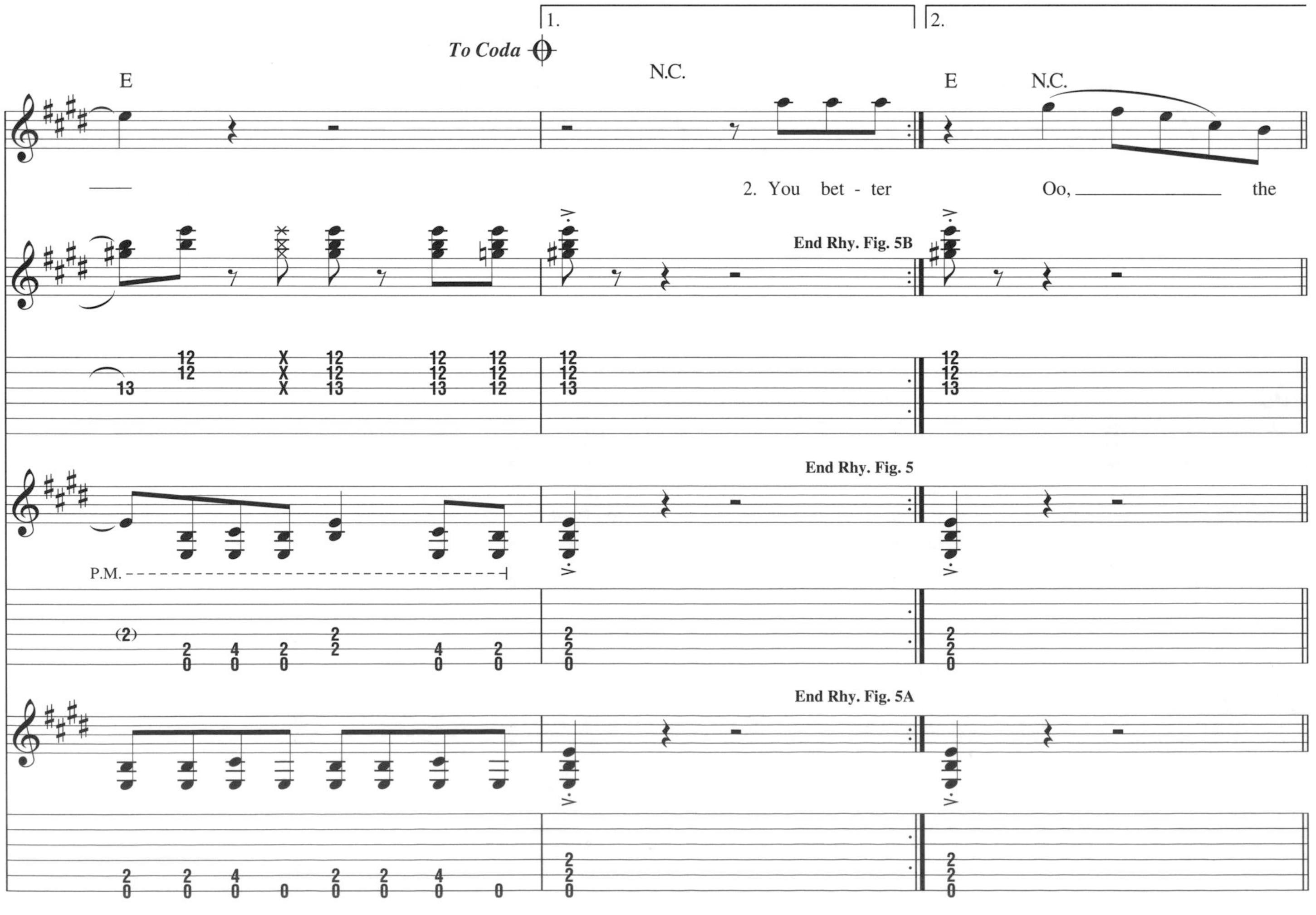
1.
2.
To Coda
E
N.C.
E
N.C.
2. You bet - ter
Oo, the
End Rhy. Fig. 5B
End Rhy. Fig. 5
P.M.
End Rhy. Fig. 5A

Bridge
Gtr. 3: w/ Rhy. Fig. 3
A E A E
band's still play - ing it loud and lean. __ Lis - ten to the gui - tar play - er
Gtr. 1
Gtr. 2
A E
mak - ing it scream. __ All ___ you got to do is just make that scene __ to - night. __
Gtr. 3: w/ Rhy. Fig. 4 (2 times)
B
__ Hey, _ to - night! __ Woo!

Guitar Solo

Gtrs. 1 & 3: w/ Rhy. Figs. 2 & 2A

F♯ F♯m E F♯

Gtr. 2

hold bend

let ring

let ring

D.S. al Coda

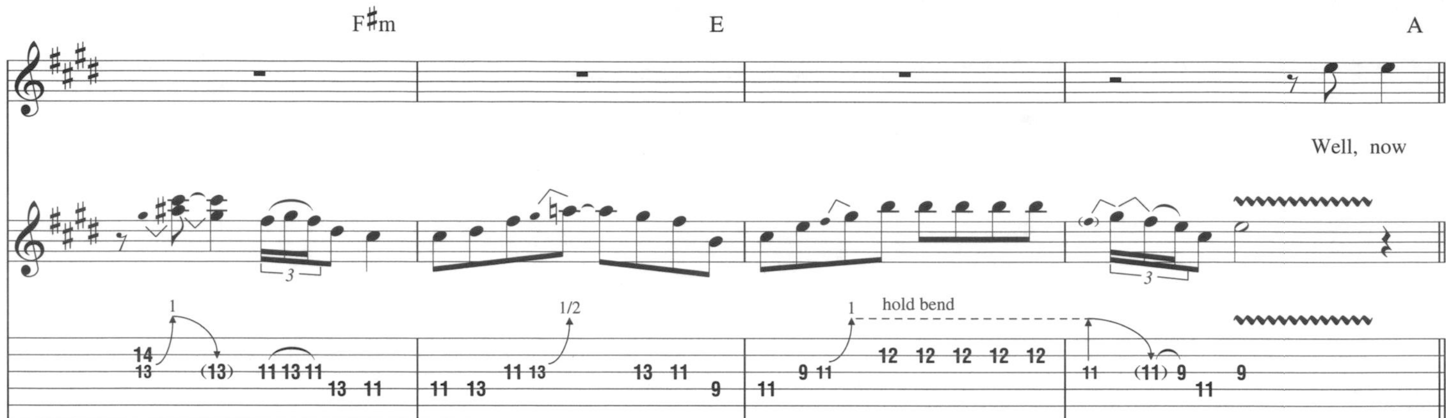

Coda

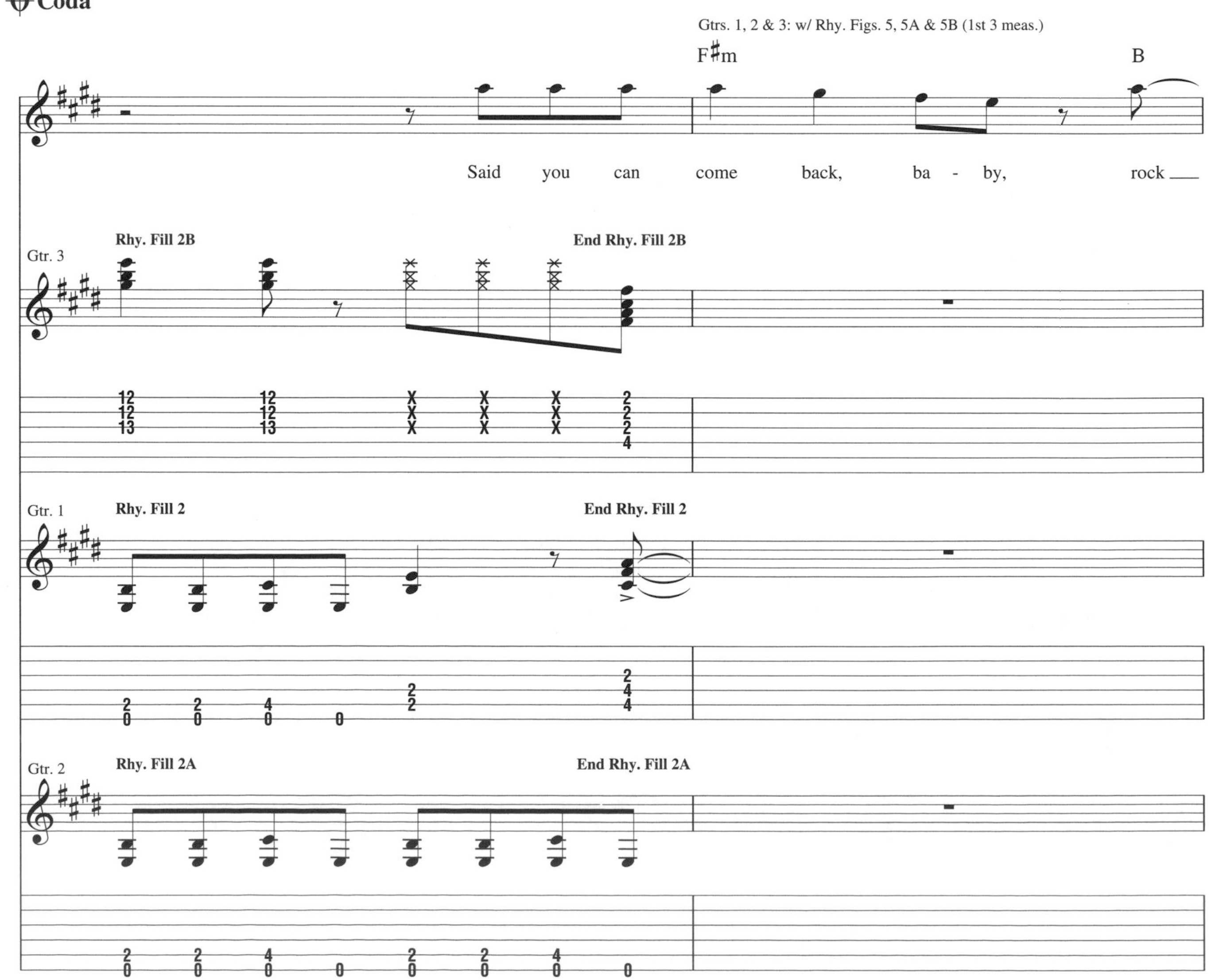

Gtrs. 1, 2 & 3: w/ Rhy. Fills 2, 2A & 2B
Gtrs. 1, 2 & 3: w/ Rhy. Figs. 5, 5A & 5B
E
F♯m
B
'n roll nev - er for - gets.
Oh, come back, ba - by, rock
E
N.C.
'n roll nev - er for - gets.
Oo.
Interlude
Gtr. 1: w/ Riff A (2 times)
Gtr. 2: w/ Rhy. Fig. 1 (2 times)
Gtr. 3: w/ Rhy. Fill 1
E5
A5
E5
Oh, yeah.
Oh, yeah.
Gtr. 3: w/ Rhy. Fill 1
A5
E5
Ha.
Uh, huh.
Uh, huh,
nev - er for - gets.
E5
A5
E5
Rhy. Fig. 6B
End Rhy. Fig. 6B
Gtr. 3
Oh, no.
Oh, no.
Oh,
nev - er for - gets.
Gtr. 1
Rhy. Fig. 6
End Rhy. Fig. 6
Gtr. 2
Rhy. Fig. 6A
End Rhy. Fig. 6A

Gtrs. 1, 2 & 3: w/ Rhy. Figs. 6, 6A & 6B

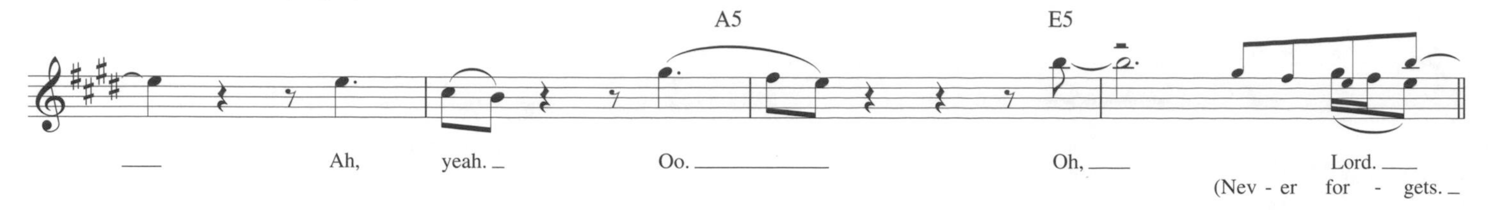

Outro-Guitar Solo

Gtrs. 1 & 3: w/ Rhy. Figs. 6 & 6B (till fade)

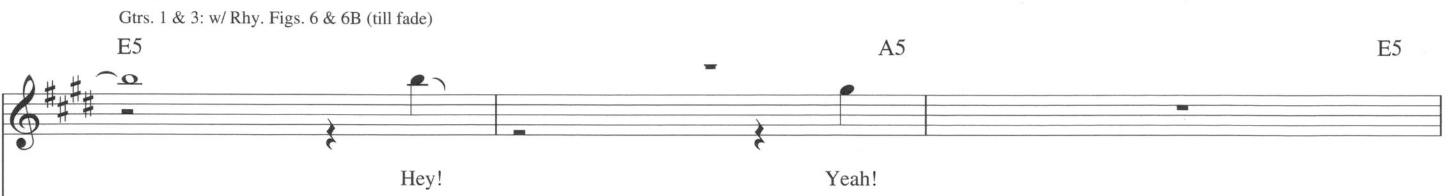

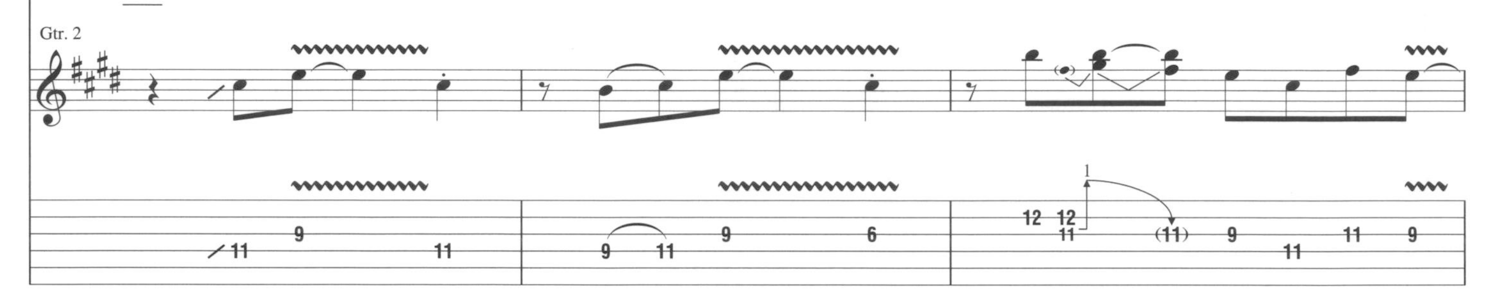

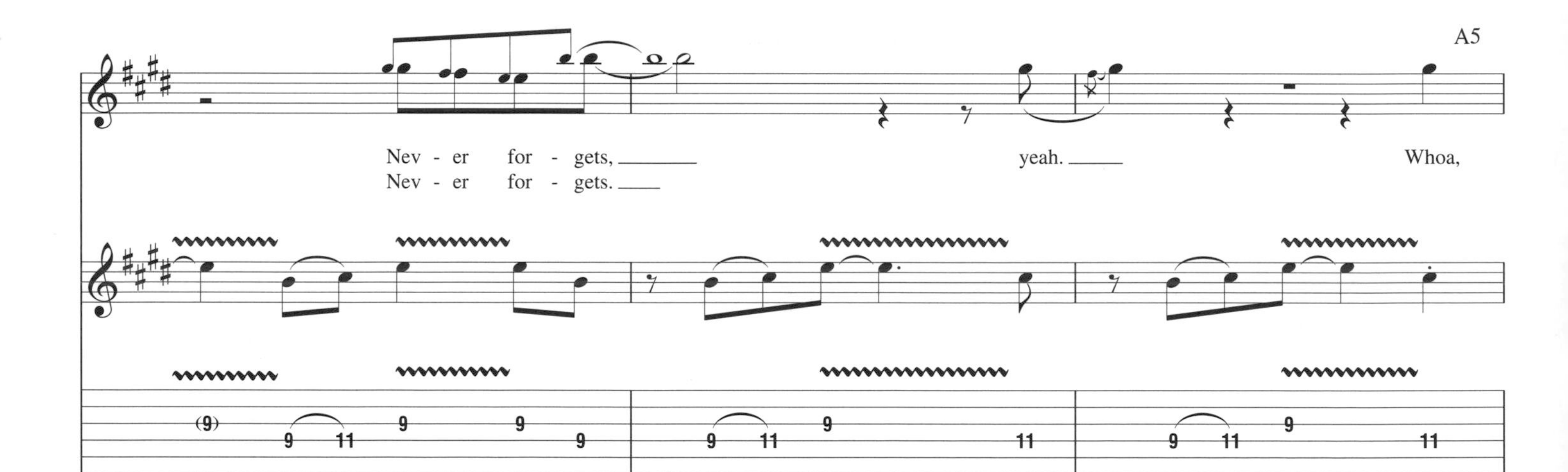

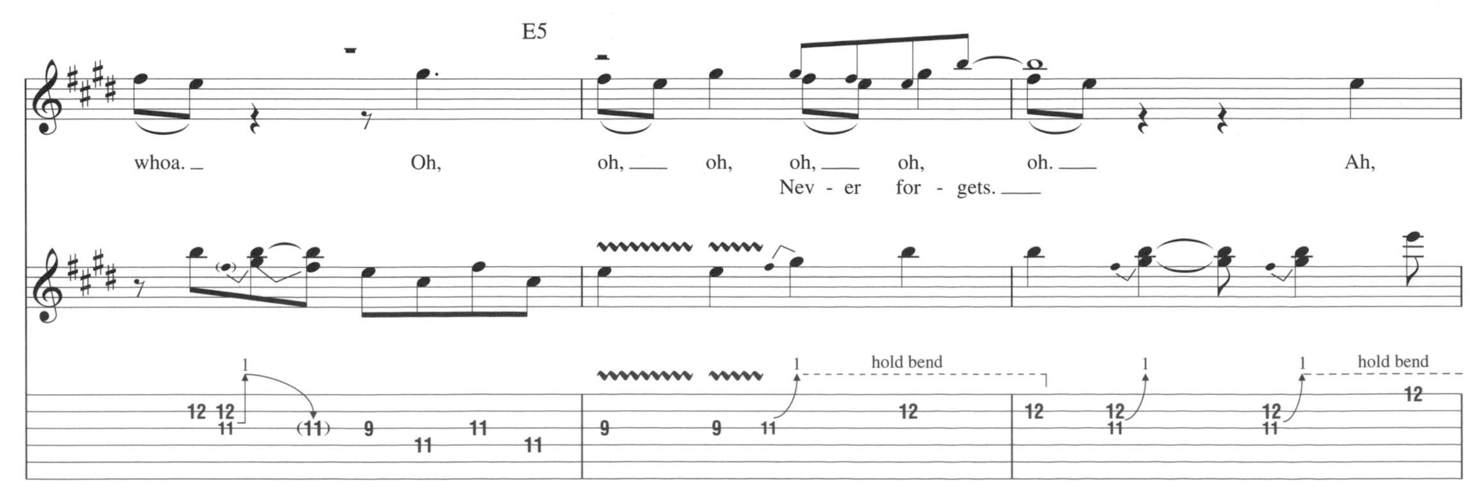

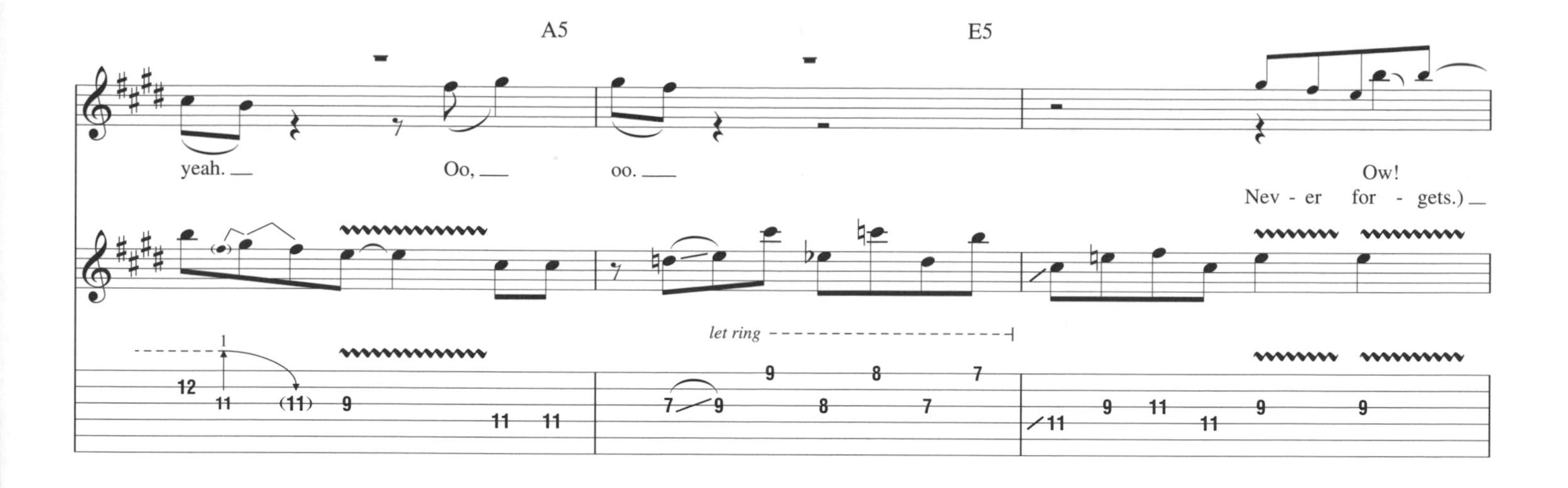
A5
E5
yeah.
Oo,
oo.
Ow!
Nev - er for - gets.)
let ring
hold bend

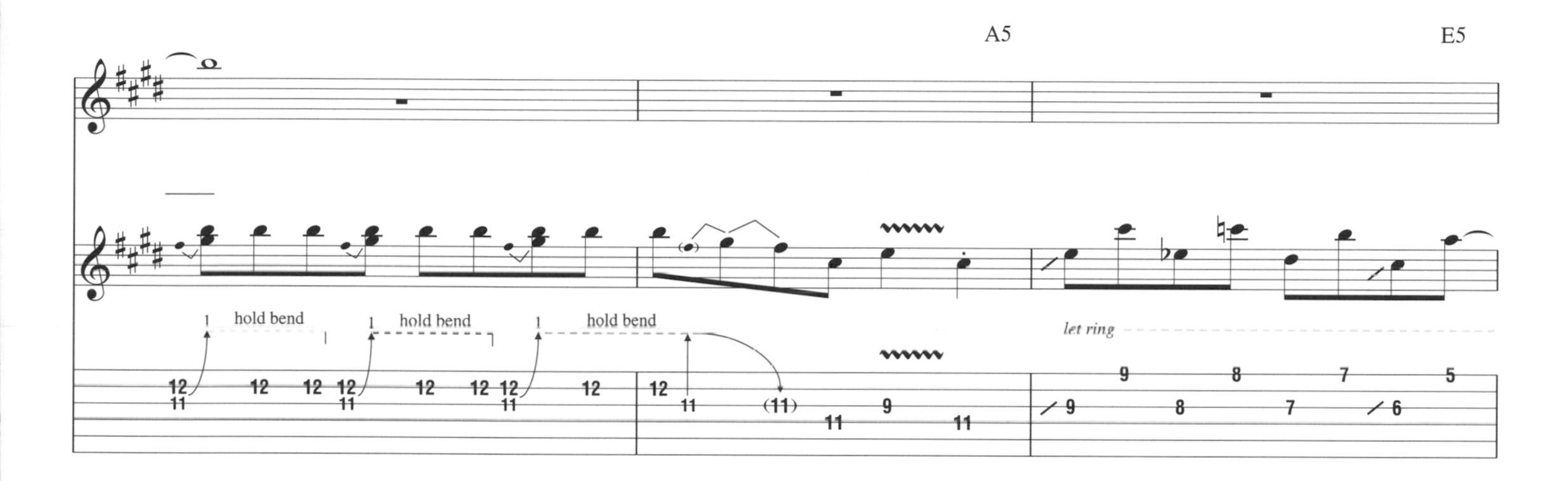
A5
E5
hold bend
hold bend
hold bend
let ring

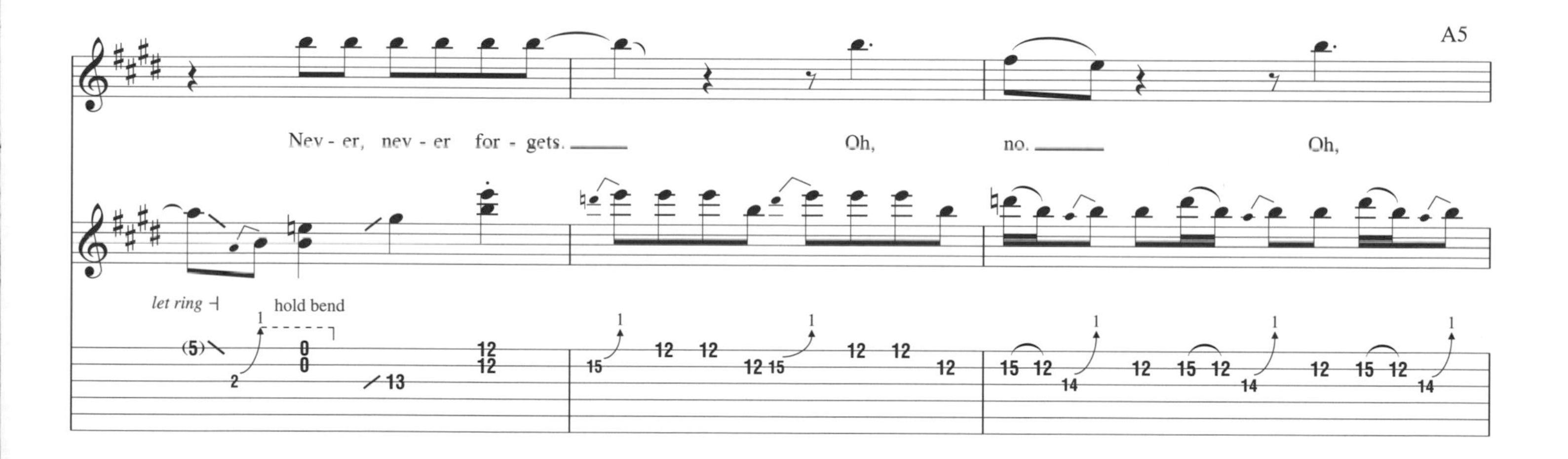
A5
Nev - er, nev - er for - gets.
Oh,
no.
Oh,
let ring
hold bend

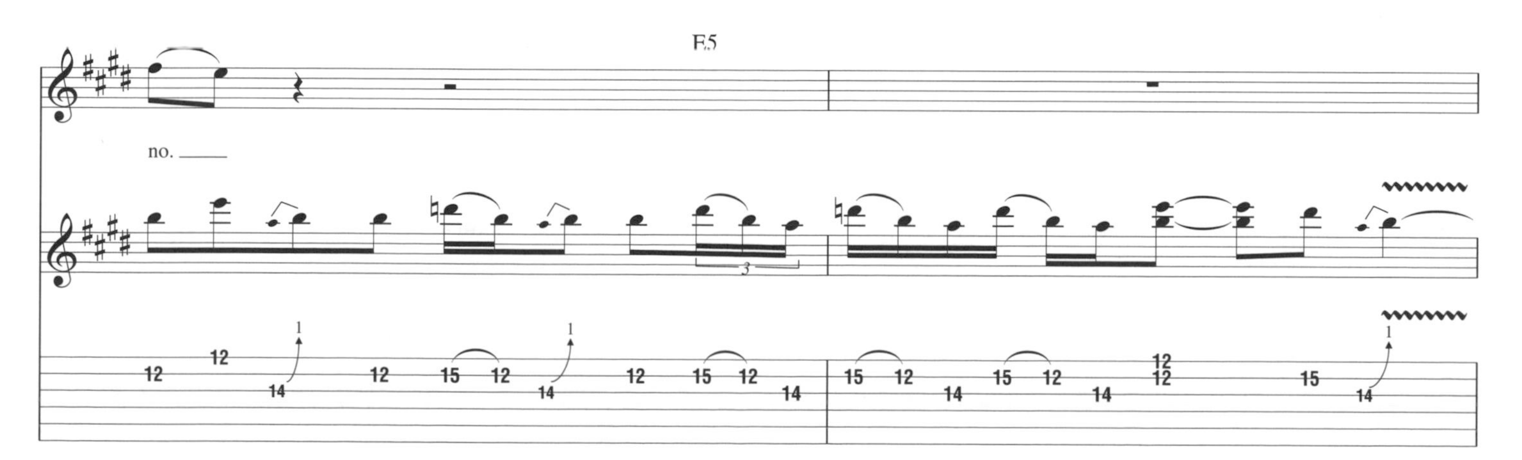
E5
no.

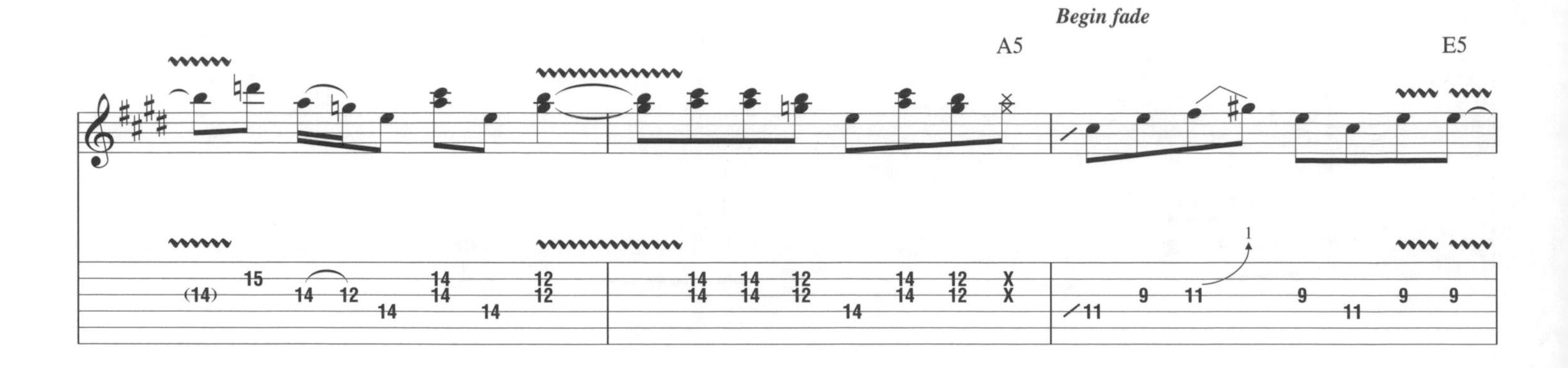
Begin fade
A5
E5

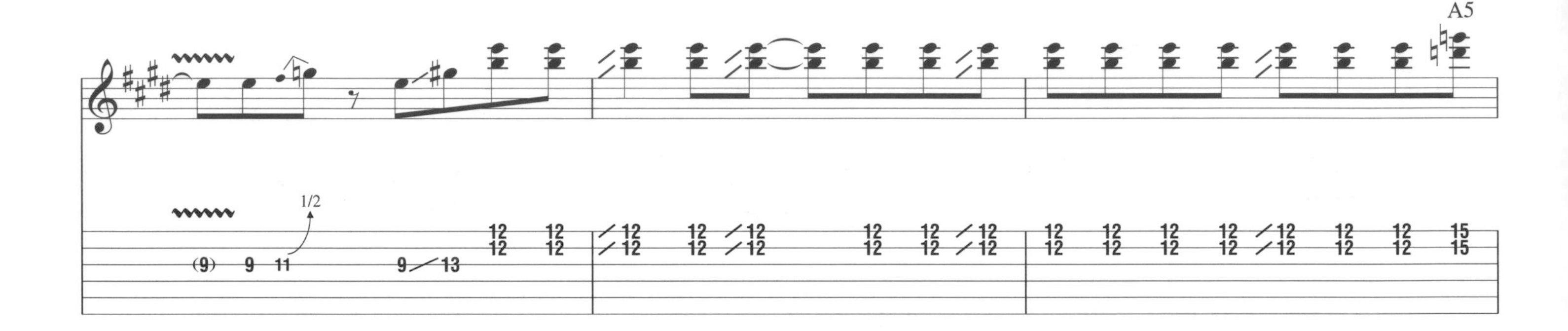
A5

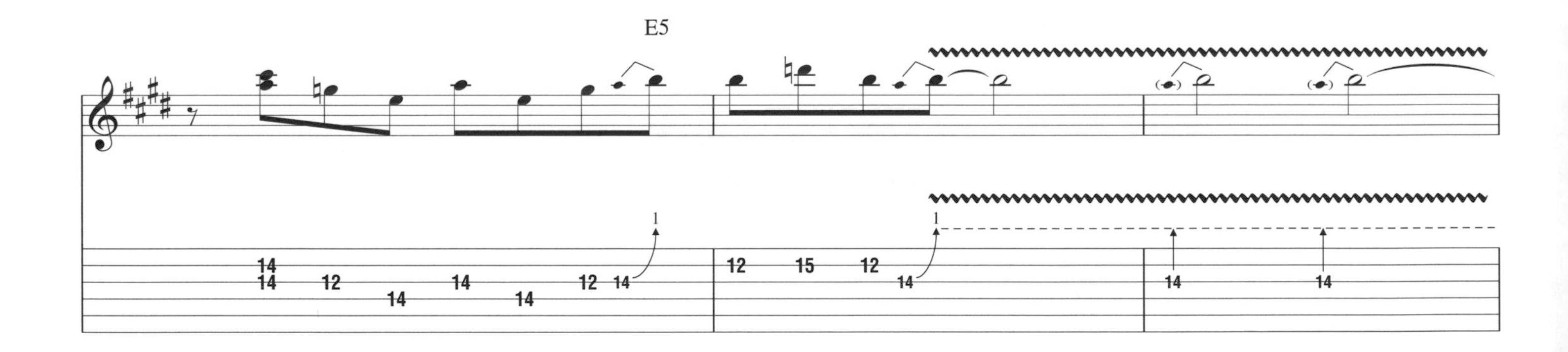
E5

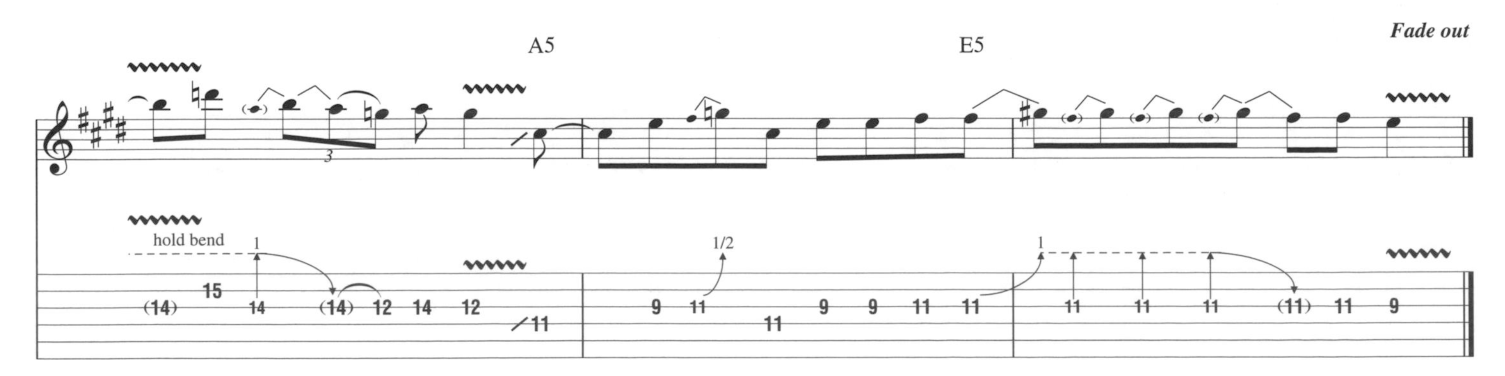
A5
E5
Fade out
hold bend

Satisfied

Words and Music by Bob Seger

(E) 231 (A/E) 3111 (A) 111 (D/A) 312 (B5) 134 (A5) 11

Capo II

Intro
Moderately ♩ = 85 (♫ = ♩♪ triplet)

N.C. (Drums) 2

Verse

F♯7 *(E7) B (A) F♯7 (E7) B (A) F♯7 (E7)

1. I need some wis - dom, __ I need some truth.

**Gtrs. 1 & 2 (acous.)

mf

P.M.

*Symbols in parentheses represent chord names respective to capoed guitar. Symbols above reflect actual sounding chords. Capoed fret is "0" in tab. Chord symbols reflect basic harmony.

**Composite arrangement

B (A) F♯7 (E7) B7 (A7) E (D) B (A)

I need some beau - ty, __ I need some proof. And in the mean - time, __

sim.

P.M.

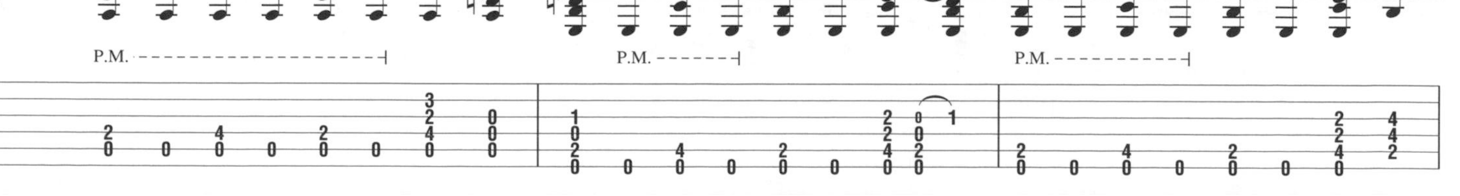

C♯5 B
(B5) (A)
E
(D)
F♯7
(E7)
B
(A)
F♯7
(E7)
If I had you, babe, I'd be sat - is - fied.
P.M.
Verse
(E)
Rhy. Fig. 1
Gtr. 3 (elec.)
mf
w/ dist. & amp tremolo
(A/E) (E)
(A/E)
2. Went to the o - cean, stood in the surf.
Gtr. 1
Gtr. 2
Gtrs. 1 & 2
(E)
(A/E) (E)
(A)
(D/A) (A)
I felt the wa - ter, I felt the earth. I heard the an - gels,

(E)
(A/E) (E)
they could-n't be de - nied.
P.M.
(B5)
(A5)
(E)
(A/E) (E)
If I had you, babe, I'd be sat - is - fied.
P.M.
Bridge
Gtr. 3 tacet
B
(A)
G♯5
(F♯5)
End Rhy. Fig. 1
Who's gon-na be-lieve me? I'm a bro-ken down dog.
P.M.

F#
(E)
But, I can still snarl with the best.
B
(A)
The train is leav - in', we can
P.M.
1/4
P.M.
G#5
(F#5)
catch it if we run.
We can
D5
(C5)
leave it all be-hind,
Bm7
(Am7)
this
C#5
(B5)
ut-ter emp-ti - ness.
P.M.

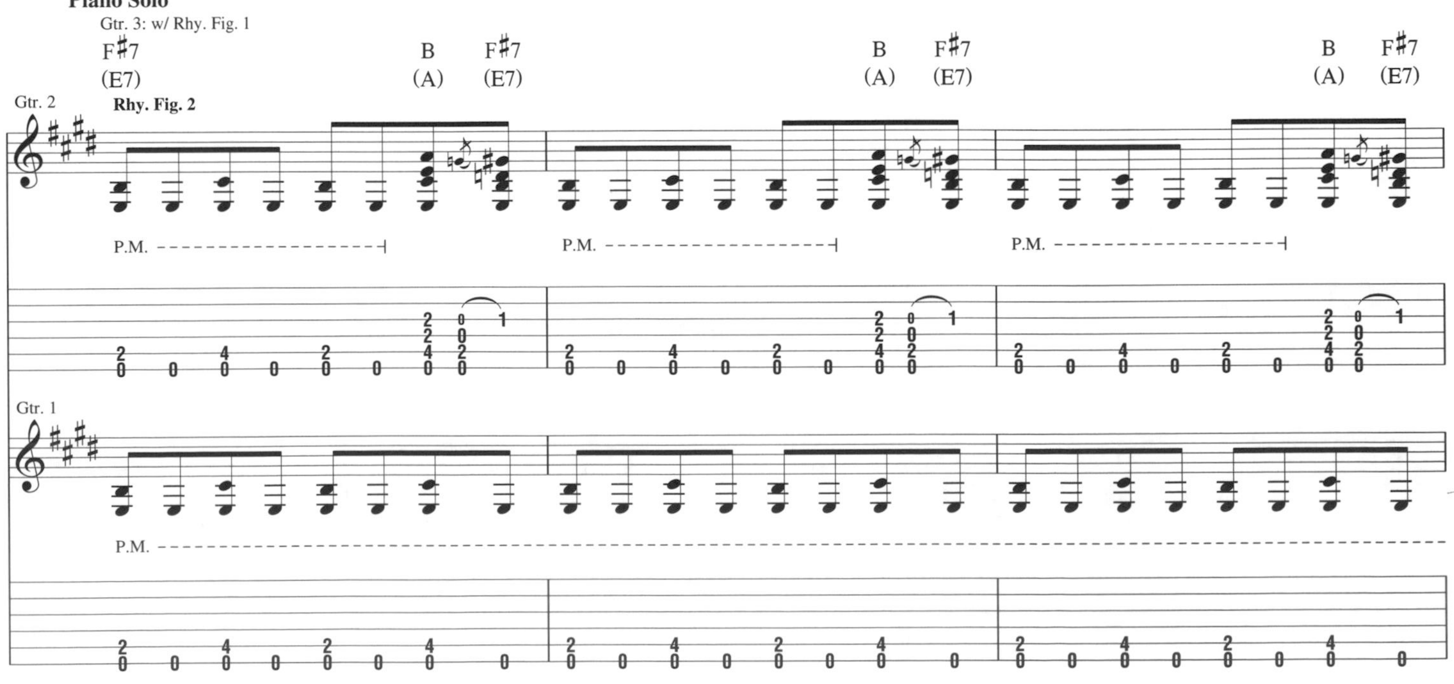
Piano Solo
Gtr. 3: w/ Rhy. Fig. 1
F#7
(E7)
B
(A)
F#7
(E7)
Gtr. 2
Rhy. Fig. 2
P.M.
Gtr. 1
P.M.

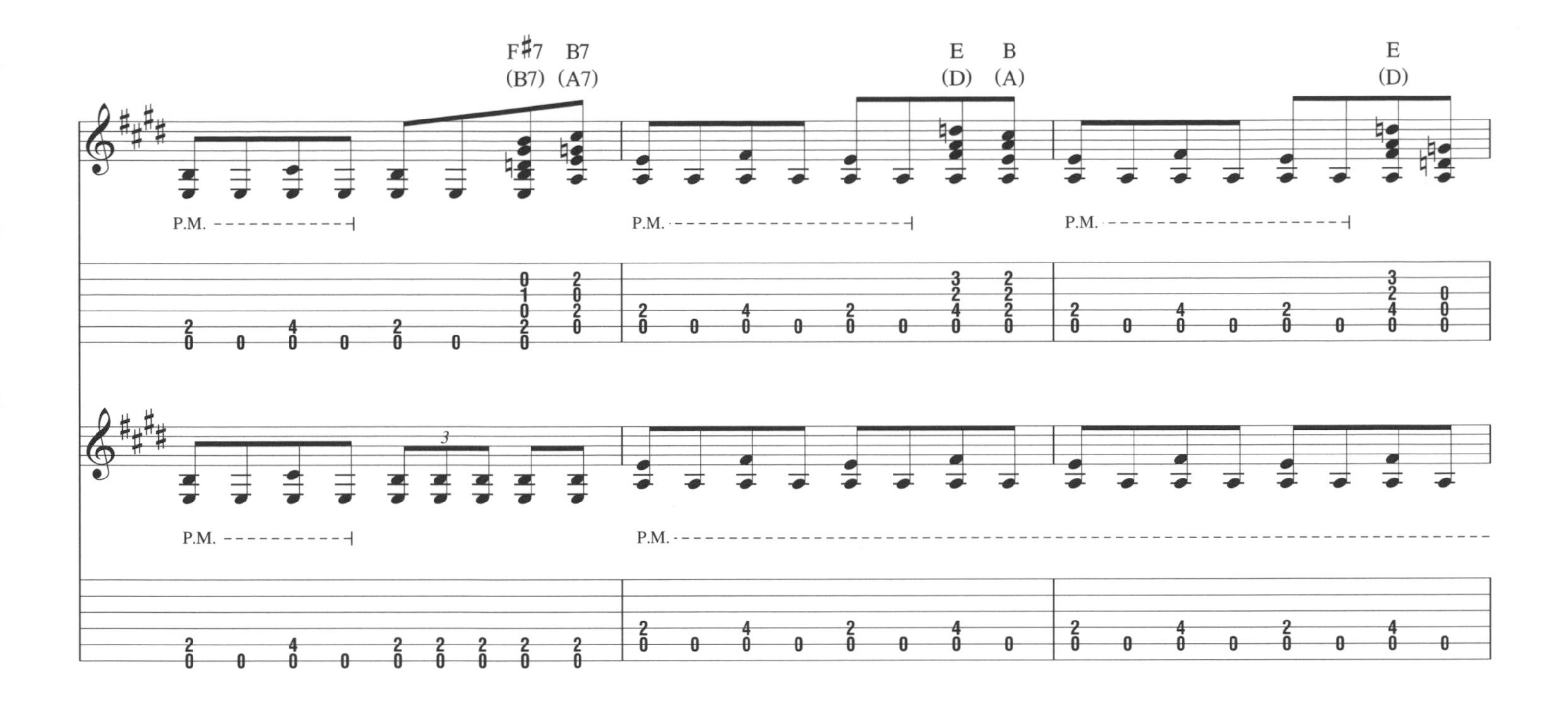
F♯7
(B7)
B7
(A7)
E
(D)
B
(A)
E
(D)
P.M.
P.M.
P.M.
P.M.
P.M.

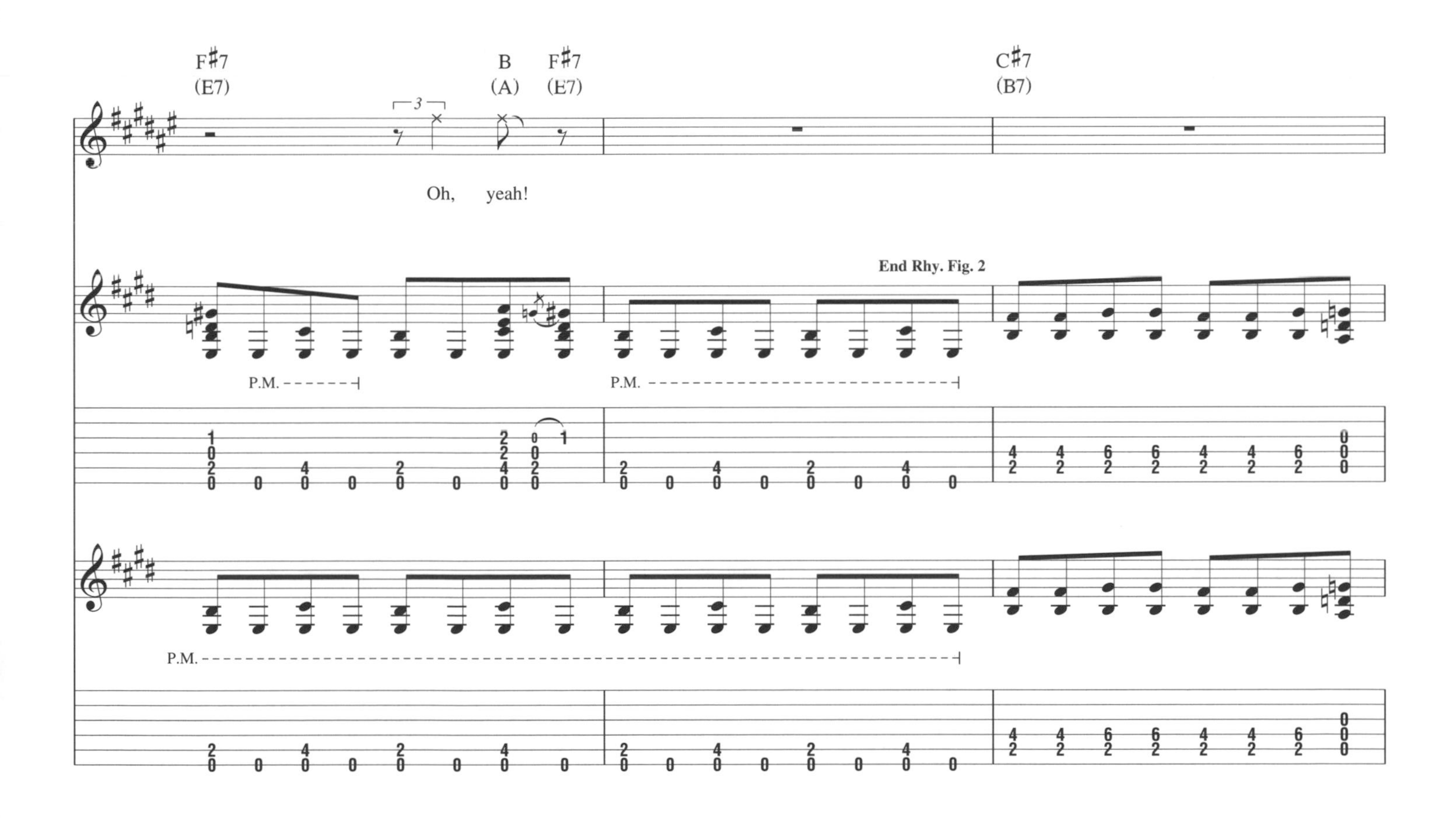
F♯7
(E7)
B
(A)
F♯7
(E7)
C♯7
(B7)
Oh, yeah!
End Rhy. Fig. 2
P.M.
P.M.
P.M.

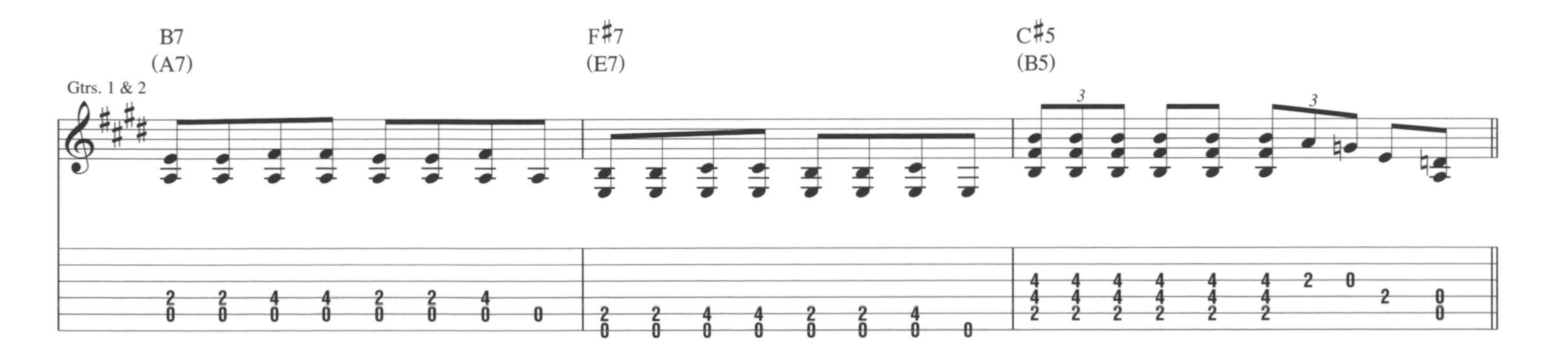
B7
(A7)
F♯7
(E7)
C♯5
(B5)
Gtrs. 1 & 2

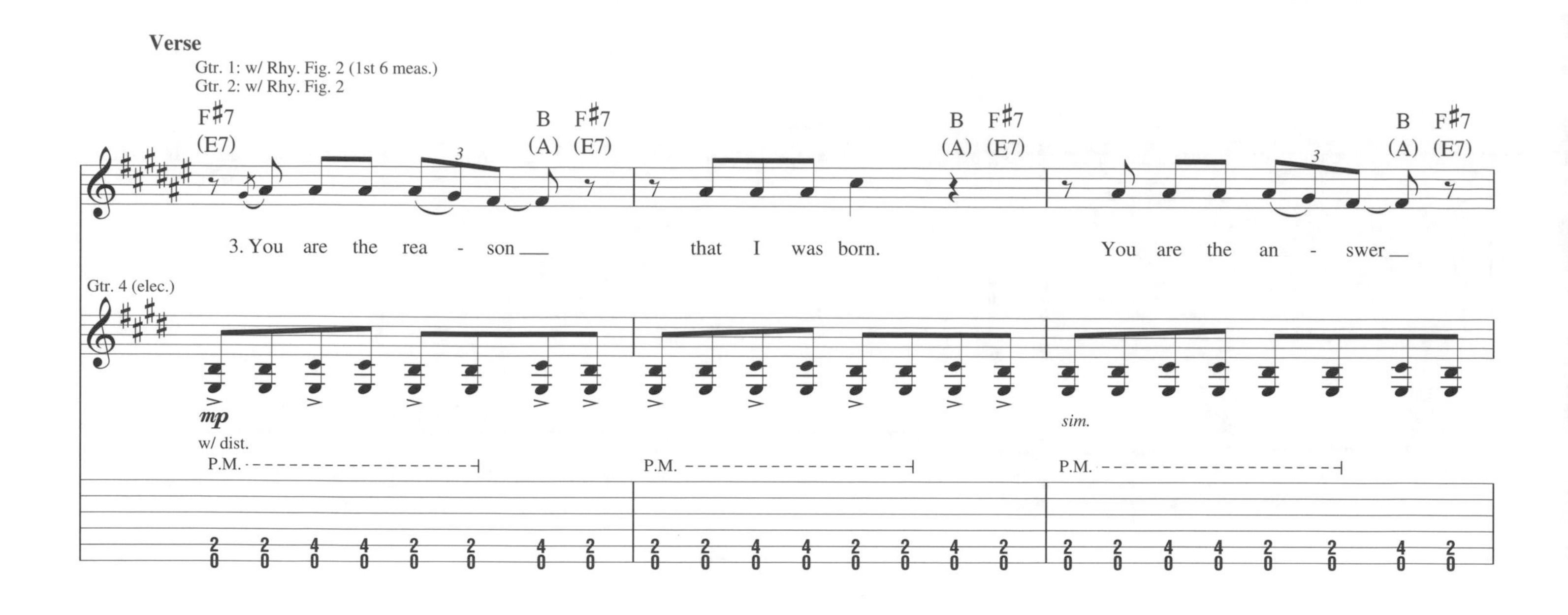
Verse
Gtr. 1: w/ Rhy. Fig. 2 (1st 6 meas.)
Gtr. 2: w/ Rhy. Fig. 2
F♯7 (E7)
B (A)
F♯7 (E7)
B (A)
F♯7 (E7)
B (A)
F♯7 (E7)
3. You are the rea - son
that I was born.
You are the an - swer
Gtr. 4 (elec.)
mp
w/ dist.
P.M.
sim.

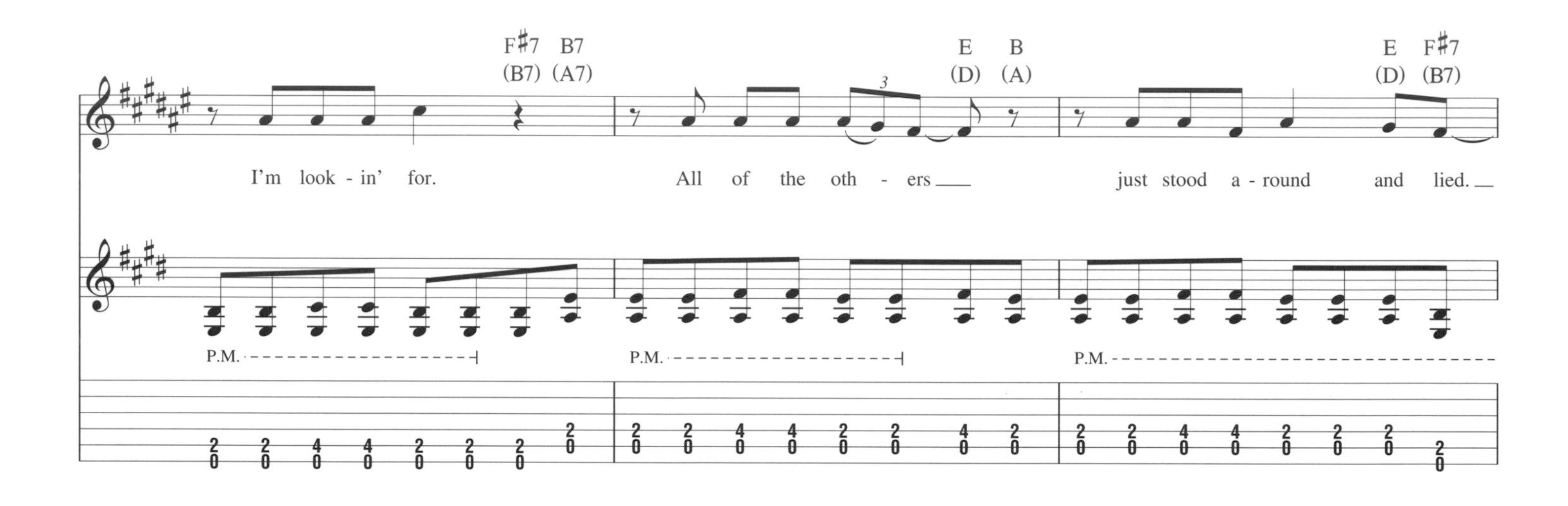
F♯7 (B7)
B7 (A7)
E (D)
B (A)
E (D)
F♯7 (B7)
I'm look - in' for.
All of the oth - ers
just stood a - round and lied.
P.M.

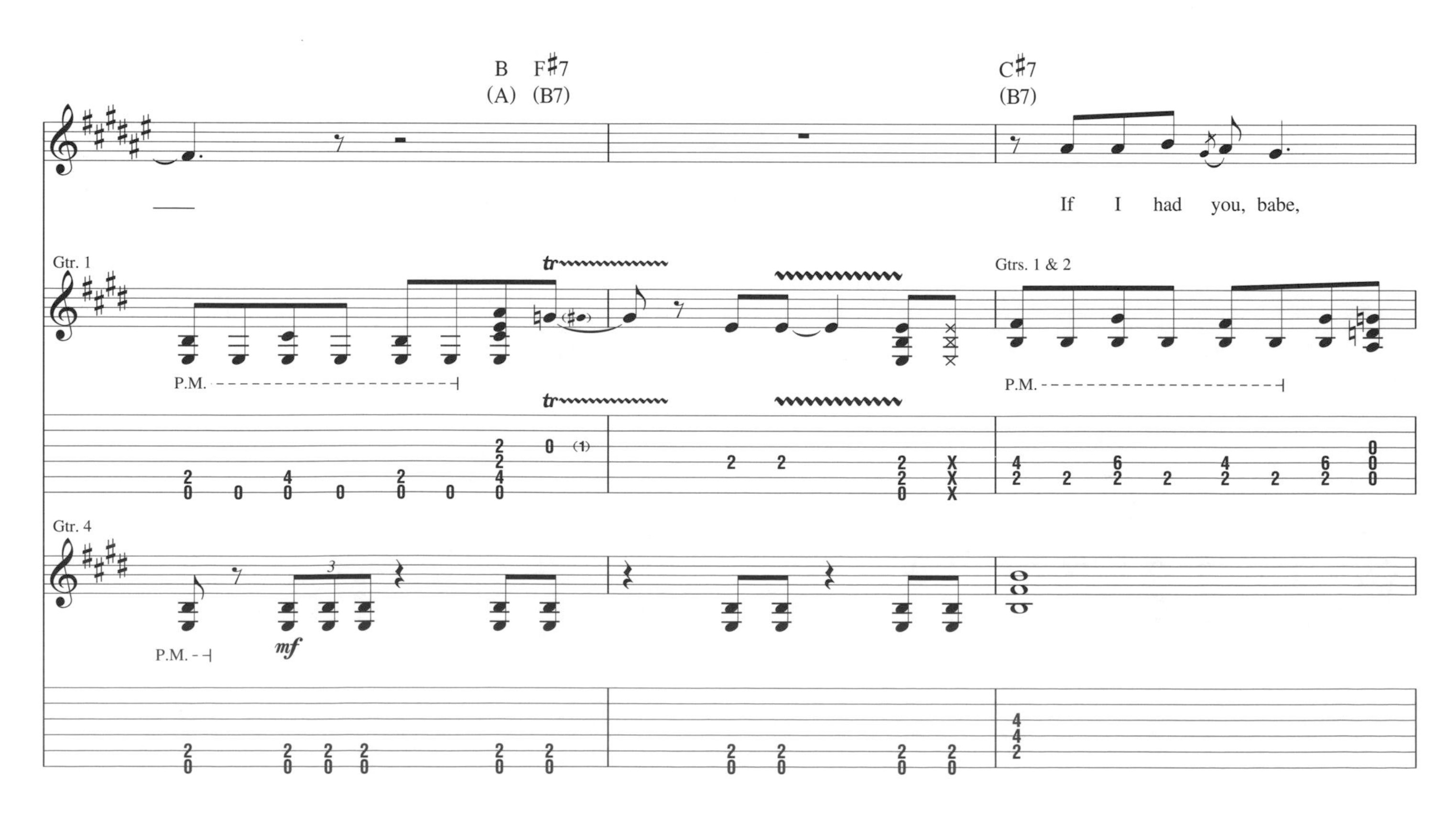
B (A)
F♯7 (B7)
C♯7 (B7)
If I had you, babe,
Gtr. 1
tr
P.M.
Gtrs. 1 & 2
Gtr. 4
mf

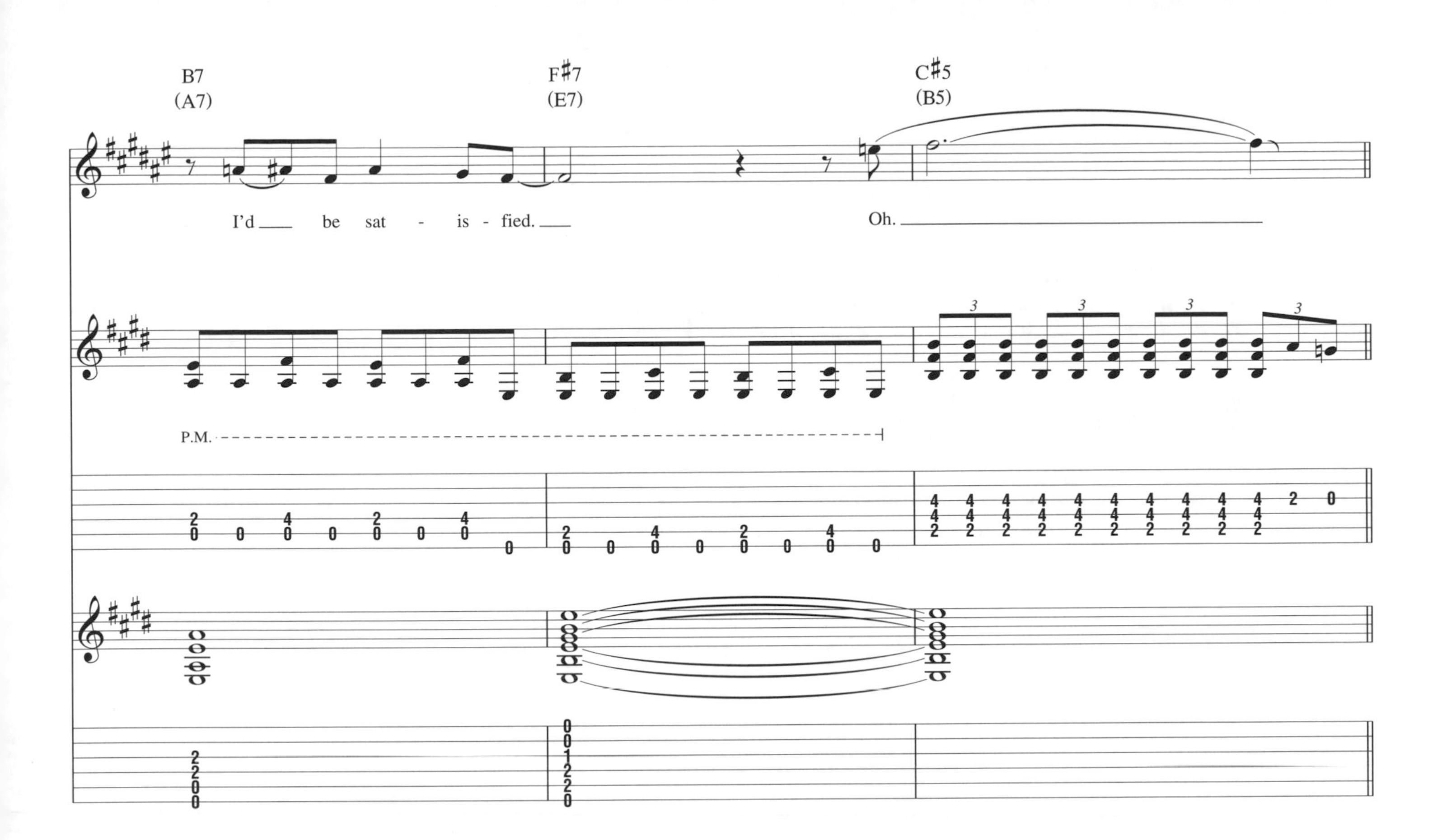

Outro-Piano Solo

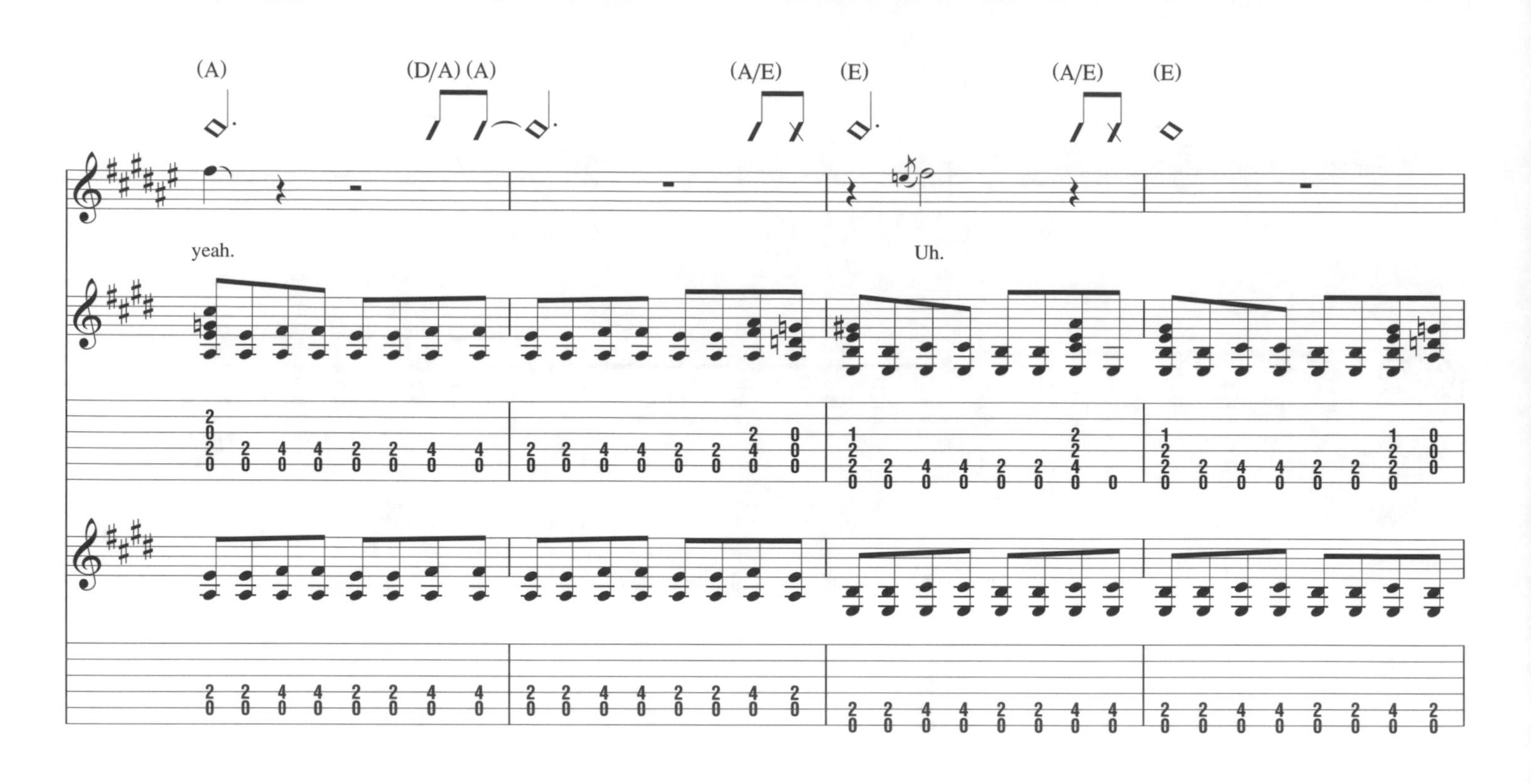
(A)
(D/A) (A)
(A/E)
(E)
(A/E)
(E)
yeah.
Uh.

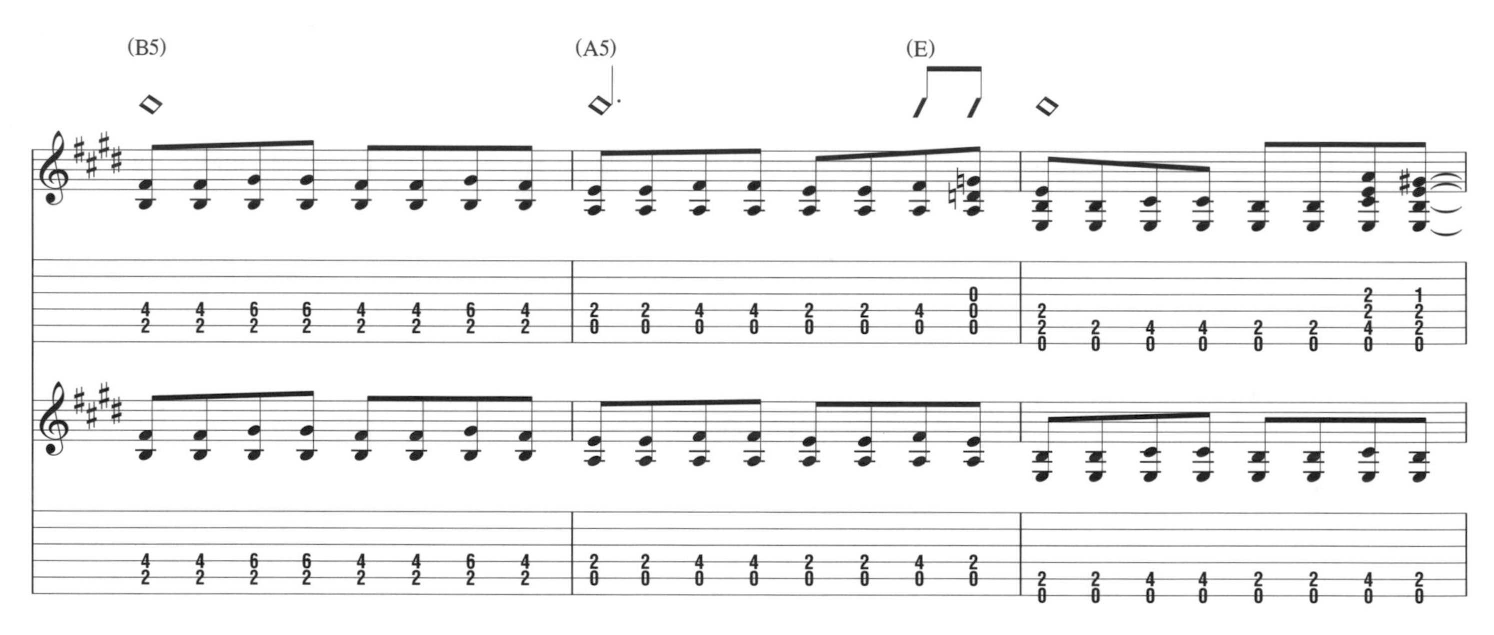
(B5)
(A5)
(E)

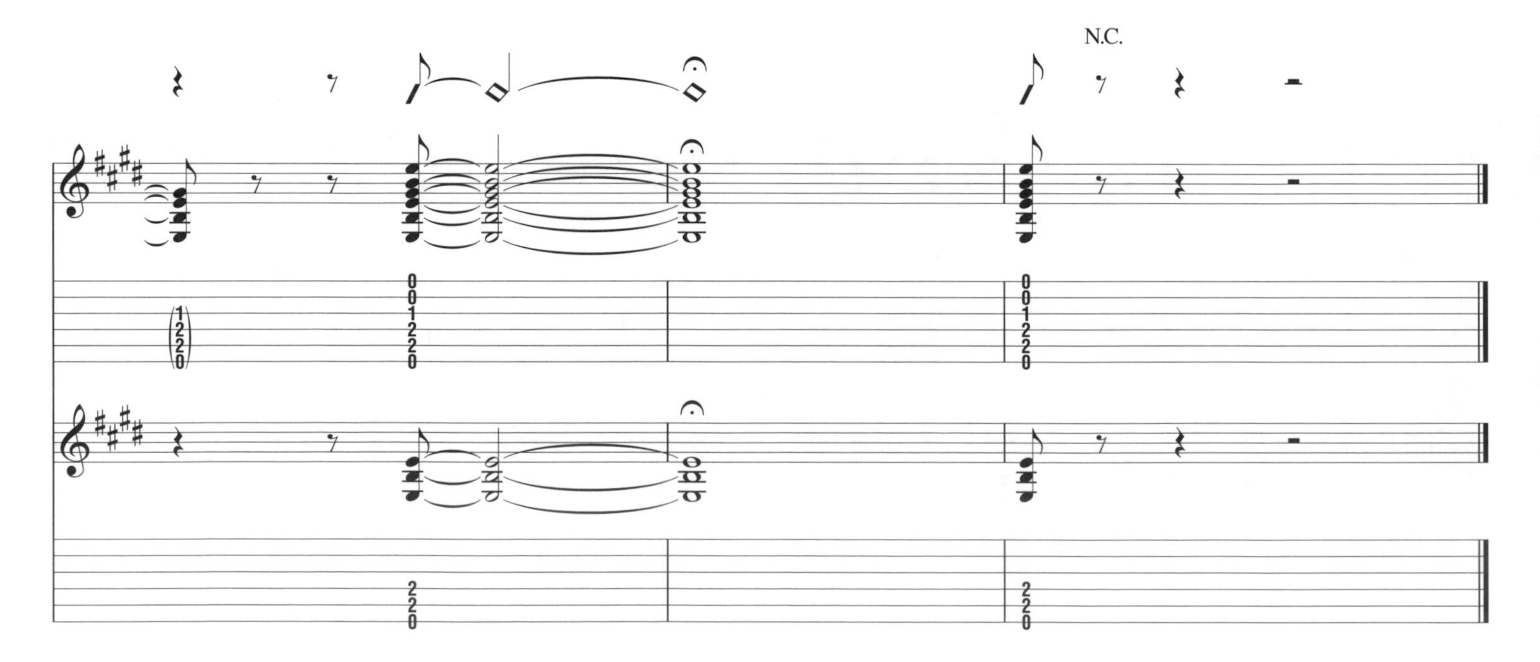
N.C.

Tomorrow

Words and Music by Bob Seger

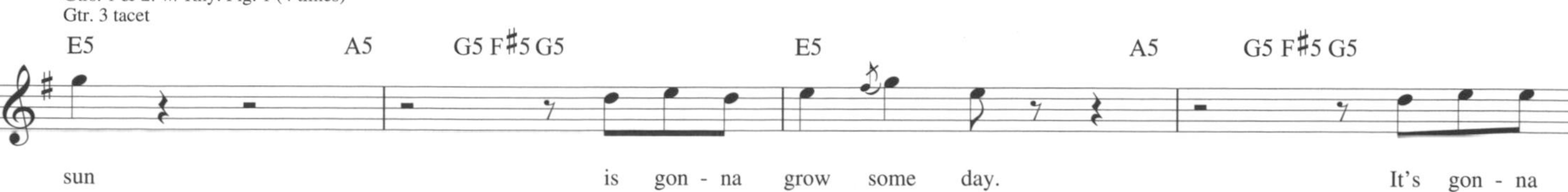

Gtr. 4 tacet
E5 A5 G5 F#5 G5 E5 A5 G5 F#5 G5
get real close, and burn us all up. No more
Gtr. 4 (dist.)
Rhy. Fill 1
End Rhy. Fill 1
mf
E5 A5 G5 F#5 G5 E5 A5 G5 F#5 G5
traf - fic in the street, no more road rage. No more pre -
Gtr. 4: w/ Rhy. Fill 1
E5 A5 G5 F#5 G5 E5 A5 G5 F#5 G5
tend - ing things are real tuff.
Chorus
D5 A5 E5
Rhy. Fig. 2
End Rhy. Fig. 2
Gtr. 1
I can't prom - ise you to - mor - row,
Gtr. 3
grad. bend
1/4
Gtr. 2
let ring

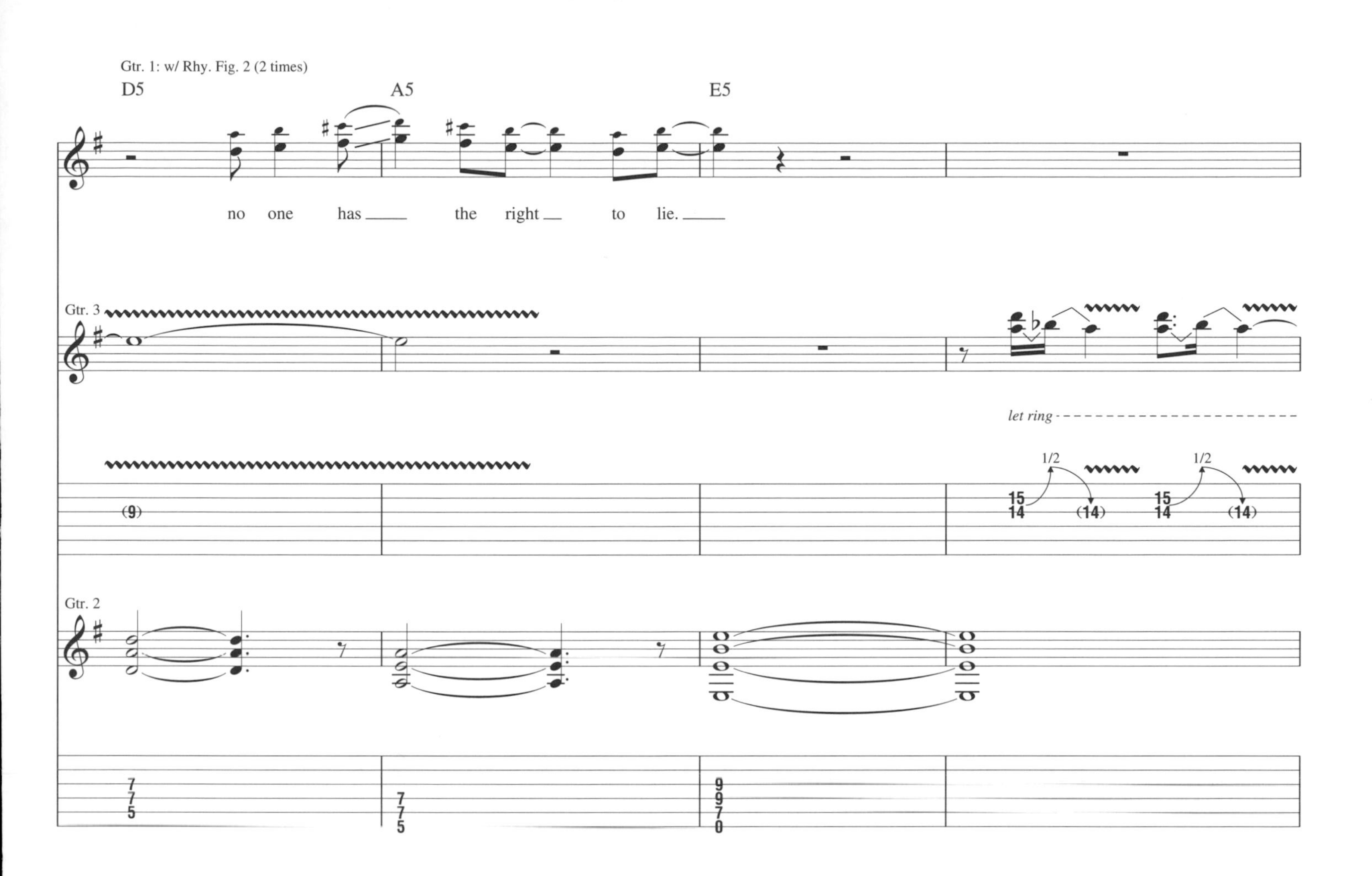
Gtr. 1: w/ Rhy. Fig. 2 (2 times)
D5
A5
E5
no one has the right to lie.
Gtr. 3
let ring
1/2
15
14
(14)
1/2
15
14
(14)
(9)
Gtr. 2
7
7
5
7
7
5
9
9
7
0

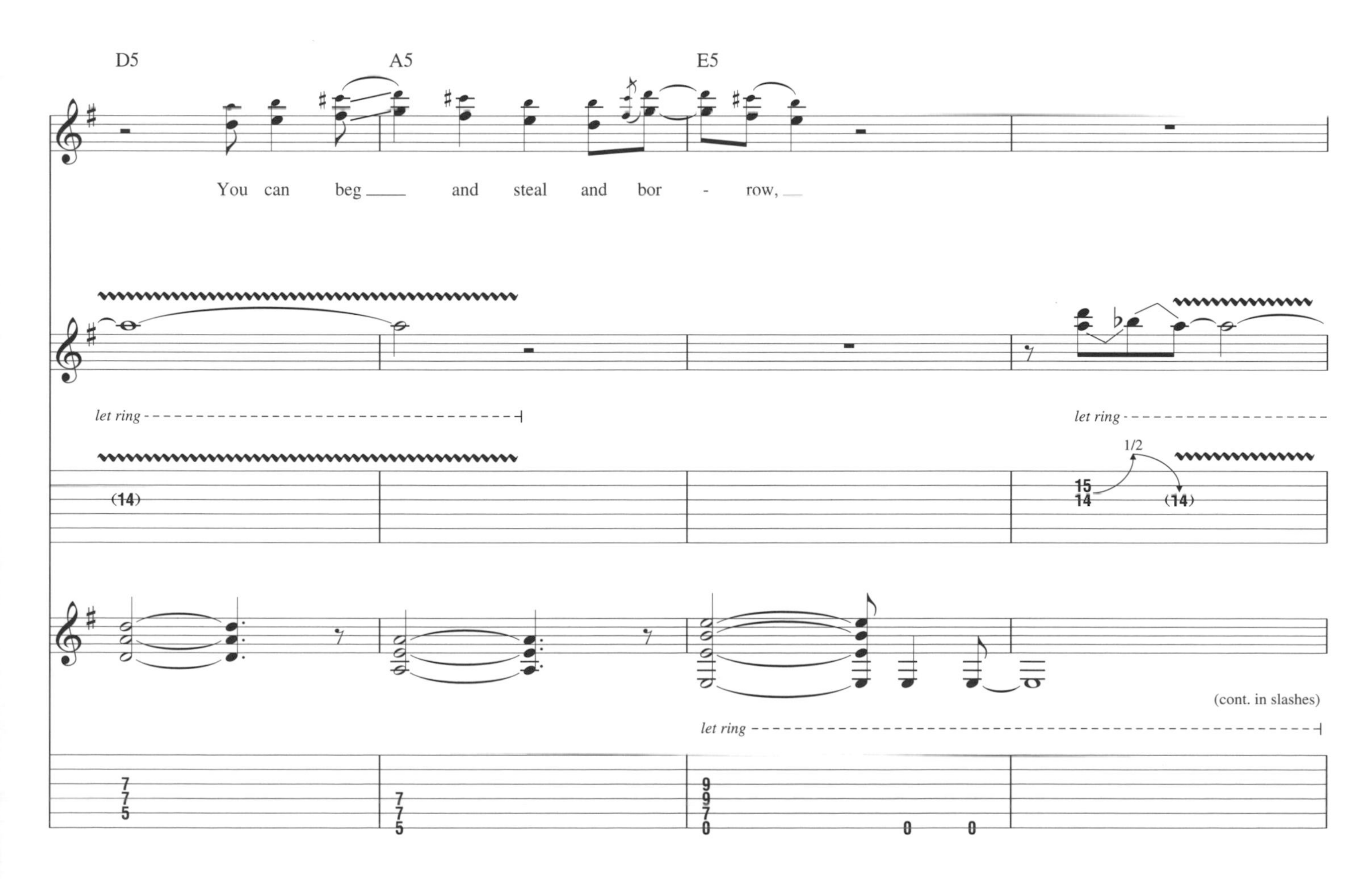
D5
A5
E5
You can beg and steal and bor - row,
let ring
let ring
1/2
(14)
15
14
(14)
(cont. in slashes)
let ring
7
7
5
7
7
5
9
9
7
0
0
0

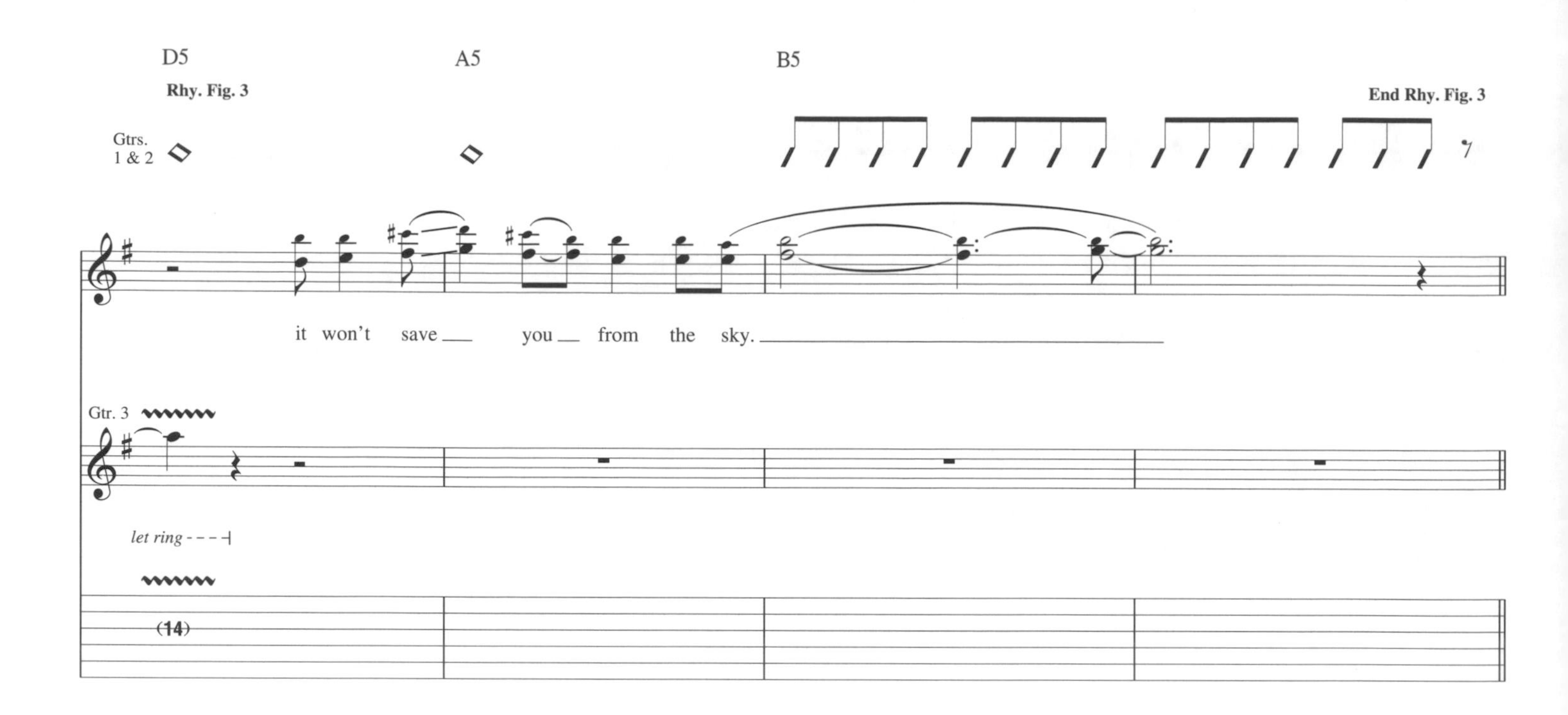
D5
A5
B5
Rhy. Fig. 3
End Rhy. Fig. 3
Gtrs. 1 & 2
it won't save you from the sky.
Gtr. 3
let ring
(14)

Guitar Solo

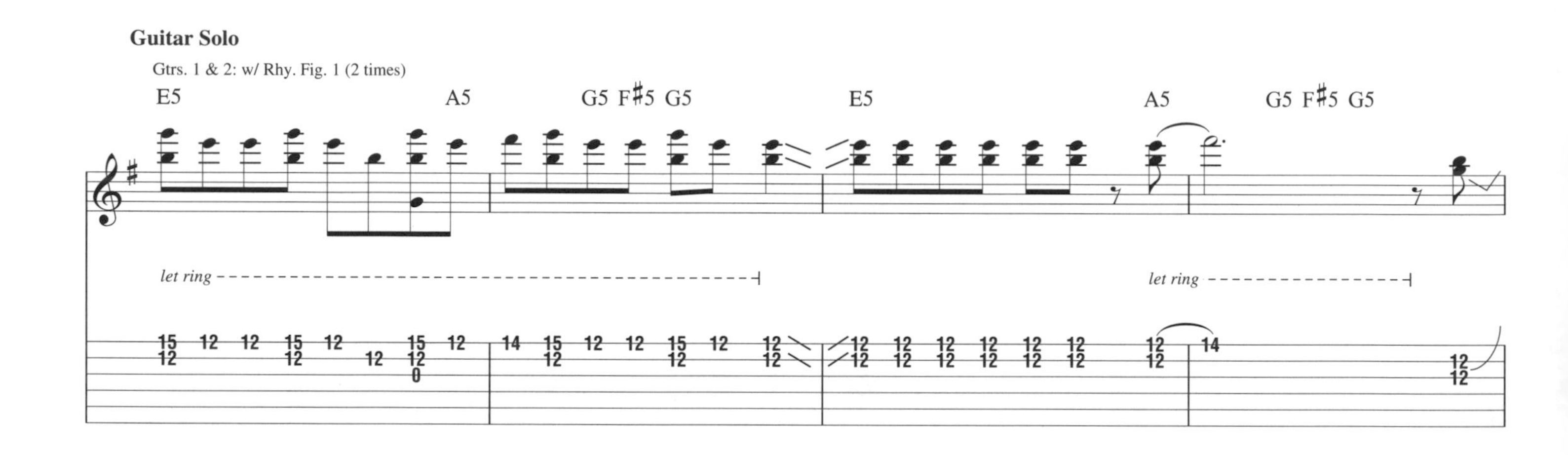
Gtrs. 1 & 2: w/ Rhy. Fig. 1 (2 times)
E5
A5
G5 F♯5 G5
let ring

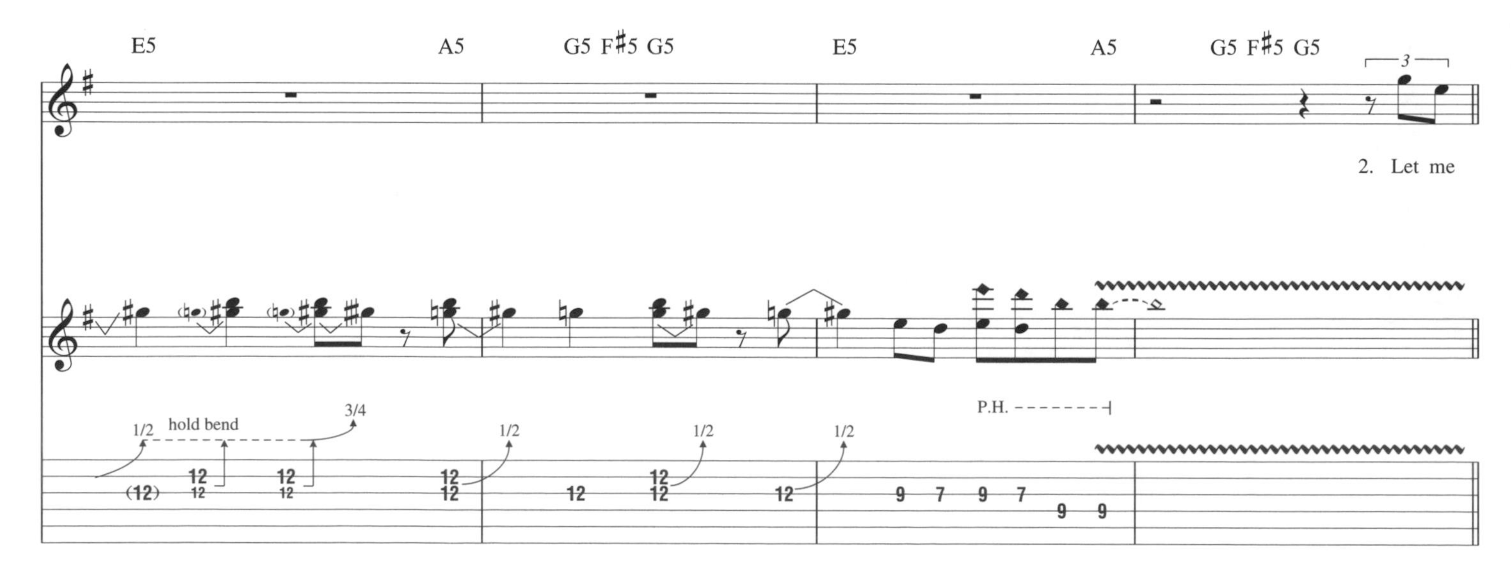
E5
A5
G5 F♯5 G5
2. Let me
hold bend
P.H.

Verse
Gtrs. 1 & 2: w/ Rhy. Fig. 1 (2 times)
Gtr. 3 tacet
E5 A5 G5 F♯5 G5 E5 A5 G5 F♯5 G5
see a show of hands,
tell me the truth now.
What
Gtr. 4: w/ Rhy. Fill 1
E5 A5 G5 F♯5 G5 E5 A5 G5 F♯5 G5
hap - pens if
neu - tri - nos have mass?
Chorus
Gtr. 1: w/ Rhy. Fig. 2 (1 1/2 times)
D5 A5 E5
I can't tell you 'bout to - mor - row,
Gtr. 3
grad. bend
1/2
Gtr. 2
let ring

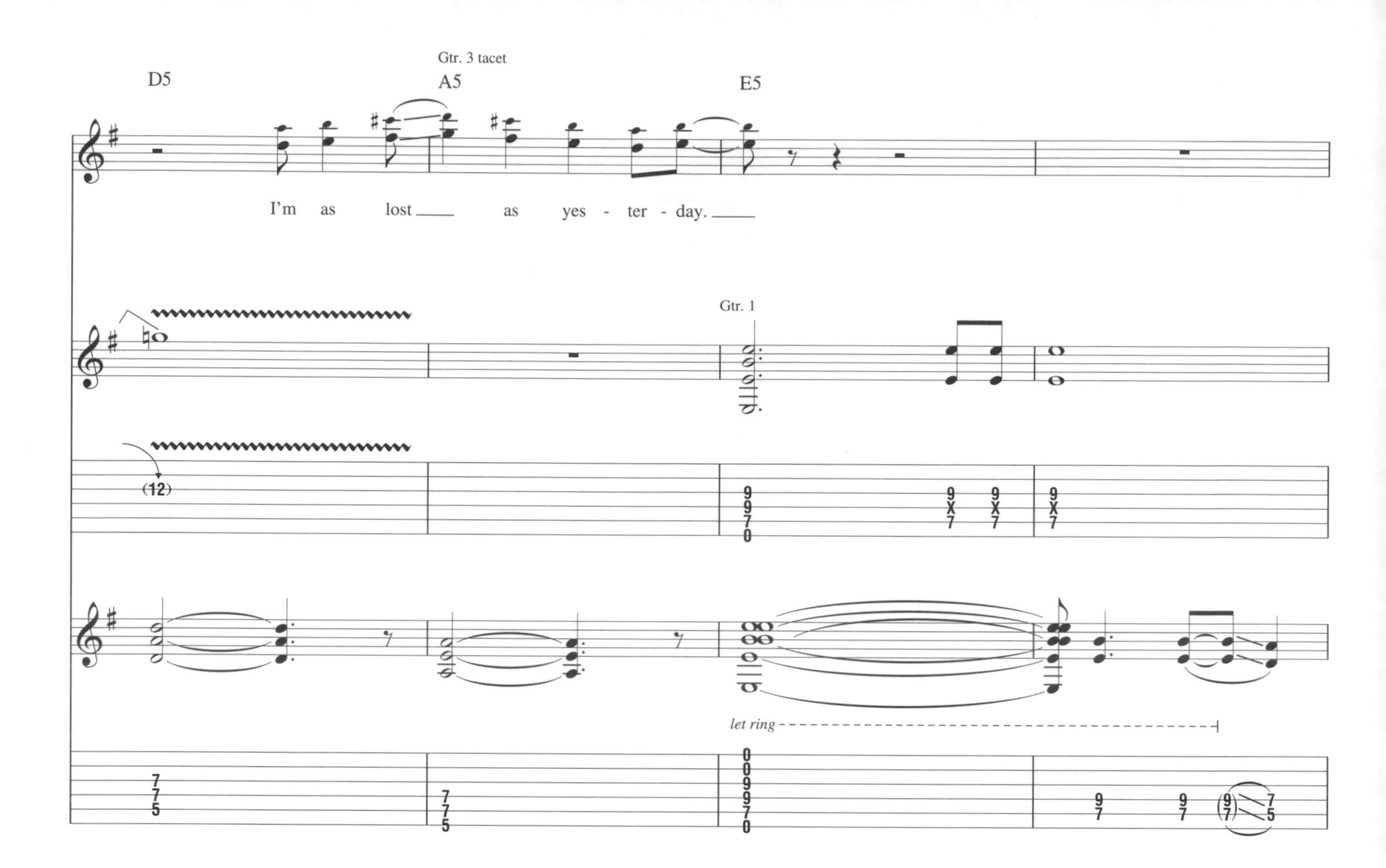
Gtr. 3 tacet
D5
A5
E5
I'm as lost as yes - ter - day.
Gtr. 1
let ring

Gtr. 1: w/ Rhy. Fig. 2
D5
A5
E5
In be - tween your joy and sor - row,
Gtr. 3
grad. bend
Gtr. 2
let ring

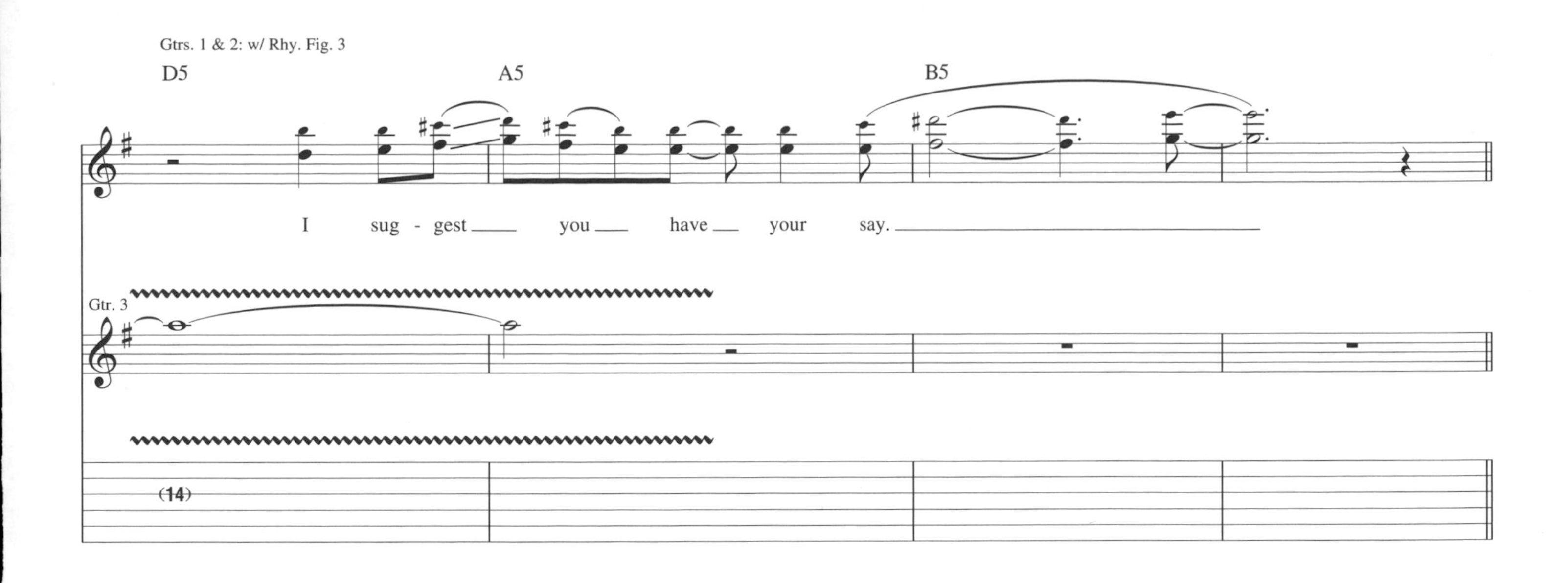
Gtrs. 1 & 2: w/ Rhy. Fig. 3
D5
A5
B5
I sug - gest you have your say.
Gtr. 3
(14)

Guitar Solo

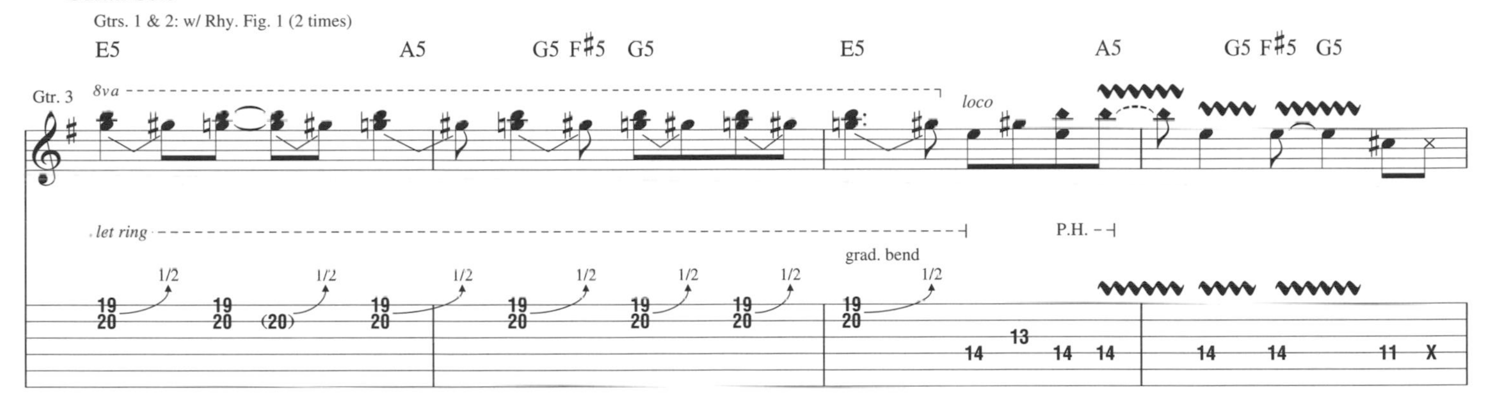
Gtrs. 1 & 2: w/ Rhy. Fig. 1 (2 times)
E5
A5
G5 F♯5 G5
E5
A5
G5 F♯5 G5
Gtr. 3
8va
loco
let ring
P.H.
grad. bend
1/2

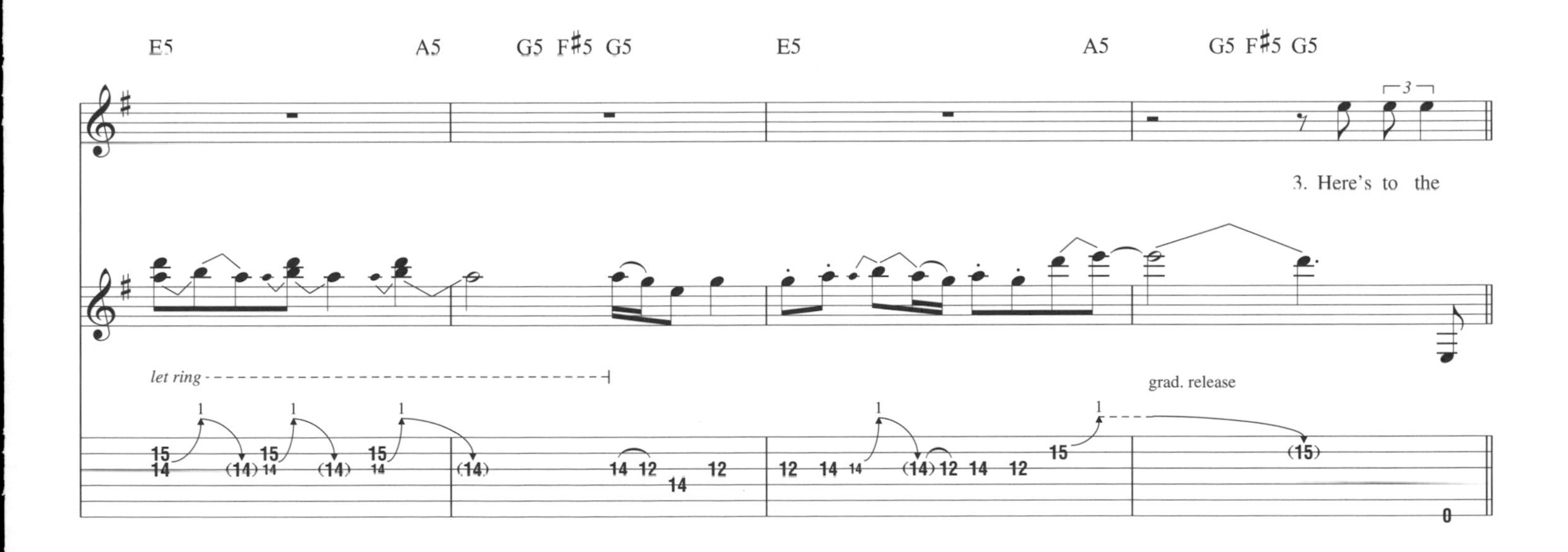
E5
A5
G5 F♯5 G5
E5
A5
G5 F♯5 G5
3. Here's to the
let ring
grad. release

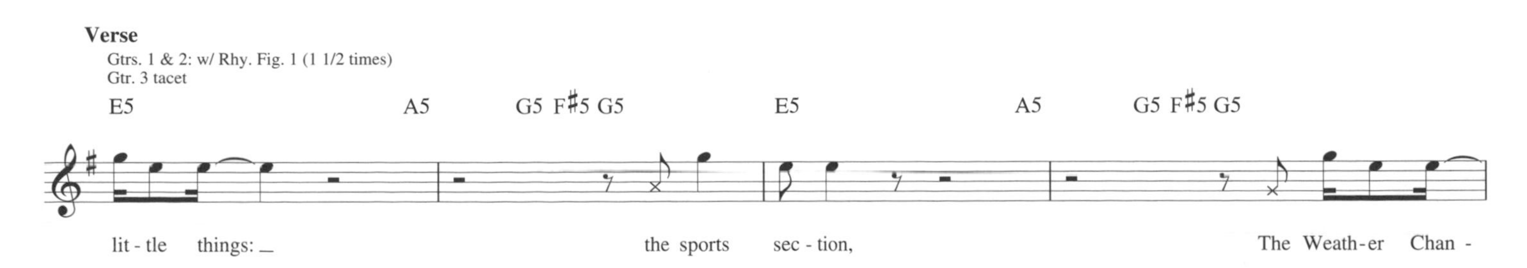
Verse
Gtrs. 1 & 2: w/ Rhy. Fig. 1 (1 1/2 times)
Gtr. 3 tacet
E5
A5
G5 F♯5 G5
E5
A5
G5 F♯5 G5
lit - tle things: the sports sec - tion, The Weath - er Chan -

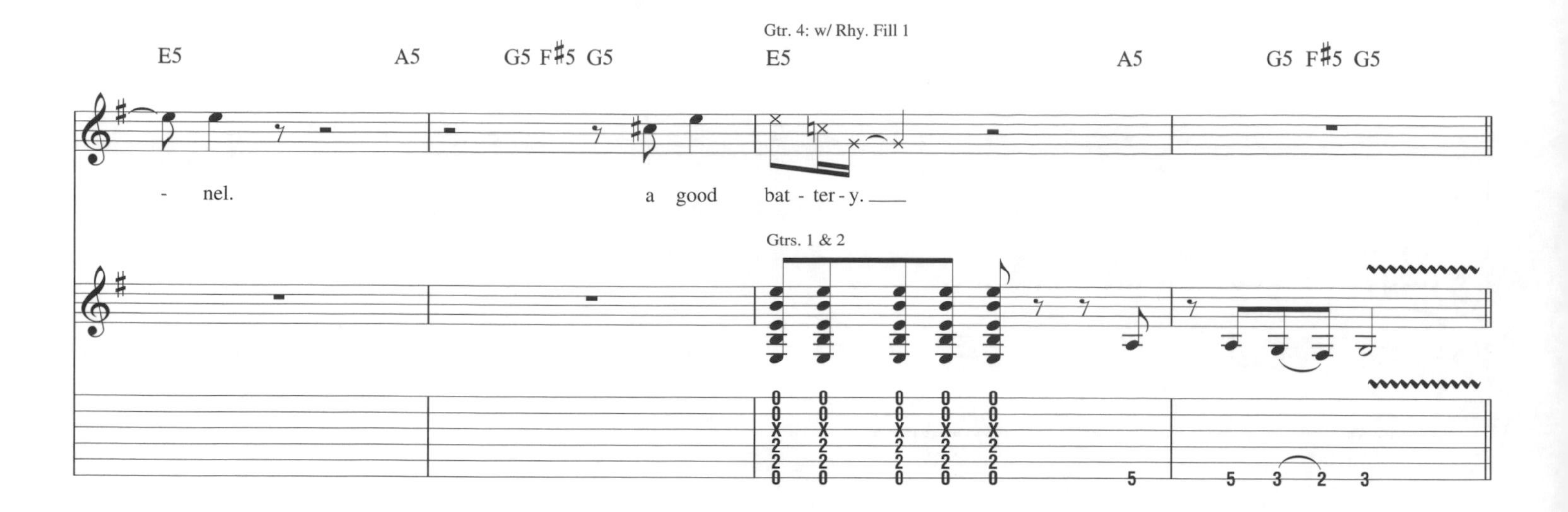
Gtr. 4: w/ Rhy. Fill 1
E5 A5 G5 F#5 G5 E5 A5 G5 F#5 G5
- nel. a good bat - ter - y.
Gtrs. 1 & 2

Outro

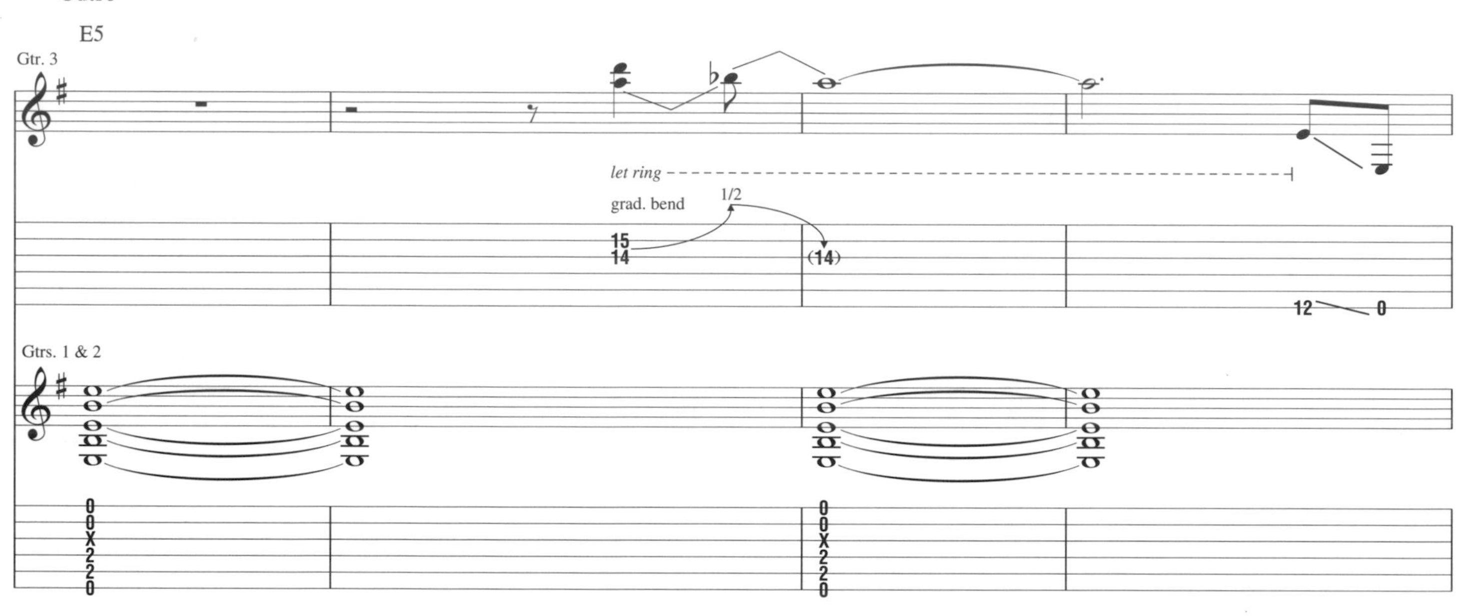
E5
Gtr. 3
let ring
grad. bend
1/2
Gtrs. 1 & 2

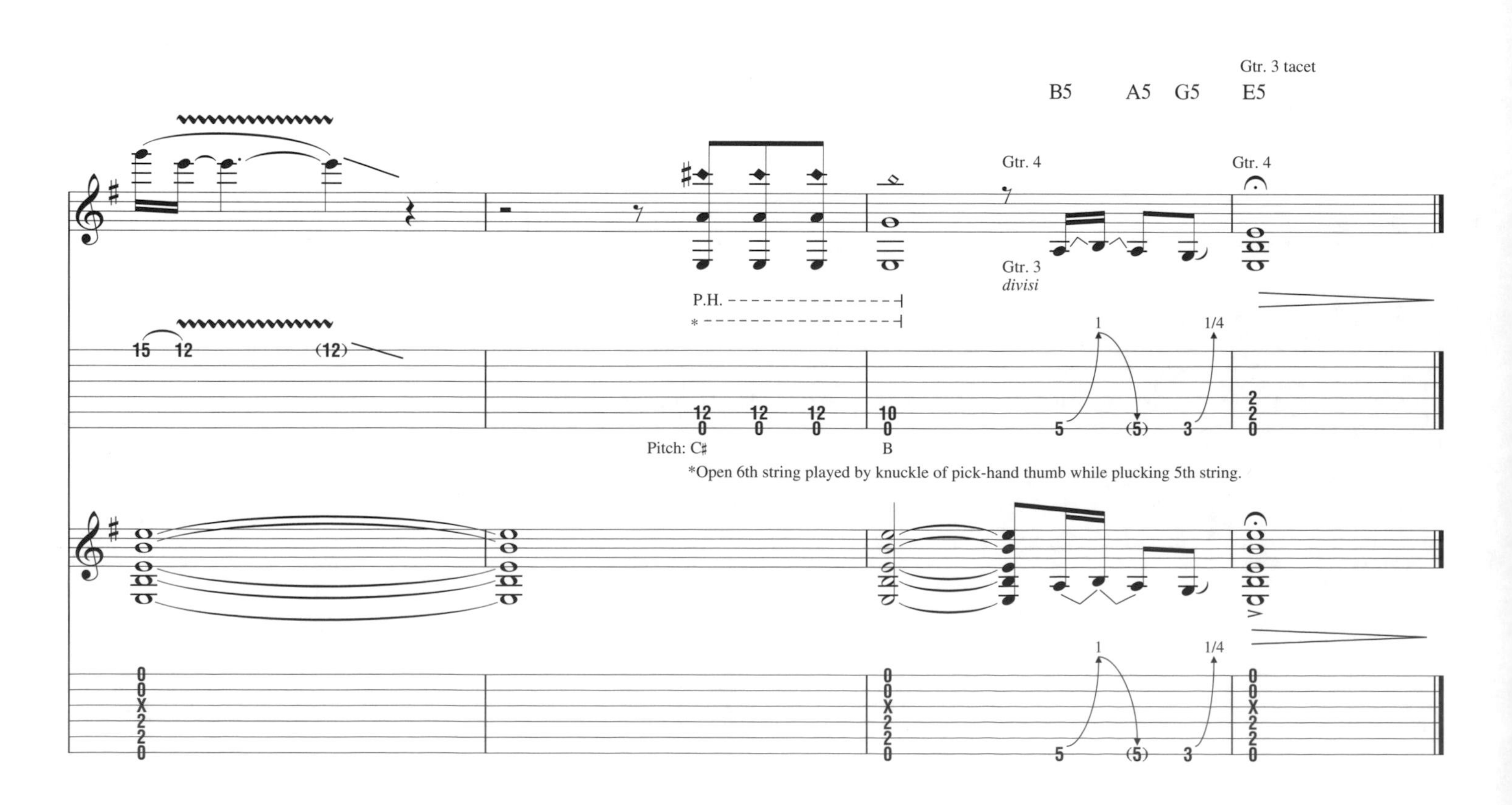
Gtr. 3 tacet
B5 A5 G5 E5
Gtr. 4
Gtr. 3
divisi
P.H.
Pitch: C#
B
*Open 6th string played by knuckle of pick-hand thumb while plucking 5th string.